MOVIE-STRUCK GIRLS

MOVIE-STRUCK GIRLS

WOMEN AND MOTION PICTURE CULTURE
AFTER THE NICKELODEON

Shelley Stamp

PRINCETON UNIVERSITY PRESS   PRINCETON, NEW JERSEY

Library of Congress Cataloging-in-Publication Data
Stamp, Shelley, 1963–
Movie-struck girls : women and motion picture culture after
the nickelodeon / Shelley Stamp
p. cm.
Includes bibliographical references and index.
ISBN 0-691-04458-9 (cloth: alk. paper.)—
ISBN 0-691-04457-0 (pbk.: alk. paper)
1. Mothion pictures and women.   2. Motion pictures for women.
3. Women in motion pictures.   I. Title.
PN1995.9.W6 S75 2000
791.43'082—dc21   99–046548

This book has been composed in Times Roman

The paper used in this publication
meets the minimum requirements of
ANSI/NISO Z39.48-1992 (R1997)
(*Permanence of Paper*)

http://pup.princeton.edu

Printed in the United States of America

10 9 8 7 6 5 4 3 2 1

10 9 8 7 6 5 4 3 2 1

For my grandmothers

Contents

Acknowledgments ——————————————————————————

ANTONIA LANT and Tom Gunning steered this project from its earliest conception, and to them I am most deeply indebted. Lauren Rabinovitz also had an enormous impact on the book, helping to shape the manuscript with detailed, perceptive commentary at several stages. Charlie Keil generously put aside his own work to give a careful, constructive reading at one crucial juncture. Many others read or heard portions of the book at various stages, offering suggestions and encouragement. Among them I am especially grateful to Richard Allen, Constance Balides, Matthew Bernstein, Scott Curtis, Anne Friedberg, Lee Grieveson, Annette Kuhn, Roberta Pearson, Vanessa Schwartz, William Simon, Ben Singer, Robert Sklar, Eric Smoodin, Janet Staiger, Kristin Thompson, and Janet Walker. My thanks to Jane Gaines, Tom Gunning, and Maureen Turim for awarding an earlier version of the manuscript first runner-up in the Society for Cinema Studies Dissertation Awards, and to the judges of the *Screen* Award and the Katherine Singer Kovacs Essay Prize for recognizing a previously published portion of chapter 2.

Without the guidance of many archivists and librarians along the way I would never have been able to navigate so smoothly through my research. Hats off to the incomparable Madeline Matz at the Library of Congress (Motion Picture, Broadcasting, and Recorded Sound Division); Charles Silver at the Museum of Modern Art's Film Study Center; Anne Coco, Scott Curtis, Sam Gill, Barbara Hall, and Warrren Sherk at the Margaret Herrick Library at the Academy of Motion Picture Arts and Sciences; Paolo Cherchi Usai in the Film Department at George Eastman House; Bryony Dixon in the National Film Archive at the British Film Institute; Lou Ellen Kramer at the UCLA Film and Television Archive; Brigitte Kueppers at UCLA Arts Special Collections; librarians at the National Board of Review of Motion Pictures Collection in the Rare Books and Manuscripts Division of the New York Public Library; the staff of the Billy Rose Theater Collection at the New York Public Library for the Performing Arts; and Ann Harris and her staff at the George Amberg Memorial Study Center at New York University. The extraordinary early-twentieth-century bound periodical collection at the University of Washington's Suzzallo and Allen Library and the comprehensive microfilm newspaper holdings at Stanford's Green Library were also most helpful in my research. Thanks to both institutions for allowing me access to their resources. Grants from the Academic Senate and the Arts Division at the University of California–Santa Cruz allowed me to travel to many of these archives and provided vital time off for research and writing. Queen's University's Research Advisory Committee awarded grants that facilitated much of the early research.

When I was not on the road, the Inter-Library Loan folks at UCSC's McHenry Library and Queen's University's Douglas Library patiently retrieved countless tomes, stacks of photocopies, and reels of microfilm, never backing down from the challenge of finding even the most obscure material. Q. David Bowers and Kay Sloan also helped by loaning me materials from their collections. Ingrid Periz kindly shared suffrage items she located during her own travels. Tamara Maloney provided able research assistance. And Don Harris in UCSC's Photo Services made the frame enlargements with great care. Students and colleagues provided enormously supportive working environments, first in the Film Studies Department at Queen's, and more recently in the Department of Film and Digital Media at UC–Santa Cruz. At Princeton University Press Mary Murrell and Lauren Lepow were most helpful in guiding me through the publication process.

In the end, it was friends who kept me laughing and sane during the long gestation of this project in New York, Kingston, Seattle, and Santa Cruz. Thanks especially to Blaine Allan, Harry Benshoff, Margaret DeRosia, Julia Erhart, Sean Griffin, Charlie Keil, Fay Plant, Cassandra Shaylor, Art Simon, and the UCSC Arts Gals. Heartfelt gratitude to Melinda Barlow, who put me up during research jaunts to New York and never remained more than a phone call away; to Leo Charney, who had confidence in the book even before I did; to Kelly Dennis, who makes a great road-trip buddy; and to Christie Milliken, who let me stay with her and Shugs (and Clover) while I was researching in L.A., and, more important, taught me how to share. Closer to home, my parents, Arlene and Robert Stamp, along with Dave, Emily, and Noah, supported my work immeasurably in ways both large and small.

Finally, the book is dedicated to my grandmothers, who influenced my thinking in ways they likely never imagined. Born at the end of the nickelodeon era, they had little opportunity to see the films discussed here. Yet my father's mother, Clarice Stamp, piqued my curiosity about women's history with her stories of working in Toronto in the 1920s when a decent lunch could be had for a dime; and my maternal grandmother, Mary Smith, enjoyed a lifelong love of the movies, a trait I have surely inherited.

MOVIE-STRUCK GIRLS

Introduction

"WHERE five years ago the attendance of the moving picture show by well-to-do people was considered a 'slumming expedition,' it has now become a standard amusement at which wives, mothers, sisters and daughters of the best classes in America are the most devoted patrons," Eustace Ball announced in his 1913 study, *The Art of the Photoplay*.[1] For Ball, the noticeable prominence of women at picture houses most eloquently registered cinema's marked transformation from a cheap, often disreputable, amusement into the nation's favorite entertainment pastime. Slipping between a description of "well-to-do people" and "wives, mothers, sisters and daughters," Ball conflates growing female patronage with cinema's ascending cultural currency in the early 1910s, an association common at the time and often repeated in subsequent accounts of the period. While it would be difficult to find a moment in American film history when female filmgoing was discussed, debated, and catered to more openly, women occupied a more complicated relation to motion picture culture than Ball's characterization would suggest. Whether as an increasingly noticeable constituency of cinema's social audience or as ever more willing participants in its new optical delights, women were not as easily accommodated into moviegoing as Ball presumes, nor were women's films and filmgoing always so readily associated with refinement. America's wives, mothers, sisters, and daughters were indeed central to the evolution of the nation's motion picture culture in the early teens but not always under the terms Ball suggests.

American cinema experienced a profound transformation, perhaps the most significant and far-reaching in its history, between the years 1908 and 1915. Cinema's visual grammar, its narrative paradigms, its industrial structure, its social standing, and its audience base all solidified during this transitional era, poised between the earliest film forms at the turn of the century and the reign of classical cinema practices and Hollywood production methods in the late 1910s. In a relatively brief span of time cinema developed from an inexpensive, fleeting, amusement into the nation's first truly mass medium, a respectable form of entertainment for people of all backgrounds, and soon to become one of the most profitable industries in the country.[2]

The escalating popularity of moviegoing was first registered by the growth of nickelodeon theaters in towns and cities across the country, beginning around 1905—venues often erected in empty storefronts hastily converted to picture showing with a projector, some folding seats, and a sheet. But by the early 1910s nickel theaters were starting to be replaced with larger, more elegant screening sites, some converted from "legitimate" theaters, others purpose-built structures exclusively devoted to motion picture exhibition.

Whereas nickelodeons, particularly those located in larger cities, had served mainly working communities, newer picture houses aimed to attract more affluent patrons. Elegant architecture and commodious service openly catered to the expectations of well-heeled clientele more accustomed to spending their leisure hours at stage plays and vaudeville houses than at penny arcades. Theaters now competed to offer patrons restrooms, uniformed ushers, sloping floors for improved visibility, and better musical accompaniment. Depending upon where movie houses were situated, in cities or rural towns, in working-class neighborhoods or upscale shopping districts, opportunities for film viewing in the transitional era varied considerably, ranging from older nickel theaters to showcase venues like the 3,500-seat Strand Theater that opened in New York in 1914.[3] With the addition of these new screening sites cinema attendance grew rapidly in the teens. Upwards of several hundred thousand movie tickets were sold each week in many cities across the country, with New York alone recording some 250,000 admissions daily. Nationwide, close to fifteen million Americans went to the pictures every day. Within less than two decades of cinema's first appearance, filmgoing had become the nation's favored pastime, "the most universally accepted of modern amusements," according to *Harper's Magazine*.[4]

If elegant screening spaces sought to draw in a broader spectrum of customers, changes in film form and content also increasingly catered to middle-class tastes and expectations in ways that helped diversify cinema's viewership. "Quality films" released by Vitagraph carefully tailored their appeal, as William Uricchio and Roberta Pearson demonstrate, reaching out to "better classes" with adaptations of literary, biblical, and historical material, while trying not to alienate cinema's core audience.[5] By 1913 outfits like the Famous Players Company, the Lasky Feature Play Company, and Bosworth, Inc., were formed solely to produce lavishly designed, upscale photoplays for cinema's growing bourgeois audience and serious dramatic films began to outweigh comedies on American screens for the first time. Often these films tackled weighty social issues of the day, wrapping them within a moral framework tailored to middle-class concerns.[6] Indeed, Sumiko Higashi and Janet Staiger argue that more open depictions of sexuality in films of the early teens, however controversial, catered to middlebrow audiences preoccupied with moral and libidinal issues in the post-Victorian era.[7]

As stories of increasing complexity made their way onto movie screens, motion picture narration evolved strategies designed to convey more intricate settings and time frames, as well as more nuanced portrayals of character psychology and motivation. Unlike early films, more dependent upon visual spectacle and sensation, styles of cinematic narration evolving in the early teens aimed to draw viewers into an apparently seamless fictional world in a more representational fashion. In the new "cinema of narrative integration," as Tom Gunning calls it, filmmakers relied more heavily on editing to shape storytelling, breaking down scenes into multiple shots, or cutting back and forth between parallel lines of action, considerably complicating cinema's depiction of time and space. Closer camera positions, more naturalistic performance styles, and growing use of dialogue intertitles were used to convey characters' subtle emotional states. These techniques allowed film narratives to stand alone, to rely less on retelling plots already familiar to audiences in other forms, and to do without the practice of lecturers in theaters explicating the story lines.[8] Films also grew in length to accommodate more complex story material, as multireel films began to replace the standard one-reel, ten-minute films of a few years earlier. By 1913 American companies began producing "feature" films of up to an hour's length or more, designed to hold an audience's sustained interest over the development of a complicated narrative.[9]

Lengthier, more intricate screen narratives transformed accustomed viewing practices as well, for they demanded a more absorbed engagement with film texts. One prolonged story became the single focus, rather than a varied program of short films and live entertainment more typical of earlier nickelodeon and vaudeville formats. Now patrons were encouraged to sit through an entire show without talking or disturbing others in the audience, their attention fixed solely on the screen. Interaction among patrons within the theater space was discouraged in favor of viewers' solitary, voyeuristic engagement with illusory cinematic space, a mode of spectatorship that veered sharply from more distracted viewing habits common to early cinema as Miriam Hansen has shown.[10]

As cinema's narrative vocabulary became increasingly codified, filmmaking companies shifted to more streamlined modes of production. Continuity shooting scripts and the division of labor within large filmmaking studios began to facilitate a rapid output of film titles to meet the ever escalating demand. The decision of several outfits to relocate in Hollywood in the early teens only confirmed the popularity of mass-production techniques, since the southern California landscape provided varied locales, year-round shooting conditions, and large, inexpensive tracts of land where elaborate indoor filmmaking studios could be built.[11] If Hollywood provided a new geographic center for film production, trade journals that circulated to production companies and theater owners also helped unify the industry around attempts to boost cinema's cultural currency. Beginning with the publication of *Moving Picture World* in 1907, trade papers promoted public acceptance of the movies, encouraging theater owners to adopt dignified exhibition customs, circulating technical information that improved the quality of film showings, leading the call for improved film quality, and beginning critical commentary on the movies at a time when few newspapers and magazines took the medium seriously. Concerned about increasingly strident calls for greater state and federal film censorship, industry leaders helped form the National Board of Censorship of Motion Pictures in 1909, hoping to prove that filmmakers were capable of regulating the moral content of their output free from governmental censorship. Always motivated by an impulse to upgrade motion pictures, the board was concerned less with stifling or censoring films than with shaping their treatment of sensitive issues, seeking instead "the gradual improvement of the quality of motion pictures."[12] By the early 1910s the board was previewing close to 85 percent of the country's film output.

Many production companies formed publicity departments during these years charged with circulating information about a given studio's output and its particular stable of players. As marketing techniques became more elaborate, individual films were adverised in posters, lobby displays, fliers, and heralds, all of which would have been uncommon in the early nickelodeon years when a more general filmgoing experience would have been promoted over the particular appeal of any one offering.[13] More sophisticated film marketing fostered a growing cult of personality surrounding motion picture players in the early 1910s. Early fan magazines, like *Motion Picture Story Magazine*, which debuted in 1911, followed by *Photoplay* in 1912, began providing moviegoers with information about upcoming releases and details about the lives and careers of performers who had remained largely anonymous in the early years of filmmaking. Soon fans were offered souvenirs of every variety bearing the likeness of their favorite players—postcards and calendars, even satin pillow tops and embossed spoons—as movie star culture began in earnest.[14]

Unquestionably popular, the movies were at last "coming to be respectable" in 1913, according to one commentator. By this point most production companies had transferred at least some of their filmmaking operations to Hollywood, where outfits like Universal were erecting huge facilities that rivaled even the most elaborate indoor studios constructed on the East Coast. Longer, multireel films were becoming the norm, rather than the exception, and American companies began to produce feature-length films to compete with European imports.

Cinema's cultural ascendance throughout these transitional years has often been yoked with the industry's campaign to build its female audience, since women, middle-class women in particular, embodied the same respectability tradesmen sought for motion pictures: social propriety, refined manners, and impeccable taste. Cinemagoing began to transform the pleasure-seeking habits of women at the turn of the century, as Kathy Peiss, Lauren Rabinovitz, and many others have demonstrated.[15] But it was during the early 1910s that women were most openly and aggressively solicited as film patrons: ladies' patronage was courted with particular diligence, for their presence announced a social cachet long sought by movie showmen; young female movie fans became a staple of many an exhibitor's business, a constituency catered to with increasing openness; and promotions and advertising campaigns wooed female customers with stories geared especially toward women's interests.

Reliable statistics about the actual composition of cinema audiences in the early period are notoriously difficult to track, but recreation surveys attentive to the demographics at amusement sites offer perhaps the best portrait of Americans at the cinema.[16] Most surveys concluded that men still outnumbered women in motion picture houses in the early teens, but often only by 5 or 10 percent. This gap narrowed even further among younger audiences, with Cleveland's report noting only slightly more men between the ages of 16 and 25 attending movies than their female counterparts, whereas many more men over 25 attended than women of that age. While women were evidently a prominent feature of audiences during the 1910s, surveys reveal that they engaged in considerably different patterns of attendance than men. Women and children tended to frequent suburban theaters more often than those located downtown, and they chose to attend in the evenings rather than the daytime hours. Men, on the other hand, overwhelmingly seemed to favor afternoon shows in downtown venues. In Madison, Wisconsin, despite "a high percentage of well-dressed women, and but few well-dressed men," male viewers outnumbered women by two to one at matinees, an even greater disparity than the weekly average.[17] Drawing upon his observations at theaters in New York and Chicago, Frank Herbert Richardson reported that daytime audiences in those cities were "composed very largely of men, with comparatively few children and a mere sprinkling of women," but theaters located in shopping districts drew matinee crowds "composed very largely of women," and the evening trade was fairly evenly divided between male and female customers.[18] Social workers visiting urban, working-class and immigrant districts also reported that the overwhelming majority of cinemagoers remained male, although Mary Heaton Vorse and fellow sociologist Olivia Howard Dunbar devoted considerable interest to women visible at these establishments.[19] Researching regional variations in film attendance, Kathryn Fuller has found that women living in smaller communities, particularly in the southern states, were less likely to frequent picture houses than their urban and midwestern counterparts, and that daughters of immigrant families were also not well represented among moviegoers, likely because of conservative ideas about suitable leisure activities for young women.[20] Though still a minority among movie viewers, women formed a growing component of audiences in the early teens and often carved out modes of filmgoing distinct from those of men and children. By the end of the decade, former *Moving Picture World* columnist W. Stephen Bush would claim that women constituted the majority of filmgoers, indicating that a remarkable transformation in American movie audiences had taken place in less than ten years.[21]

Central though they were to motion picture culture, women significantly complicated cinemas and cinemagoing throughout the formative, transitional era. Growing female patronage and increased emphasis on female subject matter did not necessarily guarantee a smooth passage to respectability, as many in the industry had hoped, for women were not always enticed to the cinema by dignified, uplifting material, and once there, they were not always seamlessly integrated into the social space of theaters or the new optical pleasures of film viewing. In fact, much about women's moviegoing habits challenged, rather than served, the industry's drive toward classical narrative construction and greater cultural legitimacy. By looking closely at the terms under which women were invited to participate in the country's new motion picture culture, the films they were offered, and the visual pleasures they enjoyed, this study seeks to complicate our understanding of women's relationship to moviegoing, challenging the usual association of female patronage with cinema's uplift. How was cinemagoing made attractive to women as a social outing? How were movie theaters transformed by expanding female audiences, and by attempts to tailor screening venues to the leisure expectations of middle-class women? What on-screen stories were offered to women about their desires and aspirations, about their own lives outside the theater? And what novel viewing perspectives might film spectatorship have offered women? Crucial to these questions is the interplay between the growing social audience of women—fostered through specifically targeted advertising and promotions, described and debated in sociological and popular observations—and the individual viewing positions offered in films that engaged women's issues and female audiences most directly.

The book begins with an examination of the specific ploys and promotional strategies exhibitors used to broaden their women's trade in the early teens. While showmen promoted a refined mode of filmgoing to upscale "ladies' " audiences, fan magazines and trade publications cheerfully lampooned the "feminization" of moviegoing, suggesting a deep ambivalence about the escalating visibility of women at the cinema. The era's caricatured "movie-struck girl," caught between her fascination with stories on screen and a narcissistic absorption in her own image, figured anxieties about women's filmgoing and female spectatorship more dramatically, suggesting that women were unsuitable patrons of the cinema and unlikely participants in its visual delights.

Chapter 2 focuses on a spate of alarmist white slave films released in the early teens which promoted the belief that women were vulnerable to sexual assault and abduction at recreation sites like the cinema, and vented broader anxieties about women's emerging social and economic independence in urban culture. The popularity of vice films, especially among young women, was cause for pronounced concern, since it was rumored that slave traffickers operated under cover of darkness at movie theaters, preying upon unsuspecting women at the very sites where they had gathered to see depictions of this "infamous traffic." These oftentimes lurid films about kidnappings and forced prostitution appealed to women with tawdry, sensational subject matter, not the high-minded topics with which exhibitors might have hoped to cultivate their female clientele. Offering women supposedly "inside exposures" of the workings of the vice trade, "slavers" catered to an openly voyeuristic, sexual gaze distinctly at odds with expectations about feminine decorum and reserve.

If white slave films attracted women whose prurient pleasures troubled many commentators, motion picture serials examined in chapter 3 represent the industry's most sustained bid to cultivate a female fan base during these years. Cunning, athletic heroines like Pauline, Elaine, and Helen, whose "perils," "exploits," and "hazards" were chronicled in regular installments, proved irresistible to many young women eager for "blood-boiling" and "nerve-wracking" thrills. Yet, with their multifaceted tie-in promotions, continuing plot lines, and ardent fan culture, serials encouraged a polymorphous, intertextual viewing practice that steered sharply away from the ever more standardized norms of classical narrative cinema. And though valued by an industry eager for such loyal patronage, fans who followed heroines' adventures from one episode to the next were also chastised for their addictive, overly invested attachment to screen narratives.

It was not only those in the film industry who seized upon the potential of female audiences at the time. Leaders of the women's suffrage movement, the era's most highly charged feminist cause, also turned to filmmaking as a key means of promoting their campaign, hoping to recruit female filmgoers for their ranks. Chapter 4 examines the sophisticated feature-length photoplays released by pro-suffrage organizations, as well as the novel exhibition strategies they utilized. As much as suffrage films might have appealed to exhibitors eager for serious-minded, educational fare, suffragists' attempts to politicize cinema's audience, to mobilize women for action outside theaters, troubled many in the industry and unleashed anxieties about the increasingly visible and vocal presence of women in society.

White slave films, sensational serial dramas, and women's suffrage photoplays all drew female audiences to the cinema with stories aimed directly at women's interests and advertising campaigns that specifically targeted female moviegoers. Even though women's films and filmgoing were so often associated with cinema's growing cultural legitimacy in the transitional era, these examples suggest that women's patronage was also built with subject matter like sexuality, action-adventure stories, and feminist agitation not normally associated with a ladylike gentility. And women evidently sought visual pleasures, like erotic voyeurism in the case of white slave films and ongoing, intertextual engagement in the case of serials, that were at odds with refined, high-brow entertainments. In each instance concerns were raised about women's conduct at cinemas and the viewing habits they enjoyed, demonstrating that women's integration into motion picture culture was neither as smooth as exhibitors might have hoped, nor as uniformly associated with cinema's uplift as subsequent historians have claimed. Competing discourses that surround women's moviegoing at the end of the nickelodeon era show us the complications that increased female patronage introduced into exhibition sites, and the problems of constructing a viewing position for women in cinema's imaginary optical field.

One

Spare Us One Evening:
Cultivating Cinema's Female
Audience

When the Star Theater opened in Newmarket, New Hampshire, in the autumn of 1913, proprietors made a concerted appeal to women of the community, distributing personal invitations and free "Ladies' Tickets" to homes throughout town.[1] Women were assured that they and their families could attend the Star "without fear," and that they would receive "courteous treatment" within. "If you spare us one evening and make use of [the enclosed tickets], we will consider it a favor," the owners declared. Like many screening venues opening throughout these years, the Star sought to bolster patronage among married, middle-class women who formed a particularly desirable segment of the market because they seemed to embody the respectability keenly sought by an industry long tarnished through its association with tawdry, urban amusements. Presumed to be patrons of particular taste and discrimination, refined ladies were also thought to be customers who could exercise considerable influence over the entertainment choices of others in their families and their communities, furnishing what Russell Merritt has called a "lifeline to the affluent bourgeoisie."[2]

Ladies were courted with matinee screenings, commodious service, prize giveaways, and theater redecorating schemes encouraging them to integrate cinemagoing into their daily routines of shopping, socializing, and child rearing. While reaching out to women, promotions of this sort also carefully tailored the expectations of cinema's expanding female constituency, crafting a culture of genteel filmgoing that furnished women of all backgrounds with clues about how to conduct themselves at the picture show, flattering their sense of social status, while also serving exhibitors' desires to upgrade the tenor of their establishments. A polite, dignified audience of the sort theater owners had in mind could not simply be imported through the patronage of bourgeois women, whatever exhibitors might have hoped. Rather, women were conscripted in broader efforts to uplift the cinema, shown how to behave at the picture show in ways that might lend an air of refinement to the enterprise as a whole.

Prized though their patronage evidently was, female filmgoers were also regularly lampooned in cartoons, poems, and satirical articles that circulated in trade papers and fan magazines of the day. Overly chatty, overdressed, or

overbearing, women in these "jests" disrupted, rather than elevated, the theaters they frequented. Ironically, it seems the very tactics used to promote
greater patronage among the "ladies" fostered modes of filmgoing—and film
viewing—that were often perceived to be inappropriate or even incorrect. Concerns about female patrons, however humorously expressed, challenge the general presumption that an expanding female audience only fueled cinema's uplift as nickelodeons gave way to more elegant screening venues in the 1910s.
In fact, women were not always seen to fit comfortably into the culture at
movie houses or the absorbed viewing position now demanded by more classical film narratives.

Playing to the Ladies

When proprietors of the Star Theater extended a special invitation to female
patrons, they suggested at once the particular desirability of married, middle-
class women and their relative absence from other screening venues in the
town of Newmarket. Bourgeois women were summoned into a realm that had
built business catering to other constituencies, especially children, single workers of both sexes, and working men who preferred cinemas to saloons for their
evening's entertainment. Personal invitations, printed tickets, use of terms like
"ladies" and "photoplay" all connoted a dignified sphere of leisure far from
the world of cheap urban amusements with which cinema might otherwise
have been associated. They invoked a milieu where, proprietors hoped, women
attentive to social decorum might feel at ease. The Star's strategy was typical of
many establishments eager for upscale business in the postnickelodeon years.
Chicago's grand new Ziegfeld Picture Playhouse touted its "sumptuously outfitted and scientifically ventilated" premises in early 1914 with a full-page
advertisement in the *Chicago Tribune* including a coupon to "Admit One
Lady" to any upcoming evening performance.[3] Like the Star, the Ziegfeld singled out bourgeois women as specific targets of address, placing equal emphasis on the elegance of the theater's accoutrements, the quality of the program
(a Richard Wagner biopic), and their eagerness to please female clientele. The
Ziegfeld pledged itself "honored to have the ladies cut out and use the coupon
below. We invite you and want you to visit our theater." Invitations conferred
esteem upon these coveted patrons, flattering women with the idea that they
were deserving of special attention and solicitation.

Delivered to women at home, invitations and coupons also bridged the distance between commercial entertainment culture and the familial sphere,
reaching out to women not normally found at picture houses in a gesture designed to express the compatibility of the two realms. Most motion picture
advertising at the time was still focused on screening sites and in the streets
immediately surrounding entertainment districts where posters, heralds, and
lobby displays were readily visible. Personalized invitations broke with this

convention, venturing beyond cinema's core audience, and targeting a segment of the market untapped by customary promotions.[4] In his 1915 guide, *Picture Theater Advertising*, Epes Winthrop Sargent repeatedly favored the use of invitations to attract well-heeled female patronage, even suggesting that male filmgoers be conscripted in the campaign to woo their female relatives and companions. Envelopes marked "For Men Only" could be distributed to gentlemen who attended pictures in the evenings, he proposed. Tucked inside, invitations good for "two ladies or one lady and child" would instruct men to "Give this to 'Her.'"[5] Men, already regular filmgoers, could serve as conduits through which to attract business from women who remained at home. Novel marketing outreaches of this kind respectfully acknowledged homemakers' domestic roles, then, while at the same time inviting them out of that domain and into theaters.[6]

Many promotions also enlisted the aid of homemakers in the task of selecting suitable recreational activities for their entire families, assigning them a preeminent role in the entertainment sphere. Viewed as influential arbiters of taste and custom, bourgeois women were attractive to theater owners precisely because of the sway they seemed to exercise over others. "We want and need your patronage," the Star Theater's management confessed, "for where you attend, so will follow the husbands and sons." If Newmarket's women could be convinced of cinema's merits, they might serve as a conduit to greater middle-class patronage on the whole, just as Russell Merritt has suggested.[7] Exhibitors evidently did not lose sight of the fact that homemakers were assuming an increasingly prominent role in the marketplace during these years through the selection and purchase of household goods for their families. Greater economic clout gave women a sense of proprietorship over their own households that extended into public life. Celebrating the unprecedented authority accorded the "woman who spends" in 1910, Bertha June Richardson maintained that "upon her rests the responsibility for the standards that govern the spending for home and community."[8]

Recognizing this, the Star Theater also flattered women's sense of bourgeois propriety, asking for their help in maintaining the community's normative values. By visiting the Star, women would be "helping us establish . . . a moving picture theater showing nothing but strictly clean, wholesome, and instructive photoplays." Ladies were assured that the theater would feature only "good, clean, moral entertainment," attractive to the entire family, and safe for their children. Programs would also be tailored to "appeal to the better qualities" of women's husbands and adult sons, who might otherwise frequent saloons or similar disreputable establishments, encouraging the men instead to "spend an evening where the atmosphere is good and the morals clean." Promises of this nature cast bourgeois wives and mothers as moral guardians within their immediate families, as well as in the community at large. Through their support of the Star, women could secure respectable recreation for their own household, while also ensuring that their Newmarket neighbors were not partaking of seedier amusements. "If you patronize us," letter recipients were reminded, "there will be no inducement for others to locate there with a less moral entertainment." By suggesting that such high-minded goals were not incompatible with actually attending the cinema, the Star's owners linked their establishment to the growing interest of reform-minded "club women" in regulating the cinema during the 1910s.[9] In the end, aims of the Star Theater's management and those of middle-class housewives were framed as coincident in a campaign that aligned women's cinemagoing with their customary maternal domain and their newer vocation as household consumer. Even the new cinema's proprietors placed themselves under the homemaker's watchful eye, pledging to honor all suggestions from this segment of the market. Assigning women a determining role over entertainment choices for family and community, the Star's promotion moved homemakers to the center of an entertainment culture from which they might otherwise have felt excluded. Bourgeois women of distinction were positioned as arbiters of taste, the central film patrons upon whose good judgment the patronage of others depended.

Women's magazines also coached their readers to oversee neighborhood screening venues, reminding them of the strength they wielded as the family's chief entertainment purveyor. The *Ladies' World* insisted that "women everywhere may now confidently call upon the local theatre patronized by her family and request the exhibitor to show pictures of the better class," insisting to its readers that "you have a duty to motion pictures, and through them, to the public." Theater owners would be "bound to listen to a plea of this nature" since wives and mothers held the power to prevent others in their family from attending the show.[10] *Woman's Home Companion* played a leading role in this campaign, urging its subscribers to "visit the little theater round the corner from your store or home." There they would find "your children, your neighbor's children, the maid who serves you at supper, the boy who delivers your meat and your bread, the young girl who clerks in the five-and-ten-cent store ... all crowded together like sardines in a huge box watching the flickering films of real life."[11] Even as they acknowledged the centrality of picture houses in most American neighborhoods and towns, these discussions were nonetheless still careful to erect class and age distinctions in order to elevate their readership above average filmgoers. The role offered to middle-class women remained essentially a proprietary one, but in order to exert their influence in the entertainment sphere, and ensure that their voices were heard, women were encouraged to make themselves visible to exhibitors: "We have never made it clear to film manufacturers that we are a majority. We have never said to them, as a body, 'Give us clean pictures and we will make it worth your while.' "[12]

By circulating a high volume of "ladies' tickets," venues like New Hampshire's Star Theater were promising much more than free admission to bargain-conscious women; promotions of this kind also helped to ensure that a noticeable portion of each audience would be female. Patrons drawn from a constituency not yet known for their regular cinemagoing habits could take comfort in the suggestion that other "ladies" were likely to be in attendance. While reaching out to middle-class women, ladies' tickets also aimed to reconfigure the dynamics of exhibition space by consciously creating a place for women in picture houses, implicitly demarcating theaters as sites of feminine congregation. Some establishments went to great lengths to guarantee that upscale women occupied a prominent and privileged position. When the Princess Theater opened in Wheeling, West Virginia, in the spring of 1914, seven rows of seats were reserved "for the exclusive use of ladies" during matinee shows.[13] Class-conscious women were thereby guaranteed that they would constitute a significant body of the audience and, perhaps more important, that they would not have to rub elbows with less cultivated patrons who might also be in attendance. Since the policy was announced in the theater's souvenir booklet, it likely also had the corollary effect of discouraging other customers who might already have formed daytime viewing habits, providing further assurance to would-be female clientele that afternoon audiences would consist mainly of other "ladies."

Promotions often instructed filmgoers about cultivated methods of attending the show. In addition to furnishing free ladies' coupons, Chicago's Ziegfeld Picture Playhouse invited regular male customers to escort female companions to the cinema, claiming their new facility was "the ideal entertainment palace to which you can go and to which you can take everybody—mothers, sisters, sweethearts, wives," suitable for female family members and loved ones of all ages on family outings, romantic get-togethers, or evenings out.[14] Male escorts were especially important for married, middle-class women, who might have been unlikely to venture to cinemas unaccompanied, particularly in the evening hours. Men then remained a vital link between proprietors and the female clientele they hoped to reach. But this appeal also subtly fostered an attitude toward the cinema that aimed to transform the dynamics of self-styled "picture playhouses" like the Ziegfeld. Instead of going to the cinema alone or with their buddies, men were coached to attend the show with a woman on their arm. Theaters were designated as spaces of refined heterosocial interaction, neither largely male purviews in which women might feel uncomfortable, nor dating enclaves for working singles that could alienate married housewives. Set against the lingering fears about heterosocial interaction at the movies examined in the next chapter, these proscriptions strictly delimited the interplay between men and women at the cinema: theaters were not cast as sites where singles could "pick up" dates, since couples were directed to arrive together; and dating relationships were cast within the same platonic, asexual realm as accompanying one's mother or sister. Exhibitors like those at the Ziegfeld evidently recognized that women, however ladylike, could not single-handedly "uplift" the cinema; rather, in the process of courting women, they also hoped to elevate the conduct of men and the interaction of couples already in motion picture audiences.

A Paramount advertising slide demonstrates how efforts to attract "better" female clientele painted a picture of affluent cinemagoing that not only solicited their patronage but helped define roles they might play in recreation culture, and postures they might adopt on visits to the local picture house. "Come here any afternoon or evening," audiences were told. "Bring the children or your visiting friends with you. You are always sure to be pleased with the Paramount program. This week's bill is exceptionally good."[15] A well-dressed man and woman sit watching a picture show in an accompanying illustration that makes no reference to the particular film program, or even to the screen, but concentrates instead on picturing upscale patrons and defining a mode of refined socializing at the cinema. Motion pictures were inscribed within a dignified sphere of activities that included visiting with friends in the afternoon hours and caring for children. Attention paid to the quality of the program and the comfort of one's surroundings, rather than the simple pleasure of diversion for its own sake, flattered the tasteful discrimination of these imagined patrons.

Yet the genteel culture of female moviegoing promoted by the industry accomplished much more than simply encouraging patronage among this desirable segment of the market. Such promotions also guided women's expectations, furnishing them with clues about how to conduct themselves in picture houses. The film industry solicited bourgeois housewives in its uplift not only by nurturing their movie habit, but by molding expectations about a refined "ladies culture" at the cinema. It was a strategy that likely influenced patrons of many constituencies who worked together to create a more cultivated atmosphere in theaters. By circulating expected models of cinemagoing, proprietors hoped to position photoplays within an urban "pleasure culture" evolving for both married, middle-class women and so-called bachelor girls of the working class. The former indulged in the city's daytime diversions—luncheons, museums, shopping, vaudeville—nearly always accompanied by women friends, while more adventuresome "bachelor girls" toured the city's delights at night, often on the arm of a male companion.[16] Thus it is important to stress that the picture of relaxed, refined filmgoing promoted to middle-class women likely embraced other women of diverse economic backgrounds as well, particularly single wage-earners and women from working-class and immigrant families eager to fantasize their own upward mobility through leisure. The genteel movie culture fashioned in these promotions, while designed to cater primarily to highbrow tastes, surely also tailored the expectations of patrons from many social strata, men and women alike, who still formed cinema's core audience.

Along with disbursing tickets and reserving seats for women, many theaters also set aside specific blocks of time, normally in the afternoons, primarily for female audiences. Taking advantage of the greater leisure hours that homemakers enjoyed during the daytime, exhibitors often marketed matinee showings almost exclusively to this clientele. Matinees had distinct economic advantages for theater owners, since identical programs could be shown afternoons and evenings with little additional cost. But as Epes Sargent emphasized in his exhibitors' guide, matinees also had the potential to capture a more socially prestigious strain of the market.[17] Women who might not otherwise frequent cinemas in the evenings, because of either family obligations or the negative associations that surrounded nighttime commercial recreation, might be enticed to visit in the afternoon. Picture houses eager to foster a family trade often charged less for women and children at matinees, as Russell Merritt has demonstrated in his research on Boston and Philadelphia venues.[18] But most matinee promotions seem to have placed more stress on the special atmosphere that prevailed in the afternoons than on bargain prices. A marketing campaign suggested by Sargent, for instance, clearly distinguished the tenor of afternoon showings from their evening counterparts. "We want to make the matinees especially attractive to the ladies," advertisements would read. "We want *you* to get the matinee habit. We want *you* for a regular patron. We want you to come in the afternoons when there is plenty of room. It will give you greater pleasure and comfort."[19] Afternoon business would be largely, if not exclusively, composed of women, Sargent's invitation implies, thereby ensuring an absence of the crowding and jostling that might have made picture houses uncomfortable for refined, suburban women. Careful to emphasize that "matinee performances are just as complete *in every way,* as the evening shows," the copy hints that the cinema's *social* climate improved considerably in the afternoons, furnishing a milieu where "ladies" visited among themselves in perfect safety, accompanied by young children.[20] What is advertised is not a change in the film program but a shift in the theater's atmosphere making it more hospitable to women and children. Theaters remained the same afternoons and evenings; their programs usually did not vary; but proprietors hoped that the presence of genteel ladies at matinees could substantially reconfigure exhibition space.

Much of the advice given to exhibitors eager to attract women's business also underscored the import of theater ambiance. As the Star Theater's promotion tells us, enterprising managers were acutely conscious of conditions inside their venues and the standing their establishments held within the community. What had been disreputable about nickelodeon culture to so many in the middle class had less to do with film fare, however vacuous it was perceived to be, than with the atmosphere that seemed to prevail inside dingy urban storefronts and the supposed conduct of patrons therein.[21] Improved theater decorum was thus a vital component in any appeal to class-conscious women. Advice manuals like John Rathbun's 1914 guide, *Motion Picture Making and Exhibiting*, repeatedly emphasized that proprietors would attract women to neighborhood theaters only by substantially elevating the tenor inside their establishments. Upgrades of this sort were far more critical, Rathbun maintained, than changes in film programming.[22] Married women, likely to sway the habits of their husbands as well, were more apt to base their film choices on advertised descriptions of theater interiors than on any particular pictures shown, proprietors were told.[23] Creating a place for middle-class women at the cinema, then, entailed much more than simply setting aside blocks of seats or hours in the day.

Lavish services that would enable women to combine picturegoing with their daily patterns of socializing, shopping, and caring for young children also aimed to recast the tenor of exhibition sites. Sargent urged proprietors to play up the comfort and accommodations provided at their establishments by inviting women to "be our guest some afternoon this week," in a campaign that cast female patrons as visitors rather than paying customers.[24] Movie houses hoping to attract afternoon shoppers should offer "retiring rooms" complete with "needles and thread, safety pins, hat and hair pins, and face powder," and if possible "a pretty writing desk well stocked with paper, correspondence cards and envelopes," Sargent suggested.[25] By providing such amenities, cinemas placed themselves among the ranks of the era's best establishments. Every restaurant, hotel, and retail outlet of any importance kept a supply of beauty products in women's dressing rooms, according to one contemporary commentator.[26] Equipped with "a women's retiring room, handsomely furnished and presided over by a maid,"the Majestic Theater in Columbus, Ohio, was thus deemed "the very latest word in motion pictures theaters" when it opened in 1914.[27] Parcel-checking services, another feature recommended to proprietors, would allow women to deposit their purchases throughout the day, then return at the end of the afternoon to watch the pictures and reclaim their packages. Accommodations of this kind were particularly important for theaters located near shopping districts, Sargent claimed, for they would encourage the matinee trade.[28] Suitable facilities for mothers with children were also a must. "Make absolutely no accommodation for baby carts," suggested a tongue-in-cheek *Motography* guide titled "How to Run a Moving Picture Show." "Give your women patrons strictly to understand that your place is a nicolette and not a nursery."[29] Checkrooms for baby carriages—even glassed-in, soundproof booths where women could retire with fretful infants—were recommended in less mocking guides. Larger, better-equipped venues sometimes offered in-house child-care centers where mothers could "check the kiddies and enjoy the performance in comfort."[30] Providing such courtesies for mothers, exhibitors were also insisting that their venues were safe for young children.

Luxurious amenities were designed to make picture houses social centers of local shopping districts, associated with comfort, attendance, and rejuvenation. By focusing on service, rather than amusement, and by integrating cinema into women's daytime patterns of shopping and visiting, proprietors hoped to dissociate matinees from the world of storefront amusements and to foster an atmosphere of indulgence that would have been familiar to many women from department stores that also catered to a largely female clientele. Clearly shopping culture furnished a powerful model of genteel female recreation outside the home that movie exhibitors eagerly grafted onto their own venues. There was, in fact, growing recognition that cinemas drew from the same constituencies that formed a department store's core clientele: young, upwardly mobile working women, urban shoppers, and well-to-do suburban housewives. One 1916 manual on motion picture advertising reminded retailers of this very intersection:

> You will find that downtown theaters attract the workers of both sexes in the lunch hours, and in the afternoon the audiences, for the most part, comprise ladies seeking relaxation after shopping tours. But out in the suburbs and residential districts business men and their wives go to the shows in the evening after supper to drive away the worries and irritations of the day.[31]

One of the chief leisure sites for women, department stores constituted a uniquely "woman-oriented center of comfort and amenity" built around ideals of service and consumption, as Susan Porter Benson has demonstrated.[32] Department stores relied heavily on "non-selling services" as a means of cultivating a steady female clientele, stressing the *experience* of shopping itself—wandering through elegant decor, surveying the products, enjoying the flattery of fawning attendants—over the act of making individual purchases. The sumptuous service culture cultivated in so many retail outlets did not cater to bourgeois clientele alone, Benson contends; rather, department stores aligned browsing and window-shopping with forms of urban gentility that working women and immigrants might have been eager to adopt in their bid for assimilation and elevated class status.[33] Cinemas, like these retail emporiums, then, aimed to create atmospheres that would cultivate an air of "distinction" in all of their patrons, not simply affluent women. Indeed, working women eager to emulate this culture might have been particularly attracted to this picture of filmgoing. Perhaps most significant, the visual spectacle offered by the array of products on display in department stores and shop windows provided woman-oriented "domains for looking" that formed an important precursor to film viewing at the turn of the century, as Anne Friedberg and Lauren Rabinovitz have shown.[34]

Exhibitors, well aware of the women's leisure culture developing around shopping, were eager to stress the connections between browsing and cinemagoing. The *Nickelodeon* recognized early on that the female consumer's growing economic might ought to be cultivated as a model for film patronage, instructing exhibitors, in the editorial of its second issue, to "play to the ladies." "Every tradesman knows that the ladies—bless 'em!—are the money spenders of any community." Exhibitors guilty of ignoring "the simple fact that most of the nickels are feminine" lost many opportunities for cultivating this untapped audience whose tastes and habits made "women's stores," "women's novels," and "women's magazines" such successful enterprises. Urging theater owners to recognize that women constituted their primary audience, the *Nickelodeon* advised them to begin marketing directly to female customers in ways that tied film patronage into their larger patterns of consumption.[35] As Jeanne Thomas Allen has argued so compellingly, this marks the period when women's movie habits were first tied to consumerism, a link that would be nursed throughout the classical era.[36]

Many establishments coordinated tie-in promotions with shopkeepers so that women going about their errands could not help but be enticed to stop in at the picture house. Local merchants frequently advertised their business on slides projected between reels, hoping to lure customers before or after the show. When owners of the Alameda Grocery in Denver bought a neighboring picture house there in 1915, they offered free movie tickets with the purchase of one dollar's worth of groceries, ensuring crossover patronage at the two establishments.[37] By sponsoring matinee screenings one day a week or distributing free tickets to their customers, retailers could exploit these connections to their advantage, Sargent proposed: rural residents might be persuaded to come into town during the week to do their shopping and attend a movie, while neighborhood women could be enticed to shop locally, rather than going downtown.[38]

Some enterprising exhibitors even went so far as to stage promotional stunts in department stores, deliberately confusing retail space with diegetic screen space. In order to publicize Universal's serial, *Lucille Love, Girl of Mystery*, owners of the Idle Hour Theatre in Sheboygan, Wisconsin, commandeered a local department store, then hired a "handsome young society woman" to appear there one afternoon each week wearing a mask. Customers were then invited to guess her identity.[39] Clearly the promotion aimed to draw patrons from the ranks of retail shoppers, to associate cinemagoing with the high-toned pursuits of "society women," but it also points up the way that exhibition venues and shopping emporiums both functioned as sites where the female body could be exhibited for the pleasure of others. Retail space and screen space coalesced in an intriguing mixture of live spectacle and motion picture excitement, as the department store became a stage upon which Lucille Love's fictional drama unfolded. In some cases the proximity of retail sites and cinemas produced a more literal intertwining of the two activities, most notably in the case of Hamburger's Department Store in Los Angeles, which constructed a one-thousand-seat movie theater on its premises in 1910 so that customers could "relax from the ardors of shopping."[40] Yet the capacity of the cinema to *arrest* the shopper's gaze, to divert her attention away from the shops, was also acknowledged in this *Moving Picture Stories* "jest":

A fair maid went to town
To buy a new hat and gown
She stopped on the way
At a good Photoplay
And is sitting there yet, I'll be boun'![41]

Here film viewing is not simply integrated into women's patterns of consumption but becomes a substitute for it.

Once at the cinema, women would have found newer theaters often outfitted to look like better retail emporiums. "Why should not a theatre take advantage by making attractive lobby displays the same as a department store derives benefits by making attractive window displays?" *Moving Picture News* asked, reminding proprietors that presentational standards imported from the best shopping establishments would be particularly appealing to female clientele.[42] Many of the modifications in theater design and layout recommended to exhibitors during this period, such as improved lighting and ventilation, mirrored common areas, perfumed deodorizers, and uniformed attendants, borrowed heavily from department store interiors.[43] Modified theater architecture might also gently steer patrons to adopt decorous standards of behavior consistent with genteel leisure habits. Decrying the often unruly behavior of customers scrambling for tickets, *Moving Picture News* proposed that handsome brass railings be installed in theater entrances to guide the flow of patrons around ticket booths. Many picture houses had likely "lost considerable business because many women will refuse to enter a throng which is disorderly to purchase tickets, and many mothers undoubtedly refused to permit their children purchasing tickets when there was such possibility of their becoming injured in the jam."[44] In this case, architectural improvements quite literally furnished a structure through which the unruly mass of film patrons could be "disciplined" to conform to the expectations of bourgeois women.

Large, open foyers where patrons gathered before and after the show were also becoming prominent in new theaters designed exclusively for motion pictures, a change from older nickelodeons that tended to contain only a single, utilitarian screening room.[45] Lobbies akin to those found in "legitimate" theaters and vaudeville houses served as liminal spaces bridging street and screening auditorium, neither fully public nor fully given over to private viewing. Since most cinemas did not have set admission times during these years, customers congregated in entranceways waiting to be seated, leaving plenty of time for socializing and surveying other patrons also gathered there. Indeed, mirrored lobbies were such an essential convenience for female patrons, Sargent insisted, that no venue would want to be without them. "A mirror, hung in a good light," he claimed, "will always attract women and may help with the matinee business. The mirror should not be frankly for feminine use, but should suggest that it is part of the decorative scheme."[46] Mirrors brought out of ladies' restrooms and fitted in common areas where patrons assembled waiting for admission invited women not only to check their appearance, as they might do with more privacy in restrooms, but also to enjoy the image of themselves circulating amid other members of the audience. Mirrors that reflected and multiplied images of customers and commodities alike had been essential features of department store interiors for many years, creating illusions of space and abundance crucial to the consumer ethos.[47]

Like the best retail entrepreneurs, then, theater designers of the era were keenly aware of creating a space where female customers could self-consciously present themselves to the public eye. A New York firm hired in 1912 to decorate a lavish new picture house in Lexington, Kentucky, suggested that "all the theaters must cater to the ladies. We must arrange things so they will be benefited, so none will be seated where there will be a harmful color effect, where every woman may feel that her own gown was thought of in arranging the lights."[48] Subtle lighting effects and color schemes, design principles long associated with department store interiors, flattered female patrons while also guaranteeing that they were being featured to best advantage.[49] Fashioning a motion picture experience suitable for women, according to this logic, meant providing facilities where they remained the center of attention, since they were imagined as patrons who associated leisure with the display of themselves and their own social status. Dressing up, or "putting on style," at leisure venues was an especially important element in working women's fantasies of social mobility during these years, Kathy Peiss demonstrates.[50] Purchasing elaborate outfits and cosmetics, then parading themselves at cinemas, dance halls, and amusement parks, allowed working women to transform themselves through consumption and exhibitionism, if only temporarily. As Bertha Richardson recognized in 1910, "A shop girl, earning seven dollars a week, has a desire to appear as if she has no connection with the conditions and life which would be consistent with her earnings."[51]

If theaters increasingly looked like retail sites, at the end of the show filmgoers were offered souvenirs and products that commodified the ephemeral photoplay experience, often in ways that explicitly connected it to shopping. Promotions and giveaways offered "advertising accessories," tangible products women could take home along with their other parcels, carrying the motion picture experience beyond theater walls. Postcards of picture players that became available at many theaters in the early 1910s furnished filmgoers with permanent mementos of the fleeting cinematic experience. For exhibitors they aided in "establishing patrons in the habit of regularity, since the desire is to obtain the complete set."[52] Fans, for their part, were advised that souvenir postcards represented a premium possession, "something rather finer than you can buy in the store."[53] Increasingly elaborate souvenirs, like pocket-size cutouts of Mary Pickford in full butterfly regalia offered for the release of *Madame Butterfly* in 1915, were designed as keepsakes produced chiefly for their appeal to women.[54] Key among the values accorded such accessories by Paramount's new publicity department was that they could easily be inserted "in a pocket or a purse, thus increasing [their] chances of preservation and insuring a measure of permanency foreign to the herald."[55] A fan culture that chiefly targeted women during these years did so by providing souvenirs and tie-ins that froze photoplays in possessable, consumable moments through the dissemination of products.

Other promotional items, more clearly domestic in orientation, tied film patronage into established patterns of household consumption. Spoons embossed with the likeness of picture players were popular keepsakes in the teens. "More than an ornament," spoons offered by the National Stars Corporation were designed for "lasting service" in the home.[56] Elegantly mounted star portraits were "just the right thing for den, room, or wall decoration," one ad claimed, persuading women to yoke their fascination with photoplayers to their facility for home decoration.[57] Satin pillow tops autographed by Eclair players were a guaranteed "matinee drawing card," sure to "please your women patrons mightily," exhibitors were promised in the studio's *Bulletin*.[58] Dishware giveaways, in which customers collected coupons in order to receive sets of china, were "particularly useful in matinee work," Sargent found, since they fostered regular, habit-forming patterns of attendance among women. He counseled exhibitors not to worry about the cost of such prizes; they would pay for themselves, he claimed, since women "will not only come themselves but urge all their friends to attend."[59] Such gimmicks insisted, rather forcefully, on the compatibility of domestic life and film culture in an attempt to leave the more sensational world of urban amusement culture far behind, as home and cinema became spheres linked through the activities of the female consumer. Care for her household, specifically envisioned as the acquisition of upmarket accessories like matching sets of china, became a model for female filmgoing. One sees here the basis upon which middle-class women appealed to theater owners: perceived as customers with regular, predictable habits whose attendance, if carefully cultivated, could be depended upon over time, like brand loyalty, they were also believed to exercise considerable influence over others. With her allegiance, her bargain-hunter's instinct, and her domestic mandate, the female consumer proved an enticing prospect.

Baby contests sponsored by theaters throughout the teens also tied women's traditional homebound pursuits to the cinema through the conduit of consumer culture. Family photographs submitted by cinemagoers were placed on slides and projected on the screen where patrons were entitled to vote for their favorite child with each ticket purchased. Baby show promotions explicitly demarcated movie houses as sites of family entertainment, by ensuring that screen images were associated—almost too literally—with domestic concerns. Designed to bring mothers into theaters, along with their children (if only symbolically), baby contests rendered motion picture venues akin to family photo

albums writ large, sites where the community-as-family staged the mutual ad-
miration of its offspring. Women would be eager to enter these contests, a
sponsor suggested, implying that female patrons were fully aware of the presentational quality of theatrical space and eager to exhibit their progeny on
the screen. In fact, baby show promotions allowed women to engage in the
presentational dynamics of both lobby and screen at one remove, showcasing
their children rather than themselves. "Who does not know the eagerness of
the young mother to display the charms of her beautiful baby?" asked the
Nickelodeon.[60] The ultimate inducement, however, remained the coveted grand
prize on exhibit in the theater lobby or ticket booth. Purchase "anything which
appeals to a mother's heart," exhibitors were advised: baby carriages, sewing
machines, dishes, and other household wares would always entice this clientele.[61] Once mothers had entered, hoping to garner prizes for their offspring,
their friends would surely follow. "Enthusiastic friends of the mothers walk
right up the ticket office and buy whole rolls of tickets and vote them for their
favorite," the *Nickelodeon* reported. "Young ladies go out after anybody they
can find, induce them to buy and vote tickets for their favorite, the baby of
their sister or brother or some dear friend."[62] In fact, baby contests were so
popular at the Lyda Theater in Grand Island, Nebraska, that proprietors were
able to beat their competitor even on days when he offered feature films.[63]
The baby show gimmick, then, configured both exhibition space and viewing
experience in terms consistent with bourgeois women's traditional spheres of
interest, for it combined the logic of display and consumption with the practice
of motherhood. With such prized giveaways in the lobby, theaters became sites
where women's eyes were tempted to wander beyond the screen, throughout
the space of exhibition, much as they would in retail space.

Women's magazines offered another forcible model of stately feminine leisure that film exhibitors also marshaled in their effort to recruit middle-class
filmgoers. Like department stores, many women's magazines fostered a culture
associated almost exclusively with the middle-class woman and organized
around her fantasies and desires.[64] If the *Nickelodeon* warned in 1909 of the
industry's tendency to overlook the large, affluent, consumer-oriented female
constituencies fostered by women's magazines, it is clear that by the midteens
the industry had heeded this call. Paramount consistently advertised in wom-
en's publications, hoping to draw female readers into theaters and to woo theater owners willing to pay Paramount's higher rental fees on the promise of
just such patronage. Slides projected in theaters reminded viewers of this connection in a circular gesture: "This Theatre Shows Paramount Pictures. The
photoplays you are reading about in the *Ladies' Home Journal*, *Saturday Evening Post*, *Woman's Home Companion*, *Ladies' World*, *American Sunday Magazine*, and the leading newspapers everywhere."[65] These same magazines
played a signal role in encouraging filmgoing among their readership by publishing fiction tie-ins for movie serials, as I will demonstrate in chapter 3. The

Ladies' World was particularly active in motion picture promotions, publishing tie-ins of major Edison serials like *What Happened to Mary?*,[66] and sponsoring "The Great Motion Picture Hero Contest" with Universal in 1913, which allowed readers to vote for their favorite male star, marking "the first time that the women voters of America have had a chance to vote in a national election."[67] "Everybody goes to the movies these days," the magazine declared, simultaneously promoting motion pictures to its readers and suggesting that any publication would be foolish not to capitalize upon such a broad audience.[68] These promotions tended to stress the compatibility of picturegoing with the twinned culture of consumption and domestic science that women's magazines celebrated.

In "A Colgate Christmas Movie," a full-page advertisement on the back cover of the *Ladies' World*'s December 1914 issue, magazine readership, film spectatorship, consumer culture, and domestic life come together in the tale of one woman's search for ideal holiday gifts. A series of panels depicts the unfolding drama in individual "shots" interspersed with descriptive titles. A smart young wife takes the trolley into town and fights her way through crowded shops only to arrive home empty-handed. Not until she espies a magazine layout for Colgate toiletries that evening is her dilemma solved. Returning to the shops the following day, she buys gifts for her entire family, then enjoys a happy Christmas with her husband and children in the final frames. Through the circularity of its story, the campaign insists upon the compatibility of shopping, browsing through magazines, and going to the cinema as related spheres of women's leisure. Fantasies of upward mobility were enacted through the woman's gaze—at product ads, at store display cases, and at the movies—as women's "inarticulate longings" were fed through consumer desire.[69]

The circulation of female desire in consumer culture, where women were themselves put on view and were invited to imagine their own commodification in the fictive space of department store interiors and women's magazines points to another aspect of women's relation to the cinema. Solicited at retail sites, spaces of fantasy and mobilization, women were also encouraged to fantasize their role as desired objects at the center of attention in a manner that mimicked their status at the cinema, where they were both paying customers and targets for consumption on exhibit in theater lobbies, as Lauren Rabinovitz points out. It is precisely this tension that gets played out in satirical portraits of female filmgoing during these years.[70]

Added Attractions: Women in the Audience

Exhibitors welcomed women into their establishments with ladies' tickets, reserved seats, matinee screenings, and elegant accommodations, all of which were designed to elevate cinemas and cinemagoing in the minds of cultivated women in the hopes that they would, in turn, lend an air of refinement to the establishments they frequented. Or, at the very least, proprietors hoped that working women among their regular clientele, already accustomed to "putting on style" at leisure outings, would adopt the graceful manner of moviegoing suggested in so many of the promotions. Trade publications and fan magazines, both relatively new to film culture in the early teens, noted with interest the marked visibility of women among moviegoers in columns, cartoons, poems, and jokes that frequently targeted female cinephiles. Yet, behind this fascination lurked a distinct unease about the presence of women at theaters. Hoping to foster an upscale audience for the movies, exhibitors eagerly reconfigured their establishments to accommodate the tastes and habits of status-conscious women; yet it seems that women themselves had to be tailored for cinemagoing, since their presence at theaters was often associated with behavior that interfered with the enjoyment of other patrons, or compromised their own viewing position.

Ironically, the attention to socializing and self-dislay that many showmen encouraged in their female clientele fostered modes of conduct that were seen as disruptive in theaters. Women who overdressed for the cinema and insisted upon parading themselves about lobbies and auditoriums distracted other patrons from the screen and became the target of many jests, as were women who chattered and gossiped throughout the show without much evident interest in the films. Feminine propriety, so welcomed by exhibitors courting respectability, was also mocked in unflattering portraits of women who put on airs at picture houses, expecting a more upscale outing than most venues could provide. Women were not as easily accommodated into exhibition space, then, as theater owners might have hoped. Indeed, they were frequently accused of being unable to adopt the viewing position demanded of classical cinema, because they were too distracted by friends or too consumed with their own appearance. While other commentators have stressed how ties to department stores and consumer culture in movie promotions and theater designs enabled new modes of female spectatorship by bridging long-standing prohibitions against women's looking, in fact ties to shopping, fashion, and socializing created filmgoing customs that were thought to be at odds with the models of classical spectatorship developing during these years. So even as Miriam Hansen, Sumiko Higashi, and Lauren Rabinovitz show how department stores "mobilized the female gaze in the service of consumption," teaching women "new ways of seeing that they put to use at the cinema," we must also stress how "the gaze distracted by the lure of consumption" often did not fit comfortably with the absorbed model of film viewing ever more prevalent in the early teens.[71]

Ladies who brought an overwrought sense of decorum to their local picture house were caricatured in *Motion Picture Magazine*'s tongue-in-cheek guide, "Etiquette: On the Proper Way for Two Women to Spend an Evening in a

Moving Picture Theater."[72] Admonishing its fictional cinemagoers to "remember that you are both ladies and that politeness is the main object," the article instead chronicles their arrogant and ostentatious behavior. Putting on social airs designed to elevate themselves above others in the audience, the women pretend to recognize society friends across the way, making it clear to anyone within hearing range that they are in the five-cent section only because more expensive seats were unavailable. Their standards are elevated to such a degree that they can find nothing but fault with their fellow patrons, from whom they are always careful to distinguish themselves: they complain about small boys who have "no business" being in the theater, and object to verbal abuse from a "brute who is rude enough to make such remarks to a lady," concluding that "motion pictures don't care who sees them, judging from the people sitting near me." Obviously having paid attention to solicitous "ladies'" promotions, the two demand a level of courtesy and service from theater staff to which they evidently feel entitled, but which their behavior ultimately does not warrant. Neither the ticket taker nor the usher treats them with the courtesy they expect, and both receive tongue-lashings as a result. Employees instructed by their class-conscious employers never to hit a lady find themselves unable to retaliate against such aggression. Somewhat paradoxically, the women's insistence upon social propriety befitting ladies' leisure disrupts rather than uplifts the theater. Women exploiting their newfound status as distinguished film patrons here become demanding and abrasive. By emphasizing the women's "performance" of refined cinemagoing, *Motion Picture*'s etiquette lesson also draws attention to the ways in which women of diverse class backgrounds might have used expectations telegraphed in ladies' promotions to stage their own uplift. Boorish behavior at the cinema is here no longer associated with such outmoded practices as eating during the show but with class pretensions that are distinctly feminized.

Particularly impertinent is the pair's inclination to chatter aloud during the films. Commenting on everything and anything, only some of which has any bearing on the material shown, they concentrate on nondiegetic details, such as fashions featured on the screen or the players' private lives, in a distracted, intertextual mode of viewing. Chatty women became one of the more familiar caricatures of the era. Mrs. McGabb, *Moving Picture World*'s ode to similarly talkative viewers, confers with her friend Mrs. Simms throughout an entire film program, keeping up a running commentary on all aspects of the experience—their choice of seats, the advertising slides, the "Mary Piquant" pictures she saw the previous evening, the piano player, the projection quality, and whether or not scantily clad actors had caught cold while filming—much to the annoyance of surrounding patrons.[73] *Motography* created a similar caricature in Mother Squeers, the "old lady in the audience," the proverbial gossiping woman, whose detailed dissection of the differences between leading film manufacturers provided the basis for a column of the same name. "Mother

Squeers, being a dyed-in-the-wool 'fan,' . . . loves to talk about the films, and it is not unusual to see her in animated conversation with an auditor in a neighboring seat."[74] She is at once the ideal patron, who attends every night and "watches the flitting photodramas with huge delight," and an object of derision whose chatter, however informed, disturbs others in the audience. The Mother Squeers column walked a particularly fine line, for it denigrated the kind of feminized intertextual consumption specifically fostered in film aficionados, while at the same time providing readers with noteworthy insider information. One poem went so far as to question why women attended movies at all, so little did they seem concerned with watching the show:

Sarah Jones and Lizzie Green
saw a movie on the screen.
During quite a friendly chat
they discussed just this and that,
conversing in a tone so clear
that all could very easy hear.
The two girls never saw the play—
they had far too much to say.
They sure enjoyed the repartee
and were as pleasant as could be.
It would really be absurd
if their neighbors lost a word!
When for talkfests ladies go,
why select a picture show?[75]

The recurring figure of a boisterous, talkative woman, a proverbial Mrs. McGabb, shows us how often women's expectations about moviegoing, fostered through advertising and promotional campaigns that stressed the social space of the theater over isolated visual pleasure, might have clashed with new conceptions of film viewing. If women coming to the cinema expected a setting where they could meet with friends and converse happily during the show, they would have found this behavior at odds with models of spectatorship that downplayed social interaction among patrons. Mrs. McGabb thus offers a gentle corrective to the practice of talking through pictures, which, Miriam Hansen has shown, was increasingly out of favor in the 1910s, replaced by viewing practices that stressed silent absorption in a manner that de-emphasized both the theater space and the viewer's body. The "rule of silence" was a learned custom during these years, Hansen argues, consistent with other modifications in viewing habits and exhibition practices that focused attention away from exhibition space and onto the film text itself.[76] Communal activities like sing-alongs, slide shows, and lectures, typical of a varied nickelodeon program only a few years earlier, also diminished, while a model of silent, absorbed spectatorship became the norm, a mode of attention more appropriate for view-

1. Mrs. McGabb, *Moving Picture World*, 1916.

ing longer, multireel films that were themselves less dependent upon extratextual information. Although women were most often figured as the "gabbers" who interfered with focused spectatorship, it is unlikely they were the only ones talking in picture houses. Instead, perhaps because they were such a visible index of expanding patronage and revised standards of conduct, female filmgoers bore the burden of constructive correction that applied to all viewers. Overly chatty ladies figured the bad habits of everybody.[77] A large women who invariably selects an aisle seat, then refuses to shift her weight to allow others to pass, Mrs. McGabb is imagined as a literal obstruction to the viewing enjoyment of others, figured through her physical girth, but manifest most profoundly in her propensity for gab. "Down in Front," the title of the *World*'s portrait, only foregrounds her status as impediment.

If distracted forms of spectatorship illustrated by Mrs. McGabb mock the social component of attending the movies that had been promoted to women, commentators also began to reconsider the appropriateness of soliciting patrons from among the ranks of retail shoppers, concerned that integrating the two activities might prompt a mode of inattentiveness that ran counter to evolving dictates of absorbed spectatorship. *Moving Picture World*'s "Our Man about Town" worried about film patrons drawn mainly from the ranks of department store customers "who have a few minutes to spare between shopping and the keeping of appointments." Picturegoing, particularly after the advent of lengthier, feature-film fare, demanded more attentive viewing habits than the distractedness typical of someone catching a show between appointments. Cinemas were "not halfway-houses," he declared, "but full-fledged places of amusement. To hold to the contrary is to class the theaters as mere nickelodeons of the former days."[78] So while ladies' matinee programs, complete with parcel-checking services and lavish retiring rooms, allowed women to integrate picturegoing into their daily shopping routines, viewing practices commanded by lengthier and more complex film texts precluded such a casual approach to attending the show.

Women were also regularly lampooned for their tendency to use visits to the local movie house as an occasion for adornment and exhibitionism. The caricatured movie enthusiast, obsessed with her own appearance at the theater, often missed the point of the enterprise. In "Too Dark to See," a cartoon featured in Paramount's *Picture Progress* fan magazine, a mother tries to entice her son to wash up before the two leave for the movies.[79] Hands buried in pockets, the boy rejects his mother's suggestion, protesting, "Oh, no, Ma; this is a moving picture show." Mother and son stand with their backs to one another: she is adjusting her hat in a mirror atop a bureau to the left; he is facing right, but looking back over his shoulder toward her. Implicit class and gender distinctions structure the joke. The boy believes that movie houses do not demand the same attention to personal hygiene as "legitimate" theaters, whereas his mother views motion picture theaters as spaces of social propriety where she will be seen and judged by others. This is evident not only in her

TOO DARK TO SEE.

Mother—Now, Willie, wash your hands and face if you
are going to the theatre.
Willie—Oh, no, Ma; this is a moving picture show.

2. *Paramount Picture Progress*, 1915.

admonition to her son but in her own position at the mirror. Going to the picture
show is, for her, associated with making *herself* presentable for public view.
The two are arranged in the frame in a manner that accentuates her exhibitionist
role, for both the mother's gaze and the son's view back over his shoulder are
directed at her mirror reflection. Humor is drawn from the misalignment of
the son's attitude toward the cinema, where looking at the pictures far out-
weighs being looked at oneself, and the mother's, where putting oneself on
display is the chief feature of attending the show. On one level, the cartoon
appears to challenge the boy's presumed hierarchy of amusements and his low
estimation of cinema's audience: movie houses were no longer the purview of
grubby little boys, the joke implies, for they now attracted an older, more
respectable clientele like his mother. Yet the caption, "Too Dark to See," also

3. *Motion Picture Magazine*, 1916.

mocks the mother's concern with her own appearance, suggesting, as her son does, that no one will notice them in the darkened theater, that her obsession is more narcissistic than practical.

"Too Dark to See" is only one of many similar figurations that poke fun at women's rituals of self-adornment prior to theater outings. A young woman preparing to leave for the pictures stands before her bureau applying face powder in a *Motion Picture Magazine* cartoon called "Added Attractions."[80] Her outlandish costume consists of perilously high-heeled shoes, provocatively short striped skirt, clashing floral blouse, wide collar, pearls, dangling ear bangles, and a broad, flower-strewn hat. Outfitted in this fashion she threatens the preeminence of anything projected on the screen. By placing the film buff in front of the mirror, the cartoon emphasizes her own construction of—and pleasure in—the vision she creates. Gazing at one's own reflection is again presented as a woman's central specular experience of the movies. Through cosmetics and costume the young fan "adds attractions" to her natural features, like a ten-cent theater manager doing everything she can to solicit interest. If the woman's pleasure in attending the show centered on making herself the magnet of attention, however, she became a potential rival of the cinema, an "added attraction" to which other customers' fascination might always be drawn. Just as gossiping and socializing in the theater suggested a mode of filmgoing that was at once too distracted for the reverent, wholly absorbed viewer favored in new models of spectatorship and too *distracting* for other patrons in the theater, overly adorned women threatened to draw eyes away from the screen while they were themselves overly focused on their own reflected image circulating in elegant screening venues. Women were unsuited to film viewing, these cartoons suggest, because of an ingrained, narcissistic absorption with their own image.

It was not simply female patrons who "added" to the show, disrupting the entertainment and distracting other viewers, but female employees were also more common at theaters in these years. Exhibitors eager to upgrade the tenor of their establishments employed a growing army of women as ticket sellers, pianists, singers, and ushers. Like female customers, these employees played a substantial role in establishing the class dynamics of screening venues, signifying either refined leisure or lowbrow amusements. Ticket sellers stationed in booths outside theaters were normally the first employees patrons encountered, and were therefore instrumental in setting the tone of these establishments. "The ticket seller should be a bright and attractive young lady, neatly dressed and wide-awake," the *Motion Picture Handbook* suggested, adding that "many a theatre loses business it might otherwise get simply because of an untidy looking ticket office presided over by an unprepossessing, gum-chewing girl."[81] Female theater owners, who were not uncommon during these years, as Eileen Bowser has shown, were often thought to lend a particular air of distinction to their establishments.[82] Bowser notes the praise lavished upon one such venue by a female customer who felt that "the refined touch of an educated woman is evident in every detail," from the ticket taker, "a quiet refined girl—not the giggling, gum chewing kind," who added poise to the front of the house, to the coat-checker inside, "a lady who might well grace a drawing-room."[83]

But in many cases female employees served only as "added attractions" to a theater's decor. "Girls ushers" introduced at the Walnut Theater in Louisville, Kentucky, as part of its improvement campaign became just another decorative feature of the house, along with a revised color scheme and architectural embellishments. Each usher wore "a party dress cut on a pretty pattern . . . [and] a black velvet, tri-cornered hat, with a rosette at each corner," outfits that produced an "effective result from the viewpoint of appearances," according to *Moving Picture World*.[84] Presented as visually pleasing adornments to exhibition space, smartly outfitted employees also ran the risk of competing with the show. Describing the ideal ticket seller, Epes Sargent stressed the fine balance that she ought to maintain between welcoming customers to the cinema and constituting herself as a rival object of fascination. She "should be attractive but not too pretty," he said, ". . . a woman with a tactful manner and a winning smile is a greater asset than a peroxide blonde who has no use for women and too much attraction for young men."[85] Piano accompanists, many of whom were women, posed a particular problem, according to the *World*, since they were themselves performers who occupied a position adjacent to the screen:

> With the coming of these girls, facilities for withdrawal from the public eye had to be provided. Even now one sees, at a few of the shows, the girl piano player boldly face the incoming audience, with the lights turned up; flirting with the ushers and

altogether comporting themselves with the same freedom as a member of a peripatetic German band; but at other places . . . the piano player slips under the stage and is not visible until the lights are turned down and the film starts again.[86]

A pianist who placed herself too near the screen, facing the audience, and who used that position to attract sexual interest, was not only presented as less respectable than an accompanist who ducked out of view; she also threatened to become the main attraction, furnishing an unruly spectacle that might override anything projected on the screen. So while female employees were thought to lend cultivation to the venues where they worked, their presence could also deflect attention away from the cinema itself.

Surely the best-known vexation associated with female filmgoers of the era was their preference for expansive, ornate hats and their reluctance to remove such headgear in theaters, a practice that prompted exhibitors to project "Ladies Please Remove Your Hats" slides between reels in an effort to urge women into compliance. Tactics of this sort evidently had little effect. An exasperated *Motography* headline complained of "Those Hats Again" in 1910, reporting that audience members were "annoyed incessantly" by women who continued to wear hats throughout the show, effectively blocking the view of those behind. Clearly more direct action was needed. So troublesome was the habit that several municipalities considered—and in some cases even passed—civic ordinances requiring that women remove headgear in motion picture theaters.[87] Irrespective of fashion trends, the inordinate attention paid to ladies' hats throughout this period signaled the appearance of well-heeled audience members dressed as they might to go shopping, attend a club meeting, visit the theater, or meet friends for a luncheon. It points, in other words, to the importance that both working women and bourgeois homemakers placed on appearing well turned out at the cinema. Women surely caused such a remarked-upon nuisance precisely because they formed such a visible component of cinema's expanding audience. Yet the hat controversy also points to a more serious struggle over the nature of exhibition space. Like images that lampooned women's obsession with their appearance, caricatures of hat-wearing filmgoers suggest that a delight in self-adornment which women were encouraged to bring to the cinema was actually at odds with evolving viewing practices that de-emphasized theater space, the viewer's body, and interaction among patrons, as Hansen contends.

Tongue-in-cheek tips in *Motion Picture*'s etiquette guide offered a gentle corrective to women's tendency to parade themselves at leisure outings:

When you sit down, be sure and do not remove your hat. That is only necessary in legitimate theaters and is not expected here. It is a good plan to raise both hands to the head with elbows held high, and utilize the next five minutes in rearranging your hair under your hat. The person in back of you can see the screen very well through the space left in the crook of your elbow. It will break the monotony for him, if it doesn't break his neck.[88]

Accompanying illustrations showed hapless male customers trying to peer through the raised elbows of a young lady adjusting her bonnet. The problem was that fashionably attired women simply prevented others from seeing the screen. *Moving Picture Stories* immortalized the fate of an unfortunate cinemagoer forced "to twist and turn behind a great big hat" in a poem that illustrates how style-conscious members of the audience interfered with normal viewing practices.

> I sit in sweet contentment, feasting eyes on scene and view,
> As mountains, land and ocean, pass before me in review.
> But the slide that pleases greatly, gives a tickle to my "slats,"
> Is one they throw on nightly, "Ladies please remove your hats."[89]

A *Motion Picture Magazine* cartoon drawn from the perspective of two gentlemen seated behind a mammoth hat figured the female viewer precisely as a visual blockage.[90] Far broader than the size of its wearer's head, the hat creates a large black space that blocks out a sizable portion of both the screen image and the cartoon frame itself. Dwarfed by her hat and rendered only in silhouette, the female filmgoer is less a distraction to the eye than an obstruction to view, an absence—literally a blank spot where vision becomes impossible. Poking fun at the lengths to which patrons were driven to avoid any disruption of cinema's spectacle, another cartoon showed a spectator using a periscope to see over the hat of an elegant matron seated in front of him.[91] Particularly hazardous were long feathers attached to grander specimens that threatened to poke out the eye of viewers seated behind. "Whether he has two eyes or four, he isn't anxious . . . to be deprived of even one of them," women were reminded.[92] Audience members frustrated by extravagant headgear were almost invariably men in these caricatures, men whose viewing pleasure was either impaired or, in the final example, actually obliterated by ladies' hats. Women were cast as those new to cinemagoing, in need of instruction about its social customs and audience sight lines, more concerned with their own appearance than with watching the screen. Lavishly adorned and bonneted women disrupted and dominated theatrical space in these caricatures, becoming "added attractions" sufficient to cast cinema itself into the shadows.

A solution to the hat conundrum, less extreme than either periscopes or legislation, was proposed in a slide offered to exhibitors, who were apparently persuaded to encourage the very stereotypes of female narcissism for which women were chastised. The slide featured a drawing of a young girl arranging her hat before a mirror, accompanied by an announcement that theater management had installed mirrors in the lobby so that ladies could readjust their hats after the show, the obvious suggestion being that headgear could be safely removed during the pictures. *Motography* cited the item with approval, noting its effective use at Chicago's new Orpheum Theater: "[T]he slide itself presents an idea to many exhibitors to provide just such a comfort for their women

Now, doesn't it seem like this when a woman in front of you "forgets" to remove her hat during an exciting picture?

4. *Motion Picture Magazine*, 1917.

patrons," reminding readers that "ladies are the backbone of any exhibitor's trade."[93] Mirrored foyers would entice well-adorned women out of screening spaces, where they threatened to draw eyes away from the screen, and into bright meeting areas where they were inspired to look their best. Like a small inscription of the screen within the lobby itself, mirrors allowed the female patron to see herself at once "on screen" and in the theater. She would be able to refocus attention toward herself after the show, by looking at her own mirror reflection and adjusting her hat so that she was once again presentable for the view of others. Her gesture was further complicated by the slide that advertised the mirror convenience in the first place, for it projected on screen an image of a woman looking in the mirror—or rather a woman figured as a charmingly self-absorbed little girl. Seeing her likeness on the screen, watching herself in a mirror, the female patron was invited to replicate this action in the lobby.

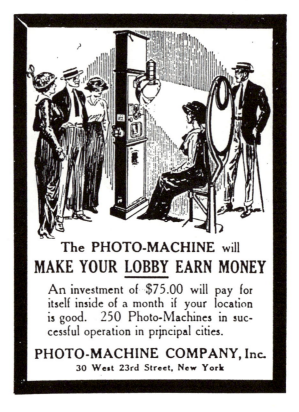

The PHOTO-MACHINE will
MAKE YOUR LOBBY EARN MONEY

An investment of $75.00 will pay for
itself inside of a month if your location
is good.   250 Photo-Machines in successful operation in principal cities.

PHOTO-MACHINE COMPANY, Inc.
30 West 23rd Street, New York

5. *Motion Picture News*, 1914.

Once again the mirror acted as a central figure through which female filmgoing
was imagined, here shifted from the home into exhibition space itself. Proprietors advised to install lobby mirrors for the comfort of female patrons were
also told how mirrors could be used to regulate the conduct of women who
interfered with the viewing pleasure of others in the audience.[94]

An automatic "Photo-Machine" advertised to exhibitors in *Motion Picture
News* offered women the opportunity to permanently fix the fleeting reflections
on view in theater foyers by photographing themselves before or after the
show.[95] Such a mechanism could turn any lobby into a profitable venture, theater owners were told, since women would be eager for the convenience. Fashionably dressed customers depicted in an illustration accompanying the ad
stand watching as a woman sits having her picture taken. Bathed in a spotlight's
glow, sitting in front of a white background screen, she squarely faces the
instrument's lens. Seated, she mimics the posture of a viewer inside the theater,
but her position is now inverted: the beam of light comes not from the projector
behind her head but from a spotlight in front of her; she no longer sits facing

the screen watching the patterns on its surface but poses before a blank field waiting to be transformed into an image herself. Reversing the very process of projection itself, she renders herself the object of the camera's gaze, while the oval screen in front of which she sits echoes the mirror so frequently evoked in representations of the female viewer, more absorbed in her own image than in anything that could be presented on the screen.

The female viewer's troubled relation to the screen is perhaps best expressed in the caricature of the "movie-struck girl" circulating widely during these years. The fan who confused her love of cinema with a desire to appear on-screen herself became a popular, if cautionary, model of film enthusiasm in the teens. With mild but rather insistent alarm *Woman's Home Companion* outlined the "epidemic," claiming that the nation's daughters were "going movie-mad at an alarming rate," and decrying "the hundreds of young girls fluttering around the movie spotlight in vain."[96] "Sentimental," "pathetic," "credulous," and "deluded" would-be actresses regularly fell prey to mail-order companies promoting useless screen acting lessons and dubious "test film" schemes that siphoned young women's savings into dead-end vanity productions, the article reported. Such crazed devotion to the medium was similarly diagnosed in *McClure's* as "Filmitis . . . the most modern of diseases."[97] Unlike the *stage*struck girl of a generation earlier, whose infatuation could be treated with "tender tolerance" since it was a passing phase that "amounted only to a disease which every girl had in the course of evolution, like croup or measles," the modern *movie*-struck condition was much more serious, reports claimed. Mothers, cousins, aunts, even male relatives now encouraged the phenomenon, pushing young women into film careers in order to live out their own dreams. Repeatedly casting female viewers as "young," "little," and "miss," the "movie-struck" caricature infantilized women's filmgoing, attributing to women an immature, narcissistic—even mad—relation to the screen, forever confused with the mirror.

Is it any wonder, then, that early movie fan magazines like *Motion Picture Magazine* and *Motion Picture Classic* carried countless advertisements for women's beauty products claiming to improve everything from hair, complexion, and eyelashes to corns and crooked spines? Fan culture increasingly catered to young women in the early 1910s, recognizing the growing component they formed in most motion picture audiences, as Kathryn Fuller has demonstrated. Information about the artistry and technology of moviemaking common to early fan publications had targeted men and women alike, she argues, while a growing emphasis on glamour, beauty, and style signaled their increased attention to women readers.[98] *Motion Picture*'s regular "Beauty Hints" column gave fans advice on how to re-create screen beauty and poise at home, Paramount's *Picture Progress* offered readers tips from the studio's stars on how to "eat and keep" and what gowns to wear "when you dance," while women's magazines began carrying ads for beauty products endorsed by early

When our dear grandmamas were girls,   Today the girlies everywhere,
They'd smile and smooth their pretty curls,   In the mirror gravely stare;
Look in the mirror then and say   "Am I fair enough," they say,
"Oh, will he think me fair today?"   "To be a movie star some day?"

6. *Motion Picture Classic*, 1916.

film celebrities like Mary Pickford.[99] So even as cartoons, often in these same magazines, chastised women for a preoccupation with their appearance at the cinema, beauty columns and product ads encouraged female fans to associate moviegoing with self-display and to scrutinize their own appearance with much the same attention that they brought to photos and close-ups of their favored screen idols.

Often the ultimate goal of such scrutiny was to end up on film oneself. "Have You a Movie Camera Face?" readers of *Motion Picture Classic* were asked in an article inviting them to devote as much time to looking at their own reflection as they did to watching the screen.[100] Cartoons satirized the movie-struck girl caught up in fantasies of her own stardom, ever-ready for the camera, performing each gesture with self-conscious theatricality. Transfixed before her mirror reflection, the cinephile no longer considered the impact she might have on prospective suitors; instead she wondered "am I fair enough to be a movie star some day?" Acting, dancing, and music lessons were offered by the dozen on the pages of early fan magazines, as if the continual task of decoration and self-improvement, cosmetic and otherwise, was one from which the movie fan must never retire. Many young women were encouraged to parlay their love of movies into an on-screen career, a fad propelled no doubt by the new star industry that celebrated the rise of "ordinary" young women to the ranks of the nation's most beloved personalities, eagerly chronicled in fan magazines that explained "How They Got In," and by magazine profiles that glamorized the culture surrounding southern California's new "motion picture land."[101] Both surely helped generate long lines of prospective employees looking for work as extras in Hollywood.

Such a misguided, naive understanding of the film industry failed to register the truth, *Woman's Home Companion* cautioned its "movie-struck" readers: factorylike filmmaking studios were already "busily engaged in manufacturing stars at low wages" and had no need of more aspiring talent. "Yes, Maude Jones, it's a long, long way to Filmland!" *Motion Picture Classic* warned. "The Romantically inclined young girl who dreams of signal honors as a screen favorite would soon be disillusioned should she visit the studio and actively engage in the profession of acting before the camera."[102] *Photoplay* published its own exposé on "breaking into the game," penned by "a girl who didn't break in."[103] Confessing to having been bitten by the "Movi-Pictoribus insect," yet another malady evidently befalling impressionable young ladies, the author recounted how she became "a rapt and driveling enthusiast of the once-despised screen," an obsession that propelled her into acting work. After spending her Sundays practicing before the mirror, she managed to land a bit part at Essanay along with several other "hope-to-be-actorines." In the end she found the work boring, mechanical, distinctly lacking in glamour, and above all, fruitless—no awaited callback ever materialized.

Deluded though she might be, the devoted film fan was nevertheless essential to the industry, as Universal's general manager, Joe Brandt, admitted when interviewed about the "movie-struck" girl. "She is at the same time the biggest asset and the biggest annoyance of the moving picture industry," Brandt confessed. "Because of the millions of movie-struck girls in America, the moving picture theatres flourish. A very large percentage of our business unquestionably comes from these young women, who eagerly flock to see every new film." The problem, Brandt pointed out, was that these women's acting ambitions threatened to displace their status as film patrons. If all interested women were hired at the studios, not only would there not be enough theaters in the country to show all the resulting films, there would no longer be audiences to see them. *Woman's Home Companion* ends predictably by suggesting that "Little Miss Movie-Struck" ought to be made to understand that "the best moving picture in which she can play a leading role is one entitled 'Home.' "

At once vital to the growing industry and a challenge to expected audience decorum, the "movie-struck" girl embodied many of the contradictions that surrounded women's filmgoing at the end of the nickelodeon period. Coveted though they might have been, female audiences were associated with a host of filmgoing habits at odds with the model of absorbed classical spectatorship evolving in the prewar years. Despite their status as prized patrons, women brought to the movies a series of associations and expectations that complicated exhibition space and accepted viewing practice just at the moment when cinemagoing began to receive broad-based appeal. Promotional strategies designed to bolster female patronage fostered modes of attending the cinema that may have been consistent with bourgeois women's leisure expectations but often proved to be inconsistent with new film-viewing norms. Women who came to the cinema to socialize, or who dropped into picture houses on the way to and from shopping expeditions, brought a distracted mode of engagement to the cinema, no longer appropriate for longer, more complex films that demanded absorbed attention. Handsomely dressed women also presented something of an obstacle at the cinema, because they threatened to deflect the gaze of other patrons away from the screen, toward themselves. And their own attention seemed to waver between a narcissistic fascination with their reflections and an interest in the shadows flickering on screen, in a peculiar confusion of screen and mirror. Even as women embodied refined patronage in many an exhibitor's eye, commentary on women's moviegoing habits and foibles suggests that they also came to symbolize much of what was disruptive in theater space and unsuited to film viewing during these years as well.

Two

Is Any Girl Safe?
Motion Pictures, Women's Leisure,
and the White Slavery Scare

"What can be done to rid the exhibiting profession of men who solicit half-grown girls to 'come in and see the only white slave film on the avenue,'" *Moving Picture World* cried in the summer of 1914, following months of controversy surrounding the depiction of white slave stories on the screen, the audiences they were attracting, and the very safety of the nation's motion picture theaters.[1] When a white slavery panic swept the country in the early 1910s, the nation's leading commercial entertainment stood at the heart of the scandal: cinemas figured prominently among those sites where women were warned that they might encounter dreaded "vice procurers," just as a rash of explicit and sensational films exploiting fears of the slave traffic began drawing sizable crowds of young women apparently unfazed by the reputed danger of movie-going. Vice films capitalized upon widely circulating tales of innocent victims forcibly abducted and sold into prostitution. Slave traffickers lurked everywhere in American cities, women were advised—outside their workplaces, at department stores where they shopped, and at recreation venues—ever ready to snatch unsuspecting prey. Even women who accompanied men on dates were told they might suddenly find themselves drugged and transported to a brothel, held there against their will. Broad currency given these largely erroneous reports suggests that they synthesized deep-rooted anxieties about the unprecedented economic and sexual latitude young, single working women enjoyed in the prewar years. Venues like the cinema figured so prominently in these tales because the new urban recreation culture they symbolized catered specifically to these women and became the chief sphere where their sexuality was given expression. Even as exhibitors promoted a genteel culture of ladies' filmgoing, then, concern raged about the wholesomeness of motion picture houses and the nature of women's interests there.

The film craze began in earnest in November 1913 with the New York premiere of *Traffic in Souls*, still the best-known of the white slave pictures.[2] It was followed closely by the release of *The Inside of the White Slave Traffic* two weeks later, a much more controversial film that stirred the interests of police, the National Board of Censorship, and vice crusaders, all the while drawing phenomenal crowds to newly converted motion picture theaters along

Broadway. The trend was solidified by the new year, as several imitators vied for places in an already-saturated market. *The Exposure of the White Slave Traffic*, *Smashing the Vice Trust*, *The House of Bondage*, *A Soul in Peril*, and *The Traffic in Girls* were among the many white slave pictures hastily released early in 1914. At the same time, *Traffic in Souls* went into nationwide release and set box office records around the country. Although the phenomenon began to wane by March of 1914, screen adaptations of vice stage plays such as *The Lure* (1914) and *The Fight* (1915), together with films like *Is Any Girl Safe?* (1916), *It May Be Your Daughter* (1916), *The Little Girl Next Door* (1916), and *Little Lost Sister* (1917), cautioned women against white slave traffickers well into the decade.

Despite their popularity, lurid screen depictions of the country's sexual underworld tested a film industry heavily invested in improving its reputation in the early teens; they alarmed progressive reformers already troubled by the cinema's moral outlook; and the films' unexpected appeal to female patrons posed a particular challenge to reigning wisdom about women's viewing habits at a time when those very customers seemed to embody the respectability so actively courted by exhibitors.

The White Slavery Scare

The country was already gripped by a fevered white slavery scare when vice films began appearing on New York screens in late 1913. By then sensational accounts of slave trafficking appeared everywhere in the popular press—in journalistic exposés, in fabricated case histories, in sociological studies, and in popular novels and stage adaptations. So pervasive were these warnings that the hyperbolic claim made in *Traffic in Souls* that "50,000 Girls Disappear Yearly" might not have seemed unwarranted. The panic had escalated sharply several years earlier in 1909 when *McClure's Magazine* published George Kibbe Turner's 1909 exposé of white slave trafficking and police corruption in New York City. His *McClure's* piece followed on the heels of similar revelations about Chicago's vice district that Turner had penned for the magazine two years earlier.[3] "New York has become the leader of the world" in slave trafficking, Turner now alleged, the conduit through which immigrant traffickers entered the country and out of which women were shipped around the nation and worldwide.[4] All tacitly condoned by the Democratic political machine at Tammany Hall, he claimed. Picking up on Turner's charges, headlines in the *New York Times* warned, "There Is a White Slave Traffic," and advised readers, "White Slave Traffic Shown to Be Real."[5] So grave were Turner's allegations that white slavery became the topic of New York municipal elections that fall. Early the following year a special grand jury, headed by local Standard Oil scion John D. Rockefeller, Jr., was formed to investigate Turner's charges further. The arrest in May of slave traffickers who had sold women to undercover grand jury investigators only fueled the panic. However, the grand jury's detailed report, made public in June, ultimately concluded that there was little evidence of an organized traffic in women, despite Turner's appearance as the star witness.[6] A preliminary report issued by the United States Immigration Commission in 1909 titled "Importing Women for Immoral Purposes" also contributed to the scare, with its suppositions concerning the role of immigrant populations in the slave trade. So pervasive were fears of white slavery and so seriously were they regarded that federal legislation seemed warranted. The Mann Act, prohibiting the transportation of women across state lines for immoral purposes, was introduced into Congress that same year and ultimately passed into law in 1910.[7] Congressional attention, immigration studies, and grand jury investigations all contributed to the perception that a monumental slave-trafficking problem existed in the nation's urban areas, one that demanded immediate action.

Vice commissions charged with investigating prostitution and white slavery were formed in many cities during this period of heightened attention; no fewer than forty-three different municipalities conducted inquiries into "the social evil" between 1910 and 1914 alone.[8] Although they found little evidence of organized trafficking rings, civic commissions reported that vast vice networks lurked beneath urban red-light districts, findings which helped shape a view of prostitution markedly different from that of previous generations. Encouraged by these studies, progressives tended to regard prostitution less as an expression of individual female perversity than as a collective enterprise where women's activities supported largely male-run networks of pimps, procurers, and saloon owners, all bolstered by police graft.[9] The Chicago Vice Commission's influential 1911 report concluded that prostitution was a "*Commercialized Business* of large proportions with tremendous profits of more than Fifteen Million Dollars per year, controlled largely by men, not women."[10] Following his New York grand jury service, an undaunted John D. Rockefeller, Jr., founded the Bureau of Social Hygiene to investigate conditions of prostitution and white slavery in that city more thoroughly. The bureau issued its first study in the summer of 1913, George Kneeland's *Commercialized Prostitution in New York City*. Famed for his investigations for the Chicago Vice Commission, Kneeland warned readers that New York's slave ring procurers lurked "wherever girls congregate for business or pleasure," ready to grab innocent victims.[11] The portraits of male-run underworlds in many of these reports fueled popular depictions of white slave kidnapping rings that played upon women's victimization. Alarmist abduction plots offered spurious accounts of the origins of prostitution that circumvented both its economic and its sexual roots. Simplifying prostitution's causes, white slave narratives also tended to simplify the solutions necessary to rectify the massive, inbred structures of urban vice documented by civic commissions. Dramatic rescues from cruel kidnappers were proposed instead of the comprehensive social and economic reforms required.

Civic commissions and grand juries found plentiful evidence of prostitution and organized vice in American cities, then, but little proof to support wild tales of white slavery rings abducting young women and holding them against their will.[12] Low salaries for female wage-earners, oppressive working conditions, and overpriced housing were far more likely to lead women to prostitution, many progressive reformers and social workers argued. The *Survey*, one of the key journals of the reform movement, frankly delineated the relationship between women's poor economic conditions and prostitution: "lack of industrial and technical training for girls, fitting them for expert employment, leaves them helpless when thrown on their own resources. The unskilled laborer becomes a tramp; the unskilled woman a prostitute."[13] Accordingly, progressives called for far-reaching social and political reform. Crusader Brand Whitlock, reported the *Survey*, "would set out on a hard course of thinking for us all, to change public opinion, to erect an equal standard for morals, to teach sex hygiene, to eliminate economic factors like low wages . . . and oppressive rents; and he would hope for much, perhaps most, from the feminist movement."[14]

Exploiting reformers' genuine fears that low wages might lead desperate young women into prostitution, tales of white slavery often simply aligned women's social and economic autonomy with moral corruption and sexual pollution, offering versions of what historian Mark Connelly calls the "wages-and-sin" theory.[15] Many alarmist tracts described women snared when answering false "room for rent" advertisements, when replying to requests for "help wanted," or when visiting leisure sites like dance halls, amusement parks, and movie houses. By exaggerating the perils of young women working and living on their own in large cities, stories of this sort registered apprehension about the migration of single women to urban centers, their entry into the workforce, and their eager participation in a growing commercial recreation culture. "Many girls are encouraged and even forced to work when it is really not necessary. They are allowed to leave home without any safeguard being placed around them . . . the number of girls in America who are procured because of these conditions is beyond belief,"[16] Clifford Roe warned in his 1910 tract, *Panders and Their White Slaves*. "The working girl who comes to the city ought to come with her eyes wide open . . . ," the Philadelphia *Public Ledger* cautioned readers in 1913. "She should be sure of an income that will enable her to preserve her self-respect without capitulation."[17]

Popular hysteria seems to have reached its peak in 1913 when two Broadway plays on the vice trade, *The Fight* and *The Lure*, appeared in late summer, barely three months before *Traffic in Souls* brought the theme to the screen.[18] New York newspapers condemned the "brothel plays" for exposing the city's underworld before its well-heeled theatergoers. "Veiled thinly with the pretense of deploring the social evil, their real purpose is to hold it up to morbid eyes," claimed the *New York Times*.[19] In a lengthy analysis for the paper's Sunday edition, famed Harvard psychologist, and later film theorist, Hugo Münsterberg argued in great detail that the presentation of such themes on the stage, in what he called a "black frame about a living picture," did more harm than good. Matters of sexual deviance were better left unspoken, he maintained.[20] Rising criticism in the city's newspapers prompted police scrutiny of both productions. Producers were summoned to appear before New York's chief police magistrate, and revisions were demanded of *The Fight*.[21] Sensational coverage also attended a police raid upon the stage production of *The House of Bondage* after it opened in December, and popular actress Cecil Spooner, the play's star, was arrested in her dressing room prior to the second evening's performance.[22] Police attention ultimately had a contradictory effect on Broadway. Intense scrutiny of *The Lure* and blow-by-blow coverage in the city's newspapers only added to the productions' popularity, resulting in overflow crowds at each performance. Just one month before the release of *Traffic in Souls*, *Moving Picture World* condemned the productions, suggesting that they were merely a "last desperate expedient to draw audiences away from the motion picture theatres. Instead of attracting the crowds, they have succeeded in attracting the police."[23]

Concerns raised about the stage productions anticipated those that would resurface in the even more contentious debate over film versions of the same material later that autumn: did dramatizations of the slave trade perform an educational service in exposing hitherto unseen aspects of the urban underworld, or did they simply cater to prurient interests? Who ought to see such productions, if they did indeed hold educational merit? And should official censorship be brought to bear upon artistic works, and in whose hands should the power of decision making rest? Attentive to the larger implications of police censorship, the *New York Dramatic Mirror* wondered "whether the New York police department is intellectually or morally fit to say whether a play shall be produced."[24] Unlike other contemporary inscriptions of white slavery, stage plays raised particularly troubling issues because of their visual enactment of scenes of prostitution and sexual behavior. As the *Mirror* suggested, audiences for such productions were "vicariously visiting a low resort and seeing the inner life of the underworld from a new angle of view."[25] These were precisely the issues that would reemerge even more insistently in the debate over white slavery on the screen.

By early 1914 one commentator observed that "the idea of 'white slavery' is not only strongly established in the popular mind, but is one in which the public veritably revels."[26] Accounts of illicit slave rings were everywhere in the popular press; scores of journalistic exposés were published in popular magazines like *Harper's* and *McClure's*, and fictionalized "case histories" chronicling the trials of individual victims appeared in women's magazines and novels. Many privately issued books warning young women and their parents about the slave trade also appeared in these years. Clifford Roe, former Illinois district attorney in Chicago, was a prolific publisher of white slave tracts, often based on his experience investigating and prosecuting alleged incidents of slave trafficking in that city.[27] "The Story of Rosalinda," a "case history" published in *Collier's* in 1913, aptly demonstrates how white slave narratives exaggerated accounts of commercial enterprise and women's victimization found in progressive reform discourse on prostitution. Purportedly "accurate in every detail," Rosalinda's story is professed to be "based on scientific investigation by the United States Government and by private authorities."[28] A young Italian immigrant living with her mother in New York City, Rosalinda visits an amusement park with a friend; there she is approached by a stranger. At first she rejects his advances, but the man pursues her, and the two begin a brief courtship followed shortly by marriage. After the wedding Rosalinda discovers that her husband has no means of supporting them and is reluctant to look for work. When he claims to have found a job in Chicago, she travels there with him, only to be sold by him to "Nino Sacco, a notorious white slaver." Enslaved in a house of prostitution for several years, Rosalinda is eventually rescued by her brothers, who bring her back to the family in New York. Rosalinda's plight indicates something of the role played by immigrant populations in tales of the slave trade, which are replete with racist references to Italian, Greek, and Jewish white slavers. Somewhat contradictorily, immigrant men were most often cast as evil slave traffickers, even as immigrant women frequently served as their pitiable victims.[29] Fears that immigrants might be particularly exploited by the slave trade were taken so seriously that the Immigrants' Protective League of Chicago enacted measures to ensure that all new arrivals in the city were met by organization members and properly directed on their way.[30] Equally telling in Rosalinda's story is the prominent place that commercial amusements held in warnings against the vice trade; here, as in other tales, sites like amusement parks furnished arenas where female patrons constantly found themselves on display and open to unsolicited attention. Attachments easily formed amid the casual interaction of young people at such sites seemed only to play into procurers' hands.

The link between women's recreation and vice, upon which many white slave narratives turned, positioned cinema at its nexus, as both site of potential entrapment and source of information. Even as films became one of the primary means by which sensational tales of the slave traffic were disseminated in the early 1910s, motion picture *theaters* featured prominently in warnings against the vice trade. Though decidedly popular recreation venues, cinemas were cast as settings where women placed themselves in particular jeopardy of encountering vice ring operatives. White slave procurers "attend steamboat excursions, are found at the sea shore and amusement parks, in moving picture shows, at the public dance halls," George Kneeland cautioned.[31] "Everywhere girls may be easily approached [procurers] hunt them," including nickel theaters, warned Clifford Roe.[32] The Chicago Vice Commission listed motion pictures "among the recreational conditions directly tributary to the increase of the victims of vice," while Philadelphia's study reported that "moving picture shows . . . are breeding-places of vice—the rendez-vous of men who entrap girls and of girls who solicit men."[33] The Rockefeller grand jury reported of cinemas that "many girls owe their ruin to frequenting them."[34] "Procurers and white slave traffickers watch for young girls at moving picture theatres or win their attention by inviting them to these places," claimed reformer Maude Miner in her study *The Slavery of Prostitution*.[35] Decrying the "menace of the movies," a New York magistrate expressed dismay at the number of indecent assaults "perpetrated in the moving picture theaters while the lights were down." He went so far as to suggest that the majority of sexual crimes against young women "have their inception through meetings with men and boys at moving picture shows." In at least one instance, he alleged, a young woman new to the city had been entrapped by a vice ring procurer on her first visit to the cinema.[36] In an oft-quoted indictment, women's suffrage leader Dr. Anna Howard Shaw dubbed dimly lit movie theaters "recruiting stations of vice" in 1910, arguing that "there should be a police woman at the entrance of every moving picture show and another inside," and citing a case in Chicago where, so she claimed, "twenty-three young girls in one month were lured from a moving picture show and shipped to Texas for immoral purposes."[37] That same year another New York magistrate declared that "more young women and girls are led astray in [moving picture palaces] than in any other way."[38] What was it about movie theaters—and women's behavior there—that prompted such strong admonitions?

Women had clearly integrated movies into emergent patterns of work and leisure by the early 1910s and had become a significant component of motion picture audiences; indeed female patronage, especially among the middle class, was energetically courted by exhibitors eager to enhance the cinema's reputation as I have shown. Yet the continuing characterization of theaters as unsafe for women suggests that their status as movie patrons and viewers remained to be negotiated, even as late as middecade. So strong was the concern that when members of the Federation of Women's Clubs met in New York in the spring of 1913, they focused special attention on conditions inside the country's motion picture theaters. "Many are very much agitated on the subject, since the white slave revelations have been published," *Moving Picture News* reported.[39]

Cinemas were described by many observers as arenas of particular carnal license, where women were alternately preyed upon by salacious men who gathered around entranceways, and themselves tempted to engage in untoward conduct. One report claimed that "vicious men and boys mix with the crowd in front of the theaters and take liberties with very young girls,"[40] another that "around the entrance of the movies a group of human vultures usually hovers waiting to flirt or to make familiar remarks or to 'pick up' girls."[41] Darkened theater interiors that offered "facilities for forming acquaintances which are often dangerous" particularly worried reformers.[42] Screenings under such conditions posed "a terrible menace to the morals of young girls," since "to these theaters with their atmosphere of darkness and obscurity flock the procurer."[43] Even more worrisome were reports of young women's participation in this dynamic. Social workers attentive to new patterns of socializing noted that women commonly made the acquaintance of unfamiliar men at movie theaters, and that in many cases these alliances led to sexual liaisons afterwards.[44] "Girls go wrong because they are movie mad and are allowed to associate with questionable young men," one Toledo reformer concluded.[45] Obviously troubled by such conduct, Jane Addams described a class of young women "who come to grief through the five-cent theaters" because they "may be induced unthinkingly to barter [their] chastity for an entrance fee."[46] In these accounts crowded lobby areas that permitted a panoply of eroticized looking, along with shadowy viewing spaces that afforded a measure of privacy and anonymity beneficial to romantic encounters, rendered women equally vulnerable. As one uneasy theater owner observed, "works of evil multiply under the cover of darkness and the danger of a poorly lighted theater to the weak-minded and weak-willed young people can hardly be exaggerated."[47] In such cautionary tales venues like the cinema were perceived to have a constant sexual undertone, one in which women's presence was immediately and perilously eroticized. These characterizations articulate the contradictory position of female viewers at the time: although their presence was thought to lend "refinement" to theater audiences, women themselves risked endangerment there. The paradoxical nature of this equation is best expressed by Lauren Rabinovitz, who argues that just as amusements like the cinema solicited the female gaze, they also confirmed woman's status as object of the gaze both on and off screen.[48] Within the exhibition space women maintained a delicate balance as both spectator and spectacle, customer and commodity. There as patrons and consumers, women were also looked at and traded upon in sexually charged recreation venues.

Reservations about the cinema echoed broader apprehensions about the emergence of a heterosexual dating culture surrounding commercial leisure in general. Dance halls, amusement parks, cafés, and motion picture theaters brought single young people together at public venues where they could escape the drudgery of their work lives, not to mention the cramped boardinghouses, apartments, and tenements where many of them lived. While traditional conceptions of female leisure had significantly curtailed both the activities and the sites available for women's recreation, entertainments like the cinema, spawned in part by wage labor, redrew such boundaries and redefined the ground upon which women might participate in urban life.[49] Recognizing this trend, a 1911 magazine commentary announced "The Passing of the Home

Daughter," content to pursue quiet pastimes by the hearth, and the ascendance of young women who felt they were "dying of asphyxiation at home!"[50] Yet, as Leslie Woodcock Tentler observes, crowded leisure sites like the cinema provided a somewhat contradictory mixture of the space and privacy lacking in so many women's lives.[51]

Commercial venues furnished locales for heterosocial interaction much different, then, from nineteenth-century models of courtship, according to which suitors would have been formally introduced, then usually entertained in family homes under the watchful eye of parental chaperones. Ironically, the public character of newer commercial venues afforded couples a measure of privacy, since their anonymity permitted a greater potential intimacy than did closely supervised "parlor" courtships of an earlier era. Modern dating habits provoked considerable consternation among social critics of the day, who worried about the free association of single, unchaperoned young people at popular establishments and the romances frequently spawned there, many of which often involved some sexual component. "The interest between girls and boys here is almost wholly one of sex," sociologist Ruth S. True observed in 1914.[52] Within this turn-of-the-century dating culture it became acceptable for single working-class women to offer sexual "favors" of one degree or another in exchange for being treated at amusement sites, historian Kathy Peiss discovered.[53] Of young women's behavior at popular venues, social worker Belle Lindner Israels observed rather delicately in her 1909 study, "one of [a young woman's] partners of the evening may exact tribute for standing treat."[54] Since women earned considerably lower salaries than men, being treated was one of the few ways many of them could partake of commercial leisure activities on a regular basis. On recreational outings, Peiss declares, "familiarity and intermingling among strangers, not decorum, defined normal public behavior among the sexes."[55] The challenges such unaccustomed comportment posed to conventional views of courtship—not to say standards of decorous femininity—were enormous. Witnessing these open displays of female sexuality, one commentator freely tied the conduct to factory labor: "Is the work of great numbers of girls at the most play-loving period of life so unsuited to them, so mechanical and exhausting that they are quite naturally feverish for excitement at night and ready to take up with anyone who can 'show them a good time'? "[56] *Collier's* magazine observed of the "working girl" in 1913 that "always her chastity has been protected by father and brother, by church, and by the watchful community. Now for the first time in history that chastity is intrusted to her young eager self for safe-keeping *or for bartering*."[57] The image of America's daughters "bartering" their bodies for trifles like movie admissions and amusement park rides, one that Addams also evoked, must have been alarming indeed. It bore the unmistakable taint of prostitution.

Within such a climate, misgivings about women's comportment on dates were readily transposed into alarmist tales of white slavery and sexual abduc-

tion. In his 1915 study, *Popular Amusements*, Richard Henry Edwards conclu-
sively linked "the amusement problem" with "the vice problem."[58] Describing
the atmosphere in establishments catering to single, working-class patrons of
both sexes, Edwards found that the "easygoing familiarity" of such settings
"frequently degenerates into promiscuous sociability" in which "a more or less
general promiscuity of relationships may emerge," concluding that "these are
the factors sought by the underworld in its recruiting stations."[59] Sexual activity
led irrevocably to sexual slavery, Edwards seemed to suggest. Tales of unwilling entrapment by vice rings hence served to mask anxieties about young wom-
en's courtship activities, while tacitly recognizing the sexual undercurrent of
recreation culture. The fictional procurer, always said to be hovering on the
margins of these sites, personified the way leisure spaces furnished arenas for
illicit sexual gazing. In the end, concern over women's safety in movie theaters
suggests less any real danger of abduction—of which there is very little evidence—than the difficulty of imagining women's willful engagement in an
eroticized milieu. Cloaking women's leisure pursuits in peril, fanciful accounts
of abduction registered mounting wariness about the dating habits of young
working men and women. They also evinced a growing discrepancy between
middle-class reformers' notions of feminine propriety and working women's
evolving expressions of sexuality, for outcry over white slavery ultimately
licensed greater control over women's leisure activities.[60] Female sexuality was
thus at once acknowledged and averted in white slave warnings.

The persistent association of cinema with sexual danger also echoes an even
older connection between female leisure patrons and prostitutes. The fact that
until the turn of the century prostitutes had been among the most mobile and
visible of women in American cities is also central to an understanding of this
controversy, for long before the white slave panic gained currency, women at
recreation sites were often assumed to be prostitutes. Throughout much of the
past century many of the women at saloons and cabarets had in fact been
prostitutes catering to the largely male clientele. So forceful were these connotations that well into the early twentieth century women's attendance at commercial recreation sites, particularly if unaccompanied, still carried strong suggestions of solicitation.[61] As late as 1908, New York City's mayor described
"a class of disorderly women who confine their activities to the moving picture
shows, which, operating with darkened rooms, afford unusual facilities for a
traffic of scandalous proportions."[62] Such allusions inflect discussions of
women attending films on white slavery, where there is a constant slippage
between descriptions of prostitutes using theaters for sexual solicitation,
women physically assaulted or abducted by traffickers, and women on dates
willingly engaging in romantic and sexual liaisons. This suggests that the last
category—women who were voluntarily sexually active, and neither prostitutes nor victims of the slave trade—was difficult for contemporary commentators to fathom. The white slave fantasy—that trafficking rings used movie

houses to procure women—simply inverted this scenario, casting women as helpless victims, while retaining the association between female patrons and prostitution. Histrionic tales of sexual abduction thus framed the growing presence of "respectable" women at the movies in terms consistent with an older model of feminine conduct that linked their attendance to solicitation.

It is no accident that motion picture theaters figured so prominently in white slave warnings, then, for cinemagoing encapsulated many aspects of working women's leisure culture that so troubled progressive reformers. Sensational stories of girls disappearing in midday certainly simplified prostitution's causes and remedies into melodramatic plots where individual virtue and vice figured large. But these frightful accounts of the hazards awaiting women who worked and lived autonomously in urban centers also gave voice to escalating alarm about the conduct of these women at recreational venues. Single, working women's growing economic independence, relative freedom from family stricture, and evolving sexual mores were all cause for concern. However shocking, tales of women's unwitting sexual entrapment by vice trafficking rings allowed society to talk about their sexual exploits in commercial leisure culture, still presenting women only as passive victims. And by repeatedly enacting the capture and enslavement of America's daughters, along with their eventual safe return home, white slave warnings also valorized traditional family structure and punished its transgressors. If, as Alice Kessler-Harris suggests, notions of women's independence and virtue were mutually exclusive during these years, then white slavery neatly correlated independence and vice.[63] Yet even as white slave warnings expressed communities' collective fears about their daughters and sisters, the stories may also have allowed young women themselves to fantasize about imagined independence and prohibited sexual encounters, at the same time rendering their participation involuntary.[64]

White Slavery and Motion Picture Audiences

Given the well-publicized danger, what pleasures did white slave films promise that might entice women to theaters, sites where they were, after all, supposedly at risk of encountering slave trade operatives? And given the saturation of alarmist vice trade warnings at the time of their release, what novel perspective might the films have offered on the situation? Like so many other accounts of white slavery, films on the vice trade harbor grave reservations about the growing visibility and autonomy of women in American cities. By presenting the perils of urban life and leisure solely in terms of sexual abduction, the films displace broader concerns about women's changing patterns of work and recreation onto fanciful accounts of sexual trafficking. Here, as elsewhere, white slavery becomes a means of distilling and negotiating unsettling aspects of prewar culture. Yet, as I will argue, films like *Traffic in Souls*, *The Inside of the White Slave Traffic*, and *Little Lost Sister* held out the possibility of an empowering view of the threatening urban terrain, one that might have had particular appeal to women already terrorized by tales of the slave trade.

The popularity of the white slave films, even amid the nationwide panic, caught both the industry and its critics off guard. The first of the white slave films, *Traffic in Souls*, was a hit the day it opened, the 24th of November, 1913, in New York, where it played to three packed houses at Joe Weber's Theater on Broadway at Twenty-ninth Street, despite the twenty-five-cent tickets.[65] Filmgoers promised a "two hour" show by this six-reel feature were evidently willing to pay the high price of admission. At nearly 1,000 seats, Weber's was triple the capacity of most motion picture venues in the city.[66] When *The Inside of the White Slave Traffic* opened a week later at the 1,800-seat Park Theater on Columbus Circle, several hundred people had to be turned away, the majority of whom were young women.[67] By the fourth week of December both films were playing simultaneously on two screens in New York. *The Inside of the White Slave Traffic* offered five additional daily showings at the Bijou Theater on Broadway, just one block north of Weber's, where *Traffic in Souls* continued to play. Further uptown, police were called in to manage crowds when *Traffic in Souls* opened additional showings at the Republic Theater.[68] Within less than a month of its opening, *Traffic in Souls* was playing simultaneously at six theaters in greater New York to no less enthusiastic audiences. At the height of their success in the city, *Traffic in Souls* and *The Inside of the White Slave Traffic* generated close to $5,000 apiece in weekly box office grosses, suggesting that upwards of 15,000 New Yorkers saw the pictures each week.[69]

With *Traffic in Souls* and *The Inside of the White Slave Traffic* doing so well, rival New York exhibitors complained that vice pictures were cutting into their receipts. Dozens of production companies across the country, eager to capitalize on the craze, reportedly had white slave films in the works.[70] "They are coming thick and fast," the *New York Clipper* reported.[71] So furious was the competition for audiences that makers of *The Inside of the White Slave Traffic* threatened to seek an injunction against any other production using the term "white slave" in its title, claiming exclusive copyright.[72] Nonetheless, imitators were so readily available that exhibitors eager to prolong the bankability of vice themes frequently replaced one white slave title with another. When the Bijou Theater abandoned trouble-plagued screenings of *The Inside of the White Slave Traffic* in the last week of December, they immediately substituted *The Exposure of the White Slave Traffic*, a cheaply made English film that had been released in theaters on the Lower East Side and Harlem three years earlier. Following the popularity of white slave pictures at relatively upscale Broadway theaters, owners of the Bijou resurrected *The Exposure of the White Slave Traffic*, adding still pictures and a lecturer, and billing it as "The European Version of the White Slave Traffic." The formula appeared to work, for *Variety* reported that "the picture did business from the outset and had a crowd waiting to gain entrance by one o'clock" on its first day, despite management's decision to double admission prices for its run.[73] So popular was this newcomer that it threatened *Traffic in Souls*, still playing at Weber's one block south. " 'Slave' Beating 'Souls,' " screamed *Variety* as it chronicled the battle for the box office.[74] After a three-week run, the Bijou replaced *The Exposure of the White Slave Traffic* with *The House of Bondage*, a screen adaptation of Reginald Wright Kauffman's wildly popular 1910 novel, by then in its fourteen printing. The film had been rushed into production in December and was released while a stage version of Kauffman's work still played in New York, a unprecedented occurrence.[75] Other quickly made imitators mentioned in the trade press in late 1913 and early 1914 all bear titles unmistakably marking them as part of the trend: *A Soul in Peril*, *The Shadows of Sin*, *The Traffic in Girls*, and *The Wages of Sin*.[76] *Traffic in Souls* eventually ended its startling eight-week run at Weber's with declining box office receipts and was itself finally replaced by a cheaply and quickly made imitator, *Smashing the Vice Trust*, in late January.[77] The ground was so well trodden by then that reviewers decried the picture as a poorly made knockoff of its predecessor—"more police pursuing outcasts and city outlaws over the roofs, more pistol plays."[78]

The white slave film sensation was ultimately short-lived, then. In less than two months the vice theme became so familiar that it invited parody. In early 1914 Universal reported that a "two-reel travesty" lampooning the plight of an "abducted country maiden" was already in production.[79] Another spoof, *Traffickers in Soles*, adhered closely to the "regulation 'vice' plot," according to *Motion Picture News*, and promised to heap "ridicule on the inside, outside, and all around the white slave traffic."[80] By early February *Moving Picture World* would report, "[H]appily the hysteria is rapidly passing away and we are even in New York City returning to sane and normal conditions."[81] While it lasted, however, the storm of controversy that gathered around the "slavers" tells us a great deal about the new role that socially conscious films were playing in urban culture, and about the struggle over motion picture exhibition in cities across the country as film became the nation's premiere entertainment form. Did feature-length white slave films herald cinema's final descent into tawdry cheap amusements? Or did they mark a point of maturity when the cinema might be able to shed light upon society's most troublesome social problems?

White slave films announced cinema's "arrival" as a major entertainment form in New York with particular force, for they helped dramatize the widespread conversion of "legitimate" theaters into moving picture houses in the early teens. Many of New York's top-ranked Broadway playhouses, including Weber's and the Republic where *Traffic in Souls* played, made the transition to motion picture exhibition with so-called vicers.[82] Fifteen major theaters had "gone into film slavery" by early 1914, according to the *New York World*, suggesting that the trope of sexual slavery came to symbolize the relationship

7. "We Are the White Slaves of the Cinema," *New York World*, January 1914.

between theater and motion pictures as a whole. The paper's comic illustration showed a new Broadway landscape now dominated by lurid movie marquees of violent traffickers and their pitiable victims. Traditional advocates of the theater were particularly unsettled. Oscar Hammerstein, owner of the Republic Theater, threatened suit against lessee David Belasco for subletting the theater to Universal during the run of *Traffic in Souls*, claiming that such "indecent" fare contravened Belasco's contract to stage "first class productions," then threatened to prevent Belasco from exhibiting motion pictures at the Republic altogether.[83] Though ultimately unsuccessful, Hammerstein's lawsuit suggests how anxieties surrounding competition between movies and stage plays crystallized around the white slave films, and how the trend allowed critics to paint the conversion of theaters in very dire terms. "We are the white slaves of the cinema," cried the *New York World*, ". . . for, like the tango, the movies have strangled the stage in every land and clime."[84]

Large Broadway theaters relatively new to the movie trade, and willing to charge twenty-five cents for feature film admissions, were also willing to advertise on Sunday newspaper pages normally reserved for stage productions.[85] *Traffic in Souls*, *The Inside of the White Slave Traffic*, and *Smashing the Vice Trust* were, it appears, the only films advertised in New York's daily papers in late 1913 and early 1914. New Yorkers who followed the city's vice scare in the daily papers would no doubt have seen film adaptations of the white slave theme advertised there as well. Ads touted spurious connections to official vice studies and boasted endorsements from respected civic leaders. *The Inside of the White Slave Traffic* was "produced from actual facts" and "based on the actual observations of a former U.S. government investigator," according to its publicity, while *Smashing the Vice Trust* was "based on District Attorney Whitman's disclosures."[86] *Traffic in Souls* professed to be "the only true and

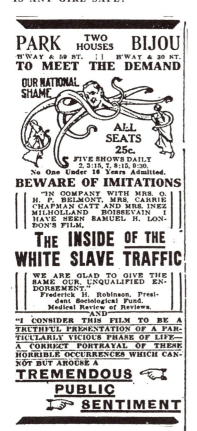

8. *New York Tribune*, December 1913.

authentic version" of the traffic in women, "the only production that has the endorsement and sanction of the many vice crusaders throughout the country."[87] If these claims seem designed to highlight the films' educational merits, simultaneous promises of visual splendor unmistakably link this verisimilitude to sexual explicitness: *Traffic in Souls* promised viewers "a two hour show depicting graphically the evils of the white slave traffic"; *Smashing the Vice Trust*, "a heart-rending spectacle in six parts and 700 scenes"; and *The Inside of the White Slave Traffic*, "A film with a moral. A film with a lesson. A film with a thrill."[88] Cloaking the films' treatment of sexual material in terms of visual spectacle, these ads suggest that film versions of the slave trade offered what no other medium could: an actual glimpse into the city's brothels and red-light districts.

Not surprisingly, it was just this aspect of the films that attracted police attention in New York, where *The Inside of the White Slave Traffic* enjoyed a particularly rocky run. *Variety* was quick to predict that the film would incur police censorship, given its portrayal of "the same scene that brought the police

9. *New York Tribune*, February 1914.

down upon two red light dramas and howling crowds to the box office" earlier that autumn.[89] *Traffic in Souls*, the paper predicted, "may escape police censorship here and elsewhere because it omits the soul of a subject it aims to reveal," whereas its racier counterpart risked the censor's knife since it "goes in for the utmost fidelity in picturing the evil which has been its inspiration."[90]

As predicted, the Park Theater's manager was summoned to police court during the second week of the film's engagement to answer charges that *The Inside of the White Slave Traffic* constituted an immoral and indecent exhibition. After a police magistrate viewed the film and heard testimony on the film's behalf from several of the city's notable social reformers, the complaint was dismissed.[91] But the headline in the *New York Press* the next morning screamed, "Police Can't Stop White Slave Film. Lose Step in Fight to Check Vice and Sex Hysteria Sweeping City."[92] Evidently unsatisfied with the magistrate's decision, the deputy police commissioner secured a warrant for the arrest of Samuel London, the film's producer, on the grounds that the film was "calculated to harm the morals of young people." Police descended upon the Park Theater on Friday evening of that same week, bringing with them a volume of officers and patrol wagons more suited to a raid on a gambling joint than to an action against a movie house, according to one observer, but they failed to arrest London, who was not on the premises.[93] When the Park Theater resumed showing *The Inside of the White Slave Traffic* the very next day, police again raided the theater in midafternoon while a screening was in progress. This time officers arrested all of the Park's employees—manager, ticket seller, ticket taker, and projectionist—and confiscated the film print. According to the *New York Sun*'s colorful account, an officer stood in the projection booth grabbing each of the five reels as it came off the projector. At midnight theater management announced to waiting crowds that a temporary injunction had been obtained preventing further police interference, and that screenings would resume the following afternoon.[94]

Two successive police raids on the Park the weekend before Christmas served as effective publicity for *The Inside of the White Slave Traffic*. The raids were front-page news in virtually all of New York's dailies. "Slave Reel Spins; Police Hands Tied," cried the *Tribune*. This attention generated intense public interest in the film, an appetite to which owners of the Park Theater readily catered. The day following the second raid, the Park offered eight showings of *The Inside of the White Slave Traffic* instead of its usual five, using duplicate prints of the confiscated material and brazenly adding a reel to the show despite the presence of police officers outside the theater. Crowds began gathering early in the afternoon, a full hour before management announced that screenings would begin.[95] "The advertising the so-called white slave films have been given through the efforts of the police to suppress them has resulted in extraordinary attendance at the Park Theatre," the *New York World* reported. Such attention "brought a crowd of fully five thousand men, women and children into Columbus Circle" that afternoon, according to the *Herald*, with the *Tribune* reporting "crowds surging in and out of the doors of the theater in increasing volumes with each succeeding exhibition."[96] By Monday a second set of daily screenings was offered at the Bijou Theater, further down Broadway at Thirtieth street, in order to accommodate audience demand. Temporarily prevented from interfering with screenings at the Park, police raided the Bijou on the second night of the film's run there, after receiving a warrant from a magistrate vowing to stem the "riot of obscene spectacles that is going on in our city." But again management obtained a temporary injunction preventing police interference.[97] Large crowds continued to attend both the Park and the Bijou all week, reportedly drawing the biggest business the film had seen since it opened.[98] In fact, front-page coverage of the police raids was thought to explain the temporary drop in attendance at *Traffic in Souls*, still playing one block south of the Bijou at Weber's and uptown at the Republic.[99]

By the last week of December, however, temporary injunctions preventing police interference at both the Park and the Bijou were vacated, giving police authorities full license to suspend the productions, which they did.[100] *The Inside of the White Slave Traffic* quickly disappeared from New York screens before the end of December, within less than a month of its opening. When Samuel London, his manager, and the manager of the Bijou were eventually convicted of exhibiting material "tending to corrupt the morals" at a closely watched March trial, the *New York Herald* declared, "[T]he happy result is that [*The Inside of the White Slave Traffic*] never can be shown again in any theatre in this city, and it is not likely other cities will take what New York has condemned."[101]

Film industry leaders were justifiably alarmed by the specter of police raid-
ing New York motion picture theaters in December of 1913, almost exactly
five years after common show licenses had been uniformly revoked by Mayor
McClellan in 1908. "The 'white slave pictures' have again this week occupied
the whole attention of the show business," *Variety* reported during the court
battles. "There has been no end to the talk, comment and arguments over
them."[102] Indeed, the trouble-plagued run of *The Inside of the White Slave
Traffic* highlighted still-lingering struggles over motion picture exhibition in
Manhattan. Just five months earlier the city had finally passed an ordinance
governing its movie theaters, after more than two years of contentious debate
initiated by newly elected mayor William Gaynor. Gaynor, who succeeded
George McClellan as mayor in 1909, was considered a supporter of the film
industry who favored liberalizing licensing laws that had restricted the growth
of motion picture venues in the past. It had in fact been Gaynor, then serving
as state supreme court justice, who issued an injunction against McClellan's
notorious Christmas Eve theater closings in 1908. In the wake of those closings, proposed revisions to civic ordinances included not only the regulation
of theatrical *sites* but also increasingly urgent discussion about appropriate
methods for regulating film *content*. Many of the city's aldermen were critical
of the National Board of Censorship, complaining that it had no power to
compel producers to submit films for review or to enforce any censorship
recommendations it made. Their favored ordinances included not only changes
in theater licensing requirements but provisions for a police censorship board
similar to one that had been operating in Chicago since 1907. Gaynor, a staunch
opponent of municipal censorship, vetoed two motion picture ordinances in
1912 and 1913 that included such provisions, arguing that public outrage, cou-
pled with already-existing obscenity laws, were sufficient to prevent the exhibition of indecent material on the city's screens. The final ordinance, signed
by Gaynor in July of 1913, included no provisions for censorship.[103] Upon the
heels of this tumultuous debate, then, the white slave films once again opened
discussions about how the cinema ought to be regulated in New York.

For a motion picture industry eager to foster a more respectable reputation
by appealing to middle-class patrons, "slavers" seemed to invite accusations
of tawdry sensationalism that exhibitors hoped to duck. Such fare threatened
the very reputation of the cinema itself, not to mention that of individual proprietors. The *New York Dramatic Mirror*, *Variety*, and *Moving Picture World*
all issued strong and repeated condemnations of the films, claiming, "[T]hey
are all bad, not alone for the public, but for the moving picture industry."[104]
Vice pictures were "a danger to the business" that would "lower the esteem in
which film plays are held" and "lessen respect for moving pictures wherever
exhibited."[105] Many of the city's exhibitors and film producers called upon the
mayor and the police to suspend exhibitions of *The Inside of the White Slave
Traffic*.[106] In January, with *Traffic in Souls* still playing, the All-Star Feature

Corporation published an open letter to Universal head Carl Laemmle in New York's Sunday papers. "In the name of the twenty-five million Americans who depend on the motion picture for their daily relaxation," the letter declared, "we protest against your company's appeal . . . to those bestial instincts which are the rebellious and destructive elements in our social life."[107]

Epes Winthrop Sargent urged exhibitors to "shun the slavers," calling the pictures "lewd" and "smutty" entertainment cloaked in the guise of educational warnings. Patrons attracted to such material were not a proprietor's regular customers and only scared away loyal, respectable clientele. "You cannot fool your decent patrons by prating about social uplift and terrible lessons," he warned. "Do not prostitute the picture business" by catering to this salacious curiosity in the interests of earning a quick profit.[108] Louis Reeves Harrison, in two *Moving Picture World* editorials on the films, also complained that vice films alienated the "family" audience and thereby risked sabotaging the industry's uplift. In a full-page discussion of "red-light films" printed several weeks prior to the release of *Traffic in Souls*, Harrison argued that there were "good business reason[s]" for keeping such films out of theaters, since motion picture exhibitions qualified as "'family' entertainment, and nearly all such places are frequented by women and children." Tying the cinema's newfound respectability and its ever more sophisticated offerings to middle-class patronage, Harrison warned of alienating this audience with dramatizations of the slave trade: "[N]o part of [a] varied program should be violently offensive to the best patrons of the place . . . [A]n appeal to the whole people does not mean an emasculated and debauching presentation of what is repulsive to decent people."[109] In a subsequent editorial he cautioned, "[I]f moving pictures become apostles of decadence, it is not unreasonable to expect that family support of the exhibitions will be alienated, and that legislation antagonistic to the entire industry will result."[110] Nonetheless, Harrison maintained that the agitation surrounding the exhibition of white slave pictures marked a "step in the evolution of the New Art," since "honest censorship and manly criticism" had been responsible for uplifting film content and gradually winning the approval of middle-class families. White slave pictures might even prove to be a "blessing in disguise," he suggested, if only because they could serve to "unite men of sane and sound purposes in this business" against "men engaged in poisoning immature minds."[111] In short, by publicly castigating and rejecting the white slave films—acting, in other words, like those reformers usually opposed to the cinema—the industry might stage its own uplift. Ironically, industry outrage over white slave films might actually champion the cause of middle-class patrons, rather than alienate them. *Variety* ultimately refused to advertise white slave films after February of 1914, claiming that they were "injurious to the public at large and the moving picture trade as a whole."[112] And *Moving Picture World* eventually proposed that exhibitors who continued to lure young women into pictures on the slave trade ought to have their licenses revoked and thus be made "thereafter ineligible for connection with any motion picture enterprise."[113]

Particularly worrisome were fears that sensational coverage of police raids in New York "stirred up the imps of censorship," as W. Stephen Bush put it, at a time when calls for state and municipal censorship boards were gaining strength.[114] Bush, who fought tirelessly against censorship during his tenure at *Moving Picture World*, actually endorsed police intervention in the exhibition of such films, arguing that existing obscenity laws could sufficiently contain vice pictures without official censorship.[115] The *New York Dramatic Mirror* feared that "when the small-city press and the small-city pulpits get their say, then the few victories that have been won in the fight to ward off local censorship will have to be fought all over again, with a strong weapon placed in the hands of the agitators."[116] Indeed, the police attention that *The Inside of the White Slave Traffic* garnered upon its New York release came exactly as Universal was preparing forty prints of *Traffic in Souls* for national distribution, and an aggressive campaign was promoting states' rights sales and direct booking of *The Inside of the White Slave Traffic*.[117] If anything, the vice films' notorious New York debut only added to their cachet. A trade ad describing "the raging sensation in New York" boasted that exhibitors "turned two thousand away the second night after the fourth show at the Park Theater."[118] A two-page trade ad for *Smashing the Vice Trust* described the picture as "the sensation of New York" and quoted from many of the New York press notices.[119] *The Inside of the White Slave Traffic* later played several cities without incident—among them Trenton, New Jersey, Allentown, Pennsylvania, and Schenectady, New York—but in many cases New York scrutiny prompted municipalities to ban the film, or shorten its run, on the principal that if the picture had been deemed unsuitable for New Yorkers, it must be wholly inappropriate for the rest of the country.[120] "The New York police stopped it, and our police should never let it open here," declared a Chicago alderman after viewing the film.[121] "If it's too bad for New York, it certainly should not be shown in Washington," said that city's mayor.[122] Exhibitors there and in Newark, New Jersey, cut runs of the film short because of police action against the production in New York.

Caught in the middle of this controversy was the fledgling National Board of Censorship of Motion Pictures.[123] Formed just four years earlier in an alliance between progressive reformers and film industry producers and exhibitors, the board sought to prove that under the guidance of moral leadership filmmakers could regulate themselves without state intervention. Tawdry white slave pictures not only threatened the industry's avowed uplift, then, they impugned the aura of responsibility and restraint fostered by the board and tested the marriage of reformers and industry leaders it celebrated.

Board of Censorship records show that the organization was acutely conscious of its role in judging the white slave films because of their particular mixture of avowedly educational content and relative sexual explicitness. Thus when they reviewed the first of the vice pictures, *Traffic in Souls*, nearly four weeks prior to its release, board members declared themselves fully aware that "a precedent would be created by any action taken" since the picture dealt "in a more deliberate and extensive way than any previous film with the so-called white slave traffic."[124] The board's Censorship Committee screened the film and, after requesting several specific alterations, found it "easy to rid [the film] of all elements which might be called suggestive." Still, mindful of the delicacy of the subject the board's general secretary, Frederic Howe, invited members of several prominent social groups to view the film with board members, requesting their help in determining "the broader question of the propriety of the treatment of these darker social problems through the medium of the stage or motion pictures," along with the question of "whether it is rightly within the province of the National Board of Censorship to interfere with such public discussions through motion pictures."[125] Ironically, then, even though members of the reform community staffed its Censorship Committee, the board felt uneasy about policing films that crossed boundaries between entertainment and sociological import.

Several community and religious leaders accepted Howe's invitation, and a screening was set up at Universal headquarters in New York. Eager to promote the film's seriousness of purpose, rather than its racy subject matter, the studio circulated a pamphlet to those who attended the showing, stressing the film's educational objectives: "It is a picture that every girl, on reaching maturity, should be taken to see by her mother." Universal touted the film's links to depictions of the vice trade in more elevated art forms—like the novel *The House of Bondage*, which had been a best-seller in 1910, and the stage plays *The Lure* and *The Fight*, which had opened on Broadway that summer—while also being careful to point out that the film did not show "any of the offensive scenes which have made these plays notorious." Moreover, it was not the studio's intent "to pander to sensationalism, or the cravings of the masses for a glimpse . . . of the so-called 'red-light' life. . . . There is nothing of a lascivious nature in the whole picture."[126]

Evidently the studio's promotion struck the right chord, for Francis Couvares has shown that those who attended the Universal screening were chiefly concerned with whether the film's portrait of vice would pose sufficient warning to vulnerable young women. One of the key debates that day centered on whether the film ought to replace its alarmist white slave abduction plot with a more nuanced consideration of the factors that led women into prostitution, echoing broader debates within the reform movement between those who fanned the flames of white slave panic and those who feared that tales of vice trafficking rings obscured very real economic and social causes of prostitution.[127] In the end the board decided to approve *Traffic in Souls* with only minimal alterations, effectively endorsing its ersatz kidnapping and rescue plot. Upholding the film's presentation of prostitution, as well as the viability of engaging motion picture audiences in the antivice crusade, committee members issued a public statement declaring their belief that "this subject [white slavery] and this method of treatment were legitimate in motion pictures," dubbing *Traffic in Souls* "a high-grade picture capable of real moral and dramatic entertainment."[128]

Board approval clearly held currency in the industry at a time when white slave pictures were "bound to arouse bitter antagonism," according to *Moving Picture World*. Noting that the "work has been carefully reviewed by the censors," and that "several eliminations have been made," the trade journal's review of *Traffic in Souls* openly touted the board's sanction: "Surely its friends, and among these are the members of the National Board of Censorship, are entitled to ask that the production be seen before it is condemned." White slavery was "dealt with so reverently," according to the *Motion Picture News*, "that even the members of the National Board of Censorship could not find fault" with *Traffic in Souls*. *Motography*'s two-page review carried a headline announcing, "Censors Have Indorsed It." Still, the latter trade viewed the board's publicly issued justification of its ruling as a defensive gesture: "[T]he action of the Censor Board in issuing this advance explanation manifestly anticipates criticism from some source," *Motography* claimed, suggesting something of the board's own uncertainty about its mandate.[129]

As *Motography* surmised, the board's cautious handling of *Traffic in Souls* exposed a lingering uncertainty about the vice films made all the more apparent in its subsequent treatment of *The Inside of the White Slave Traffic*, a much more explicit and alarming film released two weeks after its predecessor. Unlike *Traffic in Souls*, which framed a depiction of slave trafficking within a story line emphasizing punishment and redemption, *The Inside of the White Slave Traffic* promised a realistic depiction of prostitution, tantalizing viewers with an "inside" peek into the nation's vice wards and brothels, rather than lessons on how they might avoid falling prey to scurrilous slave ring operatives. The Board of Censorship's General Committee reviewed *The Inside of the White Slave Traffic* during the second week of December when it opened, voting to approve the picture only if significant eliminations and additions were made. Producers were asked to "greatly reduce" scenes shot in the New Orleans vice district and to "shorten the disorderly house sequences, leaving these scenes only long enough to show the action taking place without dwelling unnecessarily on the scene." Images of negligee-clad women in the brothel would have to be cut entirely. By allowing only those views of vice districts and brothels that advanced the film's narrative, board members were obviously concerned to curtail opportunities for prurient viewing of the film's much-touted documentary sequences. The board was also concerned to offset any potential salacious interest in sexual material with heavy-handed lessons about the downfall of those enmeshed in the slave trade. In addition to the requested cuts, producers were asked to include new scenes, precisely dictated by the board, that would castigate vice trafficking. Before the board would agree to pass *The Inside of the White Slave Traffic*, producers would have to include "scenes showing the punishment of the trafficker" and "scenes showing the downfall and end of the girl," the contours of which were outlined in some detail: "These scenes should show the kind of catastrophe which usually overtakes a girl living this kind of a life, such as becoming a down and out hag, a victim of disease, a suicide, a specimen for the doctor's dissecting table, and filling a grave in Potter's Field (or something like this)."[130] According to the board's logic, limited views of prostitution might be permitted if accompanied by clearly judgmental, fictional scenes.

Even had he agreed to make such substantial alterations to *The Inside of the White Slave Traffic*, producer Samuel H. London was not given a chance to revise the film before the board changed its ruling. Fearful that London would exploit the board's approval for publicity purposes, turning a "pass" into an open endorsement, and suspicious that the film had been submitted for its adjudication only "after being publicly and commercially exploited," the Board of Censorship voted to suspend judgment on *The Inside of the White Slave Traffic* on the 13th of December, five days after it had opened. Rather than passing or denouncing the film, the board categorized it as a "special release," a designation that left censorship decisions up to local communities.[131] Officially, the board took "no stand either for or against" *The Inside of the White Slave Traffic*.

Although the Board of Censorship attempted to diminish its jurisdiction over *The Inside of the White Slave Traffic* by designating it a "special release," the board was drawn further into the debate as the film continued to play in New York's motion picture houses, where it was receiving considerable police scrutiny. Likely motivated by the escalating fervor of police interest, Samuel London put considerable pressure on the Board of Censorship to revisit *The Inside of the White Slave Traffic*, furnishing written assurance that he would abide by its judgment and not exploit a favorable ruling in his advertising. Finally bowing to London's pressure, the board agreed to reconsider the film two weeks into its run after theater managers showing the picture had already appeared twice before police magistrates in New York. The board's General Committee convened at the Park Theater on Columbus Circle to view *The Inside of the White Slave Traffic* following a sensational weekend during which the premises had twice been closed by police raids. Although London had evidently added some new material to the film since the board had first reviewed it, every member of the General Committee, with the exception of Howe, refused to pass *The Inside of the White Slave Traffic*, citing its sensationalistic title, its portrayal of brothel interiors, and its failure to castigate the slave trade. It was, they declared, wholly unsuitable for popular audiences. In a statement released to the press that evening, committee members complained that "the picture was distinctly an illustration of the white slave traffic, thinly veiled as an attempt to educate the public. The subject is not made unattractive, does not arouse repressive action, and tends to satisfy morbid curiosity. Instead of pointing a moral, it points to an easy method of obtaining money by both men and women. This film is an illustration, rather than an education."[132]

A board ruling condemning *The Inside of the White Slave Traffic* after repeated police scrutiny—not to mention after thousands of people had already seen the film—must have been perceived by many as "too little, too late." Indeed, it was indicative of the board's hobbled posture in the midteens. After refusing to get involved for fear of controversy, it was ultimately pulled into the fray because of continuing police interventions that explicitly ignored any jurisdiction the Board of Censorship might claim. Still, hoping to solidify its position as the ultimate arbiter of film content in these matters, the Board of Censorship issued a "Special Bulletin on Social Evil" in February of 1914, carefully delineating the limited circumstances under which it would permit depictions of the vice trade.[133] Distinguishing between "indecent pictures" that simply exploited the phenomenon for the purposes of titillation (of which *The Inside of the White Slave Traffic* was likely the model) and "sex-problem photoplays" that might act as responsible agents of reform (such as *Traffic in Souls*), the board warned filmmakers that only the latter category would win its approval. Despite its attempt to exert nationwide influence over film exhibition standards, however, the board faced competition from many state and municipal censorship bodies, which either banned vice films that the board had passed, or allowed presentations of films it had censured. Even with board approval, for instance, *Traffic in Souls* was banned in many communities, including New Orleans, Chicago, Montréal, and Pittsburgh.[134] San Francisco, on the other hand, chose to defy the board's ban on *The Inside of the White Slave Traffic* when an exhibitor there drew "large throngs" to see the film in late January.[135]

Whether the National Board of Censorship could indeed speak for *national* standards from its location in New York also appears to have been of significant concern. Both Frederic Howe, by then former chairman of the board, and Orrin G. Cocks, the board's newly appointed advisory secretary and a former volunteer committee member who had been involved in the decision regarding *The Inside of the White Slave Traffic*, defended the board's decision to pass the film in articles published in New York–based reform journals, the *Outlook* and the *Survey*.[136] Evidently fearing that reports of sensational Broadway theater productions might impugn the board's standards, Cocks confessed that "though located in New York . . . the National Board does not accept as a basis of criticism the standards of the New York stage or of its complicated liberal and abnormal life."[137] Instead, Cocks and Howe stressed the contributions made by the city's prominent social organizations to the board's review committee, insisting that the organization acted "on behalf of the general conscience and intelligence of the country" and always sought "the point of view of typical Americans."[138] While the controversy still raged, Cocks even addressed a gathering of motion picture exhibitors in March of 1914 on the topic "How Moving Picture Can Be Made More Valuable to the Community."[139] Yet ultimately its unsatisfactory handling of the white slave films was indicative of the posture that the board was increasingly forced to adopt in the midteens, when its mission became more a matter of fending off proposals for state and federal censorship than one of exerting national influence over film exhibition.

Writing just over a decade after the white slave film controversy erupted, Terry Ramsaye found the films representative of a new brand of cinema, one that "had just attained the scope to share in the [progressive] movement."[140] Yet while endorsements from progressive notables helped certain films gain currency, in fact there was deep disagreement in the reform community about the merits of involving cinema and its patrons in reform efforts: many embraced the evolving view that motion pictures might serve as purveyors of both information and moral teaching in urban working-class communities; others expressed older fears about whether the constituencies addressed in the city's theaters were suitable targets of reform. "The fight long ago moved out of the range of film news and became a struggle between those who want to publish broadcast facts about the white slave traffic and the police," the *New York Dramatic Mirror* reported in late December 1913.[141]

Even as industry commentators decried the rash of white slave films, publicity material attempted to lend the pictures an air of uplift, often spuriously linking screen stories with "official" vice investigations, and boasting cases and statistics based on the findings of reform workers and civic investigations. Robert C. Allen speculates that strategies of this kind may also have been used to protect producers and exhibitors from the police scrutiny that had plagued stage productions of vice plays like *The Fight* and *The Lure* earlier in 1913.[142] Under the umbrella of such endorsements, films claimed to be presenting reform-minded, educational fare. In a publicity pamphlet accompanying its release of *Traffic in Souls*, Universal Pictures described the film as a "sermon."[143] Similar language was echoed in the *New York Dramatic Mirror*'s review of the film, which declared it "a wholesome sermon in fiction form" containing "nothing that would pander to the evil senses and everything that tends to bring out the finer feeling of the spectator."[144] *Motography* concurred, also stressing the film's educational potential and suggesting that it offered "a lesson to young and old in every foot of its length."[145] Its chief virtue for many critics was the way it revealed the "demonstrably easy fashion" in which victims were captured, alerting women and their parents to traffickers' wiles.[146] "There are contained in it warnings for the girl of the city as well as the girl from the country—and for parents, also," claimed *Moving Picture World*.[147] "Many of the methods of the 'cadets' in getting girls are demonstrated," according to one critic, "thus telling vividly of things to beware of."[148] In an otherwise cautious assessment of motion pictures, even the *Madison Recreation Survey* suggested that "the production of the so-called 'white slave traffic' subject may possibly have a good influence."[149] The prewar years mark cinema's "conscious movement into a realm of moral discourse," according to Tom Gunning.[150] Newly developing narrative codes capable of evoking complex psychological states and pointed political comparisons enabled films to present controversial subjects like sexual abduction within a moralistic frame, Gunning maintains, so that they might be more palatable to middle-class audiences. Indeed, Sumiko Higashi and Janet Staiger argue that filmic treatments of sexuality in the teens, however controversial, ushered in a middle-class audience preoccupied with moral and sexual matters in the post-Victorian era.[151]

Among those who expressed optimistic views of the white slave pictures, even in the face of police opposition, were leading members of New York's progressive elite. *The Inside of the White Slave Traffic* secured endorsements from seventeen prominent progressives listed in its title sequence, among them noted feminists Carrie Chapman Catt and Charlotte Perkins Gilman, Board of Censorship chairman Frederic Howe, "and many others, including every sociologist of note from Atlantic to Pacific." When the picture faced difficulty with police in New York, several prominent reformers—including Catt, Inez Milholland Boissevain, Mrs. O.H.P. Belmont, and Mrs. William K. Vanderbilt, Sr.—spoke out on its behalf with Vanderbilt maintaining that such films were "good for the public."[152] Placards in the Bijou Theater's lobby also reminded filmgoers of these endorsements.[153] The film's chief supporter was Frederick Robinson, head of the Sociological Fund of the *Medical Review of Reviews*. He monitored raids on theaters where the film was shown and castigated police for suppressing the film, hoping that the debate would "determine once and for all time whether the police may constitute themselves the judges and censors in our community."[154] And he appealed, unsuccessfully, to the Board of Censorship several months after the film closed, urging them to reconsider their assessment of the film.[155] Once it became clear that *The Inside of the White Slave Traffic* could not be shown commercially in the city without police interference, Robinson and several other supporters vowed to conduct private screenings of the film, during which they also planned to distribute copies of Christabel Pankhurst's banned publication "Plain Facts about a Great Evil."[156]

Not two months after the release of *Traffic in Souls*, white slave films were an issue significant enough to warrant an editorial in the progressive *Outlook*. The January 1914 piece advocated the use of "intensely democratic" media like cinema as "purveyors of social information" on prostitution, arguing that motion pictures reached a more significant segment of the population than either fiction or drama.[157] But this view was unequivocally denounced by the magazine's readers, who complained in letters published in the following issue that the very democratic constituency of movie audiences rendered cinema an unsuitable vehicle for social change.[158] Admitting that stage plays on the same subject could be equally "vulgar," one female reader insisted nevertheless that "[dramatic] theaters do not reach the same excessively impressionable class as is reached by the moving picture."[159] After attending three matinees of *The Inside of the White Slave Traffic*, a New York social worker wrote to report that the majority of audiences were composed of men, and asked, "[W]hat class of men can afford to spend two hours of an afternoon at the moving-picture show?"[160] Members of New York's reform community were particularly divided in their response to the white slave films. Speaking at the height of the controversy, Rabbi Stephen S. Wise told an audience at the Free Synagogue in Carnegie Hall that despite the educational potential of the cinema, the current crop of vice films "do nothing more than stimulate an unwholesome and morbid curiosity instead of driving home a moral lesson."[161] *The Inside of the White Slave Traffic*, in particular, caused "a row among sociological workers," according to the *New York World*.[162] Many reformers questioned the wisdom of exposing the city's vice conditions in such a vivid, lifelike manner to the moviegoing public. John D. Rockefeller, Jr., for his part, took deliberate steps to dissociate himself from productions claiming to be based upon his work at the Bureau of Social Hygiene: "I and those associated with me in this work regard this method of exploiting vice as not only injudicious but positively harmful," he claimed.[163] Even the *New York Times* entered the debate. Responding to news that films on the slave trade would be released to New York audiences, the *Times* published an editorial suggesting that it was a grave mistake "to put before the promiscuous audiences of the motion picture theaters" material on the vice trade, for information gleaned from the Rockefeller report was "meant to be circulated discreetly" and was "never meant for indiscriminate circulation, least of all in pictorial form before audiences composed of both sexes and all ages." Such pictures could have no other effect than to "pour oil upon the flames of vice," the *Times* concluded.[164] Few critics disputed the accuracy of the films' presentation of white slave trafficking, then, just the suitability of engaging motion picture patrons in matters of this gravity. Activists perceived cinema audiences as largely working-class, a segment of society they apparently considered an inappropriate target of enlightenment.

Reformers' concerns about film audiences watching sensationalized depictions of white slavery resonate with the movement's broader concerns about the general nature of working-class leisure, as well as specific fears that motion picture theaters promoted the "social evil." In addition to seriously undermining the industry's attempts to bolster its reputation, then, apprehensions about cinematic portrayals of white slavery engaged the era's larger debate about "motion picture morals," a sustained dialogue on the merits of moving picture scripts and their effects on viewers. By the midteens, cinema's already-established notoriety began to shift away from concerns about conditions at exhibition sites, emblematized in the December 1908 New York City theater closings. Instead, mounting attention focused on the virtues and vices presented *on screen*, as a series of popular articles investigated "The Morals of the Movies," "The Immoral Morality of the 'Movies,' " and "The Utter Hopelessness of the Movies."[165] Were films too violent and risqué? Were cinematic characters justifiably punished for wrongdoing? Could viewers be unduly influenced by immoral acts witnessed on the screen? Although admittedly nonplussed by the conduct of unchaperoned young people at his theater, one small-town exhibitor claimed to be far more troubled by the motion pictures themselves. There is "too much blood and thunder and crime on the screen," he reported, calling for stories on more wholesome subjects. "The movies are endlessly preoccupied with sex," lamented another observer. How such material might affect viewers, who could become "vulgarized through the eye," was also of significant concern. "It is the psychology—or rather total absence of it—in the average moving-picture play that constitutes its greatest danger to the growing mind," one writer insisted.[166] Acknowledging that motion pictures were "probably the greatest single force in shaping the American character," a 1910 magazine piece feared cinema's "suggestive" effects, citing two Pittsburgh youths who attempted to hold up a streetcar after watching a train robbery portrayed on screen, a Newark man who killed himself, emulating a film heroine's attempted suicide, and a Philadelphia man who murdered his wife after seeing a similar scene enacted at the movies the previous evening.[167]

The view that sensational depictions of white slavery somehow emblematized the larger evils of cinema is also made plain in a cartoon published in the *New York Sun* at the height of the controversy.[168] Entitled "The Movie," the cartoon depicts a man and woman purchasing tickets for a film called *The White Slave*. Although a small notice on the ticket booth proclaims the show "a great moral lesson for young and old," the overwhelming architecture of the Medusa Theater seems to contradict this view. The Medusa's head that frames the theater's portal is, of course, reminiscent of the ornate, quasi-classical facades and plasters that increasingly adorned motion picture houses in these years. But in this figuration the theater entrance becomes an engulfing feminine orifice, a visual echo of the wide, wild eyes and gaping, screaming mouth of the Medusa pictured at the top of the drawing. In this view the cinema, epitomized by the white slave pictures, becomes a horror too terrifying to view.

Evidence that attention focused less on fire hazards, ventilation systems, and promiscuity among theater patrons, as it had in the early nickelodeon era, and more often on the process of film *viewing* itself, points to broader transformations in the preclassical cinema. New concerns about spectator-text relations signify an evolving theoretization of "spectatorship" that Miriam Hansen charts in the early teens. The movement toward classical strategies of cinematic narration throughout the transitional period enabled a modified form of film viewing, Hansen maintains, one that "sought more consistently to ensure the spectator's perceptual placement *within narrative space*" and, as a conse-

The movie.

10. *New York Sun*, December 1913.

quence, "corresponded to an increased derealization of the theater space—the physical and social space of the spectator."[169] Accordingly, industry discourse moved away from generic references to the film *audience* around 1910, Hansen argues, and began conceiving of an abstract *spectator*. Film viewers were increasingly seen not just as paying customers but as individuals structured in an imaginary visual space through the act of viewing. "The term 'spectator,' " she writes, "implied a shift from a collective, plural notion of the film viewer to a singular, unified but potentially universal category. . . ."[170]

Unease about the presence of women at the white slave films noticeably registered these evolving notions of spectatorship, for chief among concerns expressed about the "slavers" was the sizable number of female patrons said to have been present at screenings, apparently eager for tales about on-screen counterparts spirited away to brothels. The *New York Times* gave special mention to the crowd of several hundred young women turned away from the premiere of *The Inside of the White Slave Traffic* in late 1913. "A large proportion of the audience was composed of young girls from sixteen to eighteen years of age," the *Times* reported, adding that "fully two-thirds of the audience were women."[171] *Variety* observed early the next year that " 'vice pictures' are attracting in the majority mostly young couples, who sit in the dark while having 'ideas' indelibly forced upon them from pictures on the sheet."[172] White slave picture attracted "half grown boys and girls" who "go to see something 'hot.' . . . They go to see sensationalism, and they go in crowds," Epes Sargent reported.[173] When *The Little Girl Next Door* opened at Chicago's LaSalle Theatre in 1916, a full-page ad in *Motion Picture News* quoted the theater owner's claim that "at 25 cents for all seats, [it] is doing the biggest business of any picture we ever played. We have a line of people waiting to get in all day and evening."[174] A photo accompanying the ad showed as many women as men visible in a crowd gathering outside the theater.

That women were attracted to material of this nature at a time when industry uplift was tied in no small measure to cinema's ability to draw in "respectable" middle-class women challenged inherent presumptions about female viewers. The films appealed to women not on the virtuous grounds exhibitors purported to uphold, but through sensationalism and titillation. "A considerable share of the two packed houses that viewed the film last night evidently expected something decidedly raw," reported one Minneapolis reviewer of the audience that greeted *Traffic in Souls* in that city.[175] The scandal surrounding women's attendance at these films suggests that, however much coveted by exhibitors, female moviegoers still posed a problem for the industry. Not only was the manner of women's participation in commercial leisure sites like the cinema contested in discussions of the white slave films, but the very nature of female spectatorship, with its suggestion of voyeurism and visual license, was also at issue.

White Slavery on the Screen

Three interwoven stories in *Traffic in Souls* delineate for viewers the varied and devious means by which trafficking rings supposedly preyed upon women particularly vulnerable in American cities. In one tale a candy store clerk is lured to a dance hall, drugged, then transported to a "house of ill repute"; in another, two Swedish immigrants just arrived at Ellis Island follow a comrade they have met aboard ship, only to find themselves trapped in a brothel temporarily disguised as a "Swedish Employment Agency"; and finally, a naive "Country Girl" unfamiliar with New York is misdirected to that same establishment, where she too is held against her will. Each scenario depicts women newly visible in the urban environment: young working women eagerly participating in the city's leisure culture; immigrants arriving in America alone, too often ill-acquainted with its language and customs; and single women migrating to cities from rural communities in search of work and accommodation outside protective family structures. By suggesting that these three groups were particularly at risk, the film raises apprehensions about the vulnerability of women newly autonomous in American cities. The film's extensive use of New York City location shooting only underscores the distinctly *urban* backdrop of these situations and enhances its realistic appeal. Exterior views staged at Battery Park, Penn Station, and on New York thoroughfares ground the stories in identifiable landmarks, while at the same time lending them a documentary flavor that guarantees their fanciful kidnapping plots an element of credibility.

Of the three scenarios, the film concentrates most intensely on the plight of the candy store clerk, known only by the name "Little Sister."[176] A detailed rendering of her procurement is measured against the more familiar stories of abduction involving immigrants and new arrivals from the country. Little Sister's narrative thread stresses the way that employment and leisure-time diversions placed working women in particular peril, for both her workplace and the city's recreation culture figure dramatically in her capture. Little Sister is first spotted by a vice ring procurer while she works behind the counter at Smyrner's Candy Store with her sister Mary. Unseen, the "cadet" watches her from the street outside, returning twice, then confirming his choice with a madam, before he enters the shop and approaches her. By flirting with the young clerk and buying her candy, he "fascinates her with his nice manners," in the words of *Motography*'s reviewer.[177] Much to her elder sister's horror, Little Sister succumbs to the cadet's flattery, agreeing to accompany him to a restaurant and dance hall where he eventually drugs her drink as she turkey-trots with his cohort. Thus incapacitated, Little Sister is easily transported to a brothel and held captive in one of its upstairs bedrooms.

To *Moving Picture World*'s critic the causal relationship between Little Sister's place of work and her eventual enslavement was immediately obvious: "To establish an acquaintance over the counter is easy. Then comes the invitation to dinner, then to a dance, then the employment of a 'safe' taxi driver, and the drugged girl is behind locked doors in the brothel."[178] Indeed, her position behind the counter at Smyrner's, on display like merchandise, allows the vice ring's cadet virtually unlimited access to her, for he may survey her through the display window as often as he pleases and chat companionably with her on the shop floor without arousing suspicion. Within the film a newspaper account of her capture draws out the wider ramifications of Little Sister's fate, asking, "Is it possible our candy stores can be used as a market for this infamous traffic?"[179] It was precisely this facet of the retail environment that prompted reformer Jane Addams to include a special warning to female sales clerks about the hazards of white slavery. "Every possible weakness in a girl is detected and traded upon" in the retail store, Addams cautioned.[180] It was not simply the nature of retail space that unnerved Addams, but the more general question of young, single women increasingly employed outside the home. Openly worried about the "girlish multitude" entering the labor force, living and working beyond reach of "the direct stimulus of family interest or affection," Addams stressed the degree to which "the superior chastity of women, so rigidly maintained during the centuries, has been a result of her domestic surroundings."[181] Positing two fundamentally opposed sectors in modern culture, Addams cast the family home, locus of morality, against an urban core constantly threatening to corrupt innocent women.

Chief among the city's temptations were commercial recreation venues that catered freely to single working women. Cafés and dance halls such as those Little Sister visits with the cadet were considered notorious hunting grounds for slave traffickers, more maligned than even the cinema. Citing the danger of café culture to retail clerks, one alarmist tract warned that "two hundred department store girls ... take the first downward step each year, in these cafés."[182] Viewers of *Traffic in Souls* are reminded of these dangers early on. A shot of Little Sister and the vice cadet laughing and enjoying themselves at the café is prefaced by an intertitle announcing "the first move of the tempter." The drinking, dancing, and wild goings-on visible in the subsequent dance hall scene only further facilitate Little Sister's capture, for the plethora of visual and physical sensations renders her blind to the perilous consequences. There "all is life and cheap gaiety but the dance music and the sight of the whirling and trotting dancers fascinates [Little Sister]," according to *Motography*.[183] O. Edward Janney described dance halls as "one of the most important recruiting grounds of the white slaver" in his monograph *The White Slave Traffic in America*. For Janney the catalyst was the "easy etiquette that prevails" there, where "too frequently an opportunity is thus afforded to lead [women] astray."[184] Another commentator observed, more bluntly, "[T]he act of dancing tends to excite sexual feeling, and no girl who wishes to make sure she will retain her virtue should visit these public traps of sin."[185] Even *Photoplay*'s narrativization of the film's story underscores Little Sister's culpability in this recreation culture, pointing out how much she enjoys "the flattering attention of her good-looking escort"; when he proposes that they move from café to dance hall, "she is quite ready to go."[186]

Even before Little Sister's drink is drugged, her presence at these sites is assigned an undercurrent of danger, for scenes depicting the rapid entrapment of the two Swedish sisters and the "Country Girl" are inserted during the early stages of Little Sister's flirtation with the cadet. Just as he enters the store for the first time, charming Little Sister, offering her candy and presumably setting up their date, we see comparable scenes where the Swedish sisters are singled out by traffickers aboard their ship off Ellis Island, and where the Country Girl is first approached by a procurer at Penn Station.[187] By the time Little Sister leaves the candy store on her supposed date, the three other women have already been locked in a brothel. Alternation among these narrative threads creates an important anticipatory device, lending the date a measure of foreboding long before Little Sister herself is aware of the threat she faces. The parallels also serve a comparative function, framing Little Sister's story within a wider context that displays the far-reaching consequences of slave trafficking. By this account she is but one of many victims caught every day around the country. But the juxtaposition also illuminates discrepancies between Little Sister's situation and those of the other women. Whereas the naïveté of the immigrant sisters and the "Country Girl" is stressed—in both cases the women rely on advice from strangers because they are unfamiliar with New York—Little Sister is partly implicated in her own misfortune. Unable to withstand the temptations of commercial recreation culture, she is lured into the slave trade by the promise of courtship, a misjudgment for which one critic labeled her a "feather-brained little girl."[188] The ongoing police investigation of the vice traffickers, and their eventual raid on the brothel where the Country Girl is held with the Swedish immigrants, also take place while Little Sister enjoys her tryst with the cadet. If alternation between the other women's captures underscores the hidden peril lurking beneath seemingly innocent leisure activities, then the parallel investigation very nearly criminalizes these same pastimes.

Significant features of Little Sister's entrapment become especially apparent when compared with the plot of the stage play *The Lure*, which premiered on Broadway just three months before the opening of *Traffic in Souls*.[189] The drama and the film bear striking similarities but diverge in notable respects as well. In the stage play the victim is looking for work to support her ailing mother and is captured when she mistakenly approaches a madam advertising "extra work for girls in the evening." Little Sister, on the contrary, is enticed sexually, agreeing to accompany her procurer to a café and then to a dance hall on a supposed date. Whereas the heroine of *The Lure* and the other victims portrayed in *Traffic in Souls* are placed above reproach, Little Sister is held somewhat accountable for her fate. Her willing participation in the dating culture that surrounds urban leisure sites puts her at particular risk. Moreover, because her sexuality comes under suspicion, she is denied the romantic interest granted the play's lead. *The Lure*'s heroine is, quite typically, reunited with her fiancé in the end, when he breaks the slave trafficking ring by leading a raid on the house where she is held captive; however, in *Traffic in Souls* it is the victim's sister Mary who is reunited with *her* fiancé, Officer Burke, after he frees Little Sister from her brothel captivity. Indeed, many of the functions customarily accorded the white slave heroine are transferred onto the victim's elder sister.[190]

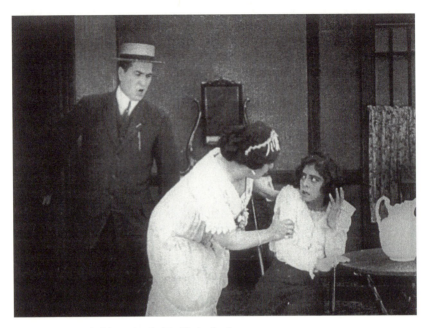

11. Little Sister held captive in *Traffic in Souls*.

The two Barton sisters are contrasted from the beginning of the film. Little Sister is shown to be rather careless and perpetually late for work, while Mary, as "head of the family," is dedicated to the girls' invalid father and exceedingly modest in her romantic relations, even refusing to kiss poor Burke in public view. Issues of desire and sexuality raised by Little Sister's plight are contained within Mary's rather asexual romance and her traditional role within the family. Crosscutting becomes the central trope of this containment in scenes matching the younger sister's enslavement with the elder sister's efforts to save her. Shots of Little Sister's limp and drugged body being dragged from the taxi to the house of prostitution, and of her being hauled up the stairs to a bedroom where her suit jacket is forcibly removed, are intercut with those of Mary at home in her own bedroom consumed with fear about her sister. Shots of Mary draped across her bed sobbing and praying for her sister's safety censor and contain the sexual associations manifest in the brothel images, transforming Little Sister's eroticized posture to one of piety and repositioning the bedroom in a domestic setting. Not surprisingly it is precisely this image that adorned the frontispiece of Eustace Hale Ball's 1914 novelization of *Traffic in Souls*.[191] Even as the film exhibits concerns about urban dating customs through the specter of sexual slavery, it attempts to contain female sexuality in the domestic sphere through the figure of Mary Barton.

12. Shots of Mary at home in her bedroom amplify *and* censor the sexual connotations of her sister's brothel scenes.

That we are invited to share Mary's perspective, rather than her younger sister's, at several key points in the narrative suggests the normative morality accorded her position. Another of these scenes occurs as the cadet first approaches Little Sister at Smyrner's. Triangulated long shot compositions place Mary in the background between the couple flirting in foreground space. Medium shots that isolate Mary's horrified reactions to this turn of events are intercut with the larger view. While not a strict point-of-view sequence (because both camera setups employ the same frontal staging and Mary appears in each shot), the compositions and cutting patterns nonetheless stress Mary's perspective and invite our participation in her concern for her younger sister's welfare. Little Sister's possible enjoyment of the procurer's flattery is thus framed throughout the scene by Mary's critical gaze. Later it is Mary who watches as her sister, drugged and lifeless, is loaded into a waiting cab; and it is she who summons the police and urges their investigation.

Although Little Sister is denied a legitimate romantic interest because of her questionable morals, the film's elaborate crosscutting strategy situates the stages of her entrapment alongside two other courtships: Mary's modest relations with Officer Burke, and wealthy Alice Trubus's engagement to "society-catch" Bobby Kopfman. Significantly, Little Sister's courtship is the only one

13. Mary watches as Little Sister is courted by the vice ring's procurer.

that takes place in the modern world of urban amusements. By insisting upon a comparison among these three couples, the film casts Little Sister's fate as a perverse romance. Her mistaken belief that the procurer is in fact courting her only adds a further element of irony. Set against such a crude seduction, the impending marriages of the two other women mock Little Sister's destiny in the brothel. A further crosscutting strategy links Little Sister's fate to a inversion of conventional domestic order, alternating among scenes in the Barton family's humble apartment, the elegant Trubus household, and the brothel where Little Sister is held. This editing pattern squarely identifies the brothel's threat by initially equating the three houses. Disguised as just another home on a residential street, the house of prostitution offers a literal transposition of the other traditional homes, with the madam and her cadet acting as surrogate mother and father to the young women they hold captive.

By elaborately framing Little Sister's entrapment in these multiple threads, *Traffic in Souls* portrays not so much a battle between Little Sister and her enslavers as a struggle between the two facets of modern urban society. The first, principally embodied by elder sister Mary Barton, represents traditional female life centered on the family home where women's sexuality and activities are contained within marriage and domesticity. The other, opposing way of life, symbolized by Little Sister's odyssey into the perverted domestic and sexual world of the brothel, equates social and romantic interests outside the home with moral and sexual decay. Here I disagree with Janet Staiger's characterization of Mary Barton as an embodiment of the era's New Woman.[192] Although she does later play a crucial role in uncovering the vice ring, Mary is associated above all with a respect for patriarchy and chaste adherence to the law; it is her younger sister who is associated with the "vices" of modernity. Far from presenting viewers with a portrait of liberated modern womanhood, *Traffic in Souls* reinforces outdated polarities between vice and virtue.

At the center of the slave ring stands William Trubus, a wealthy and respected citizen, who uses his ostensible position as head of the "International Purity and Reform League" to disguise his vice dealings. Under cover of his reform work, Trubus also runs the slave ring that preys upon the city's women, supervising a tangled network of pimps, procurers, madams, and go-betweens. It was this aspect of the film's plot that became the focus of the National Board of Censorship's review of the film. Especially sensitive to suggestions that members of the reform community might be involved in the vice traffic, the board was eager to eliminate implications that the film's vice ring leader, William Trubus, was also involved in progressive social causes. They requested that all titles describing Trubus as an "eminent philanthropist and reformer" be changed so that he was characterized only as "the man higher up." A title that cited the Travellers' Vigilance Society was also eliminated to prevent any implication that the group had endorsed the film. These were alterations clearly designed to protect the reform community by limiting its liability for the lessons learned in the film, and more important, by erasing any hint that its members might be engaged in duplicitous activities. By insisting upon the change in Trubus's character, the board was downplaying the *social* causes of prostitution in favor of dramas of individual vice and virtue.

Trubus manages his spurious reform operation from an office above the slave ring headquarters, a position that allows him to listen in on their transactions through a dictagraphic wire. Though his connection to the vice operation is thus literal, it is also obscured. A graphic match aligns Trubus sitting in his upstairs office with his go-between positioned in exactly the same way at his desk downstairs, suggesting the interconnectedness of the two enterprises and mocking the sanctity of Trubus's assumed guise. Perhaps most pointedly, the sign on Trubus's door identifying his "International Purity and Reform League" is only ever visible in reverse from the office's interior, a clear visual pun on his double-dealing existence, his posing as virtuous while acting precisely the opposite. Ironically then, the euphemism assigned to Trubus in lieu of "reformer"—"the man higher up"—describes perfectly his covert relation to the vice ring from a position of assumed social and moral superiority. And while the Board of Censorship had been scrupulous in overseeing language used in the film's titles, it did not go so far as to request changes in the film's mise-en-scène, inadvertently creating a space for this kind of irony.

Not so easily exorcised was the obvious visual resemblance between actor William Welsh (who played Trubus) and one of the era's best-known vice crusaders, John D. Rockefeller, Jr., a coincidence noted at the time.[193] Much to his displeasure, Rockefeller's name was frequently linked to vice films whose promoters were eager to cloak their salacious narratives in the guise of scientific study. Janet Staiger suggests that the characterization of Trubus offered audiences a chance to mock pious, wealthy do-gooders like Rockefeller, admittedly easy targets, while also hinting that these men controlled a capitalist sexual economy that trapped women much more effectively than the torrid vice rings they chased so publicly. Somewhat paradoxically, even though Rockefeller's own grand jury report found little evidence of organized vice trafficking, only small-scale police corruption, *Traffic in Souls* paints the opposite picture: upstanding police officers fighting a prostitution cartel headed by the city's wealthy and powerful elite.[194]

Trubus and his vice gang are associated above all with the covert surveillance that enables their sure command over the urban environment: Trubus maintains his posture as head of the reform league in order to gain privileged information about civic initiatives and police investigations; he uses a dictagraph to keep tabs on the activities of his go-between in the office below; the gang employs a magic writing pad to transcribe figures from their operation from one office to another; they send cryptic telegrams plotting the capture of the Swedish sisters; and, above all, they enjoy unusual freedom to gaze upon women at public sites. Time and again sequences stress the way that procurers survey their victims before entrapping them. Two strategies are employed to mark this action: shots of women and their predators in the same frame emphasize the women's obliviousness to their danger; and editing patterns that place women and traffickers in separate shots with the men looking out of frame emphasize the male gaze, even though not employing traditional optical point-of-view cutting. When the "Country Girl" leaves her train at Penn Station, she is immediately caught up in a network of gazes. On the platform she is watched by a rail conductor, a police officer, and a procurer, all framed in a single long shot composition that places the Country Girl, dressed in a light dress and broad-brimmed hat, at the center of attention. When she exits the station in a second shot, a cutback to the cadet on the platform (now looking out of frame) draws further attention to the way she is surveyed without her knowledge. Although an alert policeman intervenes, having spotted the procurer's approach, the cadet is merely replaced by a second operative who follows the "Country Girl" on the trolley car and misdirects her to the brothel when she becomes disoriented at the end of her journey. Like the "Country Girl," the Swedish sisters are subject to similar scrutiny aboard their ship. Even before it docks at Ellis Island, operatives look the women over, then send a coded telegram back to shore announcing, "Sweden Beautiful Country. Two." And implied point-of-view strategies are likewise employed to suggest the cadet's perusal of Little Sister at the candy store, when shots of him standing at the doorway looking out of frame are juxtaposed with those showing her in the interior of the shop. Such strategies dramatize how Trubus's syndicate occupies the position of visual mastery often attributed to procurers and vice cadets said to be haunting American cities, "everywhere looking the girls over and deciding which ones they want,"according to vice tracts. Women were warned to be on the alert for such characters, "forever lurking in your shadow . . . [where] the silent form sneaks behind you."[195] Recall here Mary's act of refusing Burke's kiss in the presence of a workman. Her gesture now seems not only to mark her modesty but to underscore the network of gazes to which all women are subject in urban space.

Police are also associated with visual surveillance in the film, a factor again emphasized through crosscutting. Images of the vice ring dispatching operatives to locations around the city are intercut with scenes in police headquarters showing officers also fanning out across town. Officers alert to cadets' tactics watch from offscreen as the men attempt to capture unsuspecting women. When the two Swedish sisters are taken to the brothel, identical locations and camera setups duplicate an earlier scene showing the entrapment of the Country Girl. The difference in this second case, however, is that Office Burke, now cognizant of the threat, follows at close range, observing the cadet's every move. The insistence upon Burke's gaze here counteracts that of the traffickers.

However clandestine they may be, Trubus still cannot prevent his vice operations from ultimately impinging on his placid home life. Emphasizing the tangible spread of corruption from public to private through prostitution and sexuality, *Traffic in Souls* stresses the physical contiguity between prostitutes, procurers, madams, go-betweens, and slave traffickers, all of whom repeatedly exchange handshakes and transfer money.[196] When Trubus's henchman shakes hands with a madam in the downstairs office, the action is echoed in the following shot where Trubus repeats the gesture with his daughter Alice's unsuspecting fiancé, introducing lingering traces of vice into the domestic realm. Such focus on the bodily transfer of contagion conflates moral contamination with physical contact and evokes the specter of venereal disease, a problem progressives readily linked with prostitution. Even Alice's engagement is compromised by Trubus's associations, the film suggests, by cutting directly from the scene of Alice and Bobby's courtship in the family home to the first scene inside one of Trubus's brothels. In the end Trubus's moral decay spreads into his own family, when a police raid disrupts a happy gathering in celebration of his daughter's engagement. The taint of corruption finally kills Trubus's upstanding wife, once she learns the true nature of her husband's business. One print of the film survives with an ending that underscores Trubus's disgrace even further: the final shot shows a garbage can containing a newspaper whose headline broadcasts details of his slave ring.[197] These connections ultimately transcended prostitution and white slavery, encompassing fears about interconnections among business, police, and vice interests in American cities, anxieties that lay at the heart of the municipal vice commissions, for whom the "social evil" meant not simply prostitution but organized urban corruption.

Connections between vice and the "man higher up" are most forcefully enacted when Mary Barton traces the dictagraphic wire linking Trubus's bogus "International Purity and Reform League" to the prostitution ring he controls downstairs.[198] Working as a secretary in Trubus's organization after having been fired from Smyrner's when Little Sister's "disgrace" is revealed, Mary casually listens in on Trubus's dictagraph, accidentally overhearing a conversation between the go-between and his cadet in the office below. When she recognizes a voice belonging to the man last seen with her sister, and when she realizes he is giving salacious details of her capture to the go-between before collecting his money, she follows the dictagraphic wire out to the fire escape and down to the office below, where she sees the two together for the first time. The importance of both her sight line and her moral perspective is again stressed in this scene as she spies on the two men through the window. The composition places her in the midground crouching by the window with the traffickers visible through the glass in the background, showing them in a camera setup not previously used. The sequence then cuts back and forth between this setup, which designates Mary's act of looking, and shots of the traffickers inside their headquarters framed by the long shot composition from which the office had been previously shown. It is an editing strategy that clearly foregrounds Mary's gaze as much as her moral perspective. The contiguity between Trubus's seemingly reputable operation and the "infamous traffic" are never more plain than in this scene.

With the help of Officer Burke and an invention of her father's, Mary eventually turns this invisible apparatus against the slave ring. Using Mr. Barton's device for "intensifying sound waves and recording dictagraphic sounds on a phonographic record" secretly installed in Trubus's office, Mary records the men's conversations on wax cylinders—tangible proof of what she has seen and heard. She then delivers the evidence to the police; urban corruption becomes a matter of public documentation as Trubus's voice is recorded and amplified in the police station, his status as "silent partner" in the prostitution ring finally exposed. Burke meanwhile trails the cadet from Trubus's office building to the brothel where Little Sister is held captive, ultimately leading a successful raid on the establishment and freeing his future sister-in-law.

The eventual triumph of her father's invention in helping to convict Little Sister's captors seems particularly noteworthy, given the way that the film links prostitution to a perversion of conventional domestic order. If Little Sister's predicament warns of the hazards awaiting modern women outside the home, then the film finds its solution in a reassertion of traditional family morality paradoxically enacted through modern technology. Although an elderly invalid who must be supported by his daughters' earnings, Mr. Barton is ultimately

14. Mary spies on vice ring operatives.

able to save his youngest and convict her captors by extending his paternal body into the public arena and employing his sound-recording mechanism to document the workings of the slave trafficking network. The prosthetic recording device resurrects the weak patriarchal body in the guise of technology. It also reverses the patterns of surveillance at work in the film, very neatly turning the surveillance back on Trubus's empire at the film's climactic moment, making him the victim of his own methods. In the end, Little Sister's rescue demonstrates that mastery over a multifarious vice conspiracy must take the form of technological reconnaissance. Although cinema is not specifically evoked in this context, allusions to its photographic properties are echoed in Barton's invention. One is given the sense that only an instrument like the cinema might be capable of rendering this invisible traffic visible, an idea I will take up further later on.

The narrative of sexual danger offered in *Traffic in Souls* ultimately charts the contours of a newly gendered urban landscape. Through a series of inversions and parallels, the film presents a city where good and evil, safety and danger, can no longer be plotted along the lines of public and private space, or indeed public and private relations: slave ring operatives pose as helpful gentlemen offering assistance to émigrés and immigrants; procurers pose as suitors; brothels pose as residential homes; and traffickers even pose as Christian reformers. This alarmist model of cosmopolitan culture envelops fears about women who work outside the home, especially in conspicuous retail sites where they find themselves exhibited along with the goods; and it dramatizes apprehensions about modern courtships taking place in commercial leisure settings, rather than the family home. *Traffic in Souls* associates these changes (almost paradoxically) with both female victimization and sexual pollution. The idea that women like Little Sister who entered the labor market or frequented popular recreation sites might be the victims of slave trafficking rings links those activities with immorality, while simultaneously abrogating women's responsibilities there.

Something of the role that documentation played in contemporary accounts of the slave trade is suggested by the part that the elder Barton's inventive recording device plays in remapping urban space in *Traffic in Souls*. Efforts to record and catalog aspects of prostitution and slave trafficking were evident mainly in vice commission reports that tallied prostitution's toll on urban life. Histrionic white slave warnings borrowed from these studies to enhance their own rather *in*credible enactments of sexual abduction, attempting to garner respectability through avowed associations with investigatory arms of the reform campaign: many authors of alarmist white slave tracts were themselves attorneys and clergymen claiming inside knowledge of the workings of red-light districts; and stories that appeared in prominent magazines were cast as "case histories" compiled by social workers, then rendered into dramatic form. Presumably, such assertions allowed family-oriented monthlies like *Collier's* to defend the publication of material on prostitution between their covers.

Films, too, made similarly inflated claims. Advance publicity for *Traffic in Souls*, for instance, promised that its events were "based upon the Rockefeller white slaves report and upon the grand jury investigation undertaken by D.A. Whitman," and that it "was staged at the suggestion of a number of prominent social workers, who felt it was the best way to make public the lessons to be drawn from the vice investigations."[199] *The Little Girl Next Door* promised "VICE . . . exposed by the Illinois State Vice Commission."[200] The ads touted fabricated connections to official vice studies and boasted endorsements from respected civic leaders. *The Inside of the White Slave Traffic* was "produced from actual facts" and "based on the actual observations of a former U.S. government investigator," according to its publicity, while *Smashing the Vice Trust* was "based on District Attorney Whitman's disclosures."[201] Proclaimed "the only production that has the endorsement and sanction of the many vice crusaders throughout the country," *Traffic in Souls* advanced its status as "the only true and authentic version" of the traffic in women.[202] *The Inside of the White Slave Traffic* quoted an endorsement from Frederick H. Robinson, president of the Sociological Research Fund; and *Smashing the Vice Trust* cited famed New York vice crusader Dr. Charles Parkhurst.[203] New York District Attorney Charles S. Whitman was even said to have appeared in the last film.[204]

When the film played in Buffalo, an exhibitor there purchased a half-page advertisement in the local newspaper featuring Whitman's photograph.[205] An industry ad for *The Inside of the White Slave Traffic* asserted that the film was "based on Real existing facts gathered by U.S. Government Investigator Samuel H. London, the man that Rockefeller uses as an authority on White Slavery."[206] London was himself the film's producer, a fact rarely omitted in promotional materials. Early publicity insisted that the project's aim, far from sensationalism, "was to disclose the entire system of degradation for the benefit of civic leagues, Y.M.C.A.s and other bodies that are working for the betterment of social conditions."[207] Claims of this sort only blurred distinctions between legitimate research about prostitution and simplistic abduction plots on the screen, giving undue credence to the latter.

Photographic studies that accompanied many published tracts manifested another, more voyeuristic, side of the documentary impulse. Alongside lurid prose descriptions of vice trafficking and brothel life, photographs of red-light districts and their inhabitants offered potent visual testimony. Readers were offered views of brothels with barred windows, male customers lurking in the streets, and mission workers attempting to rescue "fallen women." Read one caption, "Behold the skulking men with lust-mad brain, the harlot tapping on the window pane."[208] One widely reproduced series of photos depicted a staged reenactment of a young woman's entrapment during a "date," much like Little Sister's own capture in *Traffic in Souls*, all accompanied by torrid captions the likes of "Drugged and Led to Her Ruin."[209] In Mark Connelly's estimation much of avowedly reform-minded white slave literature offered exposés amounting to little more than "vicarious 'tour guides' to the red-light districts," so rich and vivid were their descriptions.[210] The title page of Rev. F. M. Lehman's study, *The White Slave Hell, or with Christ at Midnight in the Slums of Chicago*, promised "[s]tartling revelations, thrilling experiences and life stories carefully gathered from red light districts, white slave markets, segregated vice sections and midnight slum work of Chicago."[211]

Within this climate of authenticity *The Inside of the White Slave Traffic* engages a forceful documentary rhetoric in the service of voyeuristic titillation. An extremely controversial and relatively explicit film released on the heels of *Traffic in Souls*, its very title pledged unlimited access to hitherto unseen regions of American life. The implied promise of "interior" views, moreover, assured patrons a glimpse behind brothel doors. The film offers less the *dramatization* of vice, such as was provided by *Traffic in Souls* and stage plays like *The Fight* and *The Lure*, than privileged, "inside" documentation. Most important, *The Inside of the White Slave Traffic* is unique among other offerings in the way that it exploits *cinema's* specific documentary capacities. Boasting footage of actual slave trafficking and vice gathered by its own motion picture cameras, the film purports not only to verify descriptions found in white slave literature but to bring them alive. The unique *photographic* properties of the film medium guarantee the film's authenticity, for the cinema itself is presented as an investigatory tool, a revelatory machine, capable of unmasking the hidden substance of clandestine vice operations. Reports that many of the film's sequences had been shot on location in red-light districts around the country were touted conspicuously in ads and advance publicity. Two months prior to the release of *Traffic in Souls*, *The Inside of the White Slave Traffic* generated publicity about its crew's activities filming in the vice districts of notable American cities. A prominently displayed piece in the *New York Dramatic Mirror* assumed an almost boastful tone in reporting that members of the production were arrested while filming in El Paso, Texas. "Between interruptions," the story claimed, "they secured a film the likes of which, so report says, has never been approached before."[212] A week earlier in New Orleans, the item continued, crew members had been admonished for filming the city's red-light haunts, rather than its scenic locales. How much truth underlay this sensationalist publicity cannot be known; still, notices of this sort illustrate the equal emphasis that producer Samuel H. London accorded the project's "authenticity" and its scandalousness. If camera crews were arrested while shooting, as the account claimed, then the finished film promised wholly illicit views. And as I demonstrated earlier, it was precisely this aspect of *The Inside of the White Slave Traffic* that troubled the National Board of Censorship, which asked London to reduce licentious views of vice regions to only those scenes necessary to advance a plot centered on retribution. If the board had its way, viewers would not be permitted to indulge in unrestricted voyeurism.

Exactly how much of the footage included in the final version could be called "documentary" is difficult to determine from surviving reels.[213] Many dramatized sequences are staged in outdoor locations, but few explicitly "candid" scenes of urban prostitution survive. However, *Variety*'s critic identified at least three vice districts visible in the release print: West Twenty-seventh Street and West Thirty-fourth Street in New York, part of the notorious Tenderloin, and Chicago's Armour Avenue, center of that city's vice life. "The setting is real, the girls actual, the 'sailors' apparently caught by the camera . . . under the broad glare of disillusioning mid-day," he concluded.[214] With the inclusion of such scenes, *Motion Picture News* surmised, *The Inside of the White Slave Traffic* is "probably the most authoritative [of the white slave films], as it shows actual scenes in the underworld."[215] The film's portrayal of prostitution and white slavery was verifiable, in these views, because a camera had been used to record what appeared to be actual events. Boasted producer London, the film "is as near a photographic representation as possible of the great evil."[216] Portrayals were realistic enough for two New York merchants who filed suit against London when their businesses appeared in scenes depicting vice transactions in that city.[217] Throughout such accounts, and especially striking in the *Variety* commentary, a tension is evident between the galling visibility of urban prostitution, performed outdoors "under the broad glare of disillusioning midday," and the cinema's act of exposing such matters in movie theaters where they might be seen by a wider audience. If the *New York Dramatic Mirror* piece is to be believed, New Orleans officials seemed less concerned about the existence of vice activity in their communities than the possibility that these locales might be captured on celluloid. If streetwalking and open solicitation brought private sexual acts into public view, *The Inside of the White Slave Traffic* continued this enterprise, bringing activities confined to certain corners of American cities onto the screen. The unsettling reorganization of space that such footage might effect recalls Joanne Meyerowitz's discussion of the "sexual geography" of Chicago during this period. Her research suggests that urban communities were broken down into distinct quadrants, some of which might permit more open displays of sexuality and more alternative sexual practices than others.[218] In *The Inside of the White Slave Traffic* documentary cinema and location shooting attempt to break down these barriers in a manner that lent the film authority but troubled those already alarmed by the explicit nature of material presented on the screen. As Lee Grieveson points out, such documentary sequences extend to the use of settings like Ellis Island and Pennsylvania Station in *Traffic in Souls*; but *The Inside of the White Slave Traffic* delivers what is only hinted at in the earlier film's use of location shooting.[219]

The Inside of the White Slave Traffic mixes its avowedly "documentary" footage with fictional scenes, many of which were shot on location.[220] Alongside the documentary images, these scenes depict a tale of slave trafficking in keeping with many others of the genre. Despite the emphasis placed on the film's authenticity in promotional material, then, its narrative presents a perfectly routine rendering of the white slave paradigm: a young woman is lured into the sex trade by a vice ring operative through courtship and a bogus marriage; she is taken out of state and held in a brothel; eventually "traded" to another member of the gang, she is held far from her family in a community unfamiliar to her and forced to prostitute herself. By embedding the white slave narrative in what purports to be a documentary account of urban prostitution, the film legitimates exaggerated tales of sexual entrapment. Candid film footage is employed in much the same way that other investigatory elements were incorporated into more conventional tales of vice trafficking. Yet, at the same time, the film's narrative sequences present a more nuanced conception of prostitution consistent with its overall documentary impulse, an outlook that sets it apart from one-dimensional portraits of the "social evil" that appear in films like *Traffic in Souls*. Against its all-too-familiar plot line, *Inside of the White Slave Traffic* also sketches some of the social and economic circumstances that contributed to prostitution in American cities. As a result, the film's characterization of urban vice is significantly more wide-ranging than the bare abduction scenarios presented in its predecessor and common to most other renderings of the white slave myth. *The Inside of the White Slave Traffic* ultimately traces a more complicated portrait of prostitution than does *Traffic in Souls*, while still engaging the white slave scenario to voice apprehensions about the uncharted terrain of modern women's work and leisure habits.

In order to paint the permissive climate that allowed prostitution to flourish in American cities, *The Inside of the White Slave Traffic* opens with a portrait of George Fischer, a pimp at the helm of a nationwide slave ring. George runs the most public of vice operations, conducting all manner of transactions in full view: he receives telephone calls and sets up appointments at the corner store; he and a prostitute meet a client on the sidewalk outside the shop; and another prostitute delivers George's "take" of the money to a local restaurant hangout. The very bed he sleeps in, we learn, is the one used by his prostitutes for their trade. These early scenes establish how ubiquitous George's operation is; they imply that he retains the tacit complicity of shopkeepers, landlords, and even community residents, who must surely witness such transactions every day. The visibility of his organization in these opening segments counters the notion that vice rings operated in clandestine corners of the urban underworld. George's relative immobility in the opening scenes—he sits and waits while others do his bidding—is offset by the physical mobility of the two prostitutes in these scenes. The women appear and disappear at his direction, servicing clients offscreen, then delivering the money to him. Their repeated acts of entering and exiting the frame rehearse the exchange of their bodies in the sexual traffic and introduce the film's recurrent emphasis on "streetwalking." Just as the film turns prostitution on its head by exposing the inner workings of vice gangs, prostitution itself is cast as an enterprise that turns private aspects of sexuality outward, exposing them to public view and weaving them into a neighborhood's daily commercial trade. The film is typical of many reform tracts that focused attention on businesses and property owners who profited indirectly from prostitution, seeking to implicate them in the corruption of innocent women. The Minneapolis Vice Commission, for example, reported that landlords who rented rooms to pimps, as well as saloon owners who turned a blind eye to solicitation in their establishments, were "making this traffic possible" and were "helping to call into existence that vast army of professional seducers . . . who war against women's virtue, whose one business in life it is to destroy that virtue."[221]

Once this general setting has been introduced in *The Inside of the White Slave Traffic*, a more familiar white slavery narrative begins. While the tricks and ruses employed by the traffickers are quite standard for the genre, it is understood that their gang operates within the permissive urban environment delineated in the opening scenes, a feature that clearly sets the film apart from *Traffic in Souls*. Annie, a garment worker bored with her tedious job, is introduced as "The Innocent in Danger," whom George easily "recruits" for the slave trade in a swift series of brief scenes that recall the warnings of progressive activists. A shot of Annie at work in the textile factory underscores the drudgery of her job. A row of young women all working at identical sewing tables that recede seemingly endlessly into background space are shown in a diagonal composition. This demoralizing work environment seems to leave Annie particularly vulnerable to George's charms. Lurking behind a pillar, he spies Annie leaving a shop after work and makes his choice. She accepts his company, proffered as a date, but when George takes her to an outdoor café, she suddenly feels drowsy—a sure sign to knowing audience members that the man has drugged her drink. He offers to take her home, but she awakes the next morning to find herself in his apartment. Glancing back at the bed in horror, she realizes what has transpired the night before, her expression making plain what the cut has censored. When she returns home to face her parents, Annie's irate father banishes her from their home. A title warns, "Parents, beware the 'Out of My House' policy," since George has clearly counted on this outcome as the final element of his plan.

Thus before Annie is ever in the hands of George's slave traffickers, the film establishes a clear background against which her entrapment takes place: permissive and accommodating merchants in inner-city neighborhoods allow prostitution rings to operate in full view; monotonous, dead-end jobs lead young women in search of possibly dangerous leisure-time diversions; and unsupportive families abandon wayward daughters to the streets. "If [Annie's] father had not ordered her out of the house after her first step in the wrong direction, she never would have become a member of the great army of Magdalens," *Motion Picture News* concluded.[222] Indeed, white slave tracts of the period often suggest, in rather veiled terms, that families' lack of tolerance for their daughters' sexual activities may ironically force the young women into prostitution. "One of the reasons why so many girls stay in bondage," Janney reported in *The White Slave Traffic in America*, "is that they are condemned by the severe tribunal of parental indignation and social decree to banishment."[223] In *Fighting the Traffic in Young Girls* Ernest Bell argued that "the closed door of the father's home is the reason why many [young women] go deeper down in sin."[224]

With nowhere else to turn, Annie marries George, although a title warns viewers that "the marriage ceremony is seldom genuine," marking it as another ruse in the trafficking game, a further manipulation of courtship patterns earlier demonstrated in *Traffic in Souls*. Soon George advises Annie that without funds to support them both, he must temporarily "place her with friends" in a house that also clearly operates as a brothel. Once there, Annie receives word that George has left town and that she should no longer depend upon him. Viewers familiar with other "case histories" would not have been surprised. An offer of assistance from one Sam Brand, who volunteers to take Annie to New Orleans where she can have her marriage annulled, proves to be a "turn-around scheme." Brand pays George $350 for the young woman, then takes her to New Orleans where, rather than arranging the annulment she desires, he forces her to continue to prostitute herself.

Even more so than *Traffic in Souls*, *The Inside of the White Slave Traffic* emphasizes the vulnerability of its heroine. By charting her gradual introduction to prostitution through courtship, phony marriage, and promised annulment, it chronicles the stages of her deception much more forcefully than would a brutal kidnapping. At the same time, these events also hint more broadly at a critique of women's role in society. Bored with deadening, low-paying factory work, young working-class women were dependent upon courtship and marriage for excitement and social advancement. Annie's odyssey implies that the dependency inherent in such arrangements could render women vulnerable to abuse. And the film clearly demonstrates that without a family network to fall back upon, young women could quickly find themselves out on the streets, forced to rely on the marketability of their bodies. Whereas *Traffic in Souls* is quick to stage a rescue of its innocent victims, before they are actually forced into prostitution, *The Inside of the White Slave Traffic* tracks the slow "downfall" of its heroine, emphasizing less her physical incarceration—the key issue in *Traffic in Souls*—than her moral imprisonment: she cannot leave the profession because of restrictive expectations governing female sexuality. The film traces her descent into several different brothels across the country, where she is taken further and further from her family and the life she once knew.

Thinking that she can outsmart Brand, Annie eventually flees New Orleans for Denver, then Houston, but is barred from work and lodgings in both places. "The system that entrapped her, blacklists her," *Variety* explained.[225] Annie's attempted escape ultimately only highlights the network of control and surveillance exercised by the traffickers. Members of the ring send telegrams to one another warning of her "escape" and attempt to chart her journey. The code purportedly used in such telegrams is translated for viewers: "Gillette Blade" means girl, "Schmeiser" means trafficker, "Apples" means danger, and so on. In addition to using the railroad system to transport women across state borders illegally, the slave ring apparently manipulates technologies like the telegraph, creating a coded language composed of familiar words whose meanings have been altered. As in *Traffic in Souls*, the traffickers are associated with omnipotent surveillance and technological mastery. It is through this network that Brand eventually traces Annie, and although at first afraid, she is glad to see him, for without the network, she can no longer survive. Annie is next seen occupying an elaborate bedroom in fancy dress, where, a title informs us, she "slaves for him again." Plagued by fond memories of her parents and her former home life, Annie realizes that a return to this world is now no longer possible. Although she is not physically locked in a brothel as Little Sister was in *Traffic in Souls*, Annie remains just as captive, prevented by social mores and economic inequities from returning to her past life of respectability. From this virtual prison, Annie can be neither rescued nor returned to her family. Without much fanfare, the story ends bleakly: a title, likely prescribed by the

Board of Censorship, proclaims, "And in the end, she was laid away, an outcast in Potter's Field." A final shot of anonymous, numbered graves ends the film.

Like other white slave narratives, *The Inside of the White Slave Traffic* garners respectability by claiming that its portrait of prostitution is true and verifiable, not sensationalistic or exploitive. It does so in a style that is consistent with other white slave tracts by listing endorsements from noted reformers and do-gooders; but the film also solicits respectability through a novel exploitation of the photographic properties of the cinema touted in publicity material and industry discourse. Using purportedly "documentary" footage, as well as staged scenes filmed on location in various cities around the country, *The Inside of the White Slave Traffic* also attempts to present the broad social context of urban vice: an increasingly public leisure culture taking place in restaurants and cafés and on city sidewalks; changing patterns of work and recreation for young women, which place them in potentially dangerous situations; and families unwilling to confront the lives of their modern daughters. Hence *The Inside of the White Slave Traffic* expands conventional portraits of white slavery and prostitution by showing the tangled web of economic and social circumstances that permit vice rings to thrive in American cities, as well as the equally diverse circumstances that draw women into prostitution and effectively hold them captive there. What differentiates the abduction plot in *The Inside of the White Slave Traffic* from those presented in *Traffic in Souls*, then, is that emphasis shifts away from simple stories of kidnapping that center on the moral culpability of individuals like vice ring operatives, two-faced reformers, and wanton shop girls; instead, *The Inside of the White Slave Traffic* furnishes a nuanced portrait of prostitution grounded in an awareness of the cultural and economic factors that support a sexual traffic in women. Whereas Staiger argues that *The Inside of the White Slave Traffic*'s "social-structure explanation" for white slavery fails to present a plot in which individual agency plays a significant role in reforming the slave trade, I would argue that the film integrates the more traditional narrative imperative of Annie's agency within its treatment of the broad social landscape of prostitution.[226] If in *Traffic in Souls* the specter of white slavery served to curtail women's mobility through fears of urban sexual danger (real or imagined), in *The Inside of the White Slave Traffic* white slavery becomes a metaphor for larger social and economic forces that themselves restrict women's freedoms.

Like *The Inside of the White Slave Traffic*, *Little Lost Sister* works to broaden the slave trafficking scenario by delineating some of the social and economic factors that drew women into prostitution. If *Inside* links the vice trade to a range of *urban* problems, *Little Lost Sister* portrays aspects of small-town life that might have enticed women away from their rural homes and into city centers. In effect the film expands the theme of the "Country Girl" whose subplot warranted a few cursory scenes in *Traffic in Souls*. In the earlier film we are given no indication of the circumstances that brought the "Country Girl" to New York; and her capture is enacted swiftly in a single, deft ruse. In *Little Lost Sister*, however, the heroine's entrapment is presented as an elaborate seduction away from her rather stifling small-town existence. During the prewar period, the specter of rural women traveling alone to American cities became a focal point for anxieties about the evolving dynamic between urban and rural cultures.[227] Railway stations, such as the one featured in *Traffic in Souls*, were frequently cast as sites that rendered rural émigrés especially vulnerable. These points of entry proved "profitable hunting ground for the White Slavers," according to much of the literature, perhaps because they symbolized the initial encounter of country residents with metropolitan culture.[228] Women were imperiled the moment they set foot in the nation's cities, these warnings seemed to suggest. Others had more to fear from the women's own attraction to urban pleasures: "[I]nto the teeming life of [the city] they go to meet temptations for which they are unfortified." Traffickers had little trouble deceiving young women who were "mystified by the glare and light of the large cities after night," warned Clifford Roe; such victims were easily lead astray. For Jane Addams, rural migrants faced particular risk, since "from the point of view of the traffickers in white slaves, it is much cheaper and safer to procure country girls . . . because they are much more easily secreted than girls from the city." Parents were advised, "[K]eep her with you. She is far safer in the country than in the big city."[229]

The specter of America's daughters swallowed up by an omnivorous urban maw was particularly frightening to the progressive generation already alarmed by conditions in the nation's cities. In lurid tales of the slave trade aimed at rural émigrés sexuality became the locus for broad-ranging trepidation about young women's changing working and living habits. Unlike many comparable tales which detail the misfortunes that befall young women new to urban centers, *Little Lost Sister* attempts to show some of the reasons why its heroine, Elsie Welcome, a Millville factory worker, is lured to fictitious Lake City by a slave trafficker, then abandoned there to a life of prostitution. Frustrated by conditions in Millville, Elsie is captivated by the promise of cosmopolitan glamour embodied in the charming procurer, Martin Druce. The story does not offer the sentimentalized, schematic view of small-town life that characterized many tales of country daughters who venture to the city during this period. Rather, it furnishes a much more pessimistic view of industrialized America where country and city are both irrevocably altered, and where young women's lives hang in the balance.

In an opening segment reminiscent of Annie's introduction in *The Inside of the White Slave Traffic*, Elsie's factory job is shown to be monotonous and unrewarding. Three successive shots depict row upon row of female textile workers performing identical tasks at sewing tables arranged in receding diagonal compositions. Shot on location in one of Los Angeles's largest factories, it is a dehumanizing view of industrial life very like that shown in the earlier film.[230] When Elsie demands higher wages from her supervisor, she is rebuffed in an act that signals the lack of opportunities available to female workers in towns like Millville. "Then I can never earn more here?" she cries in frustration and astonishment. Elsie's bleak prospects at the textile mill are wed to a larger degradation of her moral values in other early scenes demonstrating her near-desperate search for diversion after working hours. Outside her job, the town offers Elsie little relief from her daily drudgery. Her only possibility of escape lies with procurer Martin Druce, whose bright new automobile encapsulates the power to transport her to another life. Druce's only competition seems to come from Harvey, a mild-mannered grocery boy, whose marriage proposal Elsie rejects, explaining, "I cannot marry you; I am sick of this small town." Early scenes also make it plain that Elsie's difficult family situation contributes to her sense of restlessness. Her father, an embittered alcoholic, had been an inventor who sold a lamp device to the Lake City Electric Company, which underpaid him, then subsequently made a fortune with the product. Now the elder Welcome pursues nothing but revenge against the company while neglecting his family. Again the film sends a pointed reminder that marriage represents Elsie's one avenue of escape.

Industrial labor is held accountable for much of her situation. In the film's very first scene reformer Mary Randall confronts Millville's factory owner about "the moral transformation [he has] wrought among the girls in this valley by substituting the factory for the farm." Responding angrily, the man claims, "I am not responsible for the morals of my women workers," a position the film ultimately seeks to refute. Elsie's eventual journey into the metropolitan underworld is thus prefaced by a vignette that links changing social mores to the industrial workplace. Acting as the film's conscience, the Mary Randall character voices many of the sentiments of contemporary reformers like Jane Addams, who worried openly about the female labor force. Even *Moving Picture World* made the connection, concluding that the film provided "a powerful object lesson . . . on the dangers that menace poorly-paid girls, whose home life is bereft of all that makes life worth living."[231]

A subplot involving the exploitation of Elsie's father's invention and his subsequent decline is part of a larger pattern of urban-rural exploitation portrayed in the film—a pattern that reaches its zenith in the slave ring that procures country girls for the metropolitan prostitution market. This link is embodied in the character John Boland, head of the Lake City Electric Company, but also the kingpin of a clandestine trafficking ring. Boland's son even recruits women for the vice trade on the same trips to Millville that he makes to collect (presumably overpriced) rents from town residents. Even the notion of a mill town is itself exploitive: the community's daughters provide inexpensive labor in order to produce textiles for an expanding urban consumer market. As a result, the film seems to claim, traditional farm life is destroyed. Like *Traffic in Souls*, the film traces connections between prostitution and "big business" also documented by many civic commissions at the time. Evidence of this kind fed the general suspicion of corporate capitalism in progressive America. In fact, in *Little Lost Sister*, prostitution becomes an apt metaphor for the potentially devastating effects of industrial society in the contemporary imagination.

In detailing aspects of Elsie's work and family conditions, the film does not sentimentalize its portrait of modern small-town culture. *Little Lost Sister* acknowledges the arduous conditions under which many female garment workers labored and the limited scope of opportunities open to them. It also recognizes, even more insistently than *The Inside of the White Slave Traffic*, that problems at home may drive women from their families. Thus even though Elsie's rather impetuous decision to leave for Lake City with Druce is contrasted with the modest decorum of her homebound sister, Patience, the restrictiveness of Elsie's provincial existence is made clear. In other words, the film presents a complex portrait of American society, one in which rural and urban communities are not simply polar opposites, but where changes wrought by modern industrialization affect both environments equally. Factory labor disrupted entire patterns of work and leisure activity in a manner particularly detrimental to single women. As a result, smaller towns could no longer be painted as safe havens, unaffected by twentieth-century changes, to which characters could retreat; rather, their own quiet malevolence is forcefully drawn. Still, crusader Mary Randall's comments in the opening scene suggest a longing for more traditional arrangements and, implicitly, more conventional forms of female decorum.

As expected, Elsie Welcome is eventually lured to Lake City by Martin Druce. Once there, he takes her to what she believes is his aunt's house, where a mock marriage ceremony is performed. In truth, of course, Druce has taken her to a brothel disguised as a residential home, "the house of drawn curtains"—"forbidding without and worse within," according to Selig publicity.[232] Druce's "aunt's" gaudy, ornate costume, her cascade of jewelry, and the number of young woman who inhabit the house (and wink knowingly at one another during the "wedding") alert viewers to Druce's real purpose, even though Elsie seems ignorant of the ruse. Commanding Elsie to "[d]oll yourself up and cut out the Sunday School stuff," the "aunt" thrusts a scanty dress toward the unsuspecting woman. Once again the innocent in search of romance and a little excitement finds herself in a situation for which she is totally unprepared.

Although women are presented as the primary victims of vice here, as they are in most tales of white slavery, female characters like Mary Randall are also presented as those with the power to stop the traffic. Intercut with Elsie's initiation into bordello life is a meeting of Mary's Church Vice Committee. After hearing a report on inner-city conditions, Mary declares, "The time for theory alone is over. I am going into action against the wolves of the tenderloin." Gathering evidence against property owners in the red-light district,

Mary holds them responsible for urban vice, just as she had confronted Mill-ville's factory owner at the beginning of the film about the low wages paid to women in his employ. The sentiments that she voices and the targets of her crusade echo the views of progressives who documented prostitution in the prewar era. The Philadelphia Vice Commission states plainly, "[W]e find that we are dealing with a problem more of men than of women. Commercialized vice is a business conducted largely by men, and the profits go mainly to men."[233] With the help of a concerned journalist, Mary eventually organizes a police raid on the notorious vice joint, "Café Sinister," where she frees Elsie, who is then reunited with her family.

Of all three films, *Little Lost Sister* is perhaps the most bold in the way that it yokes modern social conditions in industrial towns and inner-city neighbor-hoods to prostitution. The film portrays a heroine who is cast adrift in a land-scape scarred by industrial, economic, and social upheaval. Its evocation of "lost" sisters and daughters resonates with the deep sense of loss characteristic of many discussions of the slave trade, among them Theodore A. Bingham's 1911 treatise, *The Girl That Disappears*. The former New York police commis-sioner's study of vice trafficking begins with an anecdote that recurs in much of the white slave literature, a chilling narrative that sets into clear relief funda-mental apprehensions that guided the myth. Bingham recounts the story of a young woman killed by a trolley car during rush hour who subsequently could not be identified. When an ad seeking clues to her identity was placed in news-papers, hundreds of relatives flocked to the morgue in the hopes of finding their own "lost" daughters.[234] Although no mention of white slavery is made in the tale—nor is any foul play suggested—Bingham evokes the hazards that await young women once they venture beyond the family homestead: the pros-pect that they might become faceless, anonymous workers living in American cities, having lost all contact with their families and communities; the fear that they might vanish into an alien culture, never to be heard from again; and worst of all, the spectacle of a dead woman's limp body lying in the street, unclaimed and unidentified, then displayed at the morgue for all to see, an image rife with sexual undertones. Ultimately, Bingham's evocation of the loss of the nation's young women speaks to the disappearance of older forms of daughterly conduct now often replaced by newer (less familiar, less accept-able) ways of life.

Tales about white slave trafficking in American cities were above all about women's evolving place in urban, industrial society, a position that remained to be negotiated well into the teens. In *Traffic in Souls*, *The Inside of the White Slave Traffic*, and *Little Lost Sister*, compelling paradigms of urban peril emerge in accounts of the slave trade. As Judith Walkowitz has shown of Victorian London, narratives of sexual danger often weave a reconfiguration of city streets at times of particular cultural crisis, by charting a place for unfamiliar constituencies, like immigrants and working women, newly visible in the metropolitan landscape.[235] Because stories of white slave trafficking featured modern women who were young, single wage-earners in search of leisure-time diversions outside the home, they reverberated with grave apprehensions about changing feminine norms in prewar culture. The "little sisters" placed in danger time and again were America's daughters embarking on a course of life for which the nation remained unprepared.

Female Spectators at the White Slave Films

Ironically, although the white slave films harbored deep anxieties about women's growing participation in urban leisure culture, they succeeded in attracting scores of female patrons who gathered in movie theaters thought to be the very sites where they could find themselves prey to slave traffickers and procurers. If the white slavery scare struggled to define a place for women at screening spaces, as paying customers and leisure consumers, vice films also struggled to define a place for the female spectating subject in cinema's imaginary visual field. Commentators not only grappled with women's participation in the visual and sexual dynamics of exhibition sites; they also sought to map out a locus for women within the fictive narrative space opened up on the screen. The voyeuristic latitude granted spectators more than ever in the cinema of narrative integration was particularly pronounced for women, viewers not normally accustomed to looking freely and openly in polite society. Negotiating a place for female viewers within cinema's imaginary topography was made all the more troubling by the vice pictures: their sexually frank subject matter was assumed to repulse women, yet observers could not ignore women's evident attraction to the material. The way that cinema enabled a fictive remapping of a viewer's relation to social space—although potentially liberating for women—was for the same reason threatening to many commentators. Now an industry actively courting female *patronage* also had to consider the implications of female *spectatorship*. Indeed, the white slave film controversy shows an industry grappling with the distinction between the characterization of cinema's social audience and the various spectatorial positions that it offered.[236]

Some commentators, mostly those promoting white slave pictures, actually welcomed women in the audience at screenings. They hoped that the appearance of female patrons might lessen the taint of tawdriness that adhered to the material; that women might lend the films an air of credibility, reframing their salacious narratives as "educational" vehicles; and that the female gaze might bestow upon the films an instructional purpose and merit. Producer Samuel London opened *The Inside of the White Slave Traffic* concurrently at the relatively upscale Park Theatre on Columbus Circle in New York City and in the garment mill town of Troy, New York, claiming, "I was eager to get the picture in towns like Troy, because I wanted to get the picture before factory girls, the most frequent sufferers from the evil which we are fighting."[237] A full-page ad in *Motion Picture News* offering states' rights to *The Little Girl Next Door* billed the picture as offering "what every girl should know," simultaneously underscoring the film's educational tone and its appeal to female viewers.[238] Selig trade ads claimed that "every mother should insist that her daughters see *Little Lost Sister*."[239] Under the heading "Girls Should See It," the studio's publicity stressed that the picture had "a thrilling love romance, beautiful photography, an all-star cast, and an impressive moral lesson"—clearly all attributes designed with impressionable young women in mind.[240] A reviewer for the *Minneapolis Journal* went even further, advocating that *Traffic in Souls* not be shown to the moviegoing public but be reserved solely for immigrant women arriving at Ellis Island and for rural émigrés entering metropolitan railway stations: "[I]f its purpose were to warn, it should be exhibited to those in need of warning."[241] Chicago reformers deciding whether *The Inside of the White Slave Traffic* ought to be exhibited in that city evidently feared more from male than from female viewers: "The pictures would have a good effect on girls—to show them what they have to guard against. Especially would the effect upon factory girls be a good one, but I think it would have a different result when shown to boys," said one. Another concurred, observing that the film "might give warning of the white slave pitfalls if it could be exhibited only to girls over sixteen and their mothers. Its lesson for men—especially young men and boys—is bad, showing them how to become white slavers."[242]

Still, skeptical about the possible instructional value that dramatizations of the slave trade might hold for women, *Moving Picture World* remarked with obvious frustration, "We have repeatedly pointed out that such [motion picture] plays do not make for good and should have no place on the moving picture screen. Proper teaching at home will furnish any young girl with the best protection against the snares of the vicious."[243] "Is there any sensible person in all this country who will honestly say, after a little reflection, that even one single individual was saved from white slavery ... by means of these pictures?" the paper asked.[244] Expressing his hope that "the law forbidding obscene and indecent exhibitions will come to the rescue of the public and of our women and children especially," *Moving Picture World*'s Bush also reinforced the notion that sexually explicit material was particularly inappropriate for female viewers.[245] Young women were indeed precisely those who should be *kept* from viewing films on predatory sexual slavery, many commentators testified. Criticizing the public exhibition of films on white slavery in general, a prominent New York reformer reserved especial horror for the prospect of young *women* watching such lurid fare. A class of female moviegoers "with very little active mentality" who "are very weak and unmoral, rather than immoral" were attracted to the vice pictures, she reported, and particularly vulnerable to "what the psychologists call suggestion." Of these viewers she wrote, "[T]o [their] untrained, unbalanced and extremely susceptible mentality, the only appeal made by such pictures is one of allurement."[246] Comparing the impressionability of such women pejoratively to that of small children, the writer constructed a pathology of female viewing. Sociologist Ruth True, more inclined toward a compassionate understanding of young women's attractions to the cinema, argued that "in these girls that longing for the unreal is overlaid by much that is commonplace and sordid." Movies "spread out adventure and melodrama which are soul-satisfying" to these viewers.[247] But another observer warned of the lasting visual impact made by on-screen dramatizations of the slave trade: "[P]ictures, imprinted indelibly upon the minds of . . . girls by scenes portrayed in [photo]plays, have caused them to desire the same exciting experiences."[248] Even *Variety* wondered whether women could be swayed by the lavish brothel interiors pictured in one film, since "girls seeing it . . . might find the picture a temptation instead of a warning."[249] The *physical* vulnerability attributed to women in the white slave plots becomes in these views a kind of *mental* impressionability in which the act of viewing sexually explicit material on the screen posed more harm than sexual abduction itself.

Far from providing enlightenment or instruction, watching white slave fare placed women in greater jeopardy than they faced from actual vice traffickers, *Variety* explained in a review of the "red-lighter" *Cocaine Traffic; Or, the Drug Terror*: "There is more danger in two innocently-minded young people together watching this film, or any other of its kind, than the collar maker of Troy ever had to endure by a fellow from the city 'making a play' for her . . . the [white slave] pictures are sending more souls to hell at twenty-five cents each at the box office than were ever captured by cadets."[250] Here viewing itself became the treacherous act, not mingling with strangers in movie theater foyers, nor even tangling with vice procurers. What troubled this writer most particularly was the voyeuristic freedom white slave films licensed in women. "The enlightenment through the screen of what is, has been and always will be going on behind locked doors," he insisted, "merely means new recruits from curiosity, for *curiosity has ever been the wasting curse of pure womanhood*."[251] Although the comment seems intended to apply to matters sexual, it had the added effect of denying women access to visual pleasure at the cinema as a whole, for the logics of curiosity are precisely those which govern cinematic viewing pleasure. Spectatorship was here turned against women, framed as a position hazardous for them to occupy. Not one of these writers proposed that women be prevented from seeing white slave films because the material was inflammatory or sensational, or because it catered to unjust fears. Rather, they insisted that visual license is, in itself, incompatible with modest femininity. Voicing similar fears, a commentary on the 1916 title *Is Any Girl Safe?* complained that "the spectator is dragged through several obnoxious scenes, such as the interiors of a house of prostitution."[252] The image of viewers "dragged" from one scene to the next suggests at once mobility and coercion, absolving cinemagoers of the responsibility for watching salacious acts. The

crowds these films garnered certainly denote a keen fascination with the subject, yet viewers here are recast as passive, even unwilling, conspirators. Just
as tales of slave ring abductions cloaked fears about sexual activity in young
women, this view of female movie patrons masked their desire to see behind
brothel doors.

A discourse on female pleasure and desire is nonetheless woven throughout
accounts of female viewers at these films, for one hears in discussions of "curiosity" echoes of desire. Couched beneath questions of whether women *ought*
to be exposed to this material was the knowledge that female moviegoers evidently *wanted* to see it, and that they apparently lined up in great numbers to
do so. Issues of voyeurism and visual pleasure that might otherwise remain
tacit in examinations of female spectatorship come to the fore in assessments
of the white slave films, since the features were so brazen in their treatment of
sexual matters. The vice pictures posed the challenge of conceiving of a female
spectator-subject positioned in relation not only to sexually frank material but
also implicitly to pleasure and desire. Exploring the possibility that curiosity
might provide an alternative means of theorizing female spectatorship, one
combining scopophilia with epistemophilia, Laura Mulvey argues that an "aes-
thetics of curiosity" would link "an active look, associated with the feminine,"
with "the drive for decipherment," and "a topography of concealment and
investigation."[253] The opposite of fetishistic scopophilia, which engages the
logics of denial and "is born out of a refusal to see, a refusal to know," curiosity
engages "a compulsive desire to see and to know."[254] If curiosity did lie at the
root of women's attraction to films on the slave trade, as even *Variety* sus-
pected, then perhaps the films' appeal involved precisely their promise to reveal hitherto unseen aspects of American life.

Viewed in this light, concerns about the impressionability of female viewers
at white slave films might also be seen as fears about relinquishing to women
the powerful position of visual mastery enabled by the cinema, a position that
became all the more potent in the intricate spatial topographies created by the
cinema of narrative integration, and which in turn the vice film "exposures"
capitalized upon. In suggesting that women might see at these movies what
they had not seen elsewhere, contemporary writers also implicitly questioned
the imaginary mobility granted to women at the cinema. They decried, in other
words, the way that white slave films might extend to women, optically and
metaphorically, new freedoms of movement and association, freedoms that
figured prominently in anxieties about the vice traffic. Physical mobility could
at least be circumscribed through admonitions against the slave trade in ways
that visual curiosity could not be curtailed—especially at the cinema.

Surely part of the appeal these films held for women lay in their ability
to "transport" viewers through various regions of urban life. The illicit, but
comprehensive, surveillance of the modern cityscape promised in titles like
The Inside of the White Slave Traffic and *The Exposure of the White Slave*

Traffic might have been particularly fascinating to women, those for whom certain corners of the metropolis remained most unavailable, or unsafe. Indeed, ads promoted the films' visual breadth, one vowing to reveal the "inner workings of the organized vice interests," another promising "VICE as it actually existed in the dens of iniquity in our cities and towns."[255] Female filmgoers repeatedly warned about menacing vice rings were—at the movies—free to tour the urban underworld, to peer inside brothels, to spy upon procurers entrapping unsuspecting women, to gaze upon "the inside of the white slave traffic," and finally to traverse the streets in safety. It might also be reasonable to suspect that *middle-class* women, those most coveted by film exhibitors in the early teens, could be especially curious about commanding views of districts like New York's Tenderloin and Chicago's Armour Avenue where they might have little reason to venture otherwise. Despite plots that emphasized women's victimization, then, white slave films promised a sense of visual latitude and freedom of access to nether regions of the urban underworld.

Even while warning women that modern life was especially treacherous, white slave films offered female spectators a form of command over the urban terrain available only at the cinema. Particularly interesting in this visual economy are scenes contained in several of the films that allow viewers to observe as operatives recruiting for the slave trade spy upon unknowing potential victims: a slave ring cadet watches Little Sister while she works behind the counter at Smyrner's Candy Store in *Traffic in Souls*; lurking behind a pillar, procurer George Fischer first spots the heroine Annie leaving a shop in *The Inside of the White Slave Traffic*; and Elsie Welcome is eyed by trafficker Martin Druce, outside the factory where she works, before he approaches her in *Little Lost Sister*. These scenes, all of which take place at public sites where young women were said to be most vulnerable, might seem to reinforce the notion that women attending venues like the cinema were often objects of unwanted visual attention. However, watching these episodes on the screen, female viewers were given a sense of omnipotence—a knowledge of events that superseded that of both victim *and* procurer. Because these sequences are shot without point-of-view editing, in several cases procurer and intended target stand in the same frame, both watched over by film viewers. Even though women in the on-screen dramas are preyed upon by slave rings employing various means of covert surveillance, female spectators at the cinema reversed the dynamics of this controlling gaze.

The traffickers' command over modern technology furthers their associations with visual surveillance in both *Traffic in Souls* and *The Inside of the White Slave Traffic*. A magic writing pad and dictagraph imagined in the first film as links between the vice gang and its leader, posing as head of the "International Purity and Reform League," are added indications of the slave ring's omnipotence, as is a system of coded telegraphic messages used by the white slave syndicate in *The Inside of the White Slave Traffic*. Yet viewers are again given access to these covert machinations ahead of diegetic characters: the gang's cryptic codes are transcribed for viewers in intertitles; and the dictagraphic apparatus used by ringleaders in *Traffic in Souls* is unveiled for the audience before the heroine herself discovers it. Traffickers' associations with visual surveillance and technology are thus potentially recouped by women in the act of film viewing—glances unseen by film heroines are visible to theater viewers, and procurers' coded communiqués are decoded for spectators.

This sense of optical omnipotence is heightened even further by the interwoven crosscutting strategies employed in *Traffic in Souls* linking the three scenarios of entrapment, the three courtships, and the various levels of the clandestine trafficking ring. Tom Gunning likens the film's editing patterns to technological means of surveillance practiced by both the film's vice ring and the police squad. Like these devices, crosscutting traces patterns of power and corruption in city life no longer visible to the unaided observer. "The position from which the truth of the city can be seen and organized is no longer that of human vision," according to Gunning. "It is a purely technological position which a human can occupy only by becoming subject to an all-seeing, all-hearing technology."[256] Recall as well Mary Barton's role in watching her sister's entrapment, then enlisting the dictagraph to uncover Trubus's hidden link to the slave trade. Indeed, the suspenseful parallel editing sequence of the film's climax, which cuts back and forth between scenes in the brothel and scenes of the police raid, is metaphorically associated with Mary's gaze, so identified is she with concern for her sister and the moral surveillance of slave operatives. The sense of visual mastery over the city engaged by films like *Traffic in Souls* is for Gunning analogous to that enjoyed by the nineteenth-century *flâneur* strolling through cityscapes observing but unobserved. Yet this was a role surely open only to men. As Susan Buck-Morss insists, the *flâneur*'s female counterpart was not the "*flâneuse*" but the whore or streetwalker—a word that aptly conveys the different terms under which men and women traverse urban thoroughfares.[257] Film viewing, on the other hand, offered at least the possibility of comparable mastery to female citizens as well. Thus, although technology is associated with a resurgence of patriarchal authority in *Traffic in Souls*, and women are presented as perpetually endangered in the urban sphere, the very structure of the film itself promised female patrons commanding views of city streets and the urban underworld.

The Inside of the White Slave Traffic exploits this imaginary visual mastery even further, and perhaps best exemplifies the specular horizons that white slave films opened for women in the preclassical era. The film relies heavily on its documentary credibility, derived from candid footage shot in the red-light quadrants of notable American cities. By bringing acts tacitly condoned in certain quarters of American cities into more general view, *The Inside of the White Slave Traffic* reconfigured cityscapes in a manner that may have been particularly appealing to female spectators, many of whom, for reasons of both "respectability" and safety, could not traverse these regions *except* in the cinema's imaginary visual field. If, in the words of Griselda Pollock, "modernity was experienced spatially in terms of access to the specular city," then films like *The Inside of the White Slave Traffic* provided women with the means for a unique—even liberating—perspective on metropolitan life.[258]

Ultimately, then, the experience women might have enjoyed at the white slave films—the pleasures they might have derived from what for all intents and purposes was quite reactionary material—exemplifies characteristics of female spectatorship that both Miriam Hansen and Giuliana Bruno have identified in the transitional period. For Hansen it was at this moment that film viewing "opened up a space—a social space as well as a perceptual, experiential horizon—in women's lives."[259] Bruno stresses in particular the specular mobility women were granted at the movies, for, she argues, "the female subject's encounter with the cinema constructs a new geography, gives license to venturing. . . . Female spectatorship triggers, and participates in, women's conquest of the sphere of spatial mobility as pleasure."[260] The imaginary locomotion experienced by women at the movies held particular resonance in the white slave films, because the glimpses they provided of urban life were so risqué and so at odds with conventions of the womanly gaze, and because their visual style granted women spectacular visual license, just as the films' alarmist story lines sought to curtail the latitude women were beginning to enjoy in urban culture. Watching white slave narratives unfold on the screen, women were offered the possibility of circumventing prohibitions against both their physical mobility and their visual license. They might watch unseen as procurers spied on intended victims, crack codes used by the nefarious slave rings, and, most significant, traverse hidden regions of the nation's sexual geography in cinema's imaginary optical field.

The competing discourses that surround white slave films—about commercial recreation, female patrons, and movie morals—reveal the degree to which female filmgoing remained entangled with sexual danger in the teens, as a result of young women's participation in cinema's dating culture and, more obliquely, the specular mobility they were granted there. Woman's place in both the space of entertainment and in the illusory narrative space on-screen was by no means solidified. Thus the emphasis that Hansen and Bruno have placed upon the latitude accorded to women in preclassical cinema needs to be tempered with the recognition that, precisely for this reason, women's moviegoing remained at issue well into the 1910s. The discourse generated about women's attendance at white slave films therefore marks a significant juncture in the transitional era, when competing claims sought to define cinema's audience. Because the films engendered controversy at a time when female patronage became an explicit topic for the industry, the discussion surrounding their exhibition provides a singular instance when female spectatorship was theoretized and problematized within the industry itself. A debate about female viewers at this stage thus foregrounded notions about female filmgoing that grounded the consolidation of classical narrative and specular codes toward the latter half of the decade, as well as the potentially liberating aspects of film spectatorship open to women in this particular moment.

Three

Ready-Made Customers:
Female Movie Fans and the
Serial Craze

"Is YOUR patronage suffering from 'Serialitis'?" Kalem asked exhibitors in early 1917, three years into a craze for motion picture serials so intense that it mimicked an ailment, apparently seizing fans without warning and producing violent symptoms of withdrawal if left unattended.[1] Like the "filmitis" afflicting so many "movie-struck girls," "serialitis" named a type of compulsive film viewing at once appealing, for its capacity to hook repeat customers, and appalling, for its indulgence in abject cinephilia.

If salacious white slave films became the magnet for lingering concerns about the conduct of women in motion picture audiences and their participation in cinema's voyeuristic illusion, serials like *The Perils of Pauline* and *The Exploits of Elaine* marked the industry's first sustained, deliberate attempt to cultivate (and cater to) female patronage on a national scale. Serials celebrated cinema's potential to nurture a female fan base, even as seemingly intractable fears about the country's new commercial recreation culture dominated discussions about vice films. If anything, serials self-consciously foregrounded the commodification of the motion picture experience, packaged to produce maximum calculable effect, and the potentially endless commercial reproduction of products in the new entertainment economy. Yet, as the diagnosis "serialitis" acknowledges, serials offered female audiences ongoing narratives that contravened classical plot structures and promoted unique modes of ongoing, intertextual, even desperate, enjoyment that challenged typical viewing habits.

Serials crested in popularity during a period of marked transition in the film industry, prior to the definitive reign of feature-length subjects and before the dominance of bourgeois audiences and middlebrow taste challenged the sensationalism of serial content. In their drive toward extended film lengths, their exploitation of sophisticated promotional strategies, and their use of movie star culture to fuel interest in screen products, serials brought together nascent elements of classical filmmaking. Yet, just as serial pictures embodied many new aspects of movie culture, they also represented a marked departure from increasingly normative trends: issued in two-reel installments usually over a period of months, serials were neither feature films nor traditional shorts; their multifaceted tie-in publicity encouraged intertextual viewing practices that were distinctly at odds with models of spectatorship becoming standardized in classical narrative; and the basis upon which women were drawn to these "blood-boiling" adventure tales challenged the decorous femininity celebrated in other promotions to would-be female filmgoers.

Promoting Pauline

A reflexive prologue to Pathé's 1917 serial *The Mystery of the Double Cross* acknowledges the pivotal role that female audiences played in sustaining interest among the various intertextual discourses surrounding serials. Actress Mollie King is shown "at home" in the opening scene receiving a letter from the studio inviting her to star in the drama. Excited about playing the part of heroine Phillipa Brewster, King sits down to read the novel from which the film is to be drawn. King's shoulders begin to quiver as reaction shots register her growing interest in the tale. "I'd love to play that!" she exclaims in an intertitle. As King flips through the book, inserts show us pages containing photos of the characters and the famed "double cross," as if her imagination has brought them to life on film. King herself soon appears on the pages of the book in a split-screen matte shot. Still engrossed in the book, King rises from her chair and walks toward the camera, filling up both the book page and the right-hand portion of the frame. The image then dissolves from a shot of King, head buried in book, to King, now glamorously dressed as Phillipa. After a cut the matte shot is replaced by a full-screen image of Phillipa, no longer confined to the pages of the book, who then looks directly into the camera inviting viewers to "come with me through my adventure and try to solve the Mystery of the Double Cross."[2]

By playing upon an awareness of how King's private life might inflect her portrayal of the heroine, the prologue emphasizes an interplay between screen character and celebrity persona that was central to the evolving star system, at the same time as it acknowledges an intertextual mode of film viewing essential to early motion picture fan culture. Interestingly, King herself is depicted as an avid consumer of serialized stories, shown absorbed in a plot she will subsequently enact for viewers. King's roles as glamorous Hollywood actress, as adventurous screen heroine, and as serial aficionado are collapsed together in a gesture that recasts the fan's typically passive consumption as active engagement. Encouraged to connect together various versions of the story available in print tie-ins and on screen, asked to sustain their engagement over multiple installments, and invited to enhance their enjoyment by cultivating an interest in the star's private life, fans become the central catalyst in any serial narrative. Finally, by continually pointing outside itself—to the star's life, to other versions of the tale available in print, and to the audience watching—*The Mystery of the Double Cross*'s prologue foregrounds just how dramatically serials fostered a female audience by stepping outside classical norms.

However new to the screen, multifaceted, continuing narratives were not new to female readers, since working-class women had formed a significant portion of the audience for dime novels and story papers at the turn of the century, and serialized stories in monthly magazines already catered to a largely female readership.[3] Newspapers' Sunday supplements, with their beauty contests, fashion items, and ongoing adventures of young heroines, were cherished staples of working women's culture, according to Clara Laughlin's 1913 study, *The Work-a-Day Girl*.[4] In fact, it was likely a desire to tap into this readership that prompted the Edison Kinetoscope Company to propose the early film serial *What Happened to Mary?* in 1912 as a joint venture with *The Ladies' World*, a working women's monthly where the story was appearing.[5] Beginning with the story's second chapter in August of that year, Edison produced one-reel versions of each installment, released monthly to coincide with the magazine's publication. After Edison's *Mary* serial ended in the summer of 1913, William Selig, head of the Chicago-based Selig-Polyscope Company, approached the *Chicago Tribune* with an idea to combine biweekly film releases of *The Adventures of Kathlyn* with written installments published in the newspaper. The *Tribune*, enmeshed in a heated circulation battle, agreed, printing portions of Kathlyn's "adventures" in the "Special Features" section of its Sunday edition, beginning in the first week of January 1914, when *The Adventures of Kathlyn* was pictured on the supplement's color cover. The coordinated release of newspaper and motion picture installments of *The Adventures of Kathlyn* was an unqualified success—"the best innovation of its kind ever advanced to increase the interest, enlarge the sales and stimulate universal curiosity and cash reciprocation," according to the *New York Dramatic Mirror*.[6]

Following the *Chicago Tribune*'s victory with *The Adventures of Kathlyn*, newspapers around the country began to publish coordinated installments of motion picture serials, prompting Mutual head Philip Mindil to declare that "the movies have come into their own in the newspapers."[7] The Hearst syndicate, which owned *Tribune* rival the *Chicago American*, engaged with Pathé for its own serial, *The Perils of Pauline*, beginning in April of 1914. Thanhouser's *Million Dollar Mystery*, Edison's *The Active Life of Dolly of the Dailies*, Kalem's *Hazards of Helen* series, and Universal's *Lucille Love, Girl of Mystery* all opened later that year. "There's hardly a big concern now that isn't getting out a melodramatic series in which a young woman is the heroine and the camera has her having hairbreadth escapes by the score," *Variety* announced.[8] Indeed, most major production companies, with the notable exception of Biograph, soon had serials in production, almost all of which focused on the adventures of a strong female lead: Kalem's *Ventures of Marguerite*, Mutual's *The Girl and the Game*, and Reliance's *Runaway Jane* appeared in 1915, followed the next year by Essanay's *The Strange Case of Mary Page*. Faced with an onslaught of serial releases, some of which were of questionable quality, *Variety* eventually complained that "nearly every film maker in the country is or has been grinding out a weekly installment about the perils of a heroine or the adventures or somebody or other and the deluge has simply bored the movie fans to death."[9]

Newspaper and magazine tie-ins that almost always accompanied the serials targeted new kinds of cinema patrons, untapped by more traditional forms of motion picture publicity like posters, heralds, and lobby displays that circulated at street level. Explaining the value of such promotions, Julian Barber stressed to *Moving Picture World* readers that newspapers reached "a class of people who are interested in the pictures and who do not have an opportunity to scan the pages of the many journals devoted to the entertainment in which they are interested," concluding that "no better medium to inform these same enthusiasts can be imagined than the daily newspaper."[10] Though they might not indulge in fan magazines or trade publications, marks of the true devotee, newspaper readers retained sufficient interest in the medium to welcome news of its developments, Barber implied. The *Chicago Daily News* boasted that its film publicity efforts were literally "making 'movie fans' " from among this population.[11] Magazine readers were possibly even more coveted than newspaper readers, for women's monthlies represented a direct tie to consumer culture—"the last link in the sales system that connects the producer with the theatregoer," *Ladies' World* editor Gardner Woods maintained. Through its early promotion of *What Happened to Mary?*, Woods boasted that his publication turned its "army" of five million readers into devoted moving picture fans.[12]

From a theater owner's viewpoint, the connection to respected and widely circulated publications was, naturally, an appealing one, and trade promotions did not shy away from emphasizing this fact. Advertising its *Ventures of Marguerite* series, Kalem reminded exhibitors that 500,000 people had been introduced to the heroine in *Good Stories* magazine, where tie-ins appeared. "Many of these readers reside in your vicinity. They would be glad to see your photoplay after having read the story if you inform them that it is to be shown at your theatre."[13] Fans who followed *The Perils of Pauline* in Hearst newspapers were "ready-made customers" for the movie serials, according to Pathé: "Your patrons want it and it is up to you to give them what they want."[14] As claims became increasingly inflated with each new drama, Universal calculated that "seventy million people" were reading installments of its *Lucille Love* serial, asking exhibitors, "Are you getting your share?"[15]

Serial fans, for their part, were always encouraged to participate in all of the versions of the story available in multiple tie-ins. The *Chicago Tribune* enticed its readers to moving picture versions of *The Adventures of Kathlyn* with midweek advertisements that stressed the compound pleasures available in the diverse renditions of the heroine's escapades, promising readers "double the enjoyment" if they followed both print and film variations of the tale.[16] Similarly, movie magazines like *Photoplay* encouraged film fans to read print tie-ins of serials they had seen in theaters. "Look for the paper in your city that is running this story," then "look for the theatre showing the Universal sign," fans of *Lucille Love* were told.[17] "You *must* read it. You must *see* it," cried ads for Essanay's *The Strange Case of Mary Page*.[18] Installments of *The Perils of Pauline* printed in Hearst's *San Francisco Examiner* featured a banner embellished with mirrored images of a woman reading the serial in a chair at home, and sitting in movie theater in front of a screen. While underscoring the complementary nature of printed and screened installments, promotions also frequently stressed the specificity of cinema's visual appeal. *Examiner* readers were guaranteed that "every incident and episode" of *The Perils of Pauline* had been "enacted into real life by the famous Pathé Players," who "put it all into living, breathing reality." An "attractive and beautiful" Pauline "lives and moves" before viewers' eyes.[19] Movie versions of *The Adventures of Kathlyn* allowed fans to see the action portrayed "in all its thrilling realism" on screen. "See Kathlyn herself with your own eyes in every hair-breadth adventure and thrilling escape," the *Chicago Tribune* advised.[20] Serial promotions solicited an active female gaze, then, one that moved from its traditional sites of engagement in women's magazines and Sunday supplements to the movie screen.

Cinema's spectacular optical array was not the only feature advertised to readers of the published installments; the social experience of moviegoing was itself celebrated in promotions that glamorized the cinema. A fashionably dressed young woman is shown attending the theater on the arm of a dapper male companion in advertisements for *The Perils of Pauline*, suggesting to women that movies provided an occasion to dress up and go out for an evening with a sweetheart or husband. Of course, such images tell us little about actual audiences for serials, but they do illustrate how serial patrons were encouraged to imagine themselves in the activity of filmgoing. Cinema in general—and serial patronage in particular—is cast far from the working-class amusements with which it might otherwise be associated. Ads promoted the idea that film viewing provided women with a natural complement to contemplative reading, and that cinemagoing might provide them with an opportunity for an elegant evening out. Like the more general promotions surveyed in the first chapter, these ads offer instructive portraits of refined filmgoing, either for those unaccustomed to the experience, or for those seeking an upscale, heterosocial mode of attending the cinema. Here again women's moviegoing is framed by the dual pleasures of an active gaze and the opportunities for self-display afforded by the cinema's social arena.

Just as newspaper and magazine tie-ins yielded ready-made audiences, "pulled to the theaters by the publicity,"[21] long-running serial films also afforded proprietors opportunities for sustained promotion that most were un-

15. Social aspects of moviegoing were promoted in ads for *The Perils of Pauline*.

likely to have encountered before, since ongoing serials lent themselves to long-term publicity much more readily than did short subjects that might have played in theaters for only a day or two. Serials coincided with a marked change in film advertising and promotion during the midteens: curbside promotion using barkers and heralds gave way to elegant lobby displays inside theaters; newspaper advertisements became increasingly common; rising movie "stars" became ever more prominent in advertising campaigns; movie magazines promoted a broad-based fan culture; and product tie-ins and souvenir giveaways commercialized the film experience. In large measure these changes can be attributed to the shift away from localized, exhibitor-based promotions toward nationally coordinated publicity campaigns engineered by film production companies. In earlier years exhibitors often had little advance warning of what pictures they might have on offer, and titles usually played for no more than one or two days, so showmen rarely chose to promote individual titles. Instead, publicity tended to center on the experience of moviegoing itself, the amenities of a particular theater, or the production company whose products were shown there. As longer, multireel films, often of "feature" length, began to play in theaters in 1913 and 1914, exhibitors started to promote particular offerings. Studio magazines that circulated to theater owners, like *Universal Weekly*, the *Eclair Bulletin*, and the *Kalem Kalendar*, also began to feature ads for studio-produced promotional materials and suggestions for advertising campaigns. Companies like Mutual and Paramount formed early publicity departments designed to shift movie promotion to a national scale. Trade publications like *Moving Picture World* and *Motion Picture News* also contained extensive discussion during the midteens about the merits of different forms of publicity.[22]

Newspaper and magazine tie-ins for serial films ensured that promotional campaigns were "not only localized, but nationalized," according to the *New York Dramatic Mirror*, which, like most trade publications, applauded the move toward standardized, nationally coordinated publicity. Production companies were now guaranteed that virtually any serial could be "as big a puller in the smallest town as it is in the largest city," thanks to more uniform campaigns. Edison proudly announced to exhibitors that episodes of *What Happened to Mary?* were "the most widely advertised pictures that have ever been produced." Hearst newspaper tie ins for *The Perils of Pauline* were "getting more advertising to the public than any picture ever did before," Pathé reminded readers in its trade ads. "We are advertising for the exhibitor," claimed Thanhouser head Charles Hite of the studio's tie-in campaign for its *Million Dollar Mystery*, noting how unusual it had once been for production companies to assume a role in film promotion, normally left to exhibitors. Advance publicity for *The Million Dollar Mystery* was jointly coordinated by the studio's new publicity department and a Chicago advertising agency. In a campaign estimated to cost nearly a quarter of a million dollars, Thanhouser purchased full-page advertisements in two hundred daily newspapers across the country and erected large painted billboards in major cities.[23]

Theater owners were urged to exploit the ongoing interest in serials to their long-term advantage by fostering a dedicated audience base. "Grasp this opportunity to build and strengthen a reputation that will be lasting and will increase your regular territory," Selig encouraged licensees of its popular *Adventures of Kathlyn*.[24] After Carl Laemmle told proprietors to "ginger up" their venues during the run of *Lucille Love*, *Universal Weekly* carried stories from around the country celebrating promotions staged by local exhibitors: one enterprising showman decorated his car with *Lucille Love* banners to advertise regular Monday showings; and the Wonderland Theater in Fremont, Ohio, lavishly adorned with posters and banners, had been featured on the front page of the town's newspaper.[25]

Such strategies surely worked, for there is little doubt about the popularity of serials with film audiences. Although oftentimes skeptical about the merits of continuing chapter plays and the tenor of their melodramatic plots, trade commentators repeatedly stressed their phenomenal appeal. Many reviews juxtaposed negative comments about the sensational content of serials with an acknowledgment of their popularity, as if unable to account satisfactorily for their evident success. After complaining that the ninth installment of *What Happened to Mary?* was "most melodramatic indeed," *Moving Picture World*'s reviewer nonetheless conceded that at the screening he attended "there was not much inattention when it was on and so far as we could see the greater part of the audience found entertainment in it." And while *The Perils of Pauline* remained "rather crude when compared with the best pictures," another commentator acknowledged that it "seems to find a following." Fans of *The Million Dollar Mystery* appeared "in every locality by the hundredfold," according to *Variety*.[26] Reports from around the country confirmed reviewers' observations. The *Chicago Tribune* admonished readers to "go early today before the crowds gather," in order to see the first installment of *The Adventures of Kathlyn*, since "thousands stood in line last night." By the time the second chapter was released, the *Tribune* claimed, "all Chicago is standing in line." When the serial opened in Washington, D.C., the *Star* reported that "houses crowded to their capacity have greeted each presentation" of the film, interest in which "surpasses that which has greeted any motion picture series ever shown in this city."[27] Advertisements for film chapters of *The Perils of Pauline* in the *San Francisco Examiner* reminded readers to "Start Early for the Theater—There's Sure to be a Crowd on Hand." When the serial opened in New York, its first installment "made a big hit" with audiences on Twenty-third Street, the center of the city's entertainment district.[28] A similarly large throng gathered to see the first two installments of Thanhouser's *Million Dollar Mystery* just two months later.[29]

Crowds drawn to serial pictures became a constant theme of trade advertising, not surprisingly. Proprietors were promised "packed houses," "capacity audiences," "the biggest money getter of the decade," and "the fattest pot of gold you ever saw."[30] Signed testimonials from exhibitors around the country graced an ad for *The Perils of Pauline* during the second month of its release, boasting of box office records. The *Edison Kinetogram* offered testimony from a showman in Fairmont, Minnesota, who claimed that *What Happened to Mary?* "has been the greatest business builder that has ever come to our notice. Wherever the pictures have been run the business has been immense. In fact, the demand for Mary is now so great in this territory that we have difficulty in getting the bookings we want on the picture." Owners of the Orpheum and Grand Theatres in Baker, Oregon, pronounced *Lucille Love* "the greatest drawing card in many moons," while the owner of the Best Theatre in Hillsboro, Texas, boasted that he "jammed them in" after heavily promoting the Grace Cunard–Francis Ford offering. "I could not believe so much could be gotten into a house of 500 seating capacity—*a week's expenses in one day's receipts and some left*."[31]

So popular were the serials, and so urgent was audience desire to see them in a timely fashion, that film rental exchanges circulated an unusually high volume of prints. Four times the number of prints of *The Adventures of Kathlyn* were released in Chicago than for any film previously shown there. Even so, exhibitors had trouble keeping up with the demand from patrons.[32] Pathé also provided exchanges with many more prints of *The Perils of Pauline* than was customary at the time, hoping to ensure that exhibitors could show episodes close to the time that newspaper installments appeared. As many as thirty prints of each installment were shipped to New York, while even midsize markets like Boston and Atlanta warranted between ten and fifteen copies in simultaneous circulation. Even with such an unprecedented number of prints available, exchanges could not accommodate the demand. Two hundred theater owners in Chicago, and more than that number in New York, placed orders to show the inaugural episode of *The Perils of Pauline* within the first three days that it was offered. Some exhibitors offered installments for two or three days, an unusually long run, in order to satisfy local interest.[33] Reports circulated that audience demand for *The Adventures of Kathlyn* was so great and prints so scarce that managers eager to squeeze as much business as possible out of a single episode were ordering projectionists to run the reels more quickly than usual. Some expert projectionists apparently managed to screen a single reel in six or seven minutes, instead of the usual ten. As might be expected, the results were "not entirely satisfactory except for the crowd waiting outside anxious to get in," according to the *New York Dramatic Mirror*.[34]

The Biggest Thrills Are Yet to Come: Serial Desire and the Heterogeneous Text

If serials brought novel opportunities for promotion on a sustained, national scale that few motion pictures had exploited previously, they also introduced a new narrative format to exhibitors. With thirteen episodes released over a period of six months in one- and two-reel installments, *The Adventures of Kathlyn* marked "a new departure in production and in the method of treating a prolonged subject," according to *Moving Picture World*.[35] Episodic serials offered a compromise between traditional one- and two-reel formats and lengthier multireel "features" then appearing on the market, for serials gained in popularity just as European feature-length films like *Quo Vadis?* (1912) and

Cabiria (1914) appeared on American screens, along with early American features like *Traffic in Souls, From the Manger to the Cross* (1913), and *The Squaw Man* (1914). At one and two reels per chapter, serialized narratives could be tailored to older patterns of exhibition and distribution, while offering patrons finished narratives ultimately much longer than any of the newer features. Serials guaranteed exhibitors the best of both worlds, then: they could experiment with more sustained, developed subjects akin to those offered in feature-length products without the additional cost or risk of tying up their screens with potentially unpopular titles. Serials were "an ideal offering" suited to the needs of showmen and filmgoers alike, according to *Moving Picture World*'s Hanford C. Judson, since they provided a bridge between the audience's desire for a substantial "evening's entertainment" and the mechanical difficulties many theaters faced with longer subjects and multireel titles.[36] While serials undoubtedly capitalized upon the uncertainty of exhibition markets during the rise of features, I concur with Ben Singer in disputing the view that serialized stories furnished "a kind of training ground for feature films," since continuing chapter plays offered a wholly unique narrative form, one whose openness and intertextuality explicitly contravened the codes of classical narrative so enshrined in early features.[37]

Quite understandably, the versatility and profitability of serialized films were stressed to theater owners at a time of changing exhibition patterns. Installments of *The Great Secret* would fit into any theater "regardless of the program you are using," exhibitors were assured.[38] Kalem asked proprietors, "Why pay out all of your receipts for so-called 'features,' when *The Hazards of Helen* Railroad Series will bring you better business—and at no extra cost!"[39] Series narratives like *The Hazards of Helen*, which consisted of unconnected and interchangeable episodes, were even more flexible than proper serials whose plots built from one episode to the next in a more linear fashion: the former could be discontinued at any time if they proved unprofitable, since there was no continuing plot to be resolved; or if they turned out to be successful with audiences, the formula could be repeated indefinitely, as it apparently was with the 119 episodes of *Helen*.[40] Likewise, Kalem emphasized that episodes of *The Girl from Frisco* could be booked "in any order," ensuring theaters an added measure of control over their offerings. And though usually shorter than most features, serials still frequently boasted the production values and visual splendor associated with lengthier subjects. Every episode of *The Mystery of the Double Cross* offered "a greater feature than most of the five-reel offerings now on the market," according to Pathé, while installments of *The Hazards of Helen* gave viewers "five reels of thrills compressed into the one reel length."[41]

Series and serials alike also guaranteed a steady clientele that onetime features could not: "Show your patrons one of the *Hazards* and they will crowd your house as often as you show those that follow." With trade ads shouting,

"Every Saturday," Kalem guaranteed that each installment of *The Hazards of Helen* would be released on the same day of the week, a distribution strategy particularly appealing to theater owners who could coordinate their advertising accordingly. Indeed the consistent release schedule of many serials was frequently stressed to theater owners. "Regular releases" of *The Adventures of Kathlyn*, Selig boasted, became "regular money getters." Hence even though proprietors were told that they could invest in serials on an installment-by-installment basis with minimum financial risk, in reality exchanges tried to insist that chapter plays be shown in their entirety. Cinemas were urged to book *The Perils of Pauline* "from the start" and to "get the full series."[42] Encouraging venues to capitalize upon the possibility of repeat attendance, publicity expert Epes Winthrop Sargent endorsed the growing practice of selling "course tickets" for serial programs, allowing patrons to purchase advance tickets for an entire series at reduced cost. Such schemes were valuable, Sargent felt, "not alone because the patrons' attendance will be secured for the series, but because there will be less tendency to save money for the ticket purchase. With the ticket paid for, there will be a more liberal investment in amusements on other nights."[43]

Even as advertisements stressed the versatility of serials and their capacity to hook repeat customers, many trade commentators expressed concerns about the viability of installment narratives. Viewers who missed episodes might be robbed of key information that would prevent them from comprehending subsequent installments, trades feared, or fans' enjoyment of the story might be compromised by an interrupted plot line. The first chapter of *What Happened to Mary?* was so good that *Moving Picture World* worried about audiences' being especially frustrated if they missed future segments: "[T]he better it is the more likely it is to irritate spectators who may fail to see the ending parts." Subsequent chapters would be "meaningless except to those who have seen the others or read the story . . . [A]round us in the theater there was some feeling of discontent at continued or part pictures in general." The *World* suggested, in fact, that the appeal of serials persisted *in spite* of their episodic structure, rather than *because* of it: "We cannot deny that [*The Adventures of Kathlyn*] is making a hit even hampered as it is by the continually broken story."[44] Reviewers also found the serial format difficult to negotiate, since they felt compelled to comment upon products they considered incomplete. "Criticizing the first, sixth or seventh part of any work of art is not a very encouraging undertaking," *Moving Picture World* complained. Even by the fourth episode of *The Adventures of Kathlyn*, when it was evident that "the series seems to be attracting some attention," the *World* maintained the difficulty of assessing individual components, declaring that "as the story is incomplete, little comment is possible." In the midst of celebrating the caliber of *What Happened to Mary?*, and praising the suspenseful conclusion of its second episode, the paper still viewed the project as unfinished, suggesting that "when it is complete, it will make a splendid evening's entertainment."[45] New serialized formats even caused problems for the National Board of Censorship, since efforts to assess their moral impact were complicated by episodic plots that did not necessarily punish criminal activity within the same chapter where it was enacted. Specific mention of serials was therefore included in a 1916 pamphlet, the board's "Standards and Policy," which noted that "the temporary success of criminals is not sufficient for condemnation." A committee reviewing any given serial should therefore "reserve its judgment on the total moral effect to the end of the episodes."[46]

Not surprisingly, given industry unease about continuing stories, serials where individual episodes could be viewed independently with relative ease received the most praise from trade reviewers. "Serious objections have been made by many picture-play patrons, heretofore, that the long serials, arbitrarily chopped into reel lengths, make it hard to get any intelligent grasp of the story in its entirety," wrote Harry W. DeLong in *Moving Picture World*. "This seems to have been obviated to a great degree in *The Perils of Pauline* . . . [T]hough each installment ends at the most interesting moment, it is a complete picture in itself."[47] Studio publicity also frequently stressed the same properties of self-containment that were praised in reviews. Mutual, for instance, insisted that any given episode of *Perils of Our Girl Reporters* offered "a separate and complete two-reel thrill." Each episode of *What Happened to Mary?* was "a complete story in itself," Edison emphasized, one that "can be run absolutely independently." Kalem assured exhibitors that each installment of its *Hazards of Helen* series was "complete in itself, telling a single story with no to-be-continued feeling."[48]

Despite many misgivings, there is considerable evidence that other contemporary observers recognized the unique pleasures that prolonged and deferred story lines offered viewers. "The Biggest Thrills Are Yet to Come," ads told viewers awaiting the second installment of *The Adventures of Kathlyn* in the *Chicago Tribune*.[49] Campaigns of this sort stressed the enjoyable aspects of suspending narrative desire across and between episodes. Some trade commentators even recognized that skillfully placed ruptures in an already compelling narrative might provide audiences with pleasurable anticipation that could entice them back to theaters for subsequent escapades. The second installment of *What Happened to Mary?* was "cut short at an intensely interesting point," one reviewer noted, providing "a very strong invitation to the spectators to call at the theater to see what will follow."[50] Another recognized that the inaugural episode of *The Perils of Pauline* "stops abruptly in what appears to be the most vital spot in the narrative, and there is no doubt it will influence the audience, or a large part of it, to see what ensues, as no completed plot would do." Similarly, each of the heroine's subsequent exploits "ends at the most interesting moment."[51] Viewers of *The Exploits of Elaine*'s opening escapade were "given just enough daylight on the mysterious form and happenings . . . to arouse the most rabid interest as to what is to follow," Margaret I. MacDonald surmised in her review for the *World*. Just as detective Craig Kennedy discovers that the villainous Clutching Hand has somehow duplicated the detective's own fingerprints, the episode concludes: "[A]t this point of the story our curiosity is suspended on to the next installment," MacDonald explained, "when the hope of solving the mystery will no doubt be deferred for several succeeding releases."[52] Serial narratives increased patronage, of course, by creating an appetite for subsequent adventures. But they also fostered a particular kind of viewing pleasure, built precisely around the suspension and deferral of narrative desire. Reviewers described quite vividly the arousal of "rabid interest" these narratives provoked in such a way that "the period of waiting between installments is rather a pleasant experience" for many viewers.[53]

Many commentators also recognized the intense physiological sensations and unaccustomed mental states audiences experienced watching astonishing serial exploits enacted on screen. Ads promised that fans would be "enthralled" by "thrilling, throbbing, pulsating moving pictures" that "hold you in breathless suspense."[54] *Moving Picture World* found that "one thrill succeeds another so rapidly" in *The Adventures of Kathlyn* "that the spectator is out of breath, mentally, in trying to keep abreast of them."[55] Suspense in *The Exploits of Elaine* was so "breathless" that viewers were "launched at breakneck speed" into a rapid series of actions, while Elaine's seventh episode was "a hair raiser."[56] Universal promised *Photoplay* readers, "[Y]ou will be on the edge of your seat all the time" while watching *Lucille Love*, for each installment will be "tense, nerve-gripping, awe-inspiring."[57] Essanay ads for *The Strange Case of Mary Page* stressed the "heart-thumping escapes" viewers would witness.[58] It is as if spectators, though seated in the theater, endured something of the heart-racing, short-of-breath sensation felt by the heroine herself. Beyond a kinetic experience of speed and terror, the sheer psychological intensity of serial viewing also intrigued commentators. *The Exploits of Elaine* "fairly makes the nerves creep," and fans were likely to be "tortured" by crosscutting that both prolonged and withheld scenes of Elaine's victimization, according to Margaret I. MacDonald.[59] Such staged encounters with extreme mental and physical states were part of an early-twentieth-century interest in "hyperstimulus," as Ben Singer points out, a response to the often overwhelming challenges of urban, industrial life. As one contemporary writer observed, serialized dramas suited the temperament of "the modern spectator" who "wants variety and won't stand being wearied."[60]

In some cases the physiological and psychological intensity of serial viewing translated into vocal reactions. *Moving Picture World*'s Hanford C. Judson "shouted out good and loud" several times during one *Pauline* screening, he confessed, so compelling were the thrills. The episode, he promised, would "stir things up a bit in the picture house where it is shown."[61] Thrills presented in *The Girl and the Game* "will make your patrons gasp in sheer amazement," exhibitors were told.[62] After *The Exploits of Elaine* opened in Atlanta, a newspaper there reported that the audience "fairly rose in their chairs as the tragedy showed on the screen."[63] Testimony from the manager of the Star Theater in Deep River, Connecticut, adds flavor to these reports:

> *Lucille Love* has got our patrons simply wild. Last Friday night we ran series number nine, and if you could have seen our audience you would have thought them patients from an insane asylum. I have seen many an excited crowd at moving picture shows, but this certainly was the limit. Grace Cunard has a strong hold on our patrons, and when she momentarily got the upper hand of Francis Ford in a rough and tumble fight, the crowd was simply insane; every one was right up on his feet cheering and yelling and it is a fact throughout the last 600 feet of the second reel, I doubt if there was twenty five in the whole place in their seats.[64]

Thus far I have considered the impact that serialized, tie-in stories had on the film industry, showing how serials were used to increase cinema's audience base by drawing in readers of newspapers and women's magazines, how production companies exploited new methods of sustained, advance publicity to promote chapter plays, and how repeat audiences were fostered through the serialized tie-in format at a time when multireel features were becoming the norm. Also crucial is the impact that ongoing, intertextual narratives had on their largely female fan base, since serial films fostered unique modes of film viewing. As even contemporary reviewers acknowledged, the narrative desire engaged by ongoing plot lines distinguished serials from most other cinematic fare. Indeed, serials promoted heterogeneous forms of consumption that contravened the most fundamental dictates of classical cinema, which stressed a closed text and a contemplative, isolated film-spectator relationship. Serials, on the contrary, offered multiple sites for consumption, most of which were located outside the space of the theater; and they encouraged viewers to see themselves as part of a community of fans (entering contests, gathering to play games, singing songs together), rather than as isolated "spectators."

The conventional understanding that print tie-ins merely promoted film serials, or provided supplementary plot information, therefore needs to be tempered with a more nuanced understanding of how audiences consumed the plural versions of each narrative offered to them in printed chapters and film installments, as well as myriad other souvenirs and product tie-ins. A closer look at the heterogeneous nature of serial narratives suspended diachronically across a serialized text and synchronically across multiple, simultaneous incarnations will give us a clearer picture of the uniquely nonclassical nature of the serial-viewing experience. Although the synchronization of newspaper serializations with motion picture installments suggests an orderly relationship between discrete renditions of the story, in fact, actual patterns of distribution show that opportunities for consumption varied considerably, and that local exhibitors retained significant control over programming formats.

The Adventures of Kathlyn was released in thirteen biweekly installments in Chicago in late 1913 and early 1914, while the story was serialized weekly in Sunday editions of the *Chicago Tribune*. The first three-reel installment opened at Chicago theaters on Monday, 29 December 1913, six days prior to the publication of the first chapter in the *Chicago Tribune*'s Sunday edition. Advertisements featured daily in the paper, sometimes encompassing nearly a full page, promoted the film and alerted viewers to the fact that the story would also be serialized in the paper's Sunday supplement. The first episode played in different neighborhood theaters each night during the last week of December 1913, and again in the first week of January 1914 following the Sunday publication of the first chapter. In other words, depending upon where one lived in Chicago—or upon one's determination to see the films—customers might either see the screen version of the serial before they read the newspaper tie-in, or they might read the printed chapter before seeing the motion picture. Acknowledging that many customers saw film chapters before they read the *Tribune*'s Sunday edition, the *Tribune* boasted that their installments would be "illustrated with 'still' pictures taken from the 'Moving' Pictures you have already seen."[65] Similar announcements in the *Washington Star*, where patterns of release appear to be comparable, suggest that many viewers there might also have seen the films prior to reading the newspaper's installments. Indeed, the newspaper seems to have expected that sequence. Readers were told that biweekly film episodes "illustrate the installments of the story" that would appear in upcoming issues of the paper. Biweekly motion picture installments kept fans "just that much ahead of the publication of the story itself in the Sunday *Star*."[66]

Despite the apparent interchangeability of film and print versions of the story, fans were nonetheless advised to follow individual series in their "correct" sequence: "You won't get the full benefit of the second show unless you have previously seen the first show," and "You can't enjoy the 24 thrilling reels that follow half so well if you missed these first three!"[67] While advising patrons not to skip individual installments, newspaper tie-ins stressed the ease with which enthusiasts could keep up with the exploits of their favorite heroine. "It is not yet too late," the *Tribune* told readers. "You can still get the thread of this thrilling story" with the aid of a "synopsis, full and complete," that "will enable you to wade right into the heart of the story at once."[68]

Evidently, the *sequence* in which fans consumed print and celluloid renditions of *The Adventures of Kathlyn* was less significant than the *simultaneous* availability of varied, mutually supportive forms of the story. When the second and third installments of *The Adventures of Kathlyn* were released to theaters in January 1914, prints of the first installment were still playing in the city's outer suburbs. By the third week of release, then, there may have been patrons who had seen episode 1 prior to reading both chapters in the *Tribune*; viewers who had seen the first episode after reading chapter 1, but before reading chapter 2; and viewers who had read both chapters prior to seeing either filmed version. Given the length of each episode's run in Chicago, moviegoers were also given the option of seeing episodes several times, depending upon their inclination to travel to different venues. The length of time that elapsed between their viewings of different episodes might also vary. While the newspaper tie-ins were published regularly each week and fans were required to wait exactly seven days between installments, it would be possible for filmgoers to see two moving picture episodes of the drama on successive nights, again providing that they were willing to travel to different theaters. During the last week of January, the third episode premiered at fourteen theaters in the city, while at least six theaters continued to show episode 2, and two continued to show the first episode.[69] Two weeks later, when the fourth episode opened at theaters in downtown Chicago, viewers could also still see the previous three somewhere in the greater Chicago area.[70] One inscription of the narrative did not simply supplement the others: plural, simultaneous versions of Kathlyn's adventures allowed audiences the freedom to consume her story in disparate ways.

Unlike biweekly releases of *The Adventures of Kathlyn* and *The Perils of Pauline*, episodes of *The Exploits of Elaine* were circulated weekly to correspond with the publication of newspaper installments in the Hearst newspaper chain. And while the release of print and motion picture installments of *The Adventures of Kathlyn* was staggered, allowing different viewers to partake of the different formats in different sequences, no film installments of *Elaine* were released until after each chapter appeared in the newspaper: in the San Francisco area, where the story was serialized in Sunday editions of the *San Francisco Examiner*, lead paper of the Hearst syndicate, movie theaters began playing a new installment each Monday. Moreover, advertisements stressed a "correct" sequence of consumption: "Read it here now," the *Examiner* advised, "then see it all in motion pictures."[71] Fans were told to "begin at the beginning." Following the appearance of the first installment in the *Examiner*, readers were advised as to how they could obtain a copy of the story had they missed the Sunday edition.[72]

Yet, although there appears to have been a greater attempt to coordinate the release of film prints and newspaper tie-ins, and a greater emphasis placed on fans' reading the chapters prior to seeing the Pathé films, actual patterns of release still guaranteed that individual viewers likely saw the filmed installments at considerably varied intervals, if the distribution of prints in the San Francisco area is any indication of national trends. After the story's opening chapter appeared in the *Examiner* on the first Sunday in January 1915, the initial film installment played at centrally located theaters in downtown San Francisco and San Jose for one- or two-day runs. But viewers in smaller neighboring cities like Alameda, Oakland, and Berkeley would not have been able to see film installments until two or three weeks after chapters appeared in the

Examiner. Residents of even smaller communities like Sausalito and Palo Alto would have had to wait six weeks, until the second week of February, for the first installment of *The Exploits of Elaine* to reach their local theaters. If they had been following the novelized version of the story in the *Examiner*, they would have read six different chapters before they would have been able to see the first motion picture episode.[73] Once again, depending upon where fans lived or worked, or how willing or able they were to travel to see the films, the interval between reading newspaper installments and seeing filmed versions would vary considerably. Exhibition strategies that favored larger, inner-city theaters over those in smaller towns were typical of the period and served patrons who lived and worked near central business districts in urban centers, like the theaters along Mission Street and Market Street where *The Exploits of Elaine* first played in San Francisco. Even in its pattern of distribution *The Exploits of Elaine* facilitated an appeal to women who worked in the city or shopped in its downtown stores, but who perhaps lived somewhat farther outside the city's core.

If distribution trends in greater Chicago and the San Francisco Bay Area reveal considerable latitude in the patterns of consumption open to serial fans, there is also evidence that exhibitors may have shown separate episodes in varying sequences and arrangements. Not all screenings were presented at regular intervals coordinated with published installments; in fact, many exhibitors apparently adapted the serial format to their own needs, sometimes electing to bundle episodes together in order to give patrons a multireel experience approximating that of a feature film. Owners of the Odeon Theater on San Francisco's Market Street offered the first three episodes of *The Exploits of Elaine* in a single show during the third week of its release in early 1915.[74] Such creative programming was even promoted by studios like Edison for its *What Happened to Mary?* Toward the end of that serial's run, the *Edison Kinetogram* reported hearing from "delighted exhibitors who are running the series singly, in pairs, and in a few instances, devoting an entire performance to the 'Mary' pictures. In every case it is the same story of crowded houses and enthusiastic audiences."[75] When the company's follow-up, *Who Will Marry Mary?*, was released in the summer of 1913, Edison advised theater managers that it was "not too late" to show the first serial again, suggesting that a consecutive run of its twelve episodes over a condensed period of time might be the best way to publicize the sequel:

> Exhibitors who have already run the entire series as it came out each month are repeating it now during these "Mary" weeks and they find the interest in it just as keen as it was before. There are many people who forgot the details of one film before the next one was released, and though they enjoyed the picture when run at monthly intervals, they want to follow the story now in closer detail.[76]

Studios also played a role in repackaging installments of popular series. For the rerelease of *The Adventures of Kathlyn* in 1916 Selig edited the original thirteen episodes into eight new segments, suggesting both the flexibility of the material and its ability to stand alone without printed installments.[77]

There is also some indication that exhibitors might have broken up two-reel installments and shown them in varying arrangements. Reviews in *Moving Picture World* and *New York Dramatic Mirror* offer significantly different descriptions of two installments of *The Perils of Pauline*, suggesting that each paper's reviewer might have seen a separate configuration of these two-reel installments. In its account of the serial's twelfth chapter, the *Mirror* leaves out scenes that the *World* recounts at the beginning of the episode, and describes how the installment ends with an incident that the *World* includes at the beginning of the subsequent installment, complaining that this ending is "something like breaking off a story in the middle of a sentence."[78] It therefore appears plausible that at least one exhibitor may have shown the second reel of the twelfth episode together with the first reel of the thirteenth episode as a combined package, possibly in order to achieve a "cliff-hanger" effect. The *New York Dramatic Mirror* reviewer may simply have been mistaken, of course; but this seems unlikely, given the striking nature of the event—a poisonous snake hidden in a bouquet of flowers delivered to Pauline—and the way he remarks specifically on the abruptness of the conclusion. It seems more likely, then, that just as release dates appear to have been staggered in conjunction with newspaper supplements, the ordering and combination of separate reels might also have varied from venue to venue.

Variable patterns of distribution and exhibition require us to look more closely at the relationship between motion picture serials and published installments, as well as the patterns of consumption they facilitated among fans. Previous commentators have tended to assume that newspaper and magazine tie-ins simply promoted filmgoing to patrons who did not frequent the cinema, or that tie-ins provided summary information and background detail essential to the comprehension of filmed segments.[79] Both conclusions presuppose a pattern of consumption in which patrons read newspaper serializations before they saw the films, or consumed separate installments at regular intervals. Actual distribution and exhibition patterns suggest, on the contrary, that many followers might have enjoyed the interwoven versions of each story in quite individualized fashions. Serials were not the only films to offer plot synopses in various forms during these years, of course. "Story" versions of new multireel films were regularly published in fan publications like *Motion Picture Story Magazine* and *Photoplay*, often accompanied by stills from the films, while heralds and advertisements also frequently summarized plots for viewers. Most historians conclude that such intertextual duplication aided narrative comprehensibility, surmising that lengthier, more detailed, and psychologically

nuanced plots typical of early multireel films demanded supplementary expli-
cation. However, in the case of serials such apparent "redundancy" needs to
be viewed in relation to the intertextual duplication that pervaded serial promotions as a whole.

From the beginning motion picture episodes were embedded in a plethora
of multitextual inscriptions, making the process of consumption not only variable but extremely complex. The wide variety of story information available
in diverse formats and at staggered times suggests that printed tie-ins played
a much more complicated role than simply providing narrative "intelligibility"
and clarity. Because installments were released in episodic form, serial narratives developed synchronically; but they also multiplied diachronically, since
multifarious tie-ins offered complementary versions of the tale simultaneously.
For this reason, serials offer perhaps the most complete model of heterogeneous textuality available in the early motion picture period. Serial viewing
approaches what Michael Denning has described as the "commodification of
reading" promoted by dime novels and serialized story papers in the late nineteenth and early twentieth centuries, where the pleasure of *consuming* the narrative overrides enjoyment derived from the story line itself, particularly when
serialized texts are broken up by catchy "hooks" and elisions.[80]

Newspaper tie-ins thus represent only one form of the multiple discourses
that proliferated around film serials, offering endless repetitions and variations
of their story lines. Many serial dramas sponsored contests that asked fans to
participate in the outcome of the drama, fostering a model of interaction that
supported serialized plots by encouraging fans to suspend narrative desire
across and between episodes and to become actively involved in unfolding
events through posing questions and hypotheses about their outcome. Contests,
which had been a regular feature of women's magazine culture from the turn
of the century onward, invited viewers to fantasize within a serial's given diegetic parameters, encouraging them to integrate fictional characters and situations into their daily lives.[81] Following this tradition, contests and prize
schemes became an element of serial fanfare from the beginning, including
the earliest promotions for *What Happened to Mary?* When the story's initial
installment appeared in the *Ladies' World*, readers were asked to submit essays
speculating on the outcome of Mary's adventures. They were offered "One
Hundred Dollars For You If You Can Tell 'What Happened to Mary.'" By
stressing the enigma of Mary's adventures, in its serial format, in its very
title, and in this contest, *What Happened to Mary?* solicited direct audience
involvement. The magazine encouraged women to imagine themselves in the
heroine's position: "What do you think? You have read this story. You see the
predicament she's in. What might happen to us in her place?" Fans were invited
to chart the trajectory of Mary's story, but also to take an active interest in
crafting its conclusion: "Let your imagination have full play. Nothing is too
extraordinary to happen to our Mary." Women's agency was stressed on two

fronts, then: both the plucky heroine and her readers were involved in plotting her adventures.[82]

An even more popular contest inspired by *The Perils of Pauline* offered entrants $25,000 if they answered questions posed at the end of the story chapter printed in Hearst newspapers. "What did the Mummy say?" "What did the pirate propose?" or "What was the aged man's message?": readers were asked to speculate. "The words she spoke have not yet been written. That will be YOUR task. Read the installment, study the situations and write the 'message' that you think best fits those situations."[83] Since questions typically revolved around scenes not portrayed in either filmed or print versions, viewers were prompted to imagine hidden backstories motivating and complicating Pauline's fate. Winning answers published in subsequent editions show fans spinning highly embellished histories for Pauline and her cohorts, furnishing the heroine with a long-lost twin sister, or finding a hidden blood relation connecting Pauline and her archenemy. Winning contestants were chosen from among those entrants "showing the greatest excellence, ingenuity, imagination, inventiveness and literary skill"[84]—all traits closely aligned with those exhibited by Pauline Marvin herself, who was, among other things, an aspiring adventure writer.

With the *Pauline* promotion judged "one of the cleverest advertising campaigns ever waged," subsequent serials followed the lead.[85] *The Million Dollar Mystery* foregrounded money in its very title, offering a single $10,000 jackpot to "the man, woman or child who writes the most acceptable solution to the mystery," promising that the final installment would be produced from the winning entry. After Thanhouser's 1915 follow-up, *Zudora, The Twenty Million Dollar Mystery*, Vitagraph countered with its parody, *The Ten Billion Dollar Vitagraph Mystery Serial*. Even without a sponsored contest, fans of *The Strange Case of Mary Page* were invited to participate in the unfolding drama, since the heroine suffered amnesia: "Can you solve this mystery?" fan magazine ads asked. "Mary herself remembers nothing but the vision—the haunting vision of the giant hand on her white shoulder! She may have done it. She does not know. Do you?"[86]

Ever-popular marketing tools, contests invite fans to participate in the ongoing construction of a text in a way that sanctions and legitimates activities in which fans are often engaged on their own, encouraging them to channel their interest back into the product itself, rather than circulating competing narratives, as John Fiske points out. Mass-produced texts like the serials lend themselves particularly well to such productivity, he argues, because their "contradictions, inadequacies and superficialities" are the "very qualities that make the text open and provocative rather than completed and satisfying."[87] And by nurturing continuing dialogues about the possible outcome of story lines, serial narratives also foster an intimacy with audiences otherwise lost in mass-produced texts, according to Peter Brooks.[88] Audience involvement was facilitated by serial contests on a number of levels, then. Readers were coached to follow episodic plots closely, reading between the lines if necessary, in order to provide contest entries. They were encouraged to continue reading newspaper installments, looking for their names among the lists of winners printed each week. They were also invited to use their imagination to place themselves within the story in order to hypothesize what characters were doing and saying beyond depictions on the screen. Contests also promoted audience involvement in the construction of the story itself. They fostered the suspension of narrative desire necessary for the success of a serialized tale, encouraging viewers to distribute their investment across multiple iterations in varied formats, linking them together in a metatext. And finally, fans who entered the contests were persuaded to adopt a detecting/writing posture that echoed the heroines' own endeavors.

Exploitation stunts also stressed audiences' continuing, extratextual engagement with a narrative that was already suspended across several episodes and numerous incarnations. Lucille Love's adventures spilled out from the screen when one exhibitor placed a notice in his local newspaper announcing the disappearance of one "Lucille Love," just at the moment when the screen heroine's whereabouts were unknown. Police appeared on the scene before the manager could warn them about his publicity venture.[89] Managers of the Idle Hour Theater in Sheboygan, Wisconsin, staged a similar stunt, already described in the first chapter, when they hired a masked young woman to appear in a local department store one afternoon a week, billed, like Lucille Love, as "The Girl of Mystery." Patrons were asked to guess her identity, with five dollars offered for the correct answer.[90] Both promotions blurred the boundaries between texts and their fans' lives in a manner particularly suited to the ongoing nature of serial stories.

Alongside contests and publicity stunts, souvenir tie-ins offered in conjunction with many serials allowed film enthusiasts to prolong and commemorate their enjoyment of the stories. "Metonymy is the trope of the tie-in," Mary Ann Doane observes, since it works to disseminate the film in an endless "chain of commodities."[91] And it was undoubtedly the female star's image that circulated most widely in this chain. Serials were not the only films to offer product tie-ins, of course; this was an era when calendars, spoons, pillow tops, pin cushions, and myriad other accessories encouraged female filmgoers to decorate their homes with images of favored stars. But the scale of promotions accompanying the serials exceeded all others of the period, largely because of the extended promotional opportunities afforded by prolonged, continuing narratives. Sheet music, puzzles, and games were all offered in conjunction with the very first serial, *What Happened to Mary?*, setting the precedent for most that followed.[92]

While promotional contests fostered a mode of narrative curiosity and creativity that paralleled the actions of the heroines themselves, then, souvenir

16. Sheet music tie-ins encouraged serial fans to sustain
their engagement at home. (Courtesy of the Academy of Motion
Picture Arts and Sciences.)

tie-ins often reinscribed traditionally feminine interests in fashion, romance, and domesticity: *Motion Picture Magazine* offered paper dolls of serial queen Pearl White in conjunction with the release of *The Purple Mask*, and spoons embossed with the likeness of actress Kathlyn Williams were circulated to fans of the *Kathlyn* series.[93] Most of the serials had song tie-ins with sheet music publishers, providing exhibitors who wished to hire a singer and musicians the means to promote the pictures outside their venues, or to purchase song slides for communal sing-alongs within the theater itself for tunes like "Elaine, My Moving Picture Queen." In addition to serving these obvious promotional purposes, sheet music also allowed patrons to sustain an experience of the serial at home in their living rooms. Since sheet music also usually carried the image of the screen star, it was another medium in which her image circulated and in which her name was mentioned.[94] In a particularly novel ploy, fans of the *Mysteries of Myra*, Pathé's 1916 occult serial, were offered a cardboard "crolette," enabling them to practice some of the serial's occultist arts at home. Naturally, the device also contained announcements reminding fans of which theaters played the pictures each week, and in which newspaper the novel was serialized.[95] Users were instructed to pose questions to the spirit world, then let the device "guide" itself to write responses. "Under the influence of certain people of particularly nervous temperament, the Crolette will be found to work to greater advantage," the instructions claimed. "The best results are to be obtained if two persons, preferably of opposite sex, sit in a quiet, dimly lighted room by themselves." Everything about the crolette suggests a targeted appeal to young, unmarried women romantic enough to thrill at the prospect of a darkened, occult encounter with a young man of their acquaintance. The crolette offered devotees of the series a tangible souvenir of their experiences, one that enabled them to experiment with some of the occult practices they had seen performed on film, while also reminding them of where and when they could enjoy future installments. Like so many subsequent tie-ins, the toy promoted a form of participatory and open-ended consumption, perfectly in keeping with the ongoing nature of serialized narratives. Souvenirs like these commodified the motion picture experience, facilitating the circulation of serials by multiplying the contexts in which their story lines were disseminated. So intertwined are such products with fans' daily lives, Jane Gaines concludes, "it is impossible to tell where promotion leaves off and spontaneous cultural response begins."[96]

Serialized stories released over a course of months and endlessly reiterated in myriad formats and products generated an extremely heterogeneous text. While the continuing nature of plot lines guaranteed an ever greater propagation of material, the endless chain of accompanying tie-ins ensured an exponential reproduction of each narrative. As a result, the value fans might accord each incarnation of the tale—whether in print, on film, in song, or captured in a souvenir—diminished in relation to their overall proliferation. By promoting an endlessly regenerating form of consumption, serials not only differed from previous modes of film viewing, then; they also steered sharply away from models of classical film spectatorship increasingly prevalent in the midteens, where a closed text provided a complete experience in and of itself without relying on extratextual or intertextual support. By exploiting the suspension of viewing pleasure between and across different episodes, in time spans of several months and up to one year, serials permitted multiple, repeatable, and variable consumption, affording patrons enjoyment of interwoven versions of a tale at different moments in no fixed order; they solicited audience involvement, in the form of prizes, gimmicks, and publicity stunts that allowed customers the illusion of helping to construct the story or of actually participating in its unfolding; and they fostered a fan culture that contributed to the further proliferation of extratextual signification.

Serials offered their largely female fan base an altogether unique form of viewing pleasure, then, one that contravened the model of absorbed spectatorship increasingly normalized by classical narratives in the mid-1910s. Miriam Hansen has argued that classical viewing practices held considerable appeal for women during these years, since the sensation of mastery offered by classical cinema was not a position women normally enjoyed or were encouraged to adopt. By abandoning the closed textual model of classical cinema, serials challenged dominant models of women's spectatorship, much as white slave films' voyeuristic appeal complicated traditional notions of female viewing pleasure. Like sensational vice pictures, serials also tested assumptions about women's filmgoing tastes and habits. While trade publications encouraged exhibitors to make their theaters more commodious (and more like upscale retail outlets) to build women's patronage, and while fan magazines inscribed female viewers as objects of desire and consumption within the theater, spectatorship at the serials relied on active models of consumption both outside the theater (with all the intertextual sources) and inside the theater. Adventuresome, suspenseful antics on film also seem to have produced boisterously enthusiastic crowds, whose reported behavior was at odds with the visual inscription of female fans in ads that pictured decorous, stylishly dressed, middle-class women, patrons from whom such immodest behavior would not have been expected. Although, unlike the white slave films, serials seem to have been designed by the industry precisely to attract women, they did so on terms that sometimes clashed with expectations governing women's moviegoing practices in the midteens.

An Awful Struggle between Love and Ambition: Serial Heroines and Modern Femininity

If serial viewing offered women novel, perhaps even radical, forms of viewing pleasure, stories enacted on the screen furnished far more cautionary delights and reveal more than a little ambivalence about their famously modern heroines. Serials catered to their large female fan base with engaging portraits of plucky young women beset by harrowing adventures and blessed with unrivaled strength and bravado. Pauline Marvin, focus of the *Perils of Pauline* series named in her honor, was "the apotheosis of the old-time melodrama heroine," according to one observer, the latter having been a meek creature who "would perish ignominiously if faced by half the perils that surround her more advanced sister of the screen."[97] Like so many other female leads, Pauline manifests athletic talents and a taste for adventure that belie outmoded notions of demure "ladylike" behavior and stay-at-home femininity. These young women lead independent lives, noticeably freed from familial obligations, marital bonds, and motherhood. Still, however much they promoted a kind of modern femininity clearly tailored to appeal to their cadre of female fans, serials' woman-oriented plots offered alarmist tales in which independence is always circumscribed by the shadow of danger, the determinacy of familial ties, and the inevitability of marriage. In fact, formulaic serial plots repeatedly, even obsessively, staged the same cautionary tale in thinly disguised repetitions from episode to episode, and serial to serial, as plot lines quickly came to resemble one another.

At the beginning of many serials, a heroine's seeming independence is conspicuously marked by the loss of a parent or guardian: Pauline Marvin's beloved guardian dies in the first episode of *The Perils of Pauline*; Kathlyn Hare's father is kidnapped at the outset of her adventures, prompting her to set out in search of him; and Elaine Dodge's father is murdered in the initial chapter of her exploits, with much of the ensuing mystery embroiled in the search for his killer. Each woman's story begins, then, with her release from familial bonds, figured in each instance as paternal authority. Pauline's autonomy is especially marked. Not only are her natural parents no longer living, her legal guardian dies in the opening installment, and she refuses a marriage proposal from her guardian's son Harry, forsaking the one chance she might have for "normal" domesticity.[98] Hoping that Harry will care for Pauline after his death, guardian Stanford Marvin had urged her to accept his son's proposal, but she declines, choosing instead to strike out on a bold path of independence. Postponing marriage will allow her to travel the world and establish her name as an adventure writer, an ambition she has long cherished. "It may be that I shall consent to marry Harry some day," Pauline tells a dying Mr. Marvin, "but you know my adventurous spirit and my desire to live and realize the greatest thrills so that I can describe them in a romance of adventures." The old man reluctantly agrees to the plan, saying, "Live your life. Write your romance. And, if you love Harry, marry him." When Harry presses the issue further, Pauline insists, "No, Harry, I wish to be absolutely free for a year." Despite Harry's continued attentions, the couple make no definite plans to wed. Hence Pauline's "perils" are initiated not only by the death of her beneficent patriarch Stanford Marvin but also by her marked refusal of a conventional feminine role and her willful insistence on seeking adventure outside of marriage. "Pauline has an awful struggle between love and ambition," Pathé announced in its promotion of the series, immediately posing the terms in opposition.[99] Emphasizing both the romance and its rupture, an advertisement in the *San Francisco Examiner* bore the headline "Kiss Me, Harry, I'm Going Away!" asking readers, "What will happen to Pauline?"[100]

An even more explicit rebellion against paternal authority and marital norms is staged in the opening installment of *What Happened to Mary?*, entitled "The Escape from Bondage."[101] A prologue shows Mary Dangerfield kidnapped and abandoned as an infant, then rescued by Billy Peart, who finds five hundred dollars with the babe and a note explaining that he would be paid an additional thousand upon her marriage.[102] The story resumes when Mary is eighteen years old and Peart is encouraging the attentions of a local suitor in the hopes of marrying off his adopted daughter and collecting the reward. But, as *Moving Picture World* explained, "Mary has become a dreamer and is in no mind to marry."[103] She has struck up a friendship with an old seafarer and enjoys sailing with him and listening to his stories about the world. Mary's curiosity is aroused further when a wealthy yachting party comes to town. After seeing the vessel and catching a glimpse of its exotic passengers, Mary is enthralled. "In a moment she ceased to be the adopted daughter and general drudge in the family of Billy Peart, and her spirit faced bravely into a new world where it was possible to be happy by becoming what one might become," according to the installment printed in the *Ladies' World*.[104] Returning home, Mary discovers the money and note left with her at birth. Learning that Peart is not her biological father, she sails off in the sailor's boat at the end of the episode, while Peart is forcibly restrained on shore. "Mary sails away to freedom and the future, which will be told in some other stories," *Moving Picture World* concluded.[105] Mary's departure from traditional family structures is doubly enacted in this opening installment: kidnapped in infancy, she is forcibly removed from her parents; then as a young woman she voluntarily leaves her guardian, rejecting his claims of authority and his attempts to push her into marriage.

Thus, much as Pauline Marvin sidesteps matrimony at the opening of *The Perils of Pauline*, *What Happened to Mary?* begins with the heroine's categorical refusal to accept marriage as her preordained fate. In this case, however, marriage carries much more explicitly sinister overtones, for in encouraging Tuck Wintergreen to woo and wed his young adopted daughter, Billy Peart seeks only the thousand-dollar compensation he will receive when she marries. Stanford Marvin had urged Pauline to marry only so that she would be cared for after his death, and, unlike Mary, Pauline is fond of her betrothed and remains engaged to him throughout her adventures; she rejects married life only temporarily, choosing to stay within Harry's protective reach. Mary, on the other hand, strikes out on a much more ambitious and courageous path, without a male protector and without the security of an ongoing engagement. So the title of her first episode, "Escape from Bondage," suggests Mary's release from Peart's household as much as from the threat of marriage to Wintergreen. Sailing off at the end of the installment, Mary leaves both behind.

Like Mary and Pauline, virtually all early serial heroines are cut adrift from conventional family relationships. Although a parent's death or an infant's kidnapping often provide the dramatic pretext for a heroine's independence, her circumstances strongly echo the economic and social autonomy increasingly experienced by many women living away from their families for the first time while working in urban centers.[106] Indeed, many serials stage the heroine's "liberation" from home and family in early installments as a necessary prelude to her exploits, implying that *only* women who renounced familial and marital obligations could pursue such unconventional endeavors. At the same time, by explicitly enacting the heroine's escape from paternal control, serials drew attention to the constraints under which many women still lived, bound by the dictates of marriage and domesticity.

Despite their initial break from home life, however, heroines' lives are inevitably circumscribed by familial ties in the end, since heredity and lineage come to assume central importance in virtually all of the plots, and marriage, though initially forsaken, usually marks the conclusion of a young woman's escapades. Complex tales of hidden ancestry and cryptic inheritance schemes, favored in so many serials—where characters remain ignorant of genealogical ties that will ultimately determine their fate, a family fortune to which they are entitled, or a forgotten royal title—express the attenuated relationships that heroines have with their families.[107] Moreover, it is this lineage that causes complications in many plots: heroines often find they cannot claim their inheritance, for instance, either because they are unable to prove their lineage or because they cannot wrest the estate from the hands of a villain. Pauline spends most of her "perils" fighting off the designs of her guardian's secretary, who plots to kill her so that he can retain control of her estate. Kalem's *Ventures of Marguerite* series features a similarly orphaned heiress struggling to hold on to her fortune, as do Thanhouser's two serials *The Million Dollar Mystery* and *Zudora*. In the first story, Florence Hargreaves searches for a fortune hidden by her father; and in the subsequent tale, the heroine's guardian conceals the fact that she will inherit the rights to the profitable Zudora mine upon her eighteenth birthday.[108] In *What Happened to Mary?*, Mary Dangerfield learns not only that Billy Peart is not her natural father, but that she has a royal lineage traced through her mother, a discovery that immediately places her in danger, since Peart, her uncle, and her cousin all conspire to get their hands on Mary's money. In short, women who declare themselves freed from familial obligations usually find their fates complicated by hidden details of their ancestry. Only by claiming their lineage or their inheritance can heroines free themselves from danger.

Somewhat uncharacteristically, it is the male hero in *The Mystery of the Double Cross* who becomes embroiled in a fight to secure his inheritance. Peter Hale's father dies in the serial's opening installment, leaving a considerable fortune to his son on the condition that the young man find the woman whom the elder Hale had personally groomed to be his son's wife. "Perfect in mind and body," Mr. Hale explains in his will, the woman has been "especially trained by me to be his mate." The only clue Peter's father provides to this woman's existence is the double cross tattoo she bears on her arm. Phillipa Brewster, daughter of a wealthy businessman with whom Peter is in partnership, appears to be a likely candidate. But Peter's attempts to prove that she is his intended bride are hampered by the fact that, unbeknownst to anyone, Phillipa has a twin sister, similarly tattooed, from whom she was separated at birth, information that is revealed only at the end of the serial. It was this second, seemingly fatherless, child whom Mr. Hale had trained "mentally and physically to be the 'perfect' woman," as she explains. As in so many serials, filial estrangement and a labyrinthine inheritance tale play central roles in *The Mystery of the Double Cross*. In this case, however, many of the essential components of the plot arc are rearranged and withheld until the final moments, obscuring the fact that although the inheritance plot seems to focus uncharacteristically on the male characters, once again it is the heroine whose destiny is preordained through binding (albeit hidden) familial ties.

Even as serial heroines strike out on their own, then, kinship plots reassert the primacy of familial bonds in these women's lives. Those who considered themselves freed from domestic obligations find they are entirely circumscribed by them in the end: seemingly orphaned women discover living parents; impoverished women inherit ancestral fortunes; and ordinary women unearth astonishing royal bloodlines. That so many ordinary women find extraordinary hidden aspects of their lives suggests that serial plots provided rich fantasy terrain for many viewers. Fantasies of freedom and entitlement would have held particular appeal for single, working women otherwise lacking these elements in their lives, as Nan Enstad suggests.[109]

Pleasing though these fantasies of independence might have been for contemporary viewers, they were invariably laced with peril, for even as the absence of family ties frees serial heroines to enjoy lives of adventure, it usually also places them in grave danger. Serials demonstrate, rather paradoxically, then, that if pioneering beyond feminine norms is possible only outside of marriage and paternal authority, life beyond the safe confines of one's home remained hazardous for most women. Like white slave narratives, serials evoke the peculiar mixture of liberation and trepidation many young women might have experienced when living away from home for the first time. In both cases, new freedoms increasingly open to women were circumscribed within an aura of danger, often explicitly sexualized.[110]

Nowhere is this contradiction more pronounced than in *The Perils of Pauline*, for, ironically, it is Pauline's refusal to wed, not her taste for adventure, that repeatedly places her in jeopardy. Had she married, control of her substantial inheritance would have passed from her guardian Stanford Marvin to his son Harry, her fiancé. Since she declines to do so, her finances remain in the hands of Mr. Marvin's secretary, Owen, who obsessively and repeatedly plots the young woman's demise in the hopes of keeping the fortune for himself. By the end of the first installment the intricacies of Pauline's inheritance have been spelled out, and it is obvious that she will have no authority over her money until she marries: "[I]t is clearly to her interest to elope with almost anyone," *Moving Picture World* concluded.[111] Still Pauline declines Harry's proposal for the foreseeable future so that she can pursue her writing career unencumbered. Her willfulness draws marked attention to the constraints under which she is asked to live, for viewers are made acutely aware that Pauline does not—and will not—manage her own finances, that her assets pass, quite pointedly, through a succession of male hands: from her grandfather, to her guardian Mr. Marvin, to his executor Owen, then ultimately to a future husband. By refusing to take cover under marriage after her guardian's death, Pauline marks out a distinctly feminist stance. But Pauline's attempts to exert some influence over her fate are undercut by the perils of such a choice: unmarried, she remains a persistent target of Owen's murderous intentions.

When villains are not plotting to kill or kidnap heroines in order to hijack their assets, they are often scheming to coerce the women into wedlock, hoping to gain a more legitimate foothold. If Mary Dangerfield and Pauline Marvin escape marriage at the outset of their narratives, remaining free to pursue their adventures, many other heroines must foil attempts to force them into unseemly unions with scoundrels who are greedily eyeing their fortunes. While Mary and Pauline are imperiled when they forsake marriage, other heroines are threatened *by* marriage: Marguerite fends off her chauffeur's matrimonial designs in *The Ventures of Marguerite*; Phillipa Brewster is nearly blackmailed into marrying dastardly Bridgey Bentley, "gangster and society pet," in *The Mystery of the Double Cross*; and Kathlyn Hare, visiting the land of Allah in search of her father, is chosen to be the country's next queen and almost forced to marry a nefarious consort who has been selected for her, an outcome that leaves the heroine "stricken with terror," according to Selig's published herald.[112] Just as the wedding is about to take place, the first installment ends, leaving viewers in suspense about whether Kathlyn will elude the bonds of matrimony. The second installment resumes with the wedding about to go forward, but, as the herald explains, Kathlyn "conserves all her powers of resistance to this proceeding" and manages to postpone the ceremony for at least a week.[113]

Even as women dodge suspect nuptials with scheming villains, many of the plots drive toward marriage nonetheless, for matrimony still signals closure at the end of most heroines' endeavors. By the end of *The Adventures of Kathlyn*, the heroine's narrow escape from wedlock in early installments has been superseded by her inevitable union with sweetheart Bruce, an American hunter. In the final moments of the last episode she and her father set sail back to California, "where Kathlyn's marriage to Bruce is assured," according to the herald.[114] Indeed, marketing campaigns often stressed the romantic component of their tales in equal measure with their adventurousness: *The Exploits of Elaine* was a "thrilling story of romance, mystery and adventure"; *Lucille Love: Girl of Mystery* depicted "love, danger, intrigue and mystery"; while *The Mystery of the Double Cross* was billed as "the feature serial of perils and love."[115] The drive toward marriage allowed serial narratives, with their otherwise unorthodox plotting, to enforce some measure of closure in the end. A perpetually suspended romance plot was touted as the main continuing thread in the *Hazards of Helen* series, which otherwise stressed the integrity of its individual installments. "The only connecting link" between episodes of the heroine's adventures, the *New York Dramatic Mirror* explained, "will be Helen's love affairs, which will progress through each installment and not be finally settled until the final reel."[116] Significantly, the absence of marriage at the conclusion of *What Happened to Mary?* became the pretext for the serial's sequel, which asked, *Who Will Marry Mary?*, as if a fundamental question had been left unanswered. The final installment of Mary's first exploits serialized in the *Ladies' World* portrayed the young woman lying in bed fantasizing about how she would spend her newly discovered inheritance, but ended with her pondering, "I wonder, oh, indeed I do wonder, Who Will Marry Mary?"[117]

Again Pauline's situation is instructive, for despite her initial retreat from matrimony, her adventures are always circumscribed by her engagement to Harry Marvin. Even though she initially sidesteps the young man's proposal, even wielding a tennis racket to fend off his kisses in the opening installment, he remains at her side throughout a series of risky undertakings, often stepping into the breach just as things get rough. By introducing their betrothal at the outset, the series plants the seeds of the couple's union from the beginning; it is really only a matter of time before Pauline will agree to marry her persistent beau, for the couple's wedding becomes the inevitable conclusion to her "perils." A circular plot structure bounded by betrothal and marriage draws attention to the traditional expectations circumscribing Pauline's narrative, a pattern doubled further within individual installments, many of which stage Pauline's departure from the Marvin home, the dangerous adventures that ensue, then her eventual return to the security of this household. An identical camera setup showing Pauline safely at home with Harry is repeated at the beginning of several episodes. These establishing shots tend to be the only interior shots of each chapter and certainly the only ones at the Marvin home: in earlier installments we see Pauline sitting at the desk where her beloved guardian once worked; in later episodes she sits in the living room. With each repetition the sense of security and familiarity associated with these surroundings amplifies. Tempted away from this cocoon by some exploit or other, Pauline is inevitably reunited there with Harry in the end.

Each installment offers a double-edged pleasure, then, allowing audiences to revel in Pauline's spectacular escapades while also enjoying the comfort of seeing her back in Harry's arms in the final moments, a circular trajectory that mirrors the ultimate goal of the series as it propels the couple toward marriage. For there is no question that matrimony signals the termination of Pauline's exertions. *Moving Picture World*'s review of the twentieth and final installment announced, with some regret, that "Pauline has had the last of her perils, and her adventures that have entertained us so long are now ended—she is going

17. Pauline safely at home in Harry's arms. (Courtesy of the Academy of Motion Picture Arts and Sciences.)

to marry Harry and settle down."[118] Pauline herself declares at the end of the concluding episode, "I have once and forever finished with this life of adventure. I am quite prepared to marry you, Harry, and we shall be happy at last." The narrative thus allows us to enjoy the pleasures—and perils—of Pauline's autonomy, while also clearly circumscribing it within a temporary time frame, doubly enacted at the close of each installment and the termination of the serial itself. Thus Pauline's independence, like that of so many other serial protagonists, is carefully abridged: their autonomy places the young heroines in immediate danger; familial ties that they seem to have abandoned reassert themselves in the form of mysteries about lineage and inheritance; and although several heroines plainly decline marriage, their adventures are often framed within a betrothal or chronicled along with a budding romance that ends in matrimony. While the women appear to live beyond the strictures of domestic femininity, in fact their exploits are heavily circumscribed by the parameters of familial life.

This same paradox may be seen in the physical daring of serial heroines, for while they appear to be strong, capable women fending off extraordinary dangers, many episodes often stage the heroine's disempowerment. Pauline

Marvin is, again, a case in point, for although she willfully embarks on daring pursuits like speed racing, yachting, and flying, it is not these activities, per se, that place her in danger or elicit her exceptional feats. Rather, it is Owen's persistent attempts to sabotage these escapades that repeatedly highlight Pauline's inability to control the mechanisms with which she experiments. In the sixth episode, for instance, Owen elicits Pauline's curiosity by showing her an advertisement for an upcoming air balloon demonstration. He then accompanies her to the park, where he persuades her to climb into the basket, only to set the device loose, sending her afloat without a pilot. With Owen capitalizing upon Pauline's bravado, her boyfriend Harry tries to rein in her taste for adventure but is usually unable to prevent her from becoming embroiled in some form of derring-do. "Harry, as Pauline's self-appointed protector, is kept very busy," *Moving Picture World*'s critic observed.[119]

In fact, hero and villain often work in concert to frustrate Pauline's adventures. Unable to persuade her to adopt the more staid lifestyle he prefers, Harry thinks nothing of foiling her plans, sometimes forging an unwitting alliance with Owen as he does so. This is especially evident when Harry thwarts Pauline's attempt to fly in an airplane test in the serial's second installment. After Owen and his accomplice Hicks have convinced a pilot to take Pauline along on a flight that they plan to sabotage, Harry arrives and offers the man money *not* to take his fiancée up in the airplane. When this proves unsuccessful, and he remains unable to dissuade Pauline from her flight plans, Harry disables her car in the hopes of delaying her arrival at the airfield long enough to prevent her from boarding the plane. Acting just as Owen does, Harry seeks to control Pauline's actions through covert means, but not because he is aware of Owen's ploy; he remains as ignorant of the secretary's ruse as Pauline does. Harry simply disapproves of his sweetheart's adventuresome spirit. Given the nature of Owen's villainy, Harry's cautious attitude proves well-founded. But in the absence of any knowledge of Owen's designs, Harry's actions appear needlessly restrictive and foreshadow the strictures Pauline will experience once married. Curiously then, it is the villain who encourages Pauline's taste for the unexpected, while her fiancé attempts to restrain it.

Owen's insidious plotting is registered in compositions and editing strategies that stress his command over each situation while simultaneously underscoring Pauline's naïveté. He is, for instance, repeatedly shown lurking in the background eavesdropping on Pauline's plans. Even as she announces her intentions to be "free" in the opening installment, we are aware of the danger she faces, for Owen is visible hovering in the rear of several shots. "His face, at times, reflects gleams of wickedness which freeze the blood and make the observer shudder," one ad claimed.[120] When Pauline pens a telegram announcing her plans to visit a relative's ranch, Owen listens as Harry dictates it over the telephone; when Pauline decides to enter an automobile race in the fifteenth episode, Owen watches as she receives her entry form, then plots to sabotage the vehicle. By placing both participants in the frame at once, these compositions stress Pauline's lack of awareness and her failure to see Owen lurking in plain sight, while trumpeting Owen's command of the frame's visual and aural field. Patterns of crosscutting juxtapose scenes of the young woman, unaware of any imminent danger, with scenes of Owen and his henchmen plotting her demise, further underscoring Pauline's vulnerability while offering viewers a position of narrative omnipotence aligned with Owen's masterful deceit. Here, and throughout the series, viewers know far more about Pauline's plight than she herself does. She is forever ignorant of Owen's death plots, which always seem to be hatched just out of her sight line, but in full view of spectators. Owen's domination is rendered especially vividly in a sequence that shows him glancing out of frame to watch as Hicks throws Pauline over his shoulder and kidnaps her. Poor Harry can only stare in the foreground while Hicks disappears with his beloved into background space. Owen's command over the situation, exercised from afar and by proxy, is contrasted with Harry's relative impotence despite his proximity to the action.

In addition to stressing her lack of control over narrative and visual space, Pauline's perils repeatedly stage her entrapment in close quarters or in mechanisms over which she has little mastery. Fascinated by all manner of modern conveyance, like automobiles, airplanes, and sea vessels, Pauline is not always shown to be in command of these devices. Instead, they usually serve to imprison her, to *restrict* her movement in episodes where she finds herself prisoner in machines gone haywire: an air balloon let loose over the Palisades; an abandoned structure used as target practice by the navy; a submarine capsule submerged underwater; a boat that has sprung a leak; and a malfunctioning speedster—scenarios where her imprisonment is often doubly inscribed in images of her body bound and gagged. Pauline's ingenuity and athletic agility usually allow her to devise a means of escape, however: she slides down the air balloon's rope; she forces herself into a torpedo tube and is ejected from the sinking submarine; she sends her dog for help when fired upon by the navy. Trapped in a cave in the serial's eighth installment, Pauline remains undaunted, unafraid of a fox who enters the den, and undeterred by the physical difficulty of maneuvering out of the cave. Instead, she struggles to remove the boulders in her way, then crawls out of the cave through a fox hole. Perhaps her most spectacular escape occurs in episode 14, when she and Harry swim up the chimney of a flooded building and onto the roof, then rappel across a canal on a wire. Still, Pauline's physical prowess, however impressive in these episodes, is exercised almost solely to free herself from Owen's traps; rarely does she initiate athletic feats for any other reason. Indeed, Pauline's adventures might be said to offer a reflexive treatment of restraint and entrapment, showing how the heiress, already imperiled by her decision not to marry, is further endangered by men who seek to restrict her freedom exactly as she exercises it.

The subsequent "exploits" of Elaine Dodge, heroine of Pathé's sequel to its wildly successful *Pauline* series, go one step further, placing Elaine in much more frightening and powerless situations than those endured by Pauline Marvin. Although *The Exploits of Elaine* was named after its heroine in an alliterative formula by then familiar to viewers, and although Pearl White continued in the title part, Elaine occupies a significantly diminished position in her own story, a passivity enabled by the introduction of a more central male protagonist, Craig Kennedy, Scientific Detective, already well-known from stories published in *Cosmopolitan* magazine.[121] Craig's methods of detection are foregrounded in most episodes; it was those details that made the series "especially interesting," according to the *San Francisco Examiner*, whose reviewer expressed relief that plots did not revolve around the escapades of "pretty and attractive little Elaine, but of the wizards of science."[122] Indeed, Craig's position is much more central to the narrative of *The Exploits of Elaine* than is that of many of his counterparts. Whereas Harry Marvin stands on the sidelines throughout most of Pauline's trials, either trying in vain to get her to stay home or ending up trapped along with her and only infrequently coming to her aid, Craig is instrumental in Elaine's rescue in virtually every installment of her story, and it is Craig who solves the mystery of the "Clutching Hand" that overshadows the serial.

Throughout the story Elaine is placed in situations that underscore not simply her physical entrapment but her loss of bodily and psychological control. Unlike Pauline, Elaine can do little under the circumstances. In the serial's second installment the villainous Clutching Hand creeps through Elaine's bedroom window and injects the sleeping heroine with a potion that induces a "twilight sleep," convincing her to open her father's safe, then pen a note to detective Craig Kennedy asking him to terminate his investigation into her father's death, acts she will not recollect when awoken.[123] Strong undercurrents of sexual violation reverberate through the scenario: the young woman's bedroom is penetrated at night, she is awakened with a gun to her face, then ordered to perform acts in her nightclothes. Once it becomes clear that Elaine does not recall sending Craig the note, the detective injects her with another dose of the serum, hoping to reenact events of the previous evening, effectively repeating the assault. As was the case so often with Owen and Harry in Pauline's adventures, villain and hero again work together to incapacitate the heroine. But in Craig's hands the sexual nature of the violation is more marked and Elaine's passive victimization that much greater, a flavor that is underscored still further in the published chapter of the installment. Whereas the film chapter portrays events in sequence—the Clutching Hand drugs Elaine, she wakes with no recollection, then Craig reconstructs events with the aid of a second injection—the newspaper installment focuses on Craig's reenactment, revealing events of the night before only through Elaine's drug-induced reenactment.[124] Ironically, then, it is Craig who encourages her to perform the incidents of the night before, and Craig who induces in her the same terror she experienced at the hands of the villain. It is perhaps no coincidence that *Moving Picture World*'s reviewer notices for the first time in this episode "the glimmer of a love element to be developed" between Craig and Elaine, who looks upon the scientist with a "bewildered and admiring gaze."[125]

"The Twilight Sleep" is only one of many episodes that dramatize Elaine's physical and mental incapacitation at the hands of mysterious potions or gases that render her unconscious or delirious, as the specter of her immobilized body is repeatedly offered for display: in the tenth installment Elaine is abandoned in an underground sewer where she is felled by poisonous gases; a needle "treated with the most virulent poison" is attached to her wristwatch in "The Hour of Three," rigged to prick her at the appointed moment; Elaine's bedroom is sprayed with arsenic in the fifth installment, sickening both her and her dog as they sleep; and after having been given a drug that makes her crave water, Elaine nearly drowns trying to quench her thirst in still another episode.[126] These situations emphasize not simply her imprisonment in confined space but her inability to control bodily functions and drives in a manner that frankly mimics sexual assault. Besides "The Twilight Sleep," Elaine's bedroom is penetrated at night while she sleeps in at least two other episodes: a stone crashes through her window and onto her bed in "The Poisoned Room," and a shadowy figure appears at her bedroom window in "The Vampire."[127] Sexual violation is suggested especially vividly in the latter installment when Elaine is forcibly given a blood transfusion by the Clutching Hand and his cohorts.[128] Bound, gagged, and knocked unconscious, Elaine lies in the center of the frame while the Clutching Hand's men stand around her in the background, forming a human wall. "Elaine's life blood is fast flowing into the exhausted arteries of the desperado," *Moving Picture World* exclaimed, as her bare arm lies next to the man's.[129] Her flesh exposed and her bodily fluids forcibly exchanged, Elaine is subject to an implied sexual violation, emphasized all the more forcefully when she awakes and gasps in horror at the sight of the Clutching Hand hovering over her.

The specter of sexual assault permeates all of the Clutching Hand's encounters with Elaine, for he is repeatedly shown physically penetrating her home and her bedroom, and he regularly invades her body, injecting foreign solutions into her veins, or subjecting her respiratory system to noxious substances. The Clutching Hand's tactics find an echo in the very methods Craig uses to rescue her, again underscoring the connection between them. In one episode, Elaine is tormented at home by the Clutching Hand and saved only through the help of a "vocophone" listening instrument Craig has recently installed there, enabling him to overhear the Clutching Hand's assault from across town in his lab. The covert means by which the Clutching Hand invades Elaine's home are matched here by Craig's own controlling surveillance of that same domain. In all of these scenarios Elaine is far less an active participant than a victim or, as *Moving Picture World* noted, an "anguished spectator," forced only to witness the Clutching Hand's treachery.[130]

The passive victimization that Pauline and Elaine endure at the hands of villains who seek nothing less than their destruction was not a feature of all serials, however. In *What Happened to Mary?* and *The Hazards of Helen* heroines engage in risky ventures of their own initiation, exercising control over narrative space at every turn. Both are working women who eke out a living in the paid labor force, Mary as a stenographer in New York and Helen as a railway telegraph operator. Their adventures often stem directly from work-related situations where they volunteer their services to safeguard the lives and property of others. The eighth episode of *What Happened to Mary?*, for instance, finds Mary Dangerfield supporting herself as a stenographer after her uncle and cousin embezzle the fortune she has unexpectedly inherited in a previous episode. Opening scenes of "A Will and a Way" show Mary working in an office typing correspondence and gossiping with her coworker, much like any other young wage earner, a connection that was not lost on actress Mary Fuller, who saw direct parallels between Mary Dangerfield's life and those of her fans.[131] Confessing her love of the "Mary" and "Dollie" series she filmed at Edison, Fuller told *Photoplay* readers that she liked playing "the modern girl who has modern problems to solve, and who does this according to her own code of honor." Despite the grandeur of Mary's on screen adventures, Fuller believed that many of the situations she faced resonated with the lives of her fans: "[T]he problems of today belong only to the girl of today. She is the only one who can solve them. So whenever I'm a modern girl, on the screen, and extricate myself from modern difficulties in a perfectly practical way, I feel that maybe I am helping somebody among my spectators to solve some kind of difficulty for herself."[132]

Mary's adventures begin in this episode when she volunteers to deliver a revised will to an elderly client, Abraham Darrow, sick on his deathbed. Darrow's nefarious son Terence has thus far prevented his father's attorney from visiting, hoping that the old man will die before the son can be disinherited. Undaunted by the challenge and sure that she can get the document to the elder Darrow, Mary accepts the assignment. Her sense of purpose here immediately sets Mary apart from so many other serial heroines, who remain passive victims, preyed upon by vicious fortune seekers. Unlike Pauline Marvin, constantly subject to labyrinthine death plots orchestrated by Owen, or Elaine Dodge, forever at the mercy of schemes perpetrated by the Clutching Hand, Mary herself initiates the adventure, volunteering her skills to a stranger in need, taking calculated risks for another's benefit. While other heroines sidestep complex acts of sabotage orchestrated from afar, Mary confronts Terence Darrow directly, handily fighting him off through a combination of physical strength and cunning. She successfully gains entry to the Darrow household, obtains the elder Mr. Darrow's signature on the new will, then delivers it to the attorney's office in the nick of time—all without the help of a male accomplice.

Mary's control of the situation is registered through her command over physical space and the visual field throughout the episode. Compositions juxtapose several characters in different planes of the frame, illuminating sight lines and blind spots by showing how Mary conceals her presence or sees events that others miss. As the episode begins, Mary is initially shown at an optical disadvantage in relation to Terence. Hiding behind a pillar outside Mary's office, the greedy son overhears her conferring with her employer and is thus able to foil her first attempts to deliver the will to his father. But Mary is soon able to reverse Terence's dominance, a leverage tellingly depicted through her covert surveillance of the Darrow home. Mary takes up a position at the back of the house, watching for an opportunity to enter the dwelling. Rather than accentuating her sight line through point-of-view editing, compositions show her looking within the frame itself, much as we had seen Terence crouched behind a pillar in the earlier scene. Mary's head is visible in the foreground as she keeps watch on the back door from behind a fence that bisects the frame into two separate planes of action, one depicting the comings and goings around the Darrow's back door and the other depicting the neighbor's yard where Mary is stationed. By placing both action and onlooker in the frame, compositions draw attention to the imbalance in each character's awareness of his or her surroundings, assigning Mary an obvious advantage. Once she sees the housekeeper leave, Mary sneaks into the house but fails to reach Mr. Darrow when Terence catches her in the living room. Undaunted, Mary then borrows the housekeeper's shawl, fashioning a disguise that allows her to walk right past Terence, who does not recognize the woman he has ejected just moments earlier.[133] Mary's command of physical space and optical fields obviously sets her apart from Pauline Marvin, whose ignorance is frequently heightened in compositions where Owen lurks unseen eavesdropping on her plans. If Owen's controlling presence is set against Pauline's failure to recognize the conspiracy brewing under her nose, multiplaned compositions in *What Happened to Mary?* demonstrate Mary's authority over diegetic space and align the viewer's omniscient knowledge of the events more closely with that of the heroine, rather than the villain.

Yet even as "A Will and a Way" celebrates Mary's victory, the corresponding tie-in printed in the *Ladies' World* downplays Mary's active agency, instead showing her to be preoccupied with romance and beauty. Mary's willingness to step into the breach to help Mr. Darrow and her evident athletic prowess are tempered in the magazine installment by thoughts about how her exploits might complicate an evolving courtship. "Sometimes I wonder if it is quite womanly to climb fences and all that sort of thing," Mary speculates, suddenly self-conscious about disporting herself in an "unladylike" manner. "Anyhow,

I'm glad *he* didn't see me doing it." Then, realizing that she might have been displayed to advantage in such moments, Mary concludes, "I must have looked rather nice when my hair tumbled down. I wish *he* had seen me *then*."[134] While filmed episodes of What *Happened to Mary?* celebrate feminine athleticism, traits counterposed in so many other serials, the *Ladies' World* chapter functions to reinscribe this distinction yet again. Fans who read this chapter along with the film installment would have found Mary's accomplishments undercut by girlish concerns about her appearance. However valiant their exploits on the screen, serial heroines existed amid a plethora of extratextual products and tie-ins, many of which offset adventuresome screen antics by reinforcing more sanctioned feminine pastimes in their fans.

Even more than *What Happened to Mary?*, *The Hazards of Helen* stresses the heroine's acts of daring and physical prowess. The heroine is a humble telegrapher compelled to perform feats of extraordinary courage when she pursues runaway trains and fleeing bandits in situations that showcase her extraordinary athleticism. Leaping from one moving vehicle to another, commandeering speeding locomotives, or running over the tops of boxcars, Helen shows herself to be in command of just those machines that entrapped and imperiled lesser heroines. As Lynne Kirby suggests, "her heroism exists in the difference between not normally controlling the big machine and being able, having the resources, to do so."[135] Long shots illustrate her body in motion, showing Helen fully in command of herself, her body, and modern machinery so that the kinetic force of her actions is overlaid with cinema's own velocity. Helen's athleticism is matched by a keen intelligence. She is unusually observant about the goings-on in her station, meaning that she is often the only character cognizant of danger and the only one capable of staging a rescue. Of all female leads, Helen is most associated with control over space and the visual field, then. Episodes frequently rely upon a complex negotiation of diegetic space where viewers must deduce the relative location of characters and trains in order to gauge proximate danger within an intricate spatial and temporal matrix.[136]

One of the most interesting installments of *The Hazards of Helen* is in some ways one of the least typical, for in "The Pay Train" Helen is kidnapped and held captive in an abandoned railway car. If this is a predicament familiar to Pauline and Elaine, it is rarer for Helen, who normally finds herself rescuing others. But in this episode Helen's movements are restricted, she is forced to rescue herself rather than others, and she must rely upon her mental agility more than her athletic talents. Like many of Helen's stories the plot revolves around what characters see or do not see, and which characters know more than others; but in this case, uncharacteristically, it is Helen who is deprived of crucial information. After spying on her at the depot, bandits reroute a pay train to an abandoned track, then lock Helen in an abandoned boxcar, hoping she will not be able to prevent the robbery. But in the end Helen gains the upper hand. Even though trapped in the boxcar where she has limited range of vision and movement, Helen manages to reel in a gun lying outside the car by fashioning a rope from hairpins and shreds of her petticoat. While still trapped in the train car, she shoots down the train signal and averts the robbery. Crosscutting emphasizes Helen's sight line throughout the sequence, alternating shots of her inside the car with close shots of the gun on the ground, a juxtaposition that suggests her sight line but does not directly align our view with hers in optical point-of-view shots. Alternating scenes inside and outside the train car are also interspersed with shots of the bandits waiting to hijack the diverted train far from the site where Helen is trapped, a pattern of cutting suggesting that Helen's actions will not only lead to her release but will also enable her to thwart the robbery attempt. In fact, once she recovers the gun, she shoots down the train signal so that the pay train will not be rerouted toward the bandits. Only then does she draw attention to her own whereabouts. Thus while crosscutting initially figures Helen's lack of control, it ultimately signals her command of the situation. And although Helen is indeed rescued at the end of the episode, it is not before she saves others from danger.

Much like Mary Dangerfield, Helen is a woman of true strength and independence rare among serial heroines. Her willingness to take on adventure, her lack of male companions, and, most significant, her control of cinema's spatial and optical field all set her apart from other female leads. Helen's story runs counter to the pattern of most serials, where women are persistently endangered outside their traditional sphere in unvaried scenarios of imprisonment and rescue. Although serials engaged in radical narrative experiments, by offering multiple texts with varied points of entry, such a novel approach was not often repeated at the story level. On the contrary, continuing, intertextual narratives often served only to reproduce and reinscribe cautionary lessons about the dangers of female independence. Much like white slave films, serials frequently staged tales of female autonomy only to cloak them in menace and peril.

Yet for a complete understanding of the template serial heroines offered viewers, we must look beyond the screen exploits of Pauline and her compatriots toward the substantial star discourse that circulated around the actresses who played these women on the screen. Of all the extratextual renditions that supported serials—the myriad tie-ins, prize schemes, and souvenirs—none is more central to the address to female fans than the elaborate publicity surrounding "serial queens," some of the earliest movie stars. In profiles of these women's private lives and professional careers models of modern femininity emerge that augment the more staid, even alarmist, depictions of female independence within the films themselves.

What Sort of Fellow Is Pearl White? Serial Queens and Their Female Fans

An enormous fan culture surrounded movie serials in the mid-1910s, fueled by continuing stories that encouraged viewers to suspend curiosity beyond and between the confines of individual texts, and product tie-ins that facilitated prolonged and varied enjoyment of the material. Much of the attention focused on so-called serial queens like Pearl White, Kathlyn Williams, and Helen Holmes, actresses who appeared repeatedly in the serial dramas. Details of their private lives—their homes, their romances, their backgrounds, their beauty routines—circulated alongside contests and tie-ins in which their characters' exploits were variously inscribed. But profiles of stars' offscreen pastimes served a unique function among the multiple discourses that surrounded serials, furnishing a sustained extratextual engagement for viewers by tracing a parallel narrative to the sensational lives of heroines on the screen. Fans could measure the hyperbolic exploits of characters like Pauline Marvin and Kathlyn Hare against the "real" lives of motion picture players.

Actresses like Pearl White were among the earliest of Hollywood celebrities, for serial fan culture dovetailed neatly with the evolution of the movie star system.[137] Where motion picture performers had remained largely anonymous during the first years of the industry, by the early 1910s they began to be identified by name. As production conditions improved during these years, studios started to hire actors on permanent contract, and companies like Kalem celebrated the "stable" of players they employed. Advertisements began calling attention to particular performers, reviews began mentioning actors by name, and some companies began to provide screen credits identifying their players. Fan magazines like *Motion Picture Story* and *Photoplay*, which debuted in 1911 and 1912, also started giving readers details about favorite performers, as did inquiry columns in trade publications like *Moving Picture World* and the *New York Dramatic Mirror*. Images of favored actors also circulated among fans in slides, posters, souvenir postcards, and calendars designed to sell the products of particular studios. Closer camera positions favored during these years and new acting styles tailored to more intimate views also fostered repeat identification of the players.[138]

From this early interest in screen "personalities" developing between 1909 and 1911 Richard deCordova charts the rise of a true movie star culture in late 1913 and early 1914, just as serials began to crest in popularity. Information that had first circulated largely about performers' professional careers and accomplishments began to include more attention to their private lives. A screen star's "persona" was no longer constituted simply by her professional résumé but now included her offscreen conduct as well. Her love life, her family back-

ground, her leisure pastimes all became legitimate points of interest. This fascination was promulgated across a multiplicity of texts reaching far beyond a
star's film appearances to include publicity photos, celebrity profiles, product
tie-ins, promotional stunts, and personal appearances.[139] Once in operation,
cinema's star system was far more powerful than those in other media, for
cineasts composed the first real mass audience in history, and as so many later
theorists describe, the film image promoted an intimacy between actor and
viewer that remains unrivaled: "The player, in absence, belonged to the spectator in a closer way than would ever be possible in reality," as Eileen Bowser
suggests.[140]

Of all early film genres, serials were particularly well-suited to the development of celebrity culture: their continuing stories promoted prolonged audience fascination with a single heroine and star, and the use of compound
tie-ins invited a heterogeneous, extradiegetic mode of audience consumption
tailor-made for the cult of personality. Because plots so often centered on one
young woman's exploits, fans who saw actresses play that same character week
after week could not be blamed for conflating the two personalities, especially
given how often heroine and actress shared the same name: Mary Fuller, Kathlyn Williams, Helen Holmes, Marguerite Courtot, and Ruth Roland were only
some of the early stars for whom serials were named, or who adopted the name
of their screen character.[141] The serial format itself, where the exploits of a
single heroine, already aligned with the star, were repeated at regular intervals,
only fueled such close interest and identification. Enjoyment of motion picture
stars was already serialized to some degree, since fans eagerly followed performers like Mary Pickford or Clara Kimball Young from picture to picture;
serialized releases merely institutionalized this process, guaranteeing fans future sightings of the star in a consistent, stable persona. Viewers accustomed
to seeing beloved players in a variety of roles could now watch for the same
actress in a continuing part. And precisely because plot details were circulated
and repeated in so many forms—on the screen, in print tie-ins, in story contests—viewers were free to contemplate other elements of the texts, namely,
their stars, a point Gaylyn Studlar stresses in her examination of 1920s fan
culture.[142]

Female stars were also vital to a fan culture that increasingly targeted women
during these years. After first appealing more to men, motion picture magazines began to amend their largely technical coverage of moviemaking with a
marked concern for fashion, beauty, and performers' private lives around 1911,
signs of their growing address to women, according to Kathryn Fuller.[143] Fe-
male-centered fan cultures were by no means unprecedented in the early years
of the century, as Studlar has shown in her account of the "matinee girl" phenomenon surrounding turn-of-the-century stage actors, an important precursor
to early movie fan culture.[144] Yet "matinee girls" engaged in active, openly
libidinal attractions to male performers, while it was female stars who became

objects of fascination for the serials' largely female fan base, suggesting that the erotic attachment of earlier "matinee girls" was overlaid with a fascination for idealized role models.[145]

If serial plot lines register marked ambivalence about women's independence and physical prowess, this was rarely in evidence in fan discourse, for actresses' astonishing athletic accomplishments became one of the central features of celebrity profiles. Fans were repeatedly told that players performed their own stunts, that tremendous skill and stamina were required to execute these maneuvers, and that many stars braved incalculable dangers while filming. The fact that audiences could plainly see the peril many actresses faced added a decided level of anxiety to the viewing experience. Describing an installment of *The Hazards of Helen* where a stunt featuring actress Helen Gibson nearly went wrong, *Moving Picture World* declared, "[I]t is a tense moment to the person watching the picture and able to see clearly the girl's danger."[146] Indeed, the mettle performers summoned before the camera rivaled that of the heroines they played on film. "All over the world [Pearl White's] name has become a synonym for courage and daring," *American Magazine* reported. To her "leaps over cliffs, and dives off decks of ocean liners, are as prosaic and uneventful as her morning grapefruit."[147] Brave Mary Fuller "made the courting of danger part of her daily life" on the set of *What Happened to Mary?*[148] So hazardous were the stunts performed by Mollie King in Pathé's *Mystery of the Double Cross* series that no insurance company would assume the risk.[149] Helen Gibson, dubbed "the most daring actress in pictures," ultimately issued a challenge to other performers, vowing to prevent Kalem from promoting her in this fashion "if any other player will attempt the feats shown in 'The Girl Who Dared.'"[150] When the inevitable injuries were sustained, they were always carefully detailed in fan publications, for stars bore real traces of bravery—scars and permanent injuries their characters did not.[151] "Death is ever lurking for these daring performers," *Moving Picture World* concluded.[152]

The women's bravado extended beyond their performances on the set, for even after cameras were turned off, fans were told, many actresses pursued high-octane adventure. Well before she appeared for Pathé as Pauline Marvin and Elaine Dodge, Pearl White's publicity trumpeted her love of exploits more frequently associated with men. "For recreation I like beefsteak and aviation," the actress announced in a piece celebrating her devotion to those most modern indexes of speed and velocity, the automobile and the airplane, machines also favored by Kathlyn Williams. White had "none of the usual qualms or fears about taking risks," one publication explained, for she favored "the excitable and thrilling recreations, and prefers speeding over the country road in a six-cylinder 'gas wagon' to occupying a box at grand opera." White's rival at Universal, Grace Cunard, was described as "the perfect devotee of motoring" for whom no speed was great enough. Kalem's Ruth Roland, star of several

serials, also pursued pastimes not always associated with motion picture beau-
ties. "An expert with the rifle and shotgun," whose rooms were decorated with
"boxing gloves and fencing foils," Roland was said to be "equally proficient
with rod and line."[153] In most cases an actress's bravery and athleticism were
traced to her childhood, as in stories that stressed Helen Holmes's background
in a family of railroad workers, for instance, or Williams's early life on a
Montana ranch, an upbringing which, she said, gave her "that indefinable
'something' which allowed me to mix with wild beasts without much danger."[154] The women's accomplishments, in other words, were not skills honed
for motion picture cameras but deep-seated character traits.

Evidence that serial players carried a taste for sensationalism into their private lives blurred boundaries between their screen characters and their celebrity "personas" in a way that was elemental to the early movie star system,
since the performer was said to summon the same skills on set (and at home)
as her character was shown to embody on the screen. Stories celebrating the
women's physical prowess downplayed cinematic illusion, insisting, quite
forcefully, upon the authenticity of diegetic action sequences. Knowing that
actresses performed many stunts themselves, and that they continued such
risky undertakings on their own time, only enhanced the "hazards" and "exploits" on film: the women's exertions were real, not trickery achieved for
gullible audiences; their courage was genuine, not mimicked for the camera.
So central was this conceit that fans came to rely on the authenticity of screen
stunts. Writing to *Photo-Play Journal*, fan Helen Tarbox confessed, "[M]ost
of all, [Pearl White's] dare devil acting is what I admire."[155] Hence the acute
disappointment expressed by viewers robbed of this pleasure: "I pay my money
to see the star and not their double," one admirer complained to *Photoplay*.[156]

It was not simply that an actress's athletic skill enhanced the action sequences, or that a symbiosis between performers and screen characters bolstered the star system. Behind-the-scenes details also proved that "real"
women, not just fictional heroines, could manifest the strength and prowess
displayed in such fanciful adventure stories. Tales of hardworking motion
picture players, whose professionalism was repeatedly trumpeted in star profiles, anchored fictive exploits in actual accomplishments. Recounting the
danger Kathlyn Williams faced during the filming of the *Kathlyn* series, where
she was mauled by a tiger and nearly run over by a locomotive, *Moving Picture
World* boasted, "[S]he has never refused to risk her own safety for the sake
of a good picture."[157] In a continuing series of articles appearing under her
byline, Pearl White urged young women interested in the film business to be
strong, to learn hobbies, to be fearless, and to keep physically fit. Traits such
as these, she insisted, would boost a young woman's chances in the motion
picture industry much more readily than painstaking beauty treatments or
fancy skin creams.[158]

Proficient stunt work and ardent professionalism were matched by the dynamic role many stars assumed behind the camera as they sought artistic control over their productions. Indeed, movie actresses struggling to assert themselves in a male-dominated industry became vivid symbols of emergent womanhood in fan discourse, as potent, perhaps, as images of Helen Holmes leaping between moving railroad cars. When her husband and director, J. P. MacGowan, was hospitalized in early 1915, it was Holmes herself who took over much of the production of the *Hazards* series, writing scripts, directing episodes, and assuming a leading role in the management of Kalem studios.[159] Nor was Holmes unique in this regard. Grace Cunard trumpeted the creative role she played in serials where she appeared with Francis Ford, claiming, "I write almost every scenario which is used by Mr. Ford and myself. I play the feminine lead in some of them, and I direct some of them besides!"[160] Mary Fuller also wrote many of her own films. Several stars were outspoken in their belief that women ought to assume a much more central role in film production. Women's creative influence would be the only means of ensuring a greater diversity of female characters on the screen, since players would get strong, active roles only if they wrote them themselves, Holmes declared. "And the reason is odd: nearly all scenario-writers and authors for the films are men; and men usually won't provide for a girl things to do that they wouldn't do themselves. So if I want really thrilly action, I ask permission to write it in myself."[161] Following Holmes's lead, Kathlyn Williams argued that women were ideally suited to direct motion pictures because they were naturally "more artistic than men," and their eye for detail was well-suited to the screen's visual canvas. "I believe that women would make as big a success directing as men, if given the right chance and opportunity," she maintained.[162] While celebrating the women's directorial achievements, publicity materials often could not help but draw parallels between the courage of fictional serial heroines and that of women in the film industry. When *The Leopard's Foundling*, a film written and directed by Williams, was released two weeks after the final installment of *The Adventures of Kathlyn*, ads described how it had been "written, directed and acted by 'Kathlyn' herself," as if the screen heroine, back from fighting lions in the Land of Allah, had made her own motion picture.[163]

In the same breath with which they cheered the daring and bravado of serial queens, however, many celebrity profiles were also careful to set the stars' rugged personas against more conventional portraits of womanhood, to contrast celluloid visions of strength and tenacity with a softer femininity evident only after cameras had stopped filming. "When one meets [Pearl White] face to face, she is refreshing in her simplicity and womanly charm," *Motion Picture Classic* reported. "At home the moving picture star, who will dare anything to make her last picture the greatest, reads and plays and cooks and eats and primps like any other girl."[164] *Photoplay*'s interviewer confessed to having been taken aback upon meeting Kathlyn Williams for the first time: "So closely associated has she been of late with deeds of daring and dangerous exploits that one expects to find a dashing, mannish woman arrayed in more or less masculine attire." He professes that it was "disconcerting" to meet instead "a decidedly womanly lady." Williams was "sweet and girlish and fetching" off-camera, another reporter confessed.[165]

Certainly these stories reassured fans that stars retained their femininity even while performing feats of cinematic daring. But they also insistently marked the unaccustomed juxtaposition of feminine delicacy with might and brawn. Athleticism and beauty, perpetually twinned aspects of the serial queen persona, were almost always presented in paradoxical opposition, as many commentators noted the unlikely intersection of fragile feminine anatomy with such rough handling. One writer expressed his astonishment that Helen Holmes's "dainty figure" was "concerned chiefly with tossing itself around the tops of speeding freight trains or over yawning chasms on a horse's back" in the *Hazards of Helen* series. "You'd think a pretty girl like Helen would be afraid of spoiling her looks," Holmes's husband claimed, "but nothing worries her."[166] Indeed, many sobriquets drew attention to the uncharacteristic conjunction of femininity and physical action: Holmes was dubbed a "charming daredevil"; White became "A Pearl in the Rough."[167] Another profile of Holmes found the actress a "very pretty and very charming young lady," fond of wearing elegant gowns, but equally fond of the fact that "she can burst the sleeves of any of them by doubling up her biceps," as if she possessed an inner masculine strength forcibly, but not always successfully, contained within a ladylike shell.[168] "What Sort of Fellow Is Pearl White?" *Photo-Play Journal* asked, acknowledging the actress's disruption of conventional gender norms.[169] "Very few men, not to mention women, would risk themselves to undertake many of the feats accomplished by Kathlyn Williams," one profile declared, noting that the actress possessed traits "unusual to her sex."[170] Williams was depicted in tears as she stood between two lip-smacking lions in one *Motion Picture* cartoon, crying not because she feared the beasts, but because her two cameramen had fled in terror—only she remained brave enough to face the animals.[171] The puzzling amalgam of traditionally masculine fortitude and arresting feminine beauty was manifest most strikingly in a *Sunset* magazine portrait of the star:

> Make, in your mind, a composite picture of Roosevelt in Africa, Daniel in the lions' den, Toomai of the Elephants, Lincoln Beachey and the most daredevilish jacky in the American navy, and if it comes out all pink and white and pretty, with a row of matched pearls for teeth, big blue eyes and a mass of spun-gold hair, you will have a true portrait of Kathlyn Williams, the nerviest 'movie' lady in the land.[172]

Even as commentators struggled to reconcile the serial queens' femininity with their taste for action, Helen Holmes insisted that strength was one of the key attributes of modern femininity, appealing again to the ethic of professionalism. Performing stunts was simply "one of the demands upon a leading woman in pictures that must be met," Holmes maintained, adding that actresses ought to carry them out without "losing sympathy or that air of femininity of which we are all so proud. But by that I do not mean the frail side of woman. I mean the heroic side, deeds of valor, based upon the highest ideals."[173]

Alongside celebrations of their career highlights, accounts of actresses' domestic habits circulated widely in fan publications, furnishing details about romance, home life, and children. If at first fan culture concentrated on the professional résumés of motion picture players, celebrities' personal lives increasingly became a target of interest among movie fans in the early 1910s, as the star system grew to encompass a much broader discussion of family life. Details about intimate attachments between actresses and beloveds, husbands and wives, parents and children all became fodder for the public gaze.[174] Features on stars' homes and home lives, which quickly became central components of their publicity in the midteens, took on additional resonance in the case of serial queens because of the marked absence of domestic life in their screen stories. Were the resolutely independent exploits of fictional heroines echoed in the "real" lives of serial stars as well? Could celluloid fantasies of feminine athleticism and autonomy find parallels offscreen? One might assume that celebrations of female stars' domestic talents undermined, or at least qualified, the vigor they displayed on the screen. Yet, far from eroding the actresses' strength, publicity items on their home lives often showed them able to combine independence, physical prowess, and cunning with more expected feminine pastimes in ways that were not presented within serial plots, which tended to counterpose adventure and domesticity. On the contrary, fan culture showed actresses embracing new feminine roles at home, eking out more egalitarian relationships with men, integrating motherhood with work, and redefining the home front. Details that emerged in these write-ups thus played a key role in suggesting ways that the hyperbolic feminism of screen heroines might be extended into more prosaic, if no less revolutionary, goals. Though less spectacular, perhaps, than leaping onto speeding locomotives, small domestic revolutions in the lives of film personalities helped sketch the contours of modern womanhood for serial fans.

Some actresses explicitly rejected orthodox home life, sounding much like characters they played on film. Professing her dislike of housework, Kathlyn Williams declared a much greater fondness for baseball, fencing, and motoring. "Frankly, I am not domestic," Pearl White confessed at the height of her success, brushing aside conventional expectations.[175] White, who remained single during the early years of her fame, also promoted novel ideas about how contemporary men and women might interact, advocating new "companionate" relationships between the sexes. A complaint from the New York State Federation of Women's Clubs that "films are exerting a degenerating influence upon the young" by encouraging women to be "pals" with men prompted a strong rebuttal from the actress. Women no longer wanted to be placed on pedestals,

White insisted, claiming, "[W]e don't want to be marble; besides, there would not be enough pedestals to go around, anyway." Instead, she offered a model of partnership between the sexes based on friendship and equality. "Why not give our men the same comradeship that many of them never find outside of their clubs?" she asked.[176]

If White advocated a life that "Pauline" herself might have endorsed, other stars, many married with children, offered a more nuanced counterbalance to the resolutely independent characters they played on the screen. Although marriage signified the end of so many heroines' celluloid adventures, this was not always the case with actresses, and fan publications attentive to stars' love lives often demonstrated how marital domesticity did not interfere with the women's professional careers. An announcement of Kathlyn Williams's wedding in 1913 informed fans that the performer "did not allow her marriage to interrupt her picture work, for the day following the ceremony found her busy at work," giving no indication that a strenuous working life threatened blissful matrimony.[177] An article on Helen Holmes's marriage to J. P. MacGowan, called "How Helen Holmes Became Mrs. Mack and a Picture Star," insisted in its very title that the roles of wife and working woman were compatible, if separate. The actress's professional identity ("Helen Holmes") is clearly distinguished from her domestic role as "Mrs. Mack."[178] Some items eager to reconcile seemingly incongruous aspects of the women's lives suggested that the stars channeled their formidable talents into household chores off the set, insisting rather forcefully upon the synchronicity of domestic science and fearless professionalism: "Kathlyn Williams can bake cherry pies and many other kinds of pies after she comes in from the lion's cage," boasted a feature that included the actress's recipe for lemon custard pie.[179] *Motion Picture* supplemented a rather conventional tour of the star's home, in "Kathlyn Williams, Builder," with commentary explaining how she designed and built much of the structure herself.[180]

Helen Holmes's adopted infant daughter provided unique opportunities to feature the performer in intimate circumstances not normally associated with the fictional "Helen," but also to demonstrate how Holmes broke new ground in her maternal role. Holmes lies on the ground, wrench in hand, grease smearing her face, in a photo showing her repairing her stunt car, while daughter Dorothy sits inside an empty tire beside her. Mother and daughter pose within the tire frame in another shot parodying familiar oval-framed serial queen glamour shots.[181] Asked how she planned to rear her daughter, Holmes replied, "She will be dressed in a pair of overalls and play with a monkey wrench . . . and in time you'll see her tied to a driving rod—while the locomotive speeds on its way," as if young "Dot" embodied the promise of womanhood that "Helen" and Holmes herself only pointed toward. Yet always careful to counterpoise these statements with indications of Holmes's womanly virtues, an accompanying story told of two-year-old Dot's debut in a river-crossing stunt with her mother, reporting that the normally fearless Holmes grew nervous while filming the scene. Orthodox maternal traits, like fear for the safety of one's offspring, were held in balance with less customary feats of maternal daring, like fording a river, toddler in hand.[182]

Like star profiles that lauded an actress's delicate femininity offscreen, stories of maternal love and pie baking might have reassured audiences that serial stars still cherished ladylike pastimes in their time off. Yet these stories also served a substantial function in reconciling conventional spheres of femininity, like marriage and motherhood, with much more updated incarnations of womanly strength and autonomy, thus furnishing crucial road maps for female fans who might be trying to reconfigure their own lives beyond the customary strictures of family life. Office workers, retail clerks, and factory laborers, the likely fan base for these films, might have looked to the serial queens' offscreen lives for fresh ideas about womanhood that they could emulate in small, but meaningful ways.

Thus screen narratives that too frequently offered marriage as the conclusion to a heroine's adventures were explicitly countered by the attention paid to stars' private lives in fan publications. Stories that emphasized how actresses combined marriage and work, motherhood and professionalism, pie baking and lion taming resisted the opposition of strength and femininity, so often structurally reinforced in serial plot lines. Only outside the bounds of the text proper could "heroines" like Pearl White and Kathlyn Williams lead truly modern lives. As Gaylyn Studlar stresses in relation to 1920s fan magazines, the circulation of extratextual, biographical information in a fan culture chiefly addressed to women shifted the female gaze toward an invisible, extratextual realm hidden from the screen. Celebrity profiles encouraged reading strategies that "diversified the possibilities of women's looking, as well as their intellectual and emotional response."[183]

I began the chapter with a discussion of the reflexive prologue to *The Mystery of the Double Cross*, describing how the serial acknowledges the interplay between star personas and fictional heroines that many viewers likely folded into their experience of the story. By way of conclusion, I return to that same serial's final installment, which foregrounds the difficulty that so many serial plots have imagining strong female leads. In its concluding episode *The Mystery of the Double Cross* at last reveals the identity of the mysterious "Masked Stranger" who has executed one spectacular rescue after another throughout the unfolding drama. Dressed in male attire, face shielded by cloak and mask, the stranger has masqueraded as a man, fooling everyone, including most viewers. But she is revealed to be none other than heroine Phillipa Brewster's long-lost twin sister in this concluding chapter.

Even as the Stranger embodies much of the story's agency, her sister Phillipa remains inert throughout, captive in various interior locales while figuratively ensnared in villain Bridgey Bentley's schemes to marry her and thereby control her fortune. Poor Phillipa is trapped at home in her bedroom feigning illness during most of the eleventh episode, eventually forced to conceal herself in a closet at Bentley's request; and in the next installment Bentley holds her hostage at his office, threatening to "ruin and disgrace" her father if she does not consent to marry. Phillipa's is an acutely passive stance, compounded by her ignorance of the unfolding inheritance plot that Bentley is manipulating. Both he and hero Peter Hale have seen the telltale double cross tattoo on her arm and become convinced that she is the bride Peter's father has cultivated for his son, and through whom his inheritance will flow; both logically assume that Phillipa is herself aware of the situation, but of course she is not, a fact revealed only at the end when we—and she—discover the existence of her twin sister, similarly tattooed, and Peter's truly intended bride. Phillipa thus becomes the static object of exchange between male characters fighting for her affections: Peter, who believes she is his betrothed; Bentley, who schemes to force her into marriage; and another character, humble Dick Annesley, who truly loves her.

On the other hand, Phillipa's twin, disguised as the Masked Stranger, is a figure of remarkable strength and cunning who rescues the hapless girl on several occasions, as well as Peter Hale himself. Watching Peter and her sister from afar, the Stranger exercises an unrivaled dominance of narrative space and fields of vision. When one of Bentley's cohorts creeps into Phillipa's bedroom and tries to assault her, the Stranger is there to save her as she cowers on the bed. The Stranger also foils Bentley's attempt to poison Peter in the hopes of doing away with his rival for Phillipa's hand in marriage. When Bentley drugs Peter and ties him up to a gun rigged to a timed firing device in the serial's third installment, the Stranger frees him while he remains immobilized, either unconscious and transported around like a sack, or bound and strung up by the hands. In the serial's first spectacular stunt, the Stranger scales the roof of an adjoining building, then crosses to Peter's apartment house on a plank suspended between the buildings, cutting the board in half as she finishes, sending one of Bentley's henchmen plummeting to his death. The Stranger arrives to free Peter just before the clock strikes and the gun goes off. Shots of Phillipa safe at home interrupt the Stranger's rescue at several points, making it clear that she is not performing these feats of heroism, but also drawing a contrast between her inactivity—at one point she is shown asleep— and the Stranger's derring-do. The Stranger also knows far more than other characters, repeatedly advising Peter that Phillipa "is not the girl you seek," and vowing to do everything in her power to "keep you two apart."

So if at first *The Mystery of the Double Cross* seems to relegate Phillipa to a position even more passive than that of earlier serial heroines, eleventh-hour revelations about the Masked Stranger's identity prompt viewers to question their assumptions about feminine heroics. By disclosing the Stranger's gender so late in the story, the plot deliberately plays with audience expectations about

18. The mysterious Masked Stranger frees Peter in *The Mystery of the Double Cross*. (Courtesy of the Academy of Motion Picture Arts and Sciences.)

appropriate womanly conduct, showing us quite pointedly how willing we were to accept Phillipa's victimization and assume the rugged Stranger was male. Only when we measure Phillipa's inertia against her sister's marked intervention do we get a complete portrait of the heroine. The female lead is literally split in two here, across the bodies of the twins, one conventionally feminine and passive, the other masculine and active.

Interestingly it is this brave woman, not helpless Phillipa, who turns out to be the candidate trained as Peter's ideal wife, a mate, his father hoped, who would be "free from the weaknesses so characteristic of the modern young woman." Indeed, a flashback reveals that Mr. Hale had first spotted the girl scrapping with boys on the street, and had been moved to rescue her and prepare her to be his son's companion. One wonders if once Peter finds his intended bride, she must give up her active, masculine side in order to marry, or whether these characteristics were indeed part of the instruction his father had imparted. At first it seems as if marriage and active femininity might be compatible: after she demonstrates how she has donned the Masked Stranger's costume, Phillipa's sister takes off the mask and stands in the Brewster living room in a bifurcated costume, as her feminine head rests atop a body cloaked in masculine attire. "Are you YOU, or aren't you YOU?" Peter asks, to which she replies, "I'm I." United with her intended husband in the end, the sister embraces Peter in the Brewster living room while Phillipa and sweetheart Dick Annesley clasp together on the other side of the room. When the two couples first embrace, a mirrored composition shows Dick and Phillipa together on one side of the screen, while on the opposite side Peter puts his arm around Phillipa's twin, who is still wearing her male attire.

The Mystery of the Double Cross ultimately holds out the possibility that these two "halves" of femininity might be combined in a single woman. Before viewers learn that the Masked Stranger is Phillipa's forgotten twin, Phillipa's image dissolves slowly into the Stranger's in the concluding shot of the penultimate episode, a momentary superimposition hinting at the true nature of the relationship between the two women. Recalling the film's prologue, where an image of actress Mollie King dissolves into that of heroine Phillipa Brewster, the film's final image comes full circle, as King's visage is again superimposed, this time over an image of the Brewster twins at their wedding, dressed identically and posed on opposite sides of the frame. As the sisters move together, King appears, bidding good-bye to film audiences, suggesting that it is her persona which might hold the polarities in balance. It was King, after all, who performed both roles in the film. So while the narrative seems intent on keeping these two facets of femininity at odds, King's profession signals their point of conjunction.

Even though "love and ambition," marriage and independence, are posed as irreconcilable opposites in virtually every serial, as the ending of *The Mystery of the Double Cross* once again illustrates, audiences' growing knowledge of actresses' personal and professional lives drew attention to the novel ways in which many stars approached marriage, motherhood, and work in their off-screen experiences. If scenarios of imprisonment and rescue outweighed daring action sequences in most serial plots, and tangled familial inheritance plots quashed most heroines' ostensible liberation from family ties, celebrity profiles allowed fans to glimpse the small-scale gender "revolutions" lived by movie actresses. Indeed, fan discourse became a vital conduit between the sensational embodiments of modern womanhood viewers saw on film and more pedestrian, but no less significant, changes in the everyday lives of many of their fans. Serial queens rewrote feminine norms within a burgeoning fan culture where the integration of on screen and offscreen lives became the norm. Even if heroines like Pauline and Elaine were repeatedly victimized on the screen, fan magazines celebrated the professional accomplishments and private pastimes of their "lost twin sister," Pearl White, offering a telling counterbalance to images that circulated at the cinema. Serials must always be read against the intertextual field in which they circulated, for such extratextual discourse is fundamental to an understanding of their address to female audiences—audiences that were encouraged to translate breathtaking screen exploits into characteristics of strong femininity that they might introduce into their own lives.

If serials represent the film industry's most sustained attempt to capture and cultivate a female fan base at the end of the nickeodeon era, they do so in a manner that flies in the face of conventional assumptions about the link between increased female patronage and the growing respectability of moviegoing in the teens. Serial content was anything but tame, and reports of audience behavior suggest that fans conducted themselves in anything but a "respectable" manner. The heterogeneous, multitextual, open-ended viewing practice that serials demanded stood in direct opposition to the less distracted forms of spectatorship fostered by classical narratives.

Four

Civic Housekeeping:
Women's Suffrage, Female Viewers,
and the Body Politic

WHEN the venerable National American Woman Suffrage Association released the feature photoplay *Your Girl and Mine* in the autumn of 1914, its
members expressed confidence that the film would "become the star production of the 'movie' year, not excepting *The Adventures of Kathlyn*."[1] Suffrage
leaders, entering a pivotal phase of their campaign, had not failed to notice the
ease with which serials like *Kathlyn* captivated female audiences across the
nation and galvanized their energies around a prolific fan culture. Could such
a formidable constituency be mobilized for the suffrage fight as well? Did
daring serial heroines embody feminist ideals that might be grafted onto the
era's most pressing cause? And could the burgeoning popular appetite for motion pictures be directed toward more pointedly topical fare? Eager to test these
theories, NAWSA leaders engaged the help of serial-maker William Selig at
his Chicago studio, contracting Gibson Willets, writer of the original *Kathlyn*
series, to furnish a scenario of thrills and melodrama wrapped around the suffrage crusade. With the resulting feature, *Your Girl and Mine*, NAWSA, by
its own estimation, "boldly carried its propaganda into the moving-picture,"
booking engagements for the film around the country with speakers at every
stop.[2]

NAWSA's feature film experiment capped a tide of films on women's suffrage released in the early teens, nearly a full decade before the passage of the
Nineteenth Amendment in 1920 guaranteeing voting rights to women. In the
heated final years of the struggle film played a signal role in the debate. Comedies endlessly mocked suffragists and their opponents alike, finding humor in
the social turmoil wrought by the often bitter fight, while the nation's two
leading suffrage organizations—NAWSA and the Women's Political Union—
backed ambitious, multireel films promoting their cause. Seeking to counteract
the comic parodies, NAWSA and the WPU released four films between 1912
and 1914, making suffrage groups among the earliest advocacy bodies to exploit moving pictures at a time when the cinema's powers of social commentary were not always appreciated.[3] This was no accident. Suffrage organizations turned to cinema at a crucial juncture in their campaign: between 1910
and 1912 five states granted female voting rights (none had done so since

1896), several other states held suffrage referenda in 1912, and Congress debated women's enfranchisement for the first time in 1913.[4]

Accounts of the suffrage movement have often minimized the role that motion pictures played in the women's campaign: few historians seem aware of the existence of these films. Yet it is clear that the suffragists themselves viewed their motion picture undertakings with utmost seriousness. This is evident in the timing of the films' release during the most pivotal phase of the campaign, the choice to make feature-length dramas at a time when they remained a costly, novel form, the decision to enlist the aid of men like Selig and Willets, producers of the era's most successful female-oriented films, and the novel ways in which the films were marketed and exhibited. That films assumed such a prominent place in suffrage debates demonstrates the rhetorical sophistication and cultural prominence cinema had achieved in the early teens, enabling it to engage national issues on this level. The new medium was in fact ideally suited to the particular nuances of the suffrage dialogue, for much of the campaign was waged in visual terms through canny use of posters, pageantry, and mass media. During a vital moment in their endeavor, film, like no other medium, offered suffragists a site where modern embodiments of femininity could be visualized, where women's evolving relation to political life could be dramatized, and where a distinctly feminist community could be fostered among patrons of the nation's movie houses.

In film history, too, these early features are rarely mentioned, save by scholars chronicling the legacy of "social problem" pictures. Yet suffrage films are key to an understanding of the dynamics of filmgoing in the midteens, for they express the essential elements of "feminine uplift": stately features on educational subjects addressed to patrons attuned to current political issues. But even as suffrage features succeeded in drawing audiences of women and educated, middle-class viewers, the politicization of motion picture venues, and the audiences therein, left many contemporary commentators uneasy. If serial films had successfully marshaled female filmgoers around models of consumption, by embedding films within a larger field of images, products, and discourses, suffrage films performed a similar function in a much more tangible, and undoubtedly more threatening, arena: politics. Just as serial fans were encouraged to collect spoons, pillow covers, and movie star paraphernalia, pointed suffrage dramas invited audiences to carry lessons from the screen into the practice of their daily lives. It was a tactic that caused considerable vexation within the film industry and outside it, for cinema's place in discussions of fraught topics like enfranchisement was by no means established in the early teens, as the controversy surrounding depictions of vice in the white slave films also demonstrates. Women's suffrage films challenged a nation still grappling with the role that motion pictures might play in sensitive cultural debates, uneasy about the politicization of female audiences, indeed uncertain about women's equality.

Defining Female Citizenship in Suffrage Comedies

Well-intentioned suffrage features sponsored by NAWSA and the WPU fought against the tide of comic shorts that proliferated on the topic in the early teens. Enfranchisement was clearly so topical and so ripe for parody that few motion picture humorists could resist. It is tempting to assume that films sponsored by national suffrage organizations unequivocally endorsed the cause, while slapstick comedies merely lampooned its adherents in demeaning caricature. But this view overlooks contradictions evident in both pro- and antisuffrage campaigns and the degree to which each camp struggled to define a place for women in the political arena, a sphere from which they had long been excluded. Granting full voting rights to women would demand new conceptions of public life and the nature of women's participation there. By persistently linking sexual difference to the cultural geography of public and private life, suffrage comedies on both sides of the debate endeavored to chart the contours of an emergent female citizenship based on political equality, and in doing so often laid bare issues muted in the more high-minded features sponsored by organizations like NAWSA and the WPU.

The most conservative antisuffrage platforms stressed the doctrine that women were "separate but equal," claiming that women belonged at home, not in the civic arena. Women were expected to tend the hearth, while men acted in business and governmental affairs. Placed *above* politics, women were said to embody a realm of higher morality and sentiment beyond the political fray.[5] Within such a system, as Jean Bethke Elshtain points out, women are paradoxically deemed "morally 'superior' because they are politically inferior."[6] Those opposed to equal suffrage imagined drastic repercussions if women gained citizenship through the franchise: partisan differences would alienate husband and wife; activities outside the home would cause women to neglect children and household responsibilities; even the very bounds of femininity might be compromised. Uneasy references to an imagined dissipation of the boundaries between public and private life appeared throughout antisuffrage appeals, one of which worried that the ballot "would multiply our clubs and divide our homes" in a perverse mathematics.[7] Bestowing the vote upon wife and mother would, another traditionalist feared, "dissolve society into a heterogeneous mass of separate persons, whose individual rather than family interests would thenceforth receive political representation."[8] Other opponents of the vote, many of whom were female, did not deny women's growing contribution to social activism in the late nineteenth and early twentieth centuries. Instead they debated the conditions under which this participation could and should take place. Politics, they insisted, with its inherent power struggles and tendency toward corruption, was not a site for women. Virtuous, civic-minded reform furnished the proper context for feminine engagement in public affairs.[9]

Anxieties that course through antisuffrage texts highlight the complexities inherent in defining the nature of female citizenship just as women became increasingly prominent in progressive causes. Sexual difference challenges the body politic, Monique Canto believes, because the polity tends to define itself as socially homogeneous and distinct from private life.[10] Woman's relation to the public arena is thus complicated by her association with the home, a realm supposedly beyond the polity's domain, at the same time as woman's anatomical difference impugns the imagined homogeneity of the social body. Outdated appeals to a doctrine of separate spheres in antisuffrage rhetoric suggest the challenges that women's pronounced social activism posed to traditional conceptions of womanliness. In a world where territorial boundaries no longer successfully mapped masculine and feminine identity, antisuffrage lobbyists sought to uphold a rigidly gendered geography by aligning sexual difference with political and nonpolitical enterprise. A need to reaffirm tangible divisions between male and female domains is evident in the metaphors of dissipation used by opponents of the vote, just as alarmist caricatures of spirited suffragists betray real apprehensions about women's expanding freedoms.

Many one-reel comedies released during these years dramatize simple role-reversal scenarios where male and female domains are transposed in order to figure the disruption enacted by equal suffrage: women learn that they cannot perform "male" tasks in society, while men are demeaned through domestic labor.[11] Titles like *When Women Vote* (Lubin, 1907), *When Women Win* (Lubin, 1909), and *When Women Rule* (Selig, 1912) all imagine life after women have been granted full citizenship.[12] "Things are going to be vastly different when women win the right to vote and do other mannish things," *Moving Picture World* quipped.[13] The mere sight of women running trolley systems, delivering mail, putting out fires, policing city streets, or administering the judicial system generates comedy in a whole range of films where equal enfranchisement is figured as a feminine invasion of public space. Sometimes humor results from the flowery touches women bring to these tasks: in *When Women Win* fastidious, white-gloved ladies clean city streets, business meetings become chatty tea parties, and Friday is declared bargain day at the market.[14] More often than not, however, women's attempts to perform masculine labor fail spectacularly, and the reversal proves untenable. When Jane Higgins is declared a "justicess" in *Jane, the Justice* (Beauty, 1914), romantic interests cloud her judicial mandate, causing her to dismiss a handsome criminal after first trying his case "behind closed doors." "Even the most valiant suffragette will be forced to divest herself of her sterner moods and still more direful tightening equipment" when she sees this comedy, James McQuade told *Moving Picture World* readers.[15] Men decide to escape town rather than suffer the abuses perpetrated by women who have swept into electoral office after winning the vote in *When the Men Left Town* (Edison, 1914). Left behind, their wives are eager at first to demonstrate their independence but soon discover that "tidying up the whole town was subtly different from dusting the parlor and tying velvet bows on the what-not." Trolley cars grind to a halt because "nobody dared to monkey with the dingusses that make the car go." Realizing that they cannot run affairs on their own after all, the women stage a "monster rally" to call their husbands back, producing an ironic reversal of the usual suffrage parade. Once the men reappear, their contrite wives collectively resign from public office.[16] "After many ludicrous experiences attempting to do without the tyrant men" in *The Reformation of the Suffragettes* (Gaumont, 1911), women "find it impossible and rejoice in the return of their erstwhile hated oppressors."[17] Suffragists who attempt to commandeer a fire brigade in *Fire! Fire! Fire!* (Méliès, 1911) realize that equality is "not all their fancy painted it, and they return to their homes both wetter and wiser."[18] More pointedly, the title character in *The Suffragette's Dream* (Pathé, 1909) happily fantasizes a postenfranchisement world of equality between the sexes, then awakes from her reverie to find her husband angry and violent because no dinner has been prepared.[19] Equality in these films can be imagined only as an impossible scenario of inversion in which women usurp male roles.

Men's lives are also shown to be significantly altered when women join the body politic. Poor old Beacher Summers gets a shock when his meek wife Helen runs against him for the mayor's office, persuaded by her aunt, "a violent advocate of women's rights" who is "disgusted with Helen's contentment over domestic affairs," in *When Helen Was Elected* (Selig, 1912).[20] Much to his surprise, she wins the office right out from under him, suggesting the extent to which constitutional equality might displace male advantage. Not only do women invade public life, but the germ of suffragism infects domestic contentedness as well. In *Oh! You Suffragette* (American, 1911) a "happy little family is on the verge of rupture" when the wife becomes "inflated with the suffrage germ and feels that her mission in life lies outside of the family circle."[21] Similarly, "the quiet and peaceful home of John O'Connell has been invaded by the growing spirit of the suffragette and what was once a happy fireside now finds O'Connell doing the family washing" in *When Women Rule*.[22] Disasters result when husbands are forced to take care of children and tend to household responsibilities while their wives selfishly attend official functions. As a suffragist prepares to deliver an electoral speech in *When Women Vote*, her husband shines her shoes, brushes her coat, and minds the baby. When she returns home, the wife rudely rejects the meal her husband has so graciously prepared. Despite the apparent injustice of the situation, he cannot divorce her "when women vote" because women have taken charge of the judicial system.[23] A suffragist who "makes speeches instead of attending to her housework" leaves a young infant at home in her husband's care when she departs to address a local function in *The Baby Question* (Universal, 1913). Unable to cope with his domestic assignment, the husband rushes to the meeting hall, interrupts his wife's speech on the platform, and delivers the screaming babe into its mother's arms. The suffragist's "mother instincts" take over, and she abandons the meeting to care for her child. Returning home, she is "resolved to pay more attention to the home and let the suffrage question slide in favor of the baby question."[24] In *When Women Win* gender transposition is not merely territorial: it is biological, for men even give birth while their wives pace outside in the hospital's waiting room.[25]

Mocking the outrageous perversity of such transpositions, role-reversal comedies destabilize masculine and feminine norms, all the while insisting that traditional assumptions about separately gendered domains had a metaphysical basis. By staging these inversions so spectacularly, the comedies also unmask fears that if women gained power and a voice in society, they would orchestrate affairs to their own advantage. Still, the piteous fate that men suffer at the hands of enfranchised women hints at the inequity of a system where one sex assumes all of the household duties while the other enjoys the benefits of civic association. Denied even the most basic rights, men are finally forced to campaign for equal enfranchisement in *When Men Vote* (Universal, 1914), a horrific vision of the future where "the entire social order is reversed" and women control financial and governmental affairs.[26] Although wives oppress husbands in these alarmist dramas, their inverted structures all but acknowledge that existing divisions of labor might also be less than fair. Emphasis unquestionably falls on the restoration of traditionally gendered domains in the end, yet role reversal comedies also crystallize feminist proposals in a way that no other medium could. The prospect of female police officers, judges, and doctors, not to be fully realized for another half century, is frankly imagined in these films, even if only in jest.

If role-reversal plots attempted to visualize a world where women might be more integrated into public life, albeit with disastrous results, another body of comedies sensationalized the very prominent rallying tactics that proponents of the vote used to publicize their cause. In fact, at least two shorts—*How Women Win* (Powers, 1911) and *Was He a Suffragette* (Republic, 1912)—incorporate footage of actual suffrage demonstrations into comedic plot lines, suggesting the ease with which suffragists' methods could be used against them.[27] Partisan demonstration is equated with hysteria in *Oh! You Suffragette* when a mischief-maker liberates a cageful of mice at a suffrage rally, scattering the frightened activists and sending the title character back to the "bosom of her despised family for man's protection."[28] Imp's three-reel 1914 drama *The Militant* derives "much spectacularism" from its sensational depiction of suffrage protests. Activists destroy railroad tracks, dynamite buildings, stage counterraids on the police, and riot in a curbside brawl with men, all in a film that attempts to show the ineffectiveness of combative protests associated with the British campaign.[29] In *A Militant Suffragette* (Pathé, 1914) Asta Nielsen plays a young Englishwoman caught up in the cause. As W. Stephen Bush saw it, "the sweet harmonies of the home are vividly contrasted with the strife and turmoil of a militant suffragette." Upon hearing the "wild oratory of her older and homelier sisters," she joins "the window-smashing brigade" of "frenzied feminists."[30] Riots in Parliament, bombings, and prison force-feedings—all notorious aspects of the British fight—are carefully re-created in the film. A two-page trade ad celebrated the film's "splendid exposition of the methods of the militant suffragism that have excited the wonder of the whole world and filled the jails of England." Large photographs show how "the suffragette breaks shop windows . . . while in jail she is forcibly fed." Order is restored in the end, however, and, as Bush reports, "the last scene shows home as the true sphere of woman."[31] Thanhouser's 1913 film also called *A Militant Suffragette* staged spectacular suffrage protests on American soil, led by "one of the famous High Street Gang" imported directly from England.[32] Such films played upon the spectacle value of suffrage demonstrations, then, while at the same time indulging in fantasies of repression. But the threat that such protests posed was often barely concealed. *A Day in the Life of a Suffragette* (Pathé, 1908) depicts a group of activists rallying and speaking in public as hysterical and out of control—"drunk with their own words and getting up to battle pitch . . . screaming revolutionary songs," in one reviewer's description. At one point suffragists overpower police, and "the female wave sweeps over their prostrate bodies." Finally subdued by the militia, the women are last seen "meekly following their husbands on the way back to their domestic duties."[33] Even though conventional order is restored in the final moments, the image of prostrate policemen trampled by demonstrators suggests acute anxieties about the force that women embody when they mobilize together in public.

Other comedies trade upon the transgressiveness of women in public by rendering suffragists' rallies fodder for an eroticized male gaze. Civic demonstration collapses easily into sexual exhibitionism in *How They Got the Vote* (Edison, 1913) and *Suffragette Minstrels* (Biograph, 1913) where it assumes a decidedly carnal aura. Capitalizing on the extent to which the female body in public is, as Mary Russo suggests, "always already transgressive—dangerous and in danger," these films associate women's political agitation with an indecent display of female anatomy.[34] If the demeaning caricature of the "shrieking sisterhood"[35] so often reduced suffrage protests to a collective temper tantrum, erotic displays such as these equally transmuted suffrage strategy, which emphasized the decorum and propriety of its spokeswomen. In *Suffragette Minstrels* a band of activists seen staging a parade at the beginning of the film later perform a minstrel show "for men only" where they dance onstage. Through the point of view of two rubes armed with a powerful spyglass, we see closeups of the women's thighs as they dance in kneesocks and kilts. Suffrage demonstration, which is glimpsed only briefly at the beginning of the film, is thus recouped for male viewers as an eroticized spectacle through the very means of cinema. Spectators are offered a refiguration of potentially unsettling female activism that explicitly reestablishes masculine command over social space. Optical mastery supersedes women's empowerment in these celluloid battles.

In *How They Got the Vote* an ardent British suffragist promotes her cause by exposing herself in public. At the opening of the film she disrupts a sedate gathering by boldly removing her fur wrap to reveal a "Votes for Women" banner pinned across her shirtfront, which we are privileged to view in a cut to a medium close-up. The strategy proves temporarily ineffective, however, since men flee the room. The film concentrates on the exploits of a young man infatuated with the suffragist's daughter, but unable to win her "as he is a mere man and not much in favor of the suffrage."[36] Desperate, he seeks the help of a magician, who gives him two statuettes, one marked "Progress," the other "Sleep." With the latter he is able to halt the flow of life at London Bridge, Piccadilly Circus, and other prominent city landmarks, all rendered in freeze-frame. With their city paralyzed London's leaders are willing to do anything to restore normality, even adopt a suffrage platform as the young man advises. They do so, and holding aloft the "Progress" statue, the man brings the city back to life. "Of course he gets the girl and of course the suffragette gets the vote," quipped the *Edison Kinetogram*.[37] Like *A Suffragette in Spite of Himself* (1912), another Edison comedy shot in London at the same time, the film capitalizes upon the notoriety of the British campaign set against the grandeur of London location shooting, a feature that was played up in publicity for both films. In *How They Got the Vote*, the view of the suffragist's body on display early in the film is matched not only by that of famous London landmarks but in this case the added uniquely *cinematic* spectacle of freeze-frame photography. Even in this manifestly pro-suffrage comedy, full female citizenship entails the disruptive exhibition of women in public and the attendant disturbance of social space.

In several other films men assume the exhibitionist role so often assigned to *female* activists, but in these cases the aberration serves only to emphasize how unsuited men are for such attention. Reviews of *When Women Go on the Warpath* (1913) explain that mischievous suffragists confiscate men's trousers in order to prevent them from voting; those who show up to cast ballots must do so in their underwear. "The few men who do appear in abbreviated garments and make-shifts are run in as disorderly persons," according to *Moving Picture World*.[38] Yet however glaring a spectacle the men make of themselves, they are not reduced to erotic objects. A crotchety English antisuffragist in *A Suffragette in Spite of Himself* also finds himself at the center of attention when two pranksters pin a "VOTES FOR WOMEN" banner on his back. Strolling around London landmarks unaware, he is subjected to the same hostility as the activists he abhors when he is accosted outside a men's club and chased by police. Titles comment ironically on his situation, crying, "Is this a suffrage assault?"

19. Men make spectacles of themselves in *A Sufragette in Spite of Himself.*

and "Chained to the palings!" The man is eventually rescued by a troupe of
suffragists who recognize the banner on his back. But quickly surmising that
he is actually against their cause, the women subject him to further battery.
Although the gentleman attempts to retreat to the safety of his home at the end
of the film, he finds no solace there either, for both his wife and his maid have
hidden suffrage proclamations throughout the house, politicizing even this site.

The film, which *Moving Picture World* pronounced "a thoroughly amusing
comedy,"[39] mocks the man's denunciation of suffragism at the same time as it
allows us to recognize the trials he faces outdoors in his "altered" body. Once
he bears the suffragist banner, the gentleman can no longer be perceived as he
once was. Commonplace activities in the streets of London (buying a newspaper, walking in the park) take on new meaning under the rubric of suffragism.
Feminism here involves, quite literally, the transformation of one's body in the
public sphere. By forcing a superimposition of the activities of a suffragist
upon those of a quintessential English gentleman, complete with bowler and
umbrella, *in the same body*, the film asks us to consider how differently male
and female bodies are construed in public, and how the female body trans-
gresses there. *A Suffragette in Spite of Himself* thus speaks to the would-be
(female) suffragist, to the woman who must imagine herself in a new role in
society, who must understand that her position there will be substantially different from a man's and that her presence will meet significant challenge. In
its comic conflation of conservative gentleman and radical activist the film

reverses the portraits of "mannish" suffragists found in the nastier comedies. Where those films attempt to show that politics demands the erasure of femininity, *A Suffragette in Spite of Himself* suggests that being a feminist in public is quite a different thing from being a man in public.

It was not only the suffragists' disdain for *social* boundaries that alarmed their opponents; advocates of the vote also symbolized a dangerous transgression of anatomical norms. Caricatured "mannish" activists commonly appeared in antisuffrage rhetoric, embodiments of a femininity distorted by political agitation. Engagement in the nation's body politic could only "coarsen and contaminate the [female] sex," according to a 1912 editorial in the *Brooklyn Citizen*, for "the strong-minded and hard-featured woman, as most suffragettes are, repels the male."[40] Such views position the body as the indisputable locus of femininity, while at the same time revealing just how profoundly new female freedoms threatened common assumptions about sexual difference. If the political sphere is figured as *public space*, the female body cannot be imagined there, except as an erotic indulgence or a grotesque spectacle of freakish transsexuality. A 1915 poster opposing women's enfranchisement encapsulates these fears in clear spatial terms: "Which Do You Prefer? The Home or Street Corner for Women. Vote No on Woman Suffrage," the lettering proclaims.[41] Sketches of two women in adjacent circular frames illustrate the options proposed in the slogan. One on the left features a contented mother at home with her adoring young babe; another on the right shows a suffrage advocate hawking leaflets on a street corner, features haggard, mouth distorted in cry, hair windswept and disheveled, nose hooked and witchlike. Her hand does not support a child but wields a leaflet advertising an upcoming suffrage rally. Nor do her eyes meet the gaze of an adoring babe; they are turned upward in a semblance of madness or delusion. The transformation of womanhood potentially enacted by the franchise is imagined topographically in this poster, through the implication that politicized women will abandon their homes for the urban street corner—a site less associated with politics than with prostitution. The polarized caricatures, and the individual frames within which they are encased, enforce a further separation between the two realms. Little reference is made to female voting rights, save the suggestion that readers vote against granting women the ballot; the issue is neatly transposed into one of appropriate "womanliness" to be arbitrated solely by men. It is not simply the written text that solicits a male subject with the invocation "Which Do You prefer?" but the visual organization of the image as well. Framed in paired circles, the two women are pictured as if viewed through an instrument of enhanced vision, like a telescope or binoculars. The threatening physical mobility of women is thus recouped through the omniscience of an implied male gaze. Yet, by presenting different contemporary manifestations of femininity, the poster acknowledges the range of choices open to women in modern life,

20. Which Do You Prefer? (Rare Books Division, New York Public Library, Astor, Lennox and Tilden Foundations.)

even while it condemns nontraditional options and reveals that the debate over enfranchisement engaged issues far beyond voting rights.

Wavering boundaries between masculinity and femininity are inscribed on the body itself in another group of films, which literalize an imagined role reversal in visions of transvestism.[42] *The Suffragette's Dream, For the Cause of Suffrage* (Méliès, 1909), and *A Cure for Suffragettes* (Biograph, 1912) all feature female activists dressed in male attire.[43] Women in the last film appear in men's suits and hats with thin mustaches painted on their upper lip. The "masculinization" of the female body figured in these comedies implies women's alienation from their own anatomy in the political arena. In the case of *A Cure for Suffragettes* this is registered as an explicit alienation from the reproductive body. Transvestite suffragists abandon their babies on the sidewalk outside a meeting hall, where the infants are retrieved and cared for by policemen passing by. Such transformations might someday be written on the body itself, as one suffragist predicted in *Photoplay*'s narrativization of Thanhouser's *A Militant Suffragette*: "Women will be born to attain a height of six feet and a weight of two hundred, the great combination of both brains and brawn, a combination that is wholly lacking in man today," she tells her husband.[44] Visions of female activists parading around in men's clothing, "trying to be as masculine as possible," are echoed in at least two films where husbands don women's attire in order to infiltrate suffrage rallies.[45] In *For the Cause of Suffrage* the slight Mr. Duff disguises himself as a suffragist with the help of his cook's skirts, a wig, and plenty of padding. A quick shave of his beard, "the ornament which heretofore revealed his sex," and Duff is off to the suffragists' meeting, where the lead activist is herself dressed as a man. He takes the stage and declaims antisuffrage arguments to the assembled crowd, only to be chased from the hall, down the street, and into the water.[46] According to *Moving Picture World*, "that Mr. Duff should be under the domination of a woman of his wife's Amazonian characteristics is not to be accepted as a travesty. It is quite likely to be true."[47] Equality of the sexes is played out across the bodies of men and women in horrific visions of diminutive men and their hulking suffragist wives. Poor Mr. Bibbs, whose "four feet had no chance against his six foot wife," is dragged by the ear and forced to march in a "Votes for Women" parade in *Was He a Suffragette*.[48] Cross-dressing comedies not only dramatized fears about how partisan activity might "coarsen" women, then, but exploited corollary fears about the "emasculation" of American men at the hands of assertive women. "We are producing a generation of feminized men, who will be fit only to escort women to poll or public office," one commentator feared. Soon all distinctions between the sexes would be erased. New York, the nation's most "feminized city," was breeding "an epicene type which unites the weakness of both sexes, a sort of man-woman."[49]

The destabilization of social geography and gender identity evident in so many comedies is particularly pronounced in the 1914 Keystone short *A Busy Day*, where Charlie Chaplin appears in drag as an especially obstreperous suffragist.[50] Chaplin's performance, complete with hat, wig, voluminous skirts, and parasol, marks the logical extreme of cross-dressing episodes incorporated in other suffrage comedies. Except in this case Chaplin is neither a female suffragist who voluntarily adopts male attire, nor an angry husband who disguises himself in women's clothing. He plays an ugly, "mannish" woman of the kind so often described in antisuffrage literature. In drag, Chaplin embodies the supposedly eroded femininity of militant activists. Although nominally female, the suffragist retains Chaplin's masculine features and adopts behavior unsuited to demure womanhood: she wears heavy boots under her clothes, immodestly hikes up her petticoats to climb a set of bleachers, blows her nose into her skirt, then slugs a man sitting beside her, finally engaging in an all-out brawl before the film is through.[51] Masquerading as a woman, Chaplin brings to life the grotesque specter of androgyny so often associated with feminism in the popular imagination. Here again political equality is imagined as that which would erase all sexual difference, since Chaplin's suffragist dislocates masculine and feminine norms in a particularly frightening amalgam. Remarking on the contradictions of cross-dressing, Annette Kuhn observes that the adoption of attire associated with the opposite sex produces a distance between codes associated with one gender (through attributes like clothing) and actual anatomical difference. While the codes can be manipulated—often for comic effect in scenes where we understand a character's "true" sex while

21. Chaplin's suffragette poses for news cameras at a suffrage parade in *A Busy Day*.

diegetic characters are fooled—anatomical features cannot be so easily altered. As a result, Kuhn argues, transvestism ironically can *confirm* the body as the locus of absolute difference.[52] Misogynist impersonations of women, such as the one Chaplin performs here, experiment with gender ambiguity only to discard it.

At the same time as Chaplin's suffragist is mocked and demeaned through her association with unflattering masculine qualities, she is also characterized by excessive signifiers of femininity. Her exaggerated makeup, highly piled coiffure, and abundant petticoats register an overaccumulation of womanly attributes. Indeed, suffrage activists were often demeaned through the characterization of their behavior as hysterical, or *excessively* feminine. Massive rallies of vocal demonstrators were frequently discredited as "the shrieking sisterhood," an image of individual female psychosis writ large in agitation. An overly emotional temperament rendered women unsuited for partisan affairs, at least in the conservative imagination whose idealization of virtuous womanhood obviously depended upon the concomitant demonization of deviant femininity, which equated militancy with hysteria.

In addition to confusing gender norms, Chaplin's militant disrupts spatial and optical patterns of looking in the film. Structured through a series of reversals, *A Busy Day* begins with the suffragist perched in a crowded bleacher stand watching a parade. Crosscutting conveys an impression of point of view, alternating between shots of the audience (including Chaplin) and views of the parade. While not strictly aligned with the crowd's sight line, the cuts set up a clear pattern of alternation between onlookers and visual spectacle. Even at this stage, however, Chaplin's character threatens to unhinge the film's spectral organization, making a "spectacle" of herself in the bleachers through her obnoxious antics. She eventually leaves her seat (and her position of optical privilege) to enter the parade site, joining another suffragist who has disrupted the event in a form of protest. In doing so, Chaplin's character invades a composition previously associated with her own point of view. The association is clear: when she enters the political arena and assumes a posture of protest, she becomes an object of sensation. News cameras on hand to record the parade are now visible in these compositions as well, demonstrating how completely the suffragist's gaze has been appropriated so that she herself becomes the focus of interest. She seems to relish this role, however, pausing to pose for a newsreel camera, even lifting her skirts for the photographer in a gesture that once again reduces partisan agitation to erotic exhibitionism. Thus, in addition to inscribing a confused and confusing medley of gender norms in Chaplin's masculinized, hyperfeminine suffragette, like other suffrage comedies the film also struggles to carve out a place for women in modern life. Under pressure of producing a new feminine social space consistent with the demands of equal suffrage, the film's own optical and spatial systems collapse. Although *A Busy Day* is nominally organized around the suffragette's gaze, she persistently invades the space of action, blurring the alternation of spectator and spectacle established through patterns of crosscutting.

By exploding formerly rigid polarities of gender identity and separate spheres, comedies like *A Busy Day* at once register and resist rapidly changing expectations about women's lives that had been set in motion by the suffrage debate. A repeated emphasis on inversion and reversal in these comedies, regardless of the stance each ultimately adopts on the franchise, suggests their failure to conceive sexual difference outside patterns of binary opposition; they portray a closed system turned on its head, blind to alternative paths.

Suffrage comedies illustrate just how markedly the possibility of women's enfranchisement challenged the dominant organization of gendered space that had aligned men with public affairs, while relegating women to a private (and ostensibly nonpolitical) realm. Equal suffrage forced society to reimagine women's interactions with public life; it necessitated an entirely new conception of cultural space, one that admitted women as citizens; and it demanded a reconception of the female body at public sites, where it had most likely been construed only as an object of spectacle. Cinema became an essential instrument through which these new social topographies could be mapped in the imaginary landscape on screen. As a medium through which gendered spectators were addressed and constructed, it stood to perform a significant role in suffrage organization efforts to recruit female viewers for the cause with its potential to reach a new constituency of Americans.

Recruiting Female Viewers

Alarmed by the ridicule to which they and their cause had been subjected on America's movie screens, both the National American Woman Suffrage Association (NAWSA) and the Women's Political Union (WPU) turned to motion pictures in 1912, seeking to exploit the medium in the service of their cause. The Eclair Company released a one-reel comedy, *Suffrage and the Man*, under the auspices of the WPU in June of that year, while NAWSA cooperated with Reliance on the production of a two-reel drama, *Votes for Women*, that same month, a strategy that, according to *Photoplay*, was "looked upon as one of the best publicity moves which the Suffrage Association has yet taken."[53] Much more ambitious feature-length dramas followed. The WPU produced its four-reel picture *Eighty Million Women Want——?* in 1913, and NAWSA corresponded with a formidable eight-reel melodrama, *Your Girl and Mine*, the next year. Comparing the latter to the celebrated early features *Quo Vadis?* and *Cabiria*, one supporter declared that "*Your Girl and Mine* will be an entire evening's entertainment and will not have to dispute honors with any 'two-reel comedies.'"[54] Crafting active, likable suffragist heroines who led on screen followers in victorious campaigns for the franchise, suffragists aimed to counter satirical comedies, while at the same time drawing a female movie audience weaned on stories of action-adventure, romance, and melodrama.

In turning to film, suffrage organizations hoped to mobilize new recruits for their cause during a pivotal period when several states held suffrage referenda and Congress voted on women's enfranchisement for the first time. Indeed, *Your Girl and Mine* was rushed into release in the autumn of 1914 in the hopes that it might influence suffrage measures on the ballot in seven states that November.[55] But while the suffragists' turn to motion pictures might seem the epitome of feminized uplift so sought after by film industry leaders, in fact the use of cinema in such an overtly partisan manner and the marshaling of its viewers around such an obviously feminist cause did not sit well with many in the industry.

Cinema's capacity to attract mass audiences whose allegiances were demonstrated so forcefully in fan culture presented the suffragists with an opportunity to extend their already novel rallying tactics into the motion picture arena. Their decision to exploit film drew upon newly emboldened elements of their campaign, tactics designed to defy expectations about feminine reticence and domesticity through highly vocal and visible forms of public demonstration. Speeches, rallies, and pageants organized around the country by the WPU and NAWSA's increasingly radical Congressional Committee laid a claim for women in the national landscape, while drawing considerable attention to the cause.[56] "Trolley tours" and car journeys through the country allowed activists to promote their cause at open-air speaking stops in small towns and communities. Large-scale marches, like the delegation of several thousand women who strode up New York's Fifth Avenue in 1912, allowed suffragists to demonstrate the breadth of support for their cause, while showing the new face of modern womanhood.[57] Stage productions, such as *How the Vote Was Won*, were mounted by local groups eager to dramatize the campaign in popular form. And ambitious pageants, like the one staged on the steps of the Treasury Building in Washington the day before President Wilson's inauguration in 1913, turned national landmarks into political forums.[58] Indeed, the persuasive rhetoric of plays and open-air pageants had been credited with winning the California franchise in 1911.[59]

Highly vocal and visible tactics such as these brought "the feminine trooping into public life,"[60] as one British activist described. Marveling at the "picturesque propaganda" and "spectacular publicity" that suffragists had gained through these strategies, Bertha Damaris Knobe claimed victory: "[T]he sought-after 'man in the street' . . . who had never seen a suffraget [*sic*] except on the funny page" had been moved by such displays—"awed and interested, [his] ridicule was turned to respect."[61] Tactical invasions of public sites dramatized actual changes in women's lives, for as Martha Vicinus puts it, "freedom of movement came to symbolize the wider freedoms women were seeking through the vote."[62] Studying the imagery of the more militant British campaign (upon which the WPU based some of its tactics), Lisa Tickner observes that through the "production of their own representations" in posters, banners, leaflets, and plays, suffragists circulated positive images of female activists and activity; and by "producing themselves" in forms of public spectacle like rallies and demonstrations, suffragists "embodied" the scale of support for women's votes.[63] Visual presentation of suffrage imagery, through pageant and icon, was as important to the movement as verbal rhetoric, Tickner maintains, because the definition of womanliness was so much a visual one, and the "public expected to see the virtues and vices of femininity *written on the body*."[64]

Marches and parades also symbolized the freedoms women *did not* enjoy during these years. By insisting upon women's right to participate in communal affairs, these spectacles signified suffragists' efforts to redefine women's cultural interactions. Alone, women on city streets and in downtown parks might have been assaulted or taken for streetwalkers. Gathering in groups of thousands, however, they challenged such assumptions, as a participant in a 1913 demonstration testified: "All my girlhood mother had repeated that a lady should never allow herself to be conspicuous. To march up Fifth Avenue had promised to flout directly one's early training."[65] Such acts reappropriated female spectacle on feminist terms. They also added a decidedly political dimension to debates about women's participation in urban street culture that also circulated in discussions of white slavery and sexual danger: here the political consequences of women's engagement in public life are manifest. Suffragists' assertive rallying tactics also reveal the obstacles inherent in redefining women's relation to affairs of state, however symbolically, for prominent demonstrations did not always render public space safe for women. The ten thousand suffragists parading in Washington, D.C., on the eve of President Wilson's 1913 inauguration were mobbed by spectators along the route. Accorded little police protection, the marchers were able to push their way through the hostile crowds only with the help of sympathetic male supporters who formed a human wall. Some three hundred women required hospitalization after the onslaught.[66] Because demonstrations of this kind deliberately and defiantly "breached the social distance between men and women," according to Vicinus, they left women vulnerable to physical assault.[67]

However much maligned, aggressive public protests promoted by the Women's Political Union proved the efficacy of waging the battle for enfranchisement in visual terms and of staging the debate in conspicuous forums, a field of contest for which the cinema was ideally suited. Both NAWSA and the WPU evidently understood, when they turned to motion pictures in the early 1910s, that alternative figurations of modern womanhood in art and mass media had become an important mode of argument. Cinema, growing in popularity and influence, was a logical medium in which to document their demonstrations and through which to mobilize an expanded constituency. As suffragists' tactics shifted toward visible embodiments of the cause, then, suffragists diversified their campaign to include a novel exploitation of the new motion picture medium. In fact, coverage of rallies and demonstrations in newsreels became an important component of these events early on, in order that pageants and marches staged in one community might be brought before a much broader filmgoing audience.[68] Again, British suffragists were particularly adept at exploiting mass media publicity. Organizers invited newsreel cameras to film a Hyde Park rally in 1908, and American leaders soon followed suit. Footage of the large 1912 parade in New York appeared not only in NAWSA's *Votes for Women* but in at least one antisuffrage comedy as well. Ironically, perhaps, Gaumont newsreel footage of the 1913 march in Washington was called as evidence in the case investigating police misconduct at the parade.[69] A Brooklyn suffragist, already versed in the use of lantern slides in her oratories, excitedly seized upon the opportunity to screen footage of a 1911 march to her audiences, explaining that she hoped to "get up more films appropriate for the cause—little suffrage plays perhaps. . . . We intend to have moving picture shows in many parts of town."[70] Not content to record just the visual elements of their campaign, the movement's leaders also took advantage of Thomas Edison's pioneering Kinetophone sound-recording technology to capture various pro-suffrage speakers in early 1913, intending to screen the finished product at theaters throughout the country.[71] Chicago organizers also made good use of the medium's educational potential when women won the vote in Illinois, filming scenes that showed novice female voters how to register and cast ballots in their first election.[72]

But it was in feature-length dramas that suffragists concentrated their cinematic campaign. Well-known suffrage leaders, whom viewers might have glimpsed in newsreels, played notable roles in many of these dramas and contributed greatly to their appeal. NAWSA vice president Jane Addams was cast in *Votes for Women*, along with the organization's president, Dr. Anna Howard Shaw: "[O]n this account the film is attracting attention throughout the whole country and even abroad," *Photoplay* reported.[73] Shaw appeared again in *Your Girl and Mine* two years later, while WPU leader Harriot Stanton Blatch played herself in *Eighty Million Women Want——?*, aided by noted British activist Emmeline Pankhurst, whose screen debut caused one critic to announce that "American suffrage leaders have come around to Mrs. Pankhurst at last." Cinema's ability to picture legendary figures whom many viewers had never seen was clearly an element to be touted in publicity. Trade advertisements assured exchanges and theater owners that "world renowned personages" like Blatch and Pankhurst made *Eighty Million Women* a "self advertising" feature sure to be "the biggest money getter of a decade." One ad claimed that "no more advertised personages can be found today than those *featured* here."[74] *Moving Picture World* justifiably concluded that suffrage organizers exploited cinema "with the double object of aiding the cause and becoming personally known to thousands of women all over the world who already know them by name," when *Votes for Women* opened in 1912.[75] Indeed, cameos by leading activists proved a popular feature of suffrage dramas, according to contemporary observers. Shaw received a "warm reception as she appeared on the screen" before the audience gathered for the premiere of *Your Girl and Mine*, and Emmeline Pankhurst's debut in *Eighty Million Women* generated "more applause from the audience than all the rest of the play" at the film's premiere.[76] Screen appearances by noted activists expanded another principal arm of the suffrage struggle, then—the public "embodiment" of new feminine ideals, of which the movement's leaders were the most prominent and significant examples. Women like Addams, Shaw, Blatch, and Pankhurst bore witness to evolving definitions of womanhood in the prewar years. Challenging and broadening acceptable gender norms for these women involved not simply creating fictional prototypes but reinventing oneself.

In addition to acting on the screen in signature roles, distinguished suffrage leaders often appeared in person at screenings to introduce films and to field questions afterwards. Indeed, suffrage groups exploited novel exhibition strategies that incorporated suffrage activists' celebrated talents for public oratory and verbal argument. When the print of *Eighty Million Women Want——?* was delayed for two hours before its official premiere at the Bryant Theatre in New

York, Harriot Stanton Blatch reportedly addressed the waiting crowd with a humorous lament about "the inefficiency of mere men." Speakers then entertained the audience with calls for Blatch and Anna Howard Shaw to run for the United States Senate in New York State.[77] At the first commercial screening of the film at the Loew's Circle Theater, the hall was crowded with patrons who watched the melodrama, then "listened attentively" to speakers onstage, including Blatch herself. On-screen appearances publicized suffragists' live speaking jaunts by introducing them to a whole new public, while the appearance of reputable speakers at the films drew well-heeled viewers to the cinema. In fact, the WPU planned to have speakers present at every showing of the film across the country.[78]

A central tenet of feminist advocacy from the late nineteenth century onwards, public oratory served an integral rhetorical function in the suffrage crusade, a factor ironically underscored in Lyman Abbott's *anti*suffrage address to the National League for the Civic Education of Women in 1908. In rejecting women's enfranchisement, Abbott claimed to speak on behalf of "the great silent constituency—the wives, the mothers, the daughters, who neither strive nor cry, and whose voice is not heard in the streets": women, he argued, who "are so averse to public life that they will not even publicly protest against an endeavor to force them into public life."[79] Speaking before movie audiences, then, suffrage leaders insisted not only on having a voice in public affairs but on the right to speak for themselves. Spokeswomen who accompanied suffrage films may have also drawn upon the tradition of the movie lecturer, which had a brief revival around 1908.[80] Onstage lecturers lent the cinema claims to an educated and "cultured" status—one of the reasons that exhibitors may have welcomed lobbyists into their venues. Film lecturers were predominantly male, however. Thus while the presence of upright and articulate suffragists at the cinema furnished evidence of the medium's newfound propriety, they did so in a way that likely challenged patrons' expectations about womanly decorum. The revival of lecturers served an important narrative function during this transitional period as well, clarifying and elaborating story material as evolving cinematic vocabulary struggled to keep pace with increasingly complex narratives. By enhancing a viewer's absorption, lecturers contributed to the development of a classical diegesis in the cinema of narrative integration. Suffrage speakers who appeared before and after feature-length screenings likely had exactly the opposite effect, however. By directly addressing the audience, they hoped to incite film viewers to action beyond the theater's walls. If conventional film lecturers sought to draw spectators into a fictive screen world, suffrage oratory aimed to mobilize viewers for subsequent action outside the movie house.

When cast in silent film productions, suffrage leaders ironically had to forgo the powerful oratory for which they were renowned. Describing her experience acting in *Your Girl and Mine*, Anna Howard Shaw explained that she had

22. Emmeline Pankhurst addresses film audiences in the prologue to *Eighty Million Women Want——?*

prepared a lengthy speech for a scene where she is shown appealing to the state's lieutenant governor, only to have the director request that she limit her remarks to thirty seconds of screen time. "It would be the quickest conversion to suffrage on record," she joked.[81] However muted, suffragists' persuasive rhetoric remained an integral part of the cinematic campaigns. *Eighty Million Women Want——?* in particular incorporated an especially novel use of suffrage oratory. In addition to playing themselves in the story (and sometimes introducing the film at screenings), Harriot Stanton Blatch and Emmeline Pankhurst both appear in a short preface to the film where each is shown "speaking" directly to the audience. After an intertitle introducing Pankhurst as the "leader of the English Militants," she emerges from behind a printed curtain, bows her head slightly, then seems to speak to viewers beyond the camera, finally disappearing again behind the curtain. Pankhurst's subdued appearance and restrained manner belie her reputation for militancy and radicalism. Still, contemporary commentators noted the activist's "characteristic and decisive gestures" and "all the little familiar tricks in the use of her hands and little smiles."[82] Blatch gives a similarly modest performance in the film's preface. Following a dissolve from the Pankhurst sequence, Blatch appears seated behind a desk. Without acknowledging the camera or the audience, as Pankhurst does, Blatch makes notes to herself, then reads them "aloud." Even as each leader's screen debut alludes to her public speaking talents, it also silences her. Both women "speak," but neither sound accompaniment nor intertitles convey what they are saying. While this introductory sequence shares affinities with vignettes often used to introduce characters or players in films of the period, it clearly points beyond events on screen. Blatch and Pankhurst appear not as diegetic characters, but as themselves, just as they might introduce the film in person. Pankhurst's direct gaze, in particular, appeals to viewers in an extratextual space in an effort to marshal them for the cause. By including silent speeches in *Eighty Million Women*, suffragists evidently aimed to draw viewers out to attend rallies and demonstrations where they might match voice and image. In fact, the release of *Eighty Million Women* coincided with a speaking tour Pankhurst had organized on the East Coast. New Yorkers who had seen her on screen in November 1913 could also see her in person at Carnegie Hall later that same month.[83] Direct appeals to viewers remind us that suffrage films not only hoped to attract female customers; they also aimed to rally *feminist* viewers. If the suffrage campaign sought to have the rights of citizenship—previously held only by men—conferred upon women, then multireel suffrage dramas sought to marshal female viewership in a medium typically governed by masculine address.

Suffrage organizations thus viewed moving picture patrons as potential agents of social change, rather than its pitiable targets. They believed that movie audiences formed a potentially significant segment of the pro-suffrage lobby, but one which had not been tapped by other means. Filmgoers, then, were recruited by tactics that adapted an established element of the suffrage campaign (public oratory) into the new medium of (silent) motion pictures. Summing up NAWSA's interest in producing *Your Girl and Mine*, Ruth Hanna McCormick suggested that the group viewed cinema as both an innovative tool for broadening its audience and a novel forum in which to promote their platform. McCormick was head of NAWSA's Congressional Committee and had been instrumental in getting the film financed and produced with the help of William Selig. Movies, with their inherent appeal and easy familiarity, were perfect conduits through which to reach a broader, more popular audience, she claimed: "Realizing that the suffragists, like all other propaganda organizations, spend most of their time in talking to themselves in public, I felt it was necessary to try and originate a means of really reaching the public. . . . The aim, first of all, was to produce a photoplay that would appeal to every man and woman, regardless of whether they knew anything about the suffrage movement or cared anything about it."[84] To McCormick, supporters culled from motion picture audiences would not be as sophisticated as those drawn by speeches or published tracts, so they required suasion of a different order. "We are going to reach people who flatly refuse to read our neat, cogent little pamphlets," she declared. *Your Girl and Mine* engaged "no long-winded arguments. . . . There isn't even the familiar suffrage parade."[85]

McCormick's savvy reveals that the potential magnitude of moving picture audiences was not lost on suffragists, nor indeed on the film trade press, which noted the women's exploitation of the cinema with some interest. In fact, the use of motion picture venues for suffragist lectures and slide shows had been a significant facet of the campaign for some time.[86] A year before the first suffrage drama was released, *Moving Picture World* reported that an activist in New York had "captured a downtown moving picture theater, where she is showing lantern slides and talking the virtues of suffragism to large audiences." Citing statistics for *movie* attendance—thirty-five million weekly—the *World* proposed that "every propagandist, suffragist or otherwise, might achieve great results by getting his [or her] cause illustrated by means of lantern slides, *etc.*, before this mighty public."[87] Just three months before the release of *Votes for Women*, none other than Jane Addams herself appeared as the headline act in a vaudeville show at New York's Majestic Theater, where she was said to have delivered a "witty monologue" on equal suffrage.[88]

Given the interest of suffrage associations in the cinema, and given the novel ways they approached film exhibition, it is notable that organizers like Shaw and Addams had, just a few years earlier, loudly condemned the movies, calling theaters "recruiting stations of vice" in the highly contentious debate over white slavery.[89] The irony of their apparent reversal was not lost on industry critics. As *Moving Picture World* observed dryly, "one of the significant facts in connection with [*Votes for Women*] is that some of the ladies who appear in it at one time were to be classed as antagonistic to the moving picture."[90] Even after the release of several suffrage features, Chicago suffragists participated in a "clean-up campaign" in that city's movie houses, demonstrating how negative associations with the cinema lingered in the minds of many activists.[91] However, the suffragists' decision to exploit motion pictures reveals less an opportunistic about-face than the rapidity with which accepted opinions about the cinema and its patrons were changing. Citing the five million viewers who attended movie houses daily, one observer noted, "[I]t is no small wonder . . . that Dr. Shaw and Miss Addams rush to New York to embrace the opportunity of making the suffrage propaganda graphic." Not only was this vast audience most easily reached through the cinema, he maintained, but "the impression made by such vivid preachments as motion pictures is often deeper than those of editorials or sermons."[92] *Moving Picture World*'s W. Stephen Bush concurred, suggesting that *Your Girl and Mine* would "accomplish more for the cause than all that eloquent tongues have done since the movement was started."[93]

Many of the suffrage dramas proved quite successful in this regard. *Votes for Women* played around the country throughout 1912, 1913, and 1914, appearing not only at movie houses but at screenings organized at churches, meeting halls, and outdoor fairs. At the height of the film's popularity, NAWSA entertained ambitious plans for expanding the use of motion pictures in their drive. When *Your Girl and Mine* was completed, Ruth McCormick predicted that the picture would be financially lucrative for the organization. Unfortunately, a dispute with World Films prevented the film's national, commercial distribution, and the organization became discouraged with future prospects for the medium.[94]

Attracting female film viewers in the early teens was not only consistent with suffrage aims, of course. It was also an integral component of the film industry's attempts to remodel its image and broaden its base of support, a priority evident in *Moving Picture World*'s praise of *Eighty Million Women Want——?*: "This feature is not only a most effectual means of propaganda for the cause of Woman Suffrage, but it would, I am sure, be welcomed by any man who wants to give his patrons a high class offering with plenty of pathos and humor."[95] Suffrage features could be promoted as respectable, "high class" offerings in the hopes of attracting middle-class female viewers, who promised exhibitors the cultural cachet they sought. A female owner of the Lafayette Theater in Washington, D.C., clearly linked suffrage cinema to her ability to attract female patrons, and ultimately to provide a "healthful and pleasant" theater atmosphere. After describing efforts to keep her venue clean and well-ventilated with exhaust fans and "hourly spraying with a perfumed deodorizer," the proprietor proclaimed her undertaking a success: "Already I have been able to increase the attendance of women and the young folks. My program will include the best that can be afforded by a five-cent house. I am making arrangements to show the suffrage play *Your Girl and Mine*, and I mean to do all that I can to interest the women in the Lafayette."[96]

However coveted female patrons were, film reviews and accounts of public screenings in the industry trade press also reveal deep industry ambivalence about the suffragists' appeal to movie audiences. Describing the opening of *Your Girl and Mine* in December 1914, the *New York Dramatic Mirror*'s critic painted the presence of female activists in indecent and exhibitionist terms. He reported that "from every box scintillated the brains of the local [suffrage] organizations, not to mention a few *daring, dazzling arms*, while the *body* of the orchestra, commendably crowded, held the army." Whereas he found that other contemporary social advocacy films were "well cloaked in the dress of drama," in *Your Girl and Mine* "the *naked subject* of 'Votes for Women' stalked majestically and insistently."[97] Female viewers and opening-night speakers were reduced to objects of erotic display for this author and his readers. *Variety*'s reviewer questioned whether *Your Girl and Mine* would succeed in attracting anyone other than "the Suffragette element, who should welcome a treaty of this sort on their cause."[98] Apparently, films that appealed primarily (or exclusively) to women could irrevocably alter the dynamics of moviegoing. Admitting middle-class women into exhibition spaces was one thing; acknowledging that their presence might alter such sites was quite another.

If these reports betray a tendency to paint women's presence at screenings in exhibitionist terms, the appearance of noted suffragists on the screen itself also prompted dismissive accounts focusing on their physical attributes. When Edison's Kinetophone recording of suffrage speakers disappeared from New York theaters in 1913, the *Tribune* made great sport of its claim that mortified activists felt they had been made to look "frights and frumps" on the screen. According to a highly suspect item, suffragists decried "that talking-moving abomination" and demanded its cancellation. One complained that the film "made me look fifty years old and all askew. Telegraph to Edison and have the record or whatever smashed!"[99] Activists satirized here show an entirely narcissistic interest in exploiting cinema and betray an astonishing lack of sophistication about the medium, as the efficacy of employing motion pictures in the crusade is lost in a caricature of female vanity. Similarly, *Moving Picture World* derided the appearance of Shaw and Addams in *Votes for Women* as mere visual sensation, claiming that "pictures of wild animals in Africa and polar bears in Alaska may be popular, but soon they will have to share the limelight with the female of the species humana."[100] Besides exaggerating the spectacular value of noted activists, this account casts filmgoers as passive observers of curious phenomena, rather than active agents of political change, while it tries to neutralize the mobilization of female viewers that suffrage films aimed to achieve. A partisan appeal to audiences—unquestionably the suffragists' main intent—is elided in each account. Profound industry unease about soliciting female film patrons reveals the disparity between exhibitors' aims and those of the movement's leaders, then. On the value of female patrons they agreed. But the suffragists' desire to politicize their address to women alienated the industry.

Civic Housekeeping and the Conservative Appeal

Industry fears aside, suffrage-sponsored films actually made quite a conservative appeal for the vote, despite the movement's bold initiative to exploit motion pictures and mobilize new audiences for the cause. In fact, suffrage-sponsored films usually yoked demands for the vote to traditional representations of femininity, juggling the need to broaden expectations governing womanly conduct—in order to encompass full citizenship and suffrage—with the desire to appease the pronounced alarm that such proposals inevitably provoked. Even as they sought to inspire a newly politicized female constituency from among filmgoers, plot lines downplayed the very significance of women's impact on public life. Indeed, the complexities inherent in defining a place for women as equal citizens and recasting formerly rigid oppositions between the sexes are often manifest in the films' conflicted terms of address.

With *Suffrage and the Man*, the WPU's 1912 foray into film comedy, suffragists evidently hoped to counter antagonistic portraits of activists and their cause while still engaging the logic of inversion so common to comic shorts at the time. Here a young man breaks off his engagement when he learns of his fiancée's involvement with the women's movement. But after becoming entangled in a lawsuit over a second failed engagement, he is relieved to see his earlier sweetheart appear in court as the forewoman of the jury deciding his case, for since the two first parted, women have won the vote and along with it the right to serve as jurors. Under her guidance, the jury votes for his acquittal. "As might be expected," *Moving Picture World* added, "'suffrage wins Herbert' with a permanently happy result—in his reconciliation and marriage."[101] Like the fatalistic comedies it sought to rebut, *Suffrage and the Man* imagines a society after women have received full citizenship. But in this case men benefit from the arrangements; women such as Herbert's sweetheart, newly appointed to positions of authority, act with their hearts in aid of their loved ones. Women still cloud legal discourse with frivolous "feminine" concerns like romance, much as they did in the comedies, but here it aids rather than disrupts the hero's life. Still, like the more serious suffrage dramas that followed it, *Suffrage and the Man* hints that women's enfranchisement had the potential to divide men and women on the home front. A "comedy of votes and love," according to one advertisement, the plot foregrounds the turmoil politics might bring to domestic tranquillity, and assigns to women the task of converting their beaux to the cause.[102]

Like *Suffrage and the Man*, the subsequent multireel suffrage dramas *Votes for Women*, *Your Girl and Mine*, and *Eighty Million Women Want——?* each stage a stirring crusade for the vote but cloak demands for political equality with reassurances that traditional notions of womanhood will endure with full citizenship, and that heterosexual relations will not be destabilized. The NAWSA-sponsored film *Votes for Women* is typical of the way that all three dramas not only link voting rights to romance but present women's enfranchisement as a cause secondary to more pressing social concerns.[103] The story depicts the reformation of an irresponsible senator, who not only opposes equal suffrage but owns a rundown inner-city tenement where families live in poverty and squalor. In a plan to improve living conditions and reform Senator Herman, suffrage activists recruit his fiancée, Jane Wadsworth, to their cause. Appalled by the conditions she finds in the tenement and further shocked to learn that her fiancé is the owner, Jane tries in vain to persuade the senator to improve his tenants' surroundings. When he rebuffs her, she joins the suffragists in their crusade. When Jane's father, a department store owner, refuses to heed her warnings about sexual harassment of shop girls in his employ, the two plot lines converge; unsanitary conditions in the senator's tenement finally lead to the death of one of Mr. Wadsworth's retail clerks. But the men are won over to the suffrage cause only when Jane herself contracts scarlet fever from the wedding trousseau being prepared for her by seamstresses in Herman's tenement—when, in other words, the "contagion" of the working classes infects one of their own. In the final scenes Senator Herman and the elder Wadsworth are seen joining the women at suffragist headquarters, addressing their men's club, and marching in a suffrage parade.

If nothing else, *Votes for Women* illustrates the degree to which the suffragists' fight was contingent upon support from male politicians and business leaders—the very figures they often associated with graft and poor urban conditions—for it does not advocate women's direct political power but their ability to influence the men with whom they have intimate attachments. Jane Wadsworth and suffragist May Fillmore recruit men to the suffrage cause by drawing attention to the interconnected spheres of public and private life that the men have ignored: conditions in the tenement directly affect those in the garment factory where tenants work and in the department store where the items are sold. Women are shown to possess novel political insights, it is true, but these stem largely from traditional notions of feminine caregiving. And women's suffrage is promoted as a means of achieving larger progressive aims, like sanitary living and working conditions, equally welcomed by men, rather than women's advancement.

The cautious argument for women's enfranchisement advanced in *Votes for Women* shows how frequently suffragists exploited conservative ideas of female virtue in order to assert their rightful role as citizens. NAWSA vice president Jane Addams, one of the leading proponents of this strategy, stressed to *Ladies' Home Journal* readers in 1910 that women ought to extend their natural domestic impulses beyond their own households in a process she termed "civic housekeeping."[104] By upholding a conventional view of femininity rooted in familial and maternal activity, Addams proclaimed political activity compatible with older womanly ideals. Similarly, a NAWSA leaflet, entitled "Women in the Home," promoted the necessity of domestic virtue in urban life. "Women are by nature and training housekeepers," the text proclaimed; "let them have a hand in the city's housekeeping, even if they introduce an occasional house-cleaning."[105] Effective citizenship represented simply an extension of women's domesticity into civic life. Women, in this view, would enter electoral politics only to guarantee the sanctity of their home and children. In response to similar lines of argument, an antisuffrage treatise quipped, "Housewives! You do not need a ballot to clean out your sink spout. A handful of potash and some boiling water is quicker and cheaper."[106] Historian Aileen Kraditor finds this tactic emblematic of a major shift that suffrage arguments underwent at the beginning of the century, when lobbyists moved away from nineteenth-century claims stressing the emancipatory benefits women could achieve through the franchise. Instead, activists emphasized the advantages *society* would derive from women's electoral participation.[107] If an earlier generation of suffragists aimed to liberate women from the domestic sphere into

the political domain, twentieth-century activists helped reinstate strict segregation of these realms, arguing that "feminine" qualities ought to be introduced
into modern, urban politics.

Also eager to counter opponents' caricatures of "mannish" suffragists, more
traditionally minded elements of the movement promoted the wholesomeness
and ladylike propriety of its adherents through skillful manipulation of visual
rhetoric. In 1912 *Good Housekeeping* ran a lavishly illustrated article titled
"The Feminine Charms of the Woman Militant," which promised to demonstrate "the personal attractiveness and housewifely attainments" of suffrage
leaders.[108] A 1915 suffrage poster similarly balanced a conventional figuration
of womanhood with a call for voting rights.[109] At the top of the poster an
inscription proclaims, "Double the Power of the Home—Two Good Votes Are
Better Than One," under which appears an image of a mother seated with her
three children. A boy standing at her left reads a book balanced on her lap,
while a younger girl at her right clutches a doll as she leans upon her mother's
knee. A third child, an infant, lies cradled against the mother's breast. The
mother here is figured as the literal center of the home. A pillar of support for
her children, she is the guide who will instill in her son a keen mind and a love
of learning, and who will pass on to her daughter the nurturing skills necessary
for the girl's own future maternal role. Evidence of the woman's other domestic
accomplishments is distributed throughout the scene: a knitting basket sits on
the floor in the foreground, a kettle boils on a stove in the back, dishes are
neatly stacked in the hutch, even a "God Bless Our Home" sampler occupies
pride of place on the wall.

By offering an idealized vision of Mother and Home, the poster insists that
voting would not infringe upon customary female roles—casting a ballot
would not cause women to abandon children or disrupt the public sphere, as
opponents claimed. Instead, nurturing and caregiving associated here with
motherhood are deemed consistent with civic-mindedness. Quite significantly,
the woman is not shown engaging in partisan activities outside her home. We
can imagine that she might venture outside to vote for a candidate she and her
husband have agreed upon, but that she herself would not engage in electoral
battles or run for office. The slogan also implies that men's and women's political aims are aligned. Rather than dividing factional allegiances between husband and wife, women's enfranchisement would simply double man's vote. If
neither women nor politics would be transformed by the granting of female
suffrage, as the appeal seems to indicate, one wonders why it seemed necessary
to give women the franchise at all. Finally, this *pro*-suffrage poster reproduces
the visual rhetoric of the *anti*suffrage poster, "Which Do You Prefer?" discussed earlier. Like that idealization of maternal virtue, the woman's gaze is
unfocused, content. Her hand supports a child resting against her cheek. She
does not advance her cause directly. Her mouth closed, she does not speak.
She embodies a feminine ideal outside of politics, imported to the suffrage

DOUBLE THE POWER OF THE HOME—TWO GOOD VOTES ARE BETTER THAN ONE

23. Double the Power of the Home. (Sophia Smith Collection, Smith College.)

platform. Once again, it is men, husbands and fathers—absent from the image—who seem the intended targets of address.

If *Votes for Women* paints women's political engagement in terms consistent with a familiar caregiving ethic, maternal instincts are literally at the heart of the suffrage crusade waged in *Your Girl and Mine*.[110] While the film calls unmistakably for gender equality and for the inclusion of women as full citizens in the nation's legal process, these demands are hedged within a familiar narrative of female victimization and an appeal to maternal rights, all wrapped within a melodramatic plot. The story's heroine, Rosalind Fairlie, is a wealthy young woman who marries "a spendthrift and a man of loose morals," only to find that all of her possessions—money and children included—become his property upon marriage.[111] This she learns after he forfeits her entire fortune to gambling debts and capriciously wills away her children to his father. Unbeknownst to Rosalind, he has also abandoned a former lover, Kate Price, while she is pregnant with his child. Alone and impoverished, Kate is forced to work in sweatshops to support herself and the baby. As *Variety* dryly noted, Rosalind's husband "does nothing the brotherhood of bad men have not done in the average 'meller.'"[112] Another reviewer dubbed *Your Girl and Mine* "melodrama of the most thrilling sort, in spite of the fact that there is a moral concealed in the very title of the play. . . . But who is worried by a moral" when the plot contains thrills like a murder, "an exciting hand-to-hand fight between a man and a woman," and "an automobile abduction scene that breaks all former speed-records," he asked.[113] Yet such sensational plot lines and spectacular action were evidently part of a deliberate strategy to attract popular audiences to the cause. Surely NAWSA engaged screenwriter Gibson Willets, famed for his *Adventures of Kathlyn* series, knowing full well his intentions. The resulting film was "packed with thrills and 'action,'" NAWSA Congressional Committee chair Ruth McCormick declared triumphantly, noting that there was "not too much suffrage in the play."[114] Even Vachel Lindsay, who praised the work's efforts as a pioneer "crusading film," described *Your Girl and Mine* as "two-thirds Action Photoplay."[115]

The heroine's handling of this outworn scenario of victimization is, nonetheless, inflected with a modicum of suffrage rhetoric. Rosalind Fairlie's courtroom battle for her children shapes the climax of the film, where it provides the core of the film's case for women's voting rights. Her female attorney poses the following argument: "If women had a voice in framing the laws, would there be any law in any statute book in this broad land permitting a father to deed or will away, in spite of the mother's anguish, the children which she bore him?"[116] The crusade to have women declared equal legal guardians of their children was indeed favored by suffragists. Despite years of feminist lobbying efforts, only twelve states had enacted such legislation by 1909. Suffragists proudly proclaimed that barely one year after women won enfranchisement in Colorado, such legislation was passed.[117] However much cloaked in feminist language, the lawyer's appeal illustrates the contradictory stance that *Your Girl and Mine* adopts toward equal suffrage. Women deserve legal rights to their property and their children, the film asserts; and they will be without these rights until they are granted not only the vote but an equal hand in shaping the law. Nonetheless, the story implies that women like Rosalind enter the legal and political arena only to safeguard their private interests. Concerned chiefly to protect her marriage, her children, and her maternal bond, Rosalind is driven into the courtroom as a result of her husband's failure to live up to his obligations as patriarch and provider. The film leaves open the possibility that had he perhaps done so, she might not have had to seek recourse in the law and might have been content to defend her interests from within the home. Changes in voting laws will be most effective for women outside traditional family structures, the film implies: those who are swindled like Rosalind, and those abandoned like Kate. Although it illuminates the fate of women who live beyond the protective umbrella of the "family vote," the film nonetheless (and ironically) reinforces the notion that women ought to be protected within marriage and the family.

Just as Rosalind Fairlie embraces politics solely to protect her maternal rights, potential female voters were often described simply as "mothers" by suffragists, as if to soften the portrait of female citizenry they proposed and strictly delimit the nature of women's participation in civic affairs.[118] Indeed Addams herself was widely known as "the mother of all women" for her work toward social justice.[119] Such a narrow view of women's lives is evident in testimony given by one Denver commentator in 1909, seventeen years after women had been granted the vote in Colorado: "It does not take any mother from her home duties to spend ten minutes in going to the polls, casting her vote, and returning to the bosom of her home; but during those ten minutes she wields a power which is doing more to protect that home, and all other homes, than any other power of influence in Colorado."[120] In this view, a woman's partisan involvement is reduced to the few minutes she would spend outside her home going to the polls, a trip equated more with shopping expeditions than with full citizenship. Similarly, the attorney general of Wyoming (a state in which women were enfranchised in 1869), presented the view that the vote did not alter women's role within the family, nor did it cause them to supplant men in the affairs of state. In fact, women's new political status benefited men: "As the mother, sister, or teacher of young boys," he wrote, "the influence of woman is great. The more she knows about the obligations of citizenship, the more she is able to teach the boys"[121]—a *pro*-suffrage view of women's electoral participation nearly akin to antisuffragists' "family vote" theory.

In attempting to attract newcomers to the suffrage cause, then, *Your Girl and Mine* strikes a compromise between conventional conceptions of womanhood based on mothering and new calls for women's rights. Dual aspects of femininity alluded to in the film's title—"your girl" and "mine"—are conjoined as normative womanhood is shown to be compatible with a newly politicized identity. It is a reconciliation that the drama's resolution similarly trumpets, for the tale ends happily with Rosalind's marriage to the state's lieutenant governor. The film's attempt to address dual constituencies—moviegoers perhaps unfamiliar with pro-suffrage arguments, as well as suffrage advocates eager to see themselves portrayed favorably on the screen—is also reflected in the fractured heroine of its title. Decorous womanly traits applauded by conventionally minded spectators ("your girl") are united with those valued by suffragists ("mine"). One might even suggest that the title also acknowledges the presence of both male *and* female viewers in the audience.

The oxymoron "civic housekeeping" crystallized a number of contradictions manifest in the fight to win the franchise, then. By casting women's involvement in politics as domestic labor, NAWSA commentators assured that feminine roles would not be significantly altered by contact with public affairs, an argument not far from that tendered by opponents of the vote. Still, in advocating the vote, suffragists promoted an idea that challenged the basis on which citizenship had been conventionally practiced—traits such as care and nurturing once relegated to the private world of sentiment were, they claimed, essential to political life, a "maternal" ethic consistent with broader progressive aims.[122] A corollary of "civic housekeeping" was thus the "domestication" of America's political landscape that Paula Baker has identified in the nineteenth and early twentieth centuries. So intertwined were politics and the home by the Progressive Era, she contends, that to many equal suffrage might no longer seem unwarranted.[123] As *Votes for Women* suggested, the caretaking mandate that many suffragists embraced had become essential in modern, urban, industrial America.

The challenge of simultaneously defining women as full citizens and appeasing conservatives' fears about the feminization of public life is perhaps most evident in the WPU's signature melodrama *Eighty Million Women Want——?*, the only suffrage feature that remains extant.[124] Much like *Votes for Women* and *Your Girl and Mine*, the film pairs a dramatized rendering of the fight for voting rights with a romance involving the film's suffragist heroine, Mabel West. Mabel's beau William Travers is a fledgling attorney who initially disapproves of his sweetheart's involvement with the women's movement. But when the young man becomes entangled in corrupt local politics, Mabel and her compatriots squash the organization, saving his career from ruin, while ensuring the advance of their cause. The suffragists succeed in winning the franchise in the end, along with Travers's newfound respect and support.

The moral clarity that women could bring to urban politics is shaped by the film's portrait of Boss Kelly, a nefarious local leader, and his involvement with the naive young Travers, whose susceptibility is swiftly demonstrated at the outset of the film. Although he has few clients and could benefit from Kelly's well-placed contacts, Travers initially refuses an offer of assistance from the Boss. Unbeknownst to the struggling attorney, his first case draws him into the urban underworld, since his client is the victim of an automobile accident involving a Kelly associate, District Leader James Flynn. Kelly and Flynn plot against Travers and conspire to bribe the judge hearing the case. Unable to compete with Kelly's commanding influence, Travers loses the trial. He admits defeat and finally succumbs to temptation, allying himself with the Boss in order to succeed within the crooked legal system. Enticing Travers to join his organization, Kelly also promises to "make it possible for you to marry your pretty suffragette and give her something better to do than make street speeches," signaling his intentions to defeat the suffrage proponents. Sexism, dirty politics, and opposition to the vote are all offered as linked aspects of Kelly's character. His objection to women's enfranchisement is ultimately the logical corollary of his self-serving political aims, for their "civic housekeeping" might clean up the corruption upon which he thrives. When he and Flynn later appear in a car emblazoned with the antisuffrage slogan "Vote against Petticoat Rule," Kelly is pointedly framed in medium shot above the banner, where only the letters "GAINS" are visible beneath him. Opponents of women's enfranchisement seek only their own advancement, the composition implies.

WPU leader Harriot Stanton Blatch leads the film's suffrage organization in an effort to gather evidence that Kelly is fixing local elections. Noticing an advertisement for a secretarial position in Kelly's office, they decide to infiltrate his outfit. A handsome activist is dispatched, confident that she will land the job on the basis of her appearance, not her abilities. When this suffragist-spy reports seeing Travers in Kelly's office, Mabel fears that her sweetheart is involved with the politico, suspicions that are confirmed when she inadvertently receives a note Travers intended for Kelly in which the lawyer reveals that he has "fixed" a pivotal electoral district. Upon learning of her beau's entanglement with unscrupulous electioneering, Mabel breaks off their romance. Travers eventually reforms and decides to pursue his career free from the leader's influence but remains haunted by his early mistakes. When he confronts the Boss in Kelly's office, the two have an argument that is witnessed by a porter peering through the keyhole. Later that same night, the bitter accident victim whom Travers had unsuccessfully represented arrives at Kelly's office, where he shoots and wounds the Boss. Since no one sees the second man's visit, Travers is indicted for the assault based upon the porter's "eyewitness" testimony.

Here all three threads of the plot—love story, suffrage argument, and machine politics—converge, as Mabel's fight for the ballot is condensed into her struggle to exculpate Travers. Believing that someone other than her boyfriend visited Kelly's office that night, Mabel returns in search of clues, using a sophisticated camera to photograph suspicious fingerprints on the door handle. Seeking to exonerate Travers, Mabel devises a plan to collect prints from all those possibly implicated in the shooting, hoping to secure a match for the fingerprints she has photographed in Kelly's office. She pens a fallacious request for alms in support of a needy family, then circulates the note in Kelly's club, hoping to trap likely suspects as they handle the paper. When Mabel encounters Arthur, the accident victim, and Ruth, his girlfriend, on the street, she shows them her ruse. Unknowingly, she also obtains Arthur's fingerprint—the crucial evidence needed to clear Travers. Mabel quickly presents her proof at the district attorney's office, her beau is freed, and the couple is reunited. "Travers admires his sweetheart's ability," a title proclaims, as the two embrace in her living room, the site of their brief spat over equal suffrage at the beginning of the drama. In proving the existence of civic corruption and in working to vindicate Travers, Mabel has also won his respect for the suffrage cause.

While Mabel works to free Travers, the suffragist planted in Kelly's office gathers evidence of electoral fraud. Spying on Kelly's associates in the office, she peers into the same keyhole through which the porter had earlier glimpsed Travers fighting with the Boss. Eventually the suffragist is able to enter the office itself, where she finds "the tell-tale blotter" containing an incriminating imprint of the rigged voter list Kelly and his cohorts were concocting. Following Travers's release, the activist presents evidence of Kelly's scheme to Blatch at WPU headquarters. With this documentation Mabel and Travers monitor voters on election day and collar Kelly's repeat voters. In the final scenes of the film, Blatch and her associates are shown winning the franchise. Lest this victory taint the budding romance, the film ends traditionally with the couple's engagement.

As these events demonstrate, the fictional suffrage campaign staged in *Eighty Million Women Want——?* is intricately framed in relation to a love story involving Mabel and Travers, as well as the suffragists' crusade against a corrupt male-dominated political establishment, implying that the potential impact of women's politicization will be registered at home as much as it will be in the political sphere. In the film's opening scene, Mabel and Travers argue about her suffrage activity amid the many "Votes for Women" banners that decorate her parlor. Dramatizing friction in the couple's courtship that results from Mabel's involvement with the WPU, the film begins by posing the question of whether interpersonal attachments are compatible with women's partisan activity, and, more obliquely, whether *married* women ought to vote. Tensions in the couple's romance thus signal the conflict between dated notions about demure femininity and women's new prominence in affairs of state. By staging this quarrel in Mabel's home, the opening scene also visualizes how closely domestic and civic issues are to be intertwined in her crusade. Above all, it frames the suffrage issue as a question that must be settled between men and women on the home front.

Even as the film aims to prove the compatibility of women's sexual identity and women's political activity, however, it risks their collapse. After their reconciliation at the end of the film, Travers surprises Mabel with a marriage license, which a title proclaims "the most popular ballot for suffragette, maid, or 'mere man.'" Of this, *Motion Picture News* observed rather cynically, "[S]he seems happier by far over the marriage license than she was over the [suffrage] party badge she had worn."[125] This conflation of marriage and political enfranchisement in the film's conclusion also brings to mind the proposal so frequently heard from antisuffragists that women ought to exercise participatory citizenship through their husband's ballot, the so-called family vote. Some critics saw the love story as an opportunity to downplay the film's political agenda—one even nicknamed Mabel a "sweetheart of a suffragette."[126]

24. Mabel's suffrage politics cause discord at home.

Motion Picture News declared that "the play itself is not an advertisement of the votes-for-women movement," despite WPU endorsement.[127] And with notable relief, *Motography*'s reviewer reported that the film "was an agreeable surprise, in being not a eulogy of and a plea for suffrage, specifically, but a really and truly story with a young lawyer in love with a pretty girl."[128]

The eagerness with which contemporary commentators willfully dismissed the film's suffrage arguments in favor of the couple's courtship points to another aspect of the film's love story: the romance plot serves to inscribe and contain aspects of female desire operating implicitly at other levels of the narrative. Nowhere is this more evident than in the innuendo of film's title, *Eighty Million Women Want——?*, which confuses women's political aspirations with sexual desire. Alluding to Rheta Childe Dorr's 1910 book, *What Eight Million Women Want*, the film's title not only multiplies the number of women concerned; it also heightens tacit connections between the suffrage movement and female desire.[129] Whereas the book unequivocally defines "what women want," the film poses women's desire as an enigma. The blank line visible in the revised title suggests as much the impossibility of defining what women want as it does the obviousness of the answer; the feminine libido is at once enormous and unsignifiable. The film's title appears inarticulate, unable to speak, to utter the demand for suffrage. While the revised wording equates women's partisan objectives with a stereotypical view of their mystifying sexual insatiability, registered so graphically through the blank line, it also hints at the link between the heroine's romantic aspirations and her fight for the vote. As narrative events portray suffrage activists exposing the concealed aspects of Boss Kelly's operation, the film's title promises to expose the secrets of female desire. The plot depicts one kind of revelation, that is, while the title frames (and contains) these events within the context of another, even more tantalizing, revelation. Commenting ironically on the film's tacit inscription of desire, one critic remarked that "the average man has enough trouble trying to solve what one woman wants."[130] Noting the connection between narrative closure and the formation of the heterosexual couple, another asked, "[I]s marriage 'What Eighty Million Women Want'—or is the right of suffrage 'What Eighty Million Women Want'?" as if these aspirations might be mutually exclusive.[131] In a confused, but revealing, conflation of the two titles, *Motography*'s puzzled headline read, "What Eighty Million Women Want?"[132]

Evocations of a boundless feminine appetite pervade the discourse on women's enfranchisement, often in less subtle forms than they appear in *Eighty Million Women Want——?* "A suffragette has been defined . . . as a woman who wants something and thinks it's the vote," Edward S. Martin informed *Ladies' Home Journal* readers in 1913. "There are women who want the vote as a suitable personal attribute, as they might covet a pearl necklace, or a house, or a frock, or something that they would look well in or that would add to their personal luster or distinction," he proclaimed, reducing legitimate political claims to a trifling shopping expedition.[133] The brazen greed ascribed to suffragists, many of whom were already privileged middle- and upper-class women, is also echoed in Charles Dana Gibson's suffragist caricature, "Satan and the Suffragette," where an activist is distracted from her scholarly efforts by the arrival of a new Easter bonnet. Says Satan: "Woman's right? the right divine to be frivolous."[134] Suffragists, it seems, were merely acquisitive women.

If, as Stephen Heath suggests, a postponed kiss (whether figurative or literal) often propels film narratives toward closure and resolution,[135] then this is doubly so in *Eighty Million Women Want——?* where the couple's fractured courtship frames the political crusade. Mabel's engagement to Travers at the end of the film demonstrates the forceful closure provided by the heterosexual couple in this immediately preclassical period. But in the context of the suffrage fight, their union takes on additional resonance. It asserts the primacy of a heterosexual bond over homosocial ties among the suffragists by containing women's political aspirations within marriage, where allegiances between women (political and otherwise) might be compatible with the male establishment. Simply put, Mabel's attraction to Travers proves stronger than her ties to other women. Her marriage provides an acceptable outlet for the desires, both sexual and political, that she has expressed in the film, as so many contemporary critics slyly observed. This form of closure supplies further evidence of the perceived need to present suffragists—and all female citizens—as a group that would not seriously threaten the dominant order. Sound housekeeping is offered in lieu of radical change.

The fact that Mabel becomes engaged to an attorney, a literal embodiment of the law, also helps offset the film's critical portrait of the legal system; it suggests that while the status quo might benefit men at the expense of women, individual figures of the law were not necessarily at fault and might in fact be catalysts for change. An alliance between Mabel and the once-skeptical Travers denotes a new allegiance between female activists and progressive male leaders. In fact, both *Votes for Women* and *Your Girl and Mine* conclude with the union of a suffragist heroine and a masculine figure of the law: Senator Herman is rehabilitated by his ethical fiancée in *Votes for Women*; and in *Your Girl and Mine* Rosalind Fairlie marries the state's lieutenant governor in spite of the case she makes against its child-custody laws. Women can advocate change from *within* current systems, these unions suggest. The ballot would not displace men from positions of authority they currently hold; nor would it create a rift between men's and women's efforts at social reform. Feminist attitudes are diffused even as they are introduced, for the effects women might have on civic politics are consistently downplayed.

If the love story between Mabel and Travers in *Eighty Million Women Want——?* measures the effects of voting rights on *private* relations, as I have maintained, the film's treatment of political corruption gauges the potential impact of female citizens on public life. Suffragists seized upon tales of organized graft, widely reported in the "muck-raking" press throughout the teens, as evidence that the electoral system required fundamental reform—a moral and ethical transformation which, activists maintained, only women could provide. Noting this connection, *Motion Picture News* concluded that *Eighty Million Women Want——?* "very ably 'shows up' the modern system of machine politics . . . and brings vividly to our minds the recent exposures in the Empire State."[136] Of course, the appearance of actual organizers like Blatch and Pankhurst in the film's dramatized crusade lent credence to its condemnation of current political conditions. These respected and prominent leaders battle caricatured urban "grafters" with aplomb.

The film's timely treatment of corruption also complicates the issue of gendered spheres. Here it is *women* who are associated with public sites: suffragists speak and congregate in city parks, where they openly advocate their beliefs and prominently display banners. Men, on the other hand, are aligned with an illicit urban underworld, a secret realm that goes unnoticed in city life, yet one that the very nature of the metropolitan landscape makes possible. Offices, clubs, bars, alleyways all provide the means for this covert traffic where arrangements are unstated, but always understood. Kelly's graft involves subterfuge and covert negotiations undertaken behind the closed doors of male sanctuaries like offices and clubs. It operates in the unseen, private

25. Mabel works with Harriot Stanton Blatch at WPU headquarters.

recesses of public life. Much is made of the contrasted spheres of male and female activity. Early clandestine transactions between Kelly and cohorts in his office are intercut with shots of Mabel being welcomed into WPU headquarters by Harriot Stanton Blatch. Here we learn that Boss Kelly not only is corrupt but opposes women's voting rights as well: the suffragists locate a newspaper item revealing that the politician "promises to leave no stone unturned in his efforts to smash their organization." Two scenes follow in which Blatch visits the Boss's club in an effort to persuade him of their cause, then is nearly laughed off the premises, and where Emmeline Pankhurst meets with Kelly in his office, demanding, a title proclaims, "recognition of the rights for equal suffrage." She is accompanied by hundreds of women, who gather in support outside Kelly's building. In contrast to this rally, Kelly's office is depicted as a closeted sanctuary with dark walls, heavy window blinds, and deep leather chairs, all of which illustrate his insulation from prosecution and the secretive nature of the business he conducts within these walls.

Differences between suffragists' prominent lobbying efforts and the covert machinations of organized graft are further underscored when courtroom dealings designed to clear Flynn of charges related to the automobile accident are intercut with scenes outside the courthouse where Mabel addresses a crowded suffrage demonstration. Like Kelly's office, the seemingly public courtroom is characterized as an exclusive, all-male haven, codified by a closed-frame composition where Flynn and Kelly flank the judge's podium in a triangular figure. In contrast, an exterior long shot shows Mabel speaking to the open-air rally from an elevated platform, where she is dwarfed by the New York City skyline visible in the background. Location shooting gives the demontrsation a distinctly cosmopolitan flavor, suggesting that while graft may be endemic to civic government, urban space can also provide a uniquely *democratic* forum. If legal and electoral representation is denied to women, the sequence proposes, prominent public protest remains a viable tool of expression. Whereas Kelly and his henchmen dominate the city through an invisible network of influence and graft, the suffragists use urban sites as a means of legitimate and egalitarian congress.

Even as the film's portrait of underworld influence rewrites gendered space, by suggesting that there is a hidden field *within* public life, it still relies upon a traditional notion of separate spheres for men and women. Gendered domains are inverted, but preserved. In fact, despite the visibility of Mabel and the WPU in public life, the women retain traditional feminine traits associated with the domestic realm. Much like the antisuffragists, the film presents women's public activism as inherently moralistic and essentially nonpolitical, while male involvement in civic affairs is shown to be corrupt and politicized, lacking any moral focus. *Eighty Million Women Want——?* appears caught between an impetus to evoke new freedoms available to women—which suffragists sought to solidify and advance through the vote—and an inability to figure sexual difference apart from the trope of separate spheres. Ironically, then, the WPU's feature shares with the role-reversal comedies a desire to preserve boundaries between the sexes. Like the comic shorts, it registers the era's shifting contours of public and private space, while maintaining strict divisions between men and women.

As the investigatory plot suggests, male and female domains are negotiated primarily through surveillance and eavesdropping. Kelly's unseen network is associated with a certain control over vision at the beginning of the film. His office is used as a location from which to spy on a suffrage rally below; his cohorts secretly "fix" electoral districts to consolidate their power, and they are able to orchestrate a spurious account of Flynn's car accident in order to absolve him of responsibility for the victim's injuries. All of these activities, though covert, leave clues discernible to the vigilant suffragists: ink stains on blotters, fingerprints, fragments of conversations overheard—indexical traces that register the dirt and refuse of criminal traffic. By careful scrutiny of this detritus, the activists render invisible influence visible. The men's conspiratorial dealings become a matter of general record.

A pivotal point in the investigation occurs when the suffragist-spy catches a glimpse of the Boss's associates plotting to fix the election as she peers through the keyhole of his office door. We see the men as she does in an optical point-of-view shot, as if seen through the opening in a matte shot framed by an enlarged keyhole. Inside, the men are presented in a closed-frame medium shot that reinforces the heavily closeted nature of their dealings. The suffragist's view of Kelly's office is the only strict point-of-view image in the film, even though the porter who earlier spies Travers with Kelly looks through the same keyhole, observing a scene that he misinterprets and later uses improperly against the young attorney. The suffragist's view shows us Kelly's office from an entirely different camera setup, used only once in this shot, as if to underscore the significance of her sight line. Earlier, the porter's view of the office, for instance, is suggested through a crosscutting strategy that alternates between images showing him looking through the keyhole and shots of Kelly's office from the same camera position used to depict the room throughout the film, regardless of viewpoint.

It is important to stress the significance of the suffragist's point of view in a film that otherwise does not provide such views, where vision is such a crucial element of the plot, and where the very *visibility* of the suffragists' rallying tactics is contrasted with the *invisibility* of Kelly's network, at the same time as the women's detective work, associated with photography and visual surveillance, dramatizes their appropriation of power. By overtly spying on Kelly's operation and recording traces of his criminal activities, the women counteract the dynamics of the men's illicit transactions by reversing the politics of the gaze, inverting the organization of looking in place at the beginning of the film. They do so by entering the male business domain "invisibly" as secretaries and office clerks, positions increasingly open to women in the 1910s that enabled them to gather sensitive evidence of impropriety. Much as we saw in *Traffic in Souls*, here again women infiltrate a crooked operation, then gather evidence of wrongdoing through an innovative recording mechanism.[137] Mabel and her associates reverse conventional patterns of looking that initially pit them as objects of the male gaze, assuming an active role in the investigation, by rendering previously hidden aspects of Kelly's organization visible to all.

The reappropriation of the gaze is symbolized most forcefully in the scene where the suffragist's discovery of Kelly's office is accorded an optical point-of-view shot. Film viewers who share her insight are encouraged to turn their own investigatory gaze on urban politics. The scrutiny to which Kelly is subjected at the hands of the suffragists evokes, more generally, the ethical "vision" women were believed to bring to collective life, their ability to set politics on a truer course. In the hands of women, modern technology becomes an instrument for surveying the closed, illicit world of dirty politics. It aids and enhances the ethical superiority that women might bring into a previously all-male world, and it provides the physical conduit through which private morality might be projected onto the public domain.

If the film's narrative celebrates the power of visionary feminism to alter the American political landscape, it echoes Emmeline Pankhurst's appeal to viewers in the film's preface. By argument and example the star-studded premieres, the eloquent speakers who accompanied the film across the country, and the film's prefatory sequence all demonstrate the power of women's voices and visions. Women ought to have a say in shaping society, the film proposes, because they possess insight and ethical strength that men lack during a period of crucial progressive reform. Yet the argument maintains a delicate balance: female citizenship is presented as an extension of an older feminine caregiving role, an enterprise that will benefit society rather than women alone. Once again we confront the fundamental paradox: women are deemed essential to the body politic but can be admitted only on the condition that they do not constitute a special interest group. Women are necessary for politics, in other words, but electoral representation is not necessary for women.

Although *Eighty Million Women Want——?* posits a female viewer and even empowers her gaze with righteous morality, the film stops short of mobilizing a distinct, feminist community. The desire to attract new suffrage advocates from the ranks of filmgoers is compromised by the film's plot, which consistently seeks to appease fears about women's political status. In a narrative that links women's partisan aspirations to sexual desire, and which presents feminist politics as altruistic "civic housekeeping," threatening aspects of women's equality are suppressed. In demonstrating the effects of women's full citizenship on public and private affairs, the film strikes a conciliatory tone. Familial relations will be affected only favorably, the film suggests, since women's political aims are subordinated to sexual desire. Corruption will be eradicated in public life, it further suggests, since women's political goals are consistent with the aims of progressive society as a whole. Although the film seeks to mobilize a community of supporters, its narrative events repeatedly deny women's status as a distinct social body with aims separate from—or even potentially at odds with—those of men.

Appealing, active heroines like Mabel West or Jane Wadsworth in *Votes for Women*, as well as victims of hyperbolized tragedy, like Rosalind Fairlie in *Your Girl and Mine*, find that the suffrage campaign is secondary to the battles they must wage to protect themselves and their loved ones. Women's enfranchisement, in all cases, is offered as a route to solving other, more pressing problems. Mabel battles electoral corruption in order to exonerate her sweetheart; Rosalind fights for the vote to preserve her family interests only after her husband has abandoned them; and Jane and May hope to ameliorate impoverished inner-city conditions in *Votes for Women*. Each scenario goes out of its way to suggest, first, that political representation is not women's ultimate goal, and, second, that voting rights will not benefit women individually as much as they will benefit society as a whole. Moreover, the most vocal suffrage arguments in each film are attributed not to the heroines themselves but to secondary characters—Blatch and Pankhurst in *Eighty Million Women Want——?*, Rosalind's lawyer in *Your Girl and Mine*, and Shaw and Addams in *Votes for Women*.

The films, like so much of the suffrage campaign as a whole, reveal the conflicting demands placed upon women in the prewar years. In order to gain political advancement, advocates of the vote often appealed, quite paradoxically, to the most traditional of feminine personas. Suffrage rhetoric often upheld conventional notions of womanhood rooted in domestic life while demanding full participation for female citizens, a contradiction that suggests the difficulty of redefining norms of feminine conduct in a period of profound social upheaval. Ultimately a film like *Eighty Million Women Want——?* is caught between the desire to express new versions of femininity that could embrace full citizenship, on the one hand, and, on the other, an inability to imagine gender identities beyond outmoded tropes of spatial segregation. Suspended between the desire to mobilize a community of female film viewers and concerns about the power that such a group might wield in society, the film, like its title, fails to articulate a clear demand for women's equality.

Ironically, then, highly touted women's suffrage features were not so far from the role-reversal hilarities and cross-dressing spectacles in comedies they sought to counteract. Although they supplanted frightful, mannish suffragists with comely, vibrant heroines and stately leaders, suffrage dramas illustrate how cautiously NAWSA and the WPU promoted their cause, how unwilling they were to disturb expectations about womanly decorum. Still, the fact that so much of the suffrage debate, however vexatious, played out on the nation's movie screens testifies to the power cinema held to reach popular audiences and sway public opinion in the prewar years; it testifies to the visual and narrative sophistication of early feature filmmaking, and to the new respect in which female audiences were held.

In virtually any other context, however, the use of cinema by respectable, reform-minded women, the engagement of theaters for educational meetings, and the high-minded exploitation of feature-length photoplays around the concerns of middle-class women would have held unanimous appeal for the early film industry. But the feminist polemics of the suffrage cause and suffragists' explicit aims to mobilize film patrons demonstrate the complex negotiation of cinematic space—on the screen and in theaters—that cinema's expanding female audience provoked.

Conclusion _____

"I HAD GONE, as they had, to see pictures, but in the end I saw only them," Mary Heaton Vorse confesses in her 1911 article "Some Picture Show Audiences."[1] Admitting that most patrons at the Manhattan neighborhood theaters she visited were male, Vorse finds herself most compelled by the women gathered there. For her, it is female moviegoers who demonstrate how profoundly motion picture theaters revolutionized commercial leisure during these years, and how strongly movies captivated audiences. Women, accustomed neither to partaking so openly in urban amusements nor to gazing so freely at visual pleasures, embody, for Vorse, the precise novelty of early film culture. She notes the marked diversity of women present: young and old, married and single, many working, others child-rearing homemakers, all from varied backgrounds, some native-born, others recent immigrants. Astonished at how they have integrated picturegoing into their daily routines, Vorse watches women stopping into the movies on the way to and from work or marketing, greeting friends and neighbors there, bringing infants and children along to the show, all the while propelling movie theaters closer to the center of community life.

Vorse is struck not just by the social atmosphere at these picture houses but by the viewers she encounters transfixed by cinema's visual splendor. Seated behind her at one theater Vorse finds a woman "so rapt and entranced" with what she sees on the screen "that her voice accompanied all that happened—a little unconscious and lilting *obbligato*. It was the voice of a person unconscious that she spoke—speaking from the depths of emotion."[2] At another venue Vorse turns "again and again" to the face of "an eager little girl of ten or eleven, whose lovely profile stood out in violent relief from the dingy wall. So rapt was she, so spellbound, that she couldn't laugh, couldn't clap her hands with the others. She was in a state of emotion beyond any outward manifestation of it."[3] It is these two women, otherwise differentiated by age and background, who register cinema's extraordinary visual appeal, its unique ability to transport viewers far beyond the theater itself into an imaginary realm.

Characteristics Vorse found so remarkable about motion pictures—the new social experience cinemagoing provided for women, as well as the expanded optical field movie viewing opened up for them—remained at the forefront in discussions of women and film culture in the 1910s. Women were actively courted as valued clientele for the movies as the nickelodeon craze began to crest in the early teens. Exhibitors eager to shed the nickelodeon's associations with lowbrow amusements began to transform their theaters into sites of leisure more closely resembling the era's retail emporiums than its amusement parks or penny arcades. Matinee performances offering amenities like parcel checking and child care accommodated the rhythms of women's daily lives, while uniformed ushers and restroom attendants flattered bourgeois expectations about service and comfort. "Ladies'" promotions sold women of all backgrounds a view of moviegoing consistent with fantasies about refined leisure and socializing. Although many in the trade courted female patronage with the idea that ladies might lend an air of refinement to the cinema, in fact women did not usher in the immediate respectability that the industry had anticipated. An increasingly visible female audience and films tailored to these viewers figured prominently in the shifting dynamics of early film culture, certainly, but they did not guarantee an uncomplicated passage to legitimacy. Historical accounts that have tended to yoke cinema's uplift in the teens to an expanded female audience need to be tempered with the knowledge that women often significantly disrupted cinemas and cinemagoing during these years.

However actively courted, women remained a contested component of movie audiences well into the teens. By using theaters as sites for socializing, self-display, and consumption, women altered the tenor of exhibition space in ways that alarmed many commentators, who worried that women's tendency to parade themselves at leisure outings shifted visual attention away from the screen and onto the circulation of gazes in lobby areas and entranceways, and that women encouraged to incorporate cinemagoing into their socializing patterns might simply talk too much during the show. Even more alarming was young women's participation in an unchaperoned dating culture at picture houses. Many feared that such venues were unsafe environments for impressionable young ladies, who might be subject to solicitations from would-be suitors or, worse, assaults from vice traffickers operating under cover of darkness. The fact that cinemas were still presented as sites of danger for women, well into the teens, suggests just how problematic women's presence there continued to be.

Though patently more respectable, older women's attempts to marshal movie audiences around highly charged suffrage politics were also troubling, even to those showmen eager to enhance their venues with serious-minded educational fare of the sort suffrage films promised. Many felt that activists' efforts to cultivate their audiences for political purposes did little to align cinema with serious, progressive causes and did more to disrupt theater spaces with partisan speeches and rallies. Women who amassed at cinemas for these events were all too often mocked or eroticized by commentators clearly apprehensive about the emergence of a distinct social body of women at the cinema. Fears about the economic and political power women were assuming in society, most palpable in these discussions of suffrage screenings, also resonate with milder jokes and caricatures that ridiculed the ways women used theaters "inappropriately" for socializing and self-display. There, too, one hears echoes of apprehension about women's new prominence in cultural life.

Women's behavior at the cinema, whether circulating and mingling in lobby areas, "cuddling" with boyfriends in the dark, jumping from their seats and yelling during serial adventures, or roaring with approval at radical suffrage oratory, also frequently disrupted expectations about ladylike decorum and restraint in ways that complicated any association of female patronage with respectability and uplift. Though desirable as customers, women were clearly not seamlessly integrated into the social space of theaters; in fact, their increased visibility was frequently more troublesome than beneficial during these years. My research also complicates the view that cinemagoing provided a wholly liberating social experience for women sampling the pleasures of commercial entertainment culture in the prewar years, as social historians like Kathy Peiss, Elizabeth Ewen, and Roy Rosenzweig suggest. More specifically, Miriam Hansen's view that cinemas provided "a particularly female heterotopia" fails to account for how profoundly the congregation of women at motion picture venues changed the atmosphere of those spaces—a fact that is evident not only in humorous portraits of chatty, overdressed filmgoers but in alarmist warnings about the dangers women faced at the cinema, and uneasy discussions of explicitly feminist suffrage rallies.[4] "Bodies" of women assembling in theaters in each of these cases clearly disrupted the social and optical dynamics of viewing sites.

Moreover, women were not always enticed to the cinema by refined or uplifting material. Whether tawdry vice pictures, "blood-boiling" serials, or polemical suffrage treatises, films for women were often neither ladylike nor high-minded in their appeal. Even as white slave films were promoted as educational fare for upstanding young women in need of warning about the vast vice rings that threatened their every movement through urban space, they were simultaneously touted as forbidden "exposures" of the "inside" workings of prostitution and sexual trafficking in ways that clearly solicited sexual interest. However cloaked in seriousness of purpose, vice films were among the most explicit of the day, and their appeal to young women troubled those who associated female patronage exclusively with gentility and decorum. Even more provocative was the voyeuristic, frankly eroticized, gaze invited by the vice films, a viewing position wholly unsuited to women, many commentators felt. Still, vice films remained largely conservative, offering women fantasies of empowerment and visual mastery only within narratives that stressed the grave peril they faced walking the nation's urban thoroughfares or sampling its entertainments.

Unlike "slavers," whose appeal to women shocked so many in the industry, serials like *The Perils of Pauline* were explicitly designed to cultivate female patronage with plucky, likable heroines and the most far-reaching publicity campaigns of the era. Yet the very methods by which serials were promoted to women in published tie-ins, ongoing stories, and myriad souvenir products created narrative structures and viewing pleasures distinctly at odds with classical norms. Though they appeared alongside early multireel feature films, and to some degree capitalized on changing expectations about film form and length, serialized stories encouraged suspended narrative desire and continuing extratextual engagement in ways that more conventional motion pictures did not. Female spectatorship was cultivated, in other words, outside classical viewing norms. The abject cinephilia associated with "serialitis" simultaneously marked the desirability of "ready-made" female audiences addicted to continuing screen stories, and the aberrance of such intense filmic attachments. And while they offered fans resplendent images of female athleticism and accomplishment, serials rarely failed to illustrate how heroines' lives remained heavily circumscribed by familial, financial, and ultimately marital bonds.

Women's suffrage films went perhaps furthest in their attempts to disrupt the increasingly closed space of classical narrative cinema. Although activists usually chose the feature film format to promote their cause, because of its associations with serious culture, they used the form in a manner that relied heavily on extratextual associations. Well-known suffrage leaders appeared in photoplays, pointing beyond diegetic space to greater political struggles in the community, and women's organizations distributed films outside the usual exhibition channels, politicizing screening venues with speeches and rallies that invited audiences' direct participation. Much as women were encouraged to focus their gaze on the circulation of products that surrounded serial films, suffragists hoped to focus women's attention on the charged political climate stirring outside movie theaters. Yet while suffrage films struggled most valiantly to articulate feminist narratives and female points of entry, they often reinscribed conservative views of women's "place" in the end.

Vice pictures, serials, and women's suffrage dramas, the era's most notable women's films, all challenge the view that an expanding female audience and increased attention to female-oriented subject matter was associated with bourgeois morality and the evolution of classical narrative structures. In fact, women were attracted to sexually explicit, action-oriented, and agitational films that encouraged alternative viewing modes and extratextual engagement at a time when filmmaking was increasingly standardized toward classical norms. Nor were the kinds of viewing pleasures women engaged at these films always consistent with feminine decorum or the increasingly fixed dictates of classical cinema. The sexual voyeurism encouraged by vice films, the intertextual, ongoing engagement fostered by serials, and the extratextual mobilization marshaled by suffrage films all challenged such assumptions. Indeed, caricatures repeatedly insisted that women were unsuited, perhaps even unable, to assume the absorbed viewing position demanded by classical cinema, because they chattered through the show, daydreamed about stars' off-screen lives, or demonstrated more interest in parading their finery before other patrons than in focusing on the screen drama. "Movie-struck" girls, unable to separate film viewing from romantic dreams of their own stardom, remained hopelessly caught between their fascination with stories on the screen and a narcissistic desire to appear there themselves. In almost every case the pathologized moviegoer of these years—whether overly talkative, overly absorbed, or oversexed—was gendered female.

Thus the view that film viewing offered women a wholly novel and liberating visual perspective during these years needs to be tempered with the evidence that female spectatorship was considered problematic well into the teens. Miriam Hansen and Giuliana Bruno, for example, have both stressed how the evolving sophistication of film's visual and narrative grammar in the prewar years gave female viewers access to new optical delights, how the camera's mobile gaze, its ability to roam city streets unfettered, freed women from restraints that might otherwise have curtailed their circulation in urban landscapes. Yet commentators continued to stress that voyeurism was unsuitable for women, or that women remained either too distracted, too self-obsessed, or too star-struck to watch films "properly." And while the subjects women were offered, and the narrative formats in which they circulated, frequently worked against highbrow assumptions and classical norms, the stories women were told continued to express anxieties about their growing social, economic, and political independence during these years.

Prewar movie culture shows us that women were prized clientele for the cinema, openly catered to with specifically tailored promotions, subject matter of particular interest, and a fan culture that extended their fascination with photoplays into daily life. But women and women's films were not as easily associated with cinema's uplift as many historians have argued. Female audiences, however expanded and newly visible, did not simply transform moviegoing into a socially sanctioned, middle-American pastime. Rather, women consistently appeared at the center of debates over what constituted appropriate conduct at the picture show, who ought to see images on the screen, and what could be shown there. Though coveted and cultivated, female moviegoers provoked contradictory associations during these years, simultaneously idealized as embodiments of virtue and respectability, parodied as "movie-struck" narcissistic girls, endangered as potential victims of mashers lurking in dark auditoriums, and vilified as a politicized social body spilling beyond the confines of neighborhood theaters. While I want to complicate previous notions about the role that female audiences played in the transitional era, stressing the difficulty with which women were incorporated into cinema's social arena and its optical field, I do not mean to downplay the importance of women's patronage during these years, for there has been no other time in the history of American cinema when women's moviegoing habits, tastes, and desires were talked about, catered to, and debated so thoroughly. A closer look at this period shows us that the cultivation of a female audience for the movies, as well as textual viewing positions open to women, were not incidental to the development of classical cinema in the teens but instrumental to it.

By the 1920s, much of what had first stood as controversial about women's moviegoing and female subject matter had been incorporated into the mainstream. Cinemagoing became institutionalized in the nation's dating culture, where it no longer served as an unpleasant index of emerging female sexuality and tawdry urban amusements. Serials, once a hallmark of the industry's bid to cultivate a female fan base outside of classical norms, were relegated to Saturday afternoon fare for children, primarily boys. And the politicized suffragette, so threatening to eager-to-please showmen in the teens, gave way to the flapper—the Jazz Age's emblem of modern femininity. The female moviegoer remained instrumental to Hollywood culture in the twenties, but as Gaylyn Studlar has shown, her gaze was more often channeled toward "appropriate" interests like beauty, romance, and domesticity by a burgeoning fan culture.[5] But it is in the transitional moment, between early nickelodeon culture and Hollywood's silent "golden age," that movie-struck girls, as social audiences of women and as individual female viewers, articulate the tensions of female filmgoing most acutely.

Notes

Abbreviations

BRC   Billy Rose Theater Collection, New York Public Library for the
Performing Arts

MHL   Margaret Herrick Library, Center for Motion Picture Study, Academy
of Motion Picture Arts and Sciences

NBRMPC   National Board of Review of Motion Pictures Collection, Rare Books
and Manuscripts Division, New York Public Library

RLC   Robinson Locke Collection, New York Public Library for the
Performing Arts

RLSBC   Robinson Locke Scrapbooks, New York Public Library for the
Performing Arts

Introduction

1. Eustace Hale Ball, *The Art of the Photoplay* (New York: Veritas, 1913), 114.

2. General histories of this period can be found in Eileen Bowser, *The Transformation of Cinema, 1907–1915* (New York: Charles Scribner's Sons, 1990); Roberta Pearson, "Transitional Cinema," in *The Oxford History of World Cinema*, ed. Geoffrey Nowell-Smith (Oxford and New York: Oxford University Press, 1996), 23–42; and David Robinson, *From Peep Show to Palace: The Birth of American Film* (New York: Columbia University Press, 1996), 101–76.

3. Key sources on the transformation of screening venues during this period include Ben M. Hall, *The Best Remaining Seats: The Story of the Golden Age of the Movie Palace* (New York: Clarkson N. Potter, 1961), 26–55; Bowser, *The Transformation of Cinema*, 121–33; Douglas Gomery, *Shared Pleasures: A History of Movie Presentation in the United States* (Madison: University of Wisconsin Press, 1992), 18–56; Maggie Valentine, *The Show Starts on the Sidewalk: An Architectural History of the Movie Theatre, Starring S. Charles Lee* (New Haven: Yale University Press, 1994), 34–43; Gregory A. Waller, *Main Street Amusements: Movies and Commerical Entertainment in a Southern City, 1896–1930* (Washington: Smithsonian Institution Press, 1996), 65–122; Kathryn H. Fuller, *At the Picture Show: Small-Town Audiences and the Creation of Movie Fan Culture* (Washington: Smithsonian Institution Press, 1996), 47–74.

4. *Harper's Magazine* 125 (September 1912): 634; *Motography*, March 1912, 132; "A Booming Industry," *Outlook* 110 (21 July 1915): 645; and Alan Havig, "The Commercial Amusement Audience in Early Twentieth-Century American Cities," *Journal of American Culture* 5, no. 1 (1982): 5. See also "The Moving-Picture Shows," *Harper's Weekly* 55 (16 September 1911): 6.

5. William Uricchio and Roberta E. Pearson, *Reframing Culture: The Case of the Vitagraph Quality Films* (Princeton: Princeton University Press, 1993).

6. Tom Gunning, "From the Opium Den to the Theatre of Morality: Moral Discourse and Film Process in Early American Cinema," *Art and Text* 30 (1988): 30–40; and Gunning, *D. W. Griffith and the Origins of American Narrative Film: The Early Years*

at Biograph (Urbana and Chicago: University of Illinois Press, 1991), 151–87. On social problem films of the day, see Kay Sloan, *The Loud Silents: Origins of the Social Problem Film* (Urbana and Chicago: University of Illinois Press, 1988); and Kevin Brownlow, *Behind the Mask of Innocence. Sex, Violence, Prejudice, Crime: Films of Social Conscience in the Silent Era* (New York: Alfred Knopf, 1990).

7. Sumiko Higashi, *Cecil B. DeMille and American Culture: The Silent Era* (Berkeley and Los Angeles: University of California Press, 1994); and Janet Staiger, *Bad Women: Regulating Sexuality in Early American Cinema* (Minneapolis: University of Minnesota Press, 1995).

8. Tom Gunning, "Weaving a Narrative: Style and Economic Background in Griffith's Biograph Films," *Quarterly Review of Film Studies* 6, no. 1 (1981): 11–25; Gunning, *D. W. Griffith and the Origins of American Narrative Film*; and Bowser, *The Transformation of Cinema*, 235–72. Changes in performance style are discussed in Bowser, 87–101; Janet Staiger, " 'The Eyes Are Really the Focus': Photoplay Acting and Film Form and Style," *Wide Angle* 6, no. 4 (1985): 14–23; and Roberta E. Pearson, *Eloquent Gestures: The Transformation of Performance Style in the Griffith Biograph Films* (Berkeley and Los Angeles: University of California Press, 1992).

9. Bowser, *The Transformation of Cinema*, 191–215.

10. Miriam Hansen, *Babel and Babylon: Spectatorship in American Silent Film* (Cambridge: Harvard University Press, 1991), 34–86. See also Kathryn Helgesen Fuller, "Boundaries of Participation: The Problem of Spectatorship and American Film Audiences, 1905–1930," *Film and History* 20, no. 4 (1990): 75–86. For specific analyses of spectatorship in the teens, especially as it relates to changing film content, see Charlie Keil, "Reframing *The Italian*: Questions of Audience Address in Early Cinema," *Journal of Film and Video* 42, no. 1 (1990): 36–48; and William Uricchio and Roberta E. Pearson, " 'Films of Quality,' 'High Art Films,' and 'Films de Luxe': Intertextuality and Reading Positions in the Vitagraph Films," *Journal of Film and Video* 41, no. 4 (1989): 15–31.

11. Janet Staiger, "Dividing Labor for Production Control: Thomas Ince and the Rise of the Studio System," in *The American Movie Industry: The Business of Motion Pictures*, ed. Gorham Kindem (Carbondale and Edwardsville: Southern Illinois University Press, 1982), 94–103; and Staiger, "Blueprints for Feature Films," in *The American Film Industry*, ed. Tino Balio, 2d ed. (Madison: University of Wisconsin Press, 1985), 173–94; Staiger, "Mass-Produced Photoplays: Economic and Signifying Practices in the First Years of Hollywood," in *The Hollywood Film Industry*, ed. Paul Kerr (London: British Film Institute, 1986), 99–119; Charles Musser, "Pre-Classical American Cinema: Its Changing Modes of Film Production," *Persistence of Vision* 9 (1991): 46–65; and Bowser, *The Transformation of Cinema*, 159–65.

12. Frederic C. Howe, "What to Do with the Motion-Picture Show: Shall It Be Censored?" *Outlook* 107 (20 June 1914): 414. On the early years of the Board of Censorship, see Robert Fisher, "Film Censorship and Progressive Reform: The National Board of Censorship of Motion Pictures, 1909–1922," *Journal of Popular Film and Television* 4, no. 2 (1975): 143–56; Charles Matthew Feldman, *The National Board of Censorship (Review) of Motion Pictures, 1909–1922* (New York: Arno Press, 1977), 20–87; Kathleen D. McCarthy, "Nickel Vice and Virtue: Movie Censorship in Chicago, 1907–1915," *Journal of Popular Film* 5, no. 1 (1976): 37–56; Daniel Czitrom, "The Redemption of Leisure: The National Board of Censorship and the Rise of Motion Pictures in

New York City, 1900–1920," *Studies in Visual Communication* 10, no. 4 (1984): 2–6; Nancy J. Rosenbloom, "Between Reform and Regulation: The Struggle over Film Censorship in Progressive America, 1909–1922," *Film History* 1, no. 4 (1987): 307–25; Rosenbloom, "Progressive Reform, Censorship and the Motion Picture Industry, 1909–1917," in *Popular Culture and Political Change in Modern America*, ed. Ronald Edsforth and Larry Bennett (Albany: State University of New York Press, 1991), 41–60; Rosenbloom, "In Defense of Moving Pictures: The People's Institute, The National Board of Censorship and the Problems of Leisure in Urban America," *American Studies* 33, no. 2 (1992): 41–61; Czitrom, "The Politics of Performance: From Theater Licensing to Movie Censorship in Turn-of-the-Century New York," *American Quarterly* 44, no. 4 (1992): 525–53.

13. Leslie Midkiff DeBauche, "Advertising and the Movies, 1908–1915," *Film Reader* 6 (1985): 115–24; and Janet Staiger, "Announcing Wares, Winning Patrons, Voicing Ideals: Thinking about the History and Theory of Film Advertising," *Cinema Journal* 29, no. 3 (1990): 3–31.

14. Janet Staiger, "Seeing Stars," *Velvet Light Trap* 20 (1983): 14–23; Richard deCordova, "The Emergence of the Star System in America," *Wide Angle* 6, no. 4 (1985): 4–13; Q. David Bowers, "Souvenir Postcards and the Development of the Star System, 1912–1914," *Film History* 3, no. 1 (1989): 39–45; deCordova, *Picture Personalities: The Emergence of the Star System in America* (Urbana and Chicago: University of Illinois Press, 1990), 50–116; Bowser, *The Transformation of Cinema*, 103–20; and Fuller, *At the Picture Show*, 115–49.

15. Roy Rosenzweig, *Eight Hours for What We Will: Work and Leisure in an Industrial City, 1870–1920* (New York: Cambridge University Press, 1983), 197–98, 202; Elizabeth Ewen, *Immigrant Women in the Land of Dollars: Life and Culture on the Lower East Side, 1890–1920* (New York: Monthly Review Press, 1985), 208–24; Kathy Peiss, *Cheap Amusements: Working Women and Leisure in Turn-of-the-Century New York* (Philadelphia: Temple University Press, 1986), 140–53; Hansen, *Babel and Babylon*, 60–126; and Lauren Rabinovitz, *For the Love of Pleasure: Women, Movies and Culture in Turn-of-the-Century Chicago* (New Brunswick, NJ: Rutgers University Press, 1998), 105–77.

16. Witness the controversy sparked by Ben Singer's argument about Manhattan's movie audiences in the earlier nickelodeon period: Ben Singer, "Manhattan Nickelodeons: New Data on Audiences and Exhibitors," *Cinema Journal* 34, no. 3 (1995): 5–35; Robert C. Allen, "Manhattan Myopia; or, Oh! Iowa!" *Cinema Journal* 35, no. 3 (1996): 75–103; Sumiko Higashi, "Dialogue: Manhattan's Nickelodeons," *Cinema Journal* 35, no. 3 (1996): 72–73; Singer, "New York, Just Like I Pictured It . . . ," *Cinema Journal* 35, no. 3 (1996): 104–28; William Uricchio and Roberta E. Pearson, "New York? New York!" *Cinema Journal* 36, no. 4 (1997): 98–102; Judith Thissen, "Oy, Myopia!" *Cinema Journal* 36, no. 4 (1997): 102–7; and Singer, "Manhattan Melodrama," *Cinema Journal* 36, no. 4 (1997): 107–12.

17. Juvenile Protective Association of Cincinnati, *Recreation Survey of Cincinnati* (Cincinnati, OH, 1913), 26–27; Madison Board of Commerce, *Madison "The Four Lake City" Recreational Survey* (Madison, WI, 1915), 53–54; William Trufant Foster, *Vaudeville and Motion Picture Shows: A Study of Theatres in Portland, Oregon* (Portland: Reed College, 1914), 17; John Joseph Phelan, *Motion Pictures as a Phase of Commercialized Amusement in Toledo, Ohio* (Toledo: Little Book Press, 1919), 37–38;

and The Cleveland Foundation Committee, *Commercial Recreation* (Cleveland, OH: Cleveland Foundation Committee, 1920), 21.

18. F. H. Richardson, "Women and Children," *Moving Picture World*, 21 February 1914, 962.

19. Mary Heaton Vorse, "Some Picture Show Audiences," *Outlook* 98 (24 June 1911), 443; and Olivia Howard Dunbar, "The Lure of the Films," *Harper's Weekly* 57 (18 January 1913): 20.

20. Fuller, *At the Picture Show*, 28–46.

21. *New York Times*, 5 December 1920, n.p. Cited in Richard Koszarski, *An Evening's Entertainment: The Age of the Silent Feature Picture, 1915–1928* (New York: Charles Scribner's Sons, 1990), 30. In the absence of data confirming Bush's observation, it is wise not to overvalue his claim, especially in light of Leo Handel's argument that the film industry has consistently overestimated the actual number of female patrons in attendance. See Leo A. Handel, *Hollywood Looks at Its Audience: A Report on Film Audience Research* (Urbana: University of Illinois Press, 1950), 99–100. Key discussions of race and ethnicity among moviegoers in the transitional era include Hansen, *Babel and Babylon*, 60–76; Mary Carbine, " 'The Finest outside the Loop': Motion Picture Exhibition in Chicago's Black Metropolis, 1905–1928," *Camera Obscura* 23 (1990): 8–41; Douglas Monroy, "'Our Children Get So Different Here': Film, Fashion, Popular Culture, and the Process of Cultural Syncretization in Mexican Los Angeles, 1900–1935," *Aztlan: A Journal of Chicano Studies* 19, no. 1 (1988–90): 79–108; Junko Ogihara, "The Exhibition of Films for Japanese Americans in Los Angeles during the Silent Film Era," *Film History* 4, no. 1 (1990): 81–87; and Gregory A. Waller, "Another Audience: Black Moviegoing, 1907–1916," *Cinema Journal* 31, no. 2 (1992): 3–25.

Chapter One
Spare Us One Evening: Cultivating Cinema's Female Audience

1. *Universal Weekly*, 6 September 1913, 33.

2. Russell Merritt, "Nickelodeon Theatres, 1905–1914: Building an Audience for the Movies," in *The American Film Industry*, ed. Tino Balio, 2d ed. (Madison: University of Wisconsin Press, 1985), 83–102. For other discussions of efforts to woo female patrons during these years, see Eileen Bowser, *The Transformation of Cinema, 1907–1915* (New York: Charles Scribner's Sons, 1990), 37–47; Miriam Hansen, *Babel and Babylon: Spectatorship in American Silent Film* (Cambridge: Harvard University Press, 1991), 114–20; and Douglas Gomery, *Shared Pleasures: A History of Movie Presentation in the United States* (Madison: University of Wisconsin Press, 1992), 31.

3. *Chicago Tribune*, 10 January 1914, 7.

4. On general advertising and promotional practices in the 1910s, see Leslie Midkiff DeBauche, "Advertising and the Movies, 1908–1915," *Film Reader* 6 (1985): 115–24; Jane Gaines, "From Elephants to Lux Soap: The Programming and 'Flow' of Early Motion Picture Exploitation," *Velvet Light Trap* 25 (1990): 29–43; Richard Koszarski, *An Evening's Entertainment: The Age of the Silent Feature Picture, 1915–1928* (New York: Charles Scribner's Sons, 1990), 34–41; and Janet Staiger, "Announcing Wares, Winning Patrons, Voicing Ideals: Thinking about the History and Theory of Film Advertising," *Cinema Journal* 29, no. 3 (1990): 3–31.

5. Epes Winthrop Sargent, *Picture Theatre Advertising* (New York: Chalmers Publishing, 1915), 219.

6. A related example of marketing outreach to women at home is examined in Alexandra Keller, "Disseminations of Modernity: Representation and Consumer Desire in Early Mail-Order Catalogues," in *Cinema and the Invention of Modern Life*, ed. Leo Charney and Vanessa R. Schwartz (Berkeley and Los Angeles: University of California Press, 1995), 156–82.

7. Merritt, "Nickelodeon Theaters," 96, 95.

8. Bertha June Richardson, *The Woman Who Spends: A Study of Her Economic Function*, rev. ed. (Boston: Whitcomb and Barrows, 1910), 21–22.

9. *Motography*, April 1912, 158; *Moving Picture News*, 19 April 1913, 23; *Moving Picture World*, 27 May 1916, 1486; *Moving Picture World*, 10 June 1916, 1855; Koszarski, *An Evening's Entertainment*, 208; and Janet Staiger, *Bad Women: Regulating Sexuality in Early American Cinema* (Minneapolis: University of Minnesota Press, 1995), 96–97. The growing interest of women's clubs in the cinema during the 1910s eventually spawned the Better Films Movement of the 1920s.

10. Jane Stannard Johnson, "Woman's Duty to Motion Pictures," *Ladies' World*, January 1915, 18.

11. "The Moving-Picture Show: What It Ought to Mean in Your Town, and What It Really Does Mean," *Woman's Home Companion* 38 (October 1911): 21–22.

12. "Will You Stand with Me?" *Woman's Home Companion* 43 (May 1916). Also see "Making the Most of Moving Pictures," *Woman's Home Companion* 39 (April 1912), 12, 100; and Helen Duey, "The Movement for Better Films," *Woman's Home Companion* 42 (March 1915): 3, 64.

13. *Moving Picture World*, 16 May 1914, 961.

14. *Chicago Tribune*, 10 January 1914, 7.

15. *Paramount Progress*, 11 November 1915, 6.

16. Lois Banner, *American Beauty* (New York: Alfred Knopf, 1983), 187–90.

17. Sargent, *Picture Theatre Advertising*, 217–24.

18. Merritt, "Nickelodeon Theaters," 96.

19. Sargent, *Picture Theatre Advertising*, 218.

20. Ibid., 219.

21. On the disreputability of nickelodeons among the middle-class, see Kathleen D. McCarthy, "Nickel Vice and Virtue: Movie Censorship in Chicago, 1907–1915," *Journal of Popular Film* 5, no. 1 (1976): 37–56; Robert A. Armour, "The Effects of Censorship Pressure on the New York Nickelodeon Market, 1907–1909," *Film History* 4, no. 2 (1990): 113–21; Bowser, *The Transformation of Cinema*, 37–52; and William Uricchio and Roberta E. Pearson, *Reframing Culture: The Case of the Vitagraph Quality Films* (Princeton: Princeton University Press, 1993), 24–33. Robert C. Allen disputes this characterization of nickelodeon audiences. See his article "Motion Picture Exhibition in Manhattan, 1906–1912: Beyond the Nickelodeon," in *The American Movie Industry: The Business of Motion Pictures*, ed. Gorham Kindem (Carbondale: Southern Illinois University Press, 1982), 12–24.

22. John B. Rathbun, *Motion Picture Making and Exhibiting* (Chicago: Charles C. Thompson Co., 1914), 96.

23. *Motion Picture News*, 8 November 1913, 44–45.

24. Sargent, *Picture Theatre Advertising*, 25.

25. Ibid., 223. Douglas Gomery demonstrates that a similar service culture designed to cultivate middle-class audiences continued at movie palaces in the 1920s. See Gomery, *Shared Pleasures*, 49–50.

26. Elizabeth Reid, "What the American Woman Pays for Cosmetics," *Woman Beautiful* 4 (November 1910): 29. Quoted in Banner, *American Beauty*, 217.

27. *Moving Picture World*, 28 March 1914, 1690.

28. Sargent, *Picture Theatre Advertising*, 26.

29. *Motography*, September 1909, 86.

30. Sargent, *Picture Theatre Advertising*, 24–25.

31. Ernest A. Dench, *Advertising by Motion Pictures* (Cincinnati: Standard Publishing, 1916), 241.

32. Susan Porter Benson, *Counter Cultures: Saleswomen, Managers, and Customers in American Department Stores, 1890–1940* (Urbana: University of Illinois Press, 1986), 75–101. The quoted passage appears on 84. See also Gunther Barth, *City People: The Rise of Modern City Culture in Nineteenth-Century America* (New York: Oxford University Press, 1980); and William R. Leach, "Transformations in a Culture of Consumption: Women and Department Stores, 1890–1925," *Journal of American History* 71 (1984): 319–42.

33. Benson, *Counter Cultures*, 82–83; and William Leach, *Land of Desire: Merchants, Power, and the Rise of a New American Culture* (New York: Pantheon Books, 1993), 78–81. Jennifer Scanlon makes a similar point about women's magazines during this era. See Scanlon, *Inarticulate Longings: The Ladies' Home Journal, Gender, and the Promises of Consumer Culture* (New York: Routledge, 1995), 57.

34. Anne Friedberg, *Window Shopping: Cinema and the Postmodern* (Berkeley and Los Angeles: University of California Press, 1993), 41–44, 57–58, 65–68, 77–81; and Lauren Rabinovitz, *For the Love of Pleasure: Women, Movies and Culture in Turn-of-the-Century Chicago* (New Brunswick, NJ: Rutgers University Press, 1998), 68–79.

35. *Nickelodeon*, February 1909, 33–34.

36. Jeanne Thomas Allen, "The Film Viewer as Consumer," *Quarterly Review of Film Studies* 5, no. 4 (1980): 481–499. Key discussions of the mobilization of consumer culture later in the studio era include Charles Eckert, "The Carole Lombard in Macy's Window," *Quarterly Review of Film Studies* 3, no. 1 (1978): 1–21; Jane Gaines and Charlotte Herzog, "Puffed Sleeves before Teatime: Joan Crawford, Adrian and Women Audiences," *Wide Angle* 6, no. 4 (1985): 24–33; Mary Ann Doane, *The Desire to Desire: The Woman's Film of the 1940s* (Bloomington: Indiana University Press, 1987), 1–37; Maria La Place, "Producing and Consuming the Woman's Film: Discursive Struggle in *Now, Voyager*," in *Home Is Where the Heart Is: Studies in Melodrama and the Woman's Film*, ed. Christine Gledhill (London: British Film Institute, 1987), 138–66; Mary Ann Doane, "The Economy of Desire: The Commodity Form in/of the Cinema," *Quarterly Review of Film and Video* 11, no. 1 (1989): 23–33; Jane Gaines, "The Queen Christina Tie-Ups: Convergence of Show Window and Screen," *Quarterly Review of Film and Video* 11, no. 1 (1989): 35–60; and Jackie Stacey, *Star Gazing: Hollywood Cinema and Female Spectatorship* (New York and London: Routledge, 1994), 176–223.

37. Paul O'Malley, "Neighborhood Nickelodeons: Residential Theaters in South Denver from 1907 to 1917," *Colorado Heritage* 3 (1984): 54.

38. Sargent, *Picture Theatre Advertising*, 220–21.

39. *Universal Weekly*, 21 February 1914, 28.

40. *Edison Kinetogram*, 1 January 1910, 12. Quoted in Allen, "The Film Viewer as Consumer," 487.

41. *Moving Picture Stories*, 11 April 1913, 29.

42. *Moving Picture News*, 22 February 1913, 10. Also see *Motion Picture News*, 8 November 1913, 44–45.

43. On recommendations for theater improvements in the teens, see James F. Hodges, *Opening and Operating a Motion Picture Theatre, How It Is Done Successfully* (New York: Scenario Publishing, 1912); David S. Hulfish, *Motion-Picture Work: A General Treatise on Picture Taking, Picture Making, Photo-Plays, and Theatre Management and Operation* (Chicago: American School of Correspondence, 1913), 165–207; Rathbun, *Motion Picture Making and Exhibiting*, 96–120; Arthur S. Meloy, *Theaters and Motion Picture Houses* (New York: Architects' Supply and Publishing Company, 1916); Ben M. Hall, *The Best Remaining Seats: The Story of the Golden Age of the Movie Palace* (New York: Clarkson N. Potter, 1961), 26–55; Bowser, *The Transformation of Cinema*, 121–33; Maggie Valentine, *The Show Starts on the Sidewalk: An Architectural History of the Movie Theatre, Starring S. Charles Lee* (New Haven: Yale University Press, 1994), 34–43; and Linda Woal, "When a Dime Could Buy a Dream: Siegmund Lubin and the Birth of Motion Picture Exhibition, *Film History* 6, no. 2 (1994): 152–65. Charlotte Herzog charts the relationship between movie theater design and department store interiors in "The Movie Palace and the Theatrical Sources of Its Architectural Style," *Cinema Journal* 20, no. 2 (1981): 15–37, and "The Archaeology of Cinema Architecture: The Origins of the Movie Theater," *Quarterly Review of Film Studies* (Winter 1984): 11–32.

44. *Moving Picture News*, 22 February 1913, 10–11.

45. Koszarski, *An Evening's Entertainment*, 20.

46. Sargent, *Picture Theatre Advertising*, 18.

47. Leach, "Transformations in a Culture of Consumption," 323; and Banner, *American Beauty*, 32–36, 208–19.

48. *Lexington Leader*, 24 November 1912, 6. Quoted in Gregory Waller, *Main Street Amusements: Movies and Commercial Entertainment in a Southern City* (Washington: Smithsonian Institution Press, 1995), 103.

49. Leach, "Transformations in a Culture of Consumption," 324.

50. Kathy Peiss, *Cheap Amusements: Working Women and Leisure in Turn-of-the-Century New York* (Philadelphia: Temple University Press, 1986), chap. 4. Also see Banner, *American Beauty*, 198–99.

51. Richardson, *The Woman Who Spends*, 109.

52. *Moving Picture World*, 12 October 1912, 138. Also see Q. David Bowers, "Souvenir Postcards and the Development of the Star System, 1912–1914," *Film History* 3, no. 1 (1989): 39–45.

53. *Ladies' World*, December 1913, 1.

54. *Paramount Progress*, 11 November 1915, 7–8.

55. Ibid.

56. *Motion Picture Supplement*, September 1915, 71.

57. *Motion Picture Classic*, April 1916, 73.

58. *Eclair Bulletin*, October 1914, 2; and *Eclair Bulletin*, November 1914, 2.

59. Sargent, *Picture Theatre Advertising*, 234–35.

60. *Nickelodeon*, May 1909, 142.

61. *Nickelodeon*, June 1909, 167.

62. *Nickelodeon*, May 1909, 142.

63. *Universal Weekly*, 27 December 1913, 33. Also see DeBauche, "Advertising and the Movies," 118.

64. See Scanlon, *Inarticulate Longings*, 231–32.

65. *Paramount Progress*, 11 November 1915, 5.

66. Serializations of the *What Happened to Mary?* story appeared monthly in *Ladies' World* between August 1912 and July 1913. Ben Singer provides a useful breakdown of story tie-ins published in newspapers and women's magazines in appendix 1 of his article "Fiction Tie-Ins and Narrative Intelligibility, 1911–1918," *Film History* 5, no. 4 (1993): 500–501.

67. *Ladies' World*, February 1914, 39. Ads for slides promoting the contest appear in *Universal Weekly* throughout late 1913 and early 1914. See, for example, *Universal Weekly*, 13 December 1913, 2. Testimony from a satisfied exhibitor appears in *Universal Weekly*, 21 February 1914, 28. See ads in *Ladies' World*, December 1913, 1, 39; January 1914, 1, 34; and February 1914, 39.

68. *Ladies' World*, December 1913, 1.

69. Scanlon borrows this phrase from a *Ladies' Home Journal* copy writer of the 1920s. See Scanlon, *Inarticulate Longings*, 10.

70. Lauren Rabinovitz, "Temptations of Pleasure: Nickelodeons, Amusement Parks, and the Sights of Female Sexuality," *Camera Obscura* 23 (1991): 72. Rabinovitz develops these ideas further in *For the Love of Pleasure*, esp. 116–21.

71. Hansen, *Babel and Babylon*, 85–86, 116–25; Sumiko Higashi, *Cecil B. DeMille and American Culture: The Silent Era* (Berkeley and Los Angeles: University of California Press, 1994), 87–92; and Rabinovitz, *For the Love of Pleasure*, 79, 102. Quotations are from Hansen, 122, Rabinovitz, 79, and Hansen, 124.

72. W. A. Scranton, "Etiquette: On the Proper Way for Two Women to Spend an Evening in a Moving Picture Theater," *Motion Picture Magazine*, May 1916, 65–70.

73. *Moving Picture World*, 15 January 1916, 415.

74. *Motography*, May 1911, 77.

75. *Paste-Pot and Shears*, 12 March 1917, 3. Folder 565, William Selig Collection, MHL.

76. Hansen, *Babel and Babylon*, 95.

77. Kathryn Fuller's analysis of early fan culture leads her to a different conclusion. She finds that male fans were the focus of more criticism than women, because of perceived excesses in their attachment to screen stars. My research into theater conduct and viewing habits suggests, on the contrary, that women were more frequently singled out for criticism. See Kathryn H. Fuller, *At the Picture Show: Small-Town Audiences and the Creation of Movie Fan Culture* (Washington: Smithsonian Institution Press, 1996), 143.

78. *Moving Picture World*, 15 January 1916, 414–15.

79. *Picture Progress*, July 1915, 10.

80. *Motion Picture Magazine*, April 1916, 156.

81. Frank Herbert Richardson, *Motion Picture Handbook: A Guide for Managers and Operators of Motion Picture Theatres*, 3d ed. (New York: Moving Picture World, 1916), 662.

82. Bowser, *The Transformation of Cinema*, 45–46, 123–24.

83. *Moving Picture News*, 11 January 1913, 20. Quoted in Bowser, *The Transformation of Cinema*, 123.

84. *Moving Picture World*, 15 January 1916, 413.

85. Sargent, *Picture Theatre Advertising*, 5.

86. *Moving Picture World*, 25 May 1907, 180. I am indebted to James Lastra for sending me this item after our brief discussion in the departure lounge at the Syracuse airport in 1994.

87. *Motography*, 15 March 1910, 148. The 1909 film *Those Awful Hats* even dramatizes the issue of spectators unable to see past women's hats, ending with an intertitle declaring, "Ladies Will Please Remove Their Hats."

88. Scranton, "Etiquette," 67.

89. *Moving Picture Stories*, 18 April 1913, 9.

90. *Motion Picture Magazine*, March 1917, 138.

91. *Motion Picture Magazine*, September 1915, 139. A similar periscope cartoon from a 1916 *Photoplay* is reproduced in Koszarski, *An Evening's Entertainment*, 16.

92. Thekla D. Harrison, "On Etiquette, As It Were. Or Advice to a Young Man and a Young Lady upon Entering a Picture Show," *Motion Picture Supplement* 1, no. 1 (September 1915): 40.

93. *Motography*, 15 April 1910, 215.

94. Mirrors were also used to regulate the conduct of female department store customers who might be tempted into shoplifting by making them objects of covert surveillance. See Benson, *Counter Cultures*, and Elaine S. Abelson, *When Ladies Go A-Thieving: Middle-Class Shoplifters in the Victorian Department Store* (New York and London: Oxford University Press, 1989).

95. *Motion Picture News*, 31 January 1914, 57.

96. William A. Page, "The Movie-Struck Girl," *Woman's Home Companion* 48 (June 1918): 18, 75.

97. Anna Steese Richardson, " 'Filmitis,' the Modern Malady—Its Symptoms and Its Cure," *McClure's* 47 (January 1916): 12–14, 70.

98. Fuller, *At the Picture Show*, 115–32.

99. Marguerite Clark, "Eat and Keep Well: The Suggestions of a Famous Photoplay Star," *Picture Progress*, November 1916, 4; "When You Dance: Some Gowns and Hats. Suggestions by Florence Walton," *Picture Progress*, November 1916, 12–13; Richard deCordova, *Picture Personalities: The Emergence of the Star System in America* (Urbana and Chicago: University of Illinois Press, 1990), 110; and Fuller, *At the Picture Show*, 157.

100. Arthur Hornblow, Jr., "Have You a Movie Camera Face?" *Motion Picture Classic*, May 1916, 14–15.

101. Arthur Hornblow, Jr., "How They Got In," *Motion Picture Classic*, November 1916, 23–25; William Allen Johnson, "In Motion Picture Land," *Everybody's Magazine* 33 (October 1915): 437–48; Albert Marple, "Making Pictures in California," *Motion Picture Classic*, April 1916, 37–39, 73; Ernest A. Dench, "Extras! Extras! Extras!"

Motion Picture Classic, July 1916, 57–58; and Helen G. Smith, "The Extra Girl Is Handed a Few Snickers," *Photoplay*, March 1920, 107–8.

102. "It's a Long Way to Filmland," *Motion Picture Supplement*, October 1915, 69.

103. " 'Breaking into the Game': Told by a Girl Who Didn't Break In," *Photoplay*, August 1914, 131–35.

Chapter Two
Is Any Girl Safe? Women's Leisure, Motion Pictures, and the White Slavery Scare

1. *Moving Picture World*, 27 June 1914, 1779.

2. Although it inaugurates the white slave film craze in 1913, *Traffic in Souls* was not the first film to deal with white slavery. Kay Sloan identifies several earlier titles that include references to the theme, most notably *The Fatal Hour* (Biograph, 1908) and *Decoyed* (American Mutoscope and Biograph, 1904). See Sloan, *The Loud Silents: Origins of the Social Problem Film* (Urbana and Chicago: University of Illinois Press, 1988), 80–82. Danish cinema appears to have been among the first to exploit the panic worldwide with a series of films released several years before the American group, among them *The White Slave Girl* (1906) and *The White Slave Trade* (1910). See Ron Mottram, *Danish Film before Dreyer* (Metuchen, NJ: Scarecrow Press, 1988), 90–99. Janet Staiger also mentions three short American films released around the time of *Traffic in Souls* that seem to deal with aspects of white slavery. These include *The Fight against Evil* (Rex, 1913), *The Temptation of June* (IMP, 1913), and *By Man's Law* (Biograph, 1913). See Staiger, *Bad Women: Regulating Sexuality in Early American Cinema* (Minneapolis: University of Minnesota Press, 1995), 129–30.

3. George Kibbe Turner, "The City of Chicago: A Study of the Great Immoralities," *McClure's* 28 (April 1907): 575–92.

4. George Kibbe Turner, "The Daughters of the Poor," *McClure's* 34 (November 1909): 45. Also see "The Slave Traffic in America," *Outlook* 93 (6 November 1909): 528–29. The Committee of Fifteen, organized by New York's Chamber of Commerce, had investigated alleged connections between red-light districts and police graft in 1900. The committee's 1902 report, *The Social Evil*, prefigured vice commission reports issued by many American municipalities in the early 1910s. See Committee of Fifteen, *The Social Evil, with Special Reference to Conditions Existing in the City of New York*, 2d ed. (New York and London: G. P. Putnam's Sons, 1912).

5. *New York Times*, 9 December 1909, 10; and *New York Times* 30 April 1910, 1.

6. "Five 'White Slave' Trade Investigations," *McClure's* 35 (July 1910): 346; and "The Rockefeller Grand Jury Report: Showing the Conditions of the 'White Slave' Trade in New York City," *McClure's* 35 (August 1910): 471–73. The complete report is reproduced in O. Edward Janney, *The White Slave Traffic in America* (New York: National Vigilance Committee, 1912), 56–75.

7. Frederick K. Grittner, *White Slavery: Myth, Ideology and American Law* (New York: Garland, 1990), 83–88 and 92–102. Also see Norbert MacDonald, "The Diggs-Caminetti Case of 1913 and Subsequent Interpretation of the White Slave Trade Act," *Pacific Historian* 29, no. 1 (1985): 30–39. So vague is the wording of the Mann Act, Marlene D. Beckman contends, that well into the 1970s it was frequently misapplied to unmarried couples traveling together. See Beckman, "The White Slave Traffic Act:

Historical Impact of a Federal Crime Policy on Women," *Women and Politics* 4, no. 3 (1984): 85–101.

8. Mark Thomas Connelly, *The Response to Prostitution in the Progressive Era* (Chapel Hill: University of North Carolina Press, 1980), 14–16; Ruth Rosen, *The Lost Sisterhood: Prostitution in America, 1900–1918* (Baltimore: Johns Hopkins University Press, 1982), 43; and Roy Lubove, "The Progressive and the Prostitute," *Historian* 24, no. 3 (1962): 312–13. Also see Robert E. Riegel, "Changing American Attitudes towards Prostitution," *Journal of the History of Ideas* 29 (July–September 1968): 437–52. For information on prostitution and the social hygiene movement, see John C. Burnham, "The Progressive Era Revolution in American Attitudes towards Sex," *Journal of American History* 9, no. 4 (March 1973): 885–908.

9. Rosen, *The Lost Sisterhood*, 13; and Lubove, "The Progressive and the Prostitute," 330. The relationship that developed during this period between female prostitutes and male pimps only amplified the sexual division of labor in prostitution. For information on the rise of the pimp system documented by reformers like George Kneeland and Maude Miner, see Barbara Meil Hobson, *Uneasy Virtue: The Politics of Prostitution and the American Reform Tradition* (New York: Basic Books, 1987), 141–47. The nineteenth-century response to prostitution is chronicled in David J. Pivar, *Purity Crusade: Sexual Morality and Social Control, 1868–1900* (Westport, CT: Greenwood Press, 1973); and Laura Hapke, *Conventions of Denial: Prostitution in Late Nineteenth-Century American Anti-Vice Narrative*, Michigan Occasional Papers in Women's Studies, no. 24 (Ann Arbor: Women's Studies Program, University of Michigan, 1982). The classic nineteenth-century study is William Sanger, *The History of Prostitution: Its Extent, Causes, and Effects throughout the World* (New York: Harper and Brothers, 1858).

10. Vice Commission of Chicago, *The Social Evil in Chicago; A Study of Existing Conditions* (Chicago: Gunthorp-Warren, 1911), 311. The Chicago report received wide national distribution and formed the model for many other municipal investigations. See Grittner, *White Slavery*, 74.

11. George J. Kneeland, *Commercialized Prostitution in New York City*, rev. ed. (New York: The Century Co., 1917), 86; and "Man's Commerce in Women: Mr. Rockefeller's Bureau of Social Hygiene Issues Its First Report," *McClure's* 41 (August 1913): 185–89.

12. See, for example, Vice Commission of Minneapolis, *Report of the Vice Commission of Minneapolis* (Minneapolis, 1911), 75; and Vice Commission of Philadelphia, *A Report on Existing Conditions* (Philadelphia, 1913), 16. Both reports are reprinted in *The Prostitute and the Social Reformer: Commercial Vice in the Progressive Era* (New York: Arno Press, 1974). In contrast to my argument, Rosen finds significant instances of white slavery documented during the Progressive Era. She argues that by downplaying accounts of white slavery, we deny widespread male violence against women. For her sympathetic view of reports of white slavery, see Rosen, *The Lost Sisterhood*, 112–35. An interpretation of all prostitution as slavery is presented in Kathleen Barry, *Female Sexual Slavery* (New York: New York University Press, 1984).

13. "Social Evil in a Smaller City," *Survey* 26 (16 May 1911): 212. See also Emma Goldman, "The Traffic in Women" (1917), reprinted in *The Traffic in Women and Other Essays on Feminism* (New York: Times Change Press, 1970), 19–32. Goldman decries the public fascination with prostitution and white slavery during the prewar years,

claiming that reports of slave rings are "tales from school" which obscure the true causes of prostitution: capitalism and patriarchal notions of sexuality.

14. Editorial, *Survey* 31 (28 February 1912): 683.

15. Connelly, *The Response to Prostitution*, 31–35. This view is propagated in "Wages and Sin," *Literary Digest* 46 (22 March 1913): 621–24.

16. Clifford G. Roe, *Panders and Their White Slaves* (New York: Fleming H. Revel Co., 1910), 120–21.

17. Quoted in "A Philadelphia Warning to Girls," *Literary Digest* 46 (1 February 1913): 234.

18. *New York Dramatic Mirror*, 20 August 1913, 6; *Theatre*, September 1913, xi; *Theatre*, October 1913, 112; and *New York Dramatic Mirror*, 10 September 1913, 6, 8. Film versions of the three best-known stage productions were subsequently released: *The House of Bondage* premiered in January 1914 while the stage production continued its run. Feature-length film adaptations of both *The Lure* and *The Fight*, including players from the original stage casts, were released in August 1914 and January 1915, respectively.

19. Quoted in *New York Dramatic Mirror*, 10 September 1913, 8.

20. "Muensterberg Vigorously Denounces Red Light Drama," *New York Times*, 14 September 1913, 4.

21. "Dramatizing Vice," *Literary Digest* 47 (1913): 577–78; *New York Dramatic Mirror*, 10 September 1913, 10; and *New York Dramatic Mirror*, 17 September 1913, 7.

22. *New York Herald*, 10 December 1913, 3.

23. *Moving Picture World*, 25 October 1913. Quoted in Kathleen Karr, "The Long Square-Up: Exploitation Trends in the Silent Films," *Journal of Popular Film* 3, no. 2 (1974): 111.

24. *New York Dramatic Mirror*, 17 September 1913, 8.

25. *New York Dramatic Mirror*, 20 August 1913, 6.

26. "Popular Gullibility as Exhibited in the New White Slavery Hysteria," *Current Opinion*, February 1914, 129. See also "Sex-O'Clock in America," *Current Opinion*, August 1913, 113–14; and "Is White Slavery Nothing More Than a Myth?" *Current Opinion*, November 1913, 348.

27. Besides *Panders and Their White Slaves*, Roe's publications include a 1911 publication variously titled *The Great War on White Slavery: or, Fighting for the Protection of Our Girls, Horrors of the White Slave Trade; The Mighty Crusade to Protect the Purity of Our Homes*, and *The Prodigal Daughter; The White Slave Evil and the Remedy*. It is reprinted as *The Great War on White Slavery* (New York: Garland, 1979). Evidence suggests that Roe altered some of his data, changing accounts of consensual sex into white slave abductions. (Walter Reckless, *Vice in Chicago* [Chicago: University of Chicago Press, 1933], 36–39, as cited in Grittner, *White Slavery*, 66.)

28. Arthur Gleason, "The Story of Rosalinda," *Collier's* 51 (10 May 1913): 16. For other "case histories" in the popular press, see Harvey J. O'Higgins, "The Case of Fanny," *Collier's* 50 (2 March 1912): 11; and S. C. Rippey, "The Case of Angeline," *Outlook* 106 (31 January 1914): 255–56. Novels depicting the slave trade include Reginald Wright Kauffman, *The House of Bondage* (New York: Grosset and Dunlap, 1910); Rev. Guy F. Phelps, *Ethel Vale: The White Slave* (Chicago: The Christian Witness Co.,

1910); and Harry Coulter Todd, *The White Slave: A Novel* (New York: Neale Publishing, 1913).

29. See Egal Feldman, "Prostitution, the Alien Woman and the Progressive Imagination, 1910–1915," *American Quarterly* 19, no. 2 (1967): 192–206; and Francesco Cordasco, *The White Slave Trade and the Immigrants: A Chapter in American Social History* (Detroit: Blaire-Ethridge Books, 1981), 1–41. For an account of Jewish-American women in prostitution and the involvement of Jewish gangs in slave trafficking, see Edward J. Bristow, *Prostitution and Prejudice: The Jewish Fight against White Slavery, 1870–1939* (Oxford: Clarendon Press, 1982), 85–108. On the work of Jewish reformers in the prewar years, see Bristow, 215–80.

30. Henry B. Leonard, "The Immigrants' Protective League of Chicago, 1908–1921" *Journal of the Illinois State Historical Society* 66 (1973): 276–77.

31. Kneeland, *Commercialized Prostitution*, 86.

32. Roe, *The Great War on White Slavery*, 106. See also Ernest A. Bell, *Fighting the Traffic in Young Girls; or, War on the White Slave Trade* (Chicago: L. S. Ball, 1910), 110–11; and Rev. Frederick M. Lehman, *The White Slave Hell; or, With Christ at Midnight in the Slums of Chicago* (Chicago: The Christian Witness Co., 1910), 369.

33. Vice Commission of Chicago, *The Social Evil in Chicago*, 230; and Vice Commission of Philadelphia, *A Report on Existing Conditions*, 21.

34. Reprinted in Janney, *The White Slave Traffic*, 66.

35. Maude Miner, *The Slavery of Prostitution: A Plea for Emancipation* (New York: Macmillan, 1916), 85.

36. *New York World*, 15 March 1914, E1. Ironically, it was Swann who presided at several of the New York court hearings involving films on the slave trade.

37. Quoted in *Moving Picture World*, 12 March 1910, 370–71. For the record, *Moving Picture World* characterized Shaw's comments as "most uncharitable slander," claiming that "no greater nonsense was ever talked" and calling upon exhibitors to refute her charges.

38. Quoted in Eileen Bowser, *The Transformation of Cinema, 1907–1915* (New York: Charles Scribner's Sons, 1990), 38.

39. *Moving Picture News*, 19 April 1913, 23. See also *Motography*, April 1912, 158.

40. Vice Commission of Chicago, *The Social Evil in Chicago*, 247.

41. "The Morals of the Movies: From the Standpoint of the Manager in the Small Town," *Survey* 33 (4 March 1916): 662.

42. Janney, *The White Slave Traffic*, 99.

43. Theodore A. Bingham, *The Girl That Disappears: The Real Facts about the White Slave Traffic* (Boston: R. G. Badger, 1911), 60.

44. Lauren Rabinovitz, "Temptations of Pleasure: Nickelodeons, Amusement Parks and the Sights of Female Sexuality," *Camera Obscura* 23 (1991): 71, 73; and Rabinovitz, *For the Love of Pleasure: Women, Movies and Culture in Turn-of-the-Century Chicago* (New Brunswick, NJ: Rutgers University Press, 1998), 116–21.

45. Quoted in John Joseph Phelan, *Motion Pictures as a Phase of Commercialized Amusement in Toledo, Ohio* (Toledo: Little Book Press, 1919), 265.

46. Jane Addams, *A New Conscience and an Ancient Evil* (New York: Macmillan, 1912), 111.

47. "The Morals of the Movies: From the Standpoint," 662.

48. Rabinovitz, "Temptations of Pleasure," 72.

49. Kathy Peiss, *Cheap Amusements: Working Women and Leisure in Turn-of-the-Century New York* (Philadelphia: Temple University Press, 1986), 45; and Peiss, "Commercial Leisure and the 'Woman Question,' " in *For Fun and Profit: The Transformation of Leisure into Consumption*, ed. Richard Butsch (Philadelphia: Temple University Press, 1990), 105–17.

50. Marion Harland, "The Passing of the Home Daughter," *Independent* 71 (13 July 1911): 90, quoted in James McGovern, "The American Woman's Pre–World War I Freedom in Manners and Morals," *Journal of American History* 55, no. 2 (September 1968): 320. Also see Annette Austin, "The Drifting Daughter: Why Many Girls Leave Home to Work in the City and Why They and Many Others Do Not Marry," *Ladies' World*, October 1912, 5–6.

51. Leslie Woodcock Tentler, *Wage-Earning Women: Industrial Work and Family Life in the United States, 1900–1930* (New York: Oxford University Press, 1979), 110–12.

52. Ruth S. True, *The Neglected Girl* (New York: Russell Sage Foundation, 1914), 68–69.

53. Kathy Peiss, " 'Charity Girls' and City Pleasures: Historical Notes on Working-Class Sexuality, 1880–1920," in *Passion and Power: Sexuality in History*, ed. Kathy Peiss and Christina Simmons (Philadelphia: Temple University Press, 1989), 57–69.

54. Belle Lindner Israels, "The Way of the Girl," *Survey* 22 (3 July 1909): 486–88.

55. Peiss, " 'Charity Girls,' " 58.

56. Richard Henry Edwards, *Popular Amusements* (New York: Association Press, 1915), 22.

57. "The Working Girl," *Collier's* 51 (28 June 1913): 13. Emphasis added.

58. Edwards, *Popular Amusements*, 19.

59. Ibid., 69.

60. Judith R. Walkowitz makes a similar point about white slavery scandals in Victorian London. See *Prostitution and Victorian Society: Women, Class and the State* (New York: Cambridge University Press, 1980), 247–52.

61. Lary May, *Screening Out the Past: The Birth of Mass Culture and the Motion Picture Industry*, 2d ed. (Chicago: University of Chicago Press, 1982), 45; and Claudia D. Johnson, "That Guilty Third Tier: Prostitution in Nineteenth-Century American Theaters," in *Victorian America*, ed. Daniel Walker Howe (Philadelphia: University of Pennsylvania Press, 1976), 111–20.

62. *New York Tribune*, 29 December 1908. Quoted in Daniel Czitrom, "The Redemption of Leisure: The National Board of Censorship and the Rise of Motion Pictures in New York City, 1900–1920," *Studies in Visual Communication* 10, no. 4 (1984): 3.

63. Alice Kessler-Harris, "Independence and Virtue in the Lives of Wage-Earning Women: The United States, 1870–1930," in *Women in Culture and Politics: A Century of Change*, ed. Judith Friedlander, Blanche Wiesen Cook, Alice Kessler-Harris, and Carroll Smith-Rosenberg (Bloomington: Indiana University Press, 1986), 3–17.

64. Kathleen Odean offers this latter reading of contemporary white slave myths in "White Slavers in Minnesota: A Psychological Reading of the Legend," *Midwestern Journal of Language and Folklore* 11, no. 1 (1985): 27. Odean interprets white slave stories that spread in various European and American cities in the 1960s and 1970s, concentrating on those centered on the Twin Cities area. In these modern variants the

shopping mall becomes the site where young women are said to be most likely to encounter slave traffickers.

65. *New York Times*, 25 November 1913, 11.

66. *Moving Picture World*, 6 December 1913, 1135. Information about seating capacity at Weber's was found in Michael M. Davis, *The Exploitation of Pleasure: A Study of Commercial Recreation in New York City* (New York: Russell Sage Foundation, 1911), 26. Seating capacity for the Park is provided in *New York World*, 22 December 1913, 3.

67. *New York Times*, 9 December 1913, 8.

68. *New York Tribune*, 21 December 1913, sec. 3, 8; and *New York Dramatic Mirror*, 24 December 1913, 29.

69. *Variety*, 19 December 1913, 17.

70. Ibid.; and *New York Clipper*, 20 December 1913, 15.

71. *New York Clipper*, 13 December 1913, 10.

72. *Variety*, 9 January 1914, 12.

73. *Variety*, 2 January 1914, 14. *Variety* also suggests that *The Exposure of the White Slave Traffic* might have been a "general model" for *Traffic in Souls*, since a climactic rooftop raid appears in the earlier film as well as in its later, better-known counterpart.

74. *Variety*, 9 January 1914, 12.

75. *Variety*, 19 December 1913, 16, 17; *New York Dramatic Mirror*, 7 January 1914, 38; and Connelly, *The Response to Prostitution*, 115. The original novel was Kauffman, *The House of Bondage*.

76. *Variety*, 19 December 1913, 16; *Variety*, 30 January 1914, 25; *Variety*, 20 February 1914, 25; and *Variety*, 27 February 1914, 22.

77. *Variety*, 23 January 1914, 14, 24; and *Variety*, 20 February 1914, 23.

78. *Variety*, 20 February 1914, 23.

79. *Universal Weekly*, 7 February 1914, 9.

80. *Motion Picture News*, 7 February 1914, 10; and *Motion Picture News*, 21 February 1914, 36. See ads in *Moving Picture World*, 7 February 1914, 717; *Motion Picture News*, 7 February 1914, 10; *Moving Picture World*, 14 February 1914, 5, 881; and *Motion Picture News*, 21 February 1914, 36.

81. *Moving Picture World*, 7 February 1914, 653.

82. *Moving Picture World*, 6 December 1913, 1135; and *New York World*, 15 March 1914, M2. See also *New York Times*, 3 November 1913, 9. Also see Daniel Frohman, "The 'Movies' and the Theatre," *Woman's Home Companion* 40 (November 1913): 5.

83. *Variety*, 19 December 1913, 17; *New York World*, 17 January 1914, 14; *New York Dramatic Mirror*, 21 January 1914, 26; and *Variety*, 23 January 1914, 14. The *Dramatic Mirror* hinted that Hammerstein might also have been suffering financially as a result of the theater's conversion, since his commission on box office receipts from twenty-five cent movie admissions could be considerably less than that generated by stage prices upwards of $2.50 a seat, even taking the film's popularity into account.

84. *New York World*, 15 March 1914, M2.

85. On advertising practices during this period, see Leslie Midkiff DeBauche, "Advertising and the Movies, 1908–1915," *Film Reader* 6 (1985): 115–24; and Janet Staiger, "Announcing Wares, Winning Patrons, Voicing Ideals: Thinking about the History and Theory of Film Advertising," *Cinema Journal* 29, no. 3 (1990): 7.

86. *New York Tribune*, 7 December 1913, sec. 3, 8; *New York Tribune*, 14 December 1913, sec. 3, 8; and *New York Tribune*, 22 February 1914, sec. 3, 8.

87. *New York Tribune*, 21 December 1913, sec. 3, 8.

88. Ibid.; *New York Tribune*, 22 February 1914, sec. 3, 8; and *New York Tribune*, 7 December 1913, sec. 3, 8.

89. *Variety*, 12 December 1913, 12.

90. Ibid.

91. *New York World*, 17 December 1913, 11; *Variety*, 19 December 1913, 16, 17; and *New York Tribune*, 22 December 1913, 4. The *World* later reported that Justice Ten Eyck had requested the elimination of some material from the film, and that cuts were subsequently made. It is the only source to report that information. The cuts referred to were likely those made at the request of the National Board of Censorship. See *New York World*, 22 December 1913, 3.

92. Quoted in the *New York Dramatic Mirror*, 24 December 1913, 28.

93. *New York Sun*, 20 December 1913, 1; *New York Clipper*, 27 December 1913, 14.

94. *New York Sun*, 21 December 1913, 1; *New York World*, 21 December 1913, 1,2; *New York Clipper*, 27 December 1913, 14.

95. *New York Tribune*, 22 December 1913, 1, 4; and *New York World*, 22 December 1913, 3.

96. *New York World*, 22 December 1913, 3; *New York Herald*, 22 December 1913, 5; and *New York Tribune*, 22 December 1913, 4.

97. *New York Tribune*, 24 December 1913, 1; *New York World*, 24 December 1913, 3; *New York Herald*, 24 December 1913, 4; and *New York World*, 25 December 1913, 5.

98. *New York Herald*, 23 December 1913, 11; *New York World*, 23 December 1913, 3; and *New York Clipper*, 27 December 1913, 14.

99. *Variety*, 2 January 1914, 14.

100. *New York Tribune*, 28 December 1913, 10; *New York World*, 30 December 1913, 16; *New York Clipper*, 3 January 1914, 14; and *Moving Picture World*, 10 January 1914, 156.

101. Quoted in *Variety*, 13 March 1914, 23. For coverage of the trial, see *New York World*, 17 January 1914, 14; *Variety*, 23 January 1914, 15; *Moving Picture World*, 31 January 1914, 530; *New York World*, 4 March 1914, 1; *New York World*, 5 March 1914, 7; *New York World*, 6 March 1914, 9; *New York Dramatic Mirror*, 11 March 1914, 31; and *Variety*, 13 March 1914, 23. Other employees of the Park and Bijou originally arrested were not indicted.

102. *Variety*, 19 December 1913, 17.

103. Martin F. Norden, "New York Mayor William J. Gaynor and His City's Film Industry," *Film Reader* 6 (1985): 79–91; Nancy J. Rosenbloom, "Between Reform and Regulation: The Struggle over Film Censorship in Progressive America, 1909–1922," *Film History* 1, no. 4 (1987): 314–17; and Daniel Czitrom, "The Politics of Performance: From Theater Licensing to Movie Censorship in Turn-of-the-Century New York," *American Quarterly* 44, no. 4 (1992): 544–48. For information on earlier nickelodeon-era struggles, see Robert A. Armour, "The Effects of Censorship Pressure on the New York Nickelodeon Market, 1907–1909," *Film History* 4, no. 2 (1990): 113–21; and William Uricchio and Roberta E. Pearson, *Reframing Culture: The Case of the Vitagraph Quality Films* (Princeton: Princeton University Press, 1993), 24–33. Mayor

Gaynor did not live to participate in the debate surrounding the white slave films, having died of a heart attack in September of 1913.

104. *Variety*, 27 February 1914, 23.

105. *Variety*, 12 December 1913, 12; *Moving Picture World*, 11 October 1913, 133; and *New York Dramatic Mirror*, 24 December 1913, 28.

106. *Variety*, 19 December 1913, 17.

107. Quoted in the *New York Dramatic Mirror*, 14 January 1914, 57.

108. *Moving Picture World*, 14 October 1916, 227.

109. *Moving Picture World*, 11 October 1913, 133.

110. *Moving Picture World*, 17 January 1914, 265.

111. Ibid.

112. *Variety*, 27 February 1914, 21.

113. *Moving Picture World*, 27 June 1914, 1779.

114. *Moving Picture World*, 7 February 1914, 653. Particularly notable in this regard was the ongoing case between Mutual and the state of Ohio, which had created a censorship body in the spring of 1913. Mutual pursued its case all the way to the Supreme Court, which issued a landmark 1915 ruling upholding the rights of states to censor motion pictures, a decision that was not reversed until the 1952 ruling guaranteeing films protection under the First Amendment. See Garth S. Jowett, " 'A Capacity for Evil': The 1915 Supreme Court Mutual Decision," *Historical Journal of Film, Radio and Television* 9, no. 1 (1989): 59–78; and John Wertheimer, "Mutual Film Reviewed: The Movies, Censorship, and Free Speech in Progressive America," *American Journal of Legal History* 37, no. 2 (1993): 158–89.

115. *Moving Picture World*, 17 January 1914, 276. On Bush's anticensorship philosophy, see Richard L. Stromgren, "The *Moving Picture World* of W. Stephen Bush," *Film History* 2, no. 1 (1988): 19–20.

116. *New York Dramatic Mirror*, 24 December 1913, 28. Also see *New York Dramatic Mirror*, 19 November 1913, 28.

117. *Variety*, 19 December 1913, 17.

118. *Variety*, 12 December 1913, 25.

119. *Motion Picture News*, 28 February 1914, 58–59.

120. *Variety*, 2 January 1914, 14; and *New York World*, 23 December 1913, 3.

121. *Moving Picture World*, 10 January 1914, 155.

122. *New York Herald*, 22 December 1913, 5.

123. On the early years of the Board of Censorship, see Robert Fisher, "Film Censorship and Progressive Reform: The National Board of Censorship of Motion Pictures, 1909–1922," *Journal of Popular Film and Television* 4, no. 2 (1975): 143–56; Charles Matthew Feldman, *The National Board of Censorship (Review) of Motion Pictures, 1909–1922* (New York: Arno Press, 1977), 20–87; Kathleen D. McCarthy, "Nickel Vice and Virtue: Movie Censorship in Chicago, 1907–1915," *Journal of Popular Film* 5, no. 1 (1976): 37–55; Czitrom, "The Redemption of Leisure," 2–6; Rosenbloom, "Between Reform and Regulation," 307–25; Rosenbloom, "Progressive Reform, Censorship and the Motion Picture Industry, 1909–1917," in *Popular Culture and Political Change in Modern America*, ed. Ronald Edsforth and Larry Bennett (Albany: State University of New York Press, 1991), 41–60; Rosenbloom, "In Defense of Moving Pictures: The People's Institute, The National Board of Censorship and the Problems of Leisure in Urban America," *American Studies* 33, no. 2 (1992): 41–61; Czitrom, "The Politics of

Performance," 525–53. For a more detailed treatment of the board's handling of white slave pictures, see Shelley Stamp, "Moral Coercion, or the Board of Censorship Ponders the Vice Question," in *Regulating Hollywood: Censorship and Control in the Studio Era*, ed. Matthew Bernstein (New Brunswick, NJ: Rutgers University Press, 1999), 41–58.

124. A statement released by John Collier, the Board of Censorship's general secretary, is reprinted in "To Censor or Not," *Motography*, 15 November 1913, 339–40.

125. Box 107, Controversial Films Correspondence, NBRMPC.

126. Ibid. Even Frederic Howe was quoted in the pamphlet defending the stage production of *The Fight* earlier that year.

127. Francis G. Couvares, "The Good Censor: Race, Sex, and Censorship in the Early Cinema," *Yale Journal of Criticism* 7, no. 2 (1994): 243.

128. "To Censor or Not," 339.

129. *Moving Picture World*, 22 November 1913, 849; *Motion Picture News*, 22 November 1913, 34; *Motography*, 29 November 1913, 397–98; and *Motography*, 15 November 1913, 339.

130. Box 105, Controversial Films Correspondence, NBRMPC. Existing prints suggest that London did finally incorporate some of these suggestions, following them more according to the letter than in spirit. As my subsequent analysis demonstrates, the film continues to frame the bald moralizing demanded by the Board of Censorship within a broad critique of American social and economic institutions.

131. Ibid. The board's own use of the "special release" category to describe *The Inside of the White Slave Traffic* appears to contravene normal practice, where producers themselves would adopt the term in order to sidestep board scrutiny. See Jowett, " 'A Capacity for Evil,' " 65.

132. Box 105, Controversial Film Correspondence, NBRMPC. Samuel London returned to the board with a further revised print in early February of 1914 after police had closed screenings in New York, evidently hoping that with board approval he might successfully exhibit the film without further police interference. Viewed again and discussed at length, *The Inside of the White Slave Traffic* still failed to win the board's sanction, despite the addition of new scenes, enacting the vice ring's capture, that the board had initially requested.

133. Box 171, Subjects Papers, NBRMPC.

134. *Moving Picture World*, 3 January 1914, 53; *Variety*, 6 February 1914, 22; *Variety*, 13 February 1914, 23; *Variety*, 20 February 1914, 25; *Variety*, 27 February 1914, 22; and McCarthy, "Nickel Vice and Virtue," 45.

135. *Variety*, 30 January 1914, 24.

136. Frederic C. Howe, "What to Do with the Motion-Picture Show: Shall It Be Censored?" *Outlook* 107 (20 June 1914): 412; and Orrin G. Cocks, "Applying Standards to Motion Picture Films," *Survey* 32 (27 June 1914): 338. See also John Collier, "Censorship and the National Board," *Survey* 35 (2 October 1915): 9–14. Francis G. Couvares provides an excellent overview of the board's decisions on controversial subjects in "The Good Censor," 233–51.

137. Cocks, "Applying Standards," 338.

138. Howe, "What to Do," 415; and Cocks, "Applying Standards," 338.

139. *Moving Picture World*, 28 March 1914, 1668.

140. Ramsaye, *A Million and One Nights*, 612.

141. *New York Dramatic Mirror*, 31 December 1913, 23.

142. Robert C. Allen, "*Traffic in Souls*," *Sight and Sound* 44, no. 1 (Winter 1974–75): 52.

143. Quoted in Couvares, "The Good Censor," 242.

144. *New York Dramatic Mirror*, 19 November 1913, 33.

145. *Motography*, 29 November 1913, 397.

146. *Moving Picture World*, 22 November 1913, 849.

147. Ibid.

148. *Motion Picture News*, 22 November 1913, 34.

149. Madison Board of Commerce, *Madison Recreational Survey* (Madison, WI, 1915), 57.

150. Tom Gunning, "From the Opium Den to the Theatre of Morality: Moral Discourse and Film Process in Early American Cinema," *Art and Text* 30 (1988): 31.

151. Sumiko Higashi, *Cecil B. DeMille and American Culture: The Silent Era* (Berkeley and Los Angeles: University of California Press, 1994); and Staiger, *Bad Women*.

152. *New York Tribune*, 22 December 1913, 1, 4; and *New York Tribune*, 19 January 1914, 9.

153. *New York World*, 24 December 1913, 3.

154. *New York World*, 29 December 1913, 3; and *New York Sun*, 29 December 1913, 9.

155. Box 105, Controversial Films Correspondence, NBRMPC.

156. *New York Sun*, 21 December 1913, 1; and *New York Dramatic Mirror*, 31 December 1913, 23.

157. "The White Slave Films," *Outlook* 106 (17 January 1914): 121.

158. "The White Slave Films: A Review," *Outlook* 106 (14 February 1914): 347–48, 350.

159. Ibid., 348.

160. Ibid., 347.

161. *New York Herald*, 22 December 1913, 5.

162. *New York World*, 25 December 1913, 5.

163. *New York Dramatic Mirror*, 17 December 1913, 30; and *New York Clipper*, 20 December 1913, 15.

164. The *New York Times* editorial is reproduced in *Motion Picture News*, 15 November 1913, 41. The trade paper acknowledged that views expressed in the *Times* editorial "closely conform" to those held by *Motion Picture News*.

165. In addition to the articles cited below, see "The Morals of the Movies," *Outlook* 107 (20 June 1914), 387–88; "Movie Crimes against Good Taste," *Literary Digest* 51 (18 September 1915): 591–92; "The Immoral Morality of the 'Movies,' " *Current Opinion*, October 1915, 244; and "The Utter Hopelessness of the Movies," *Life*, 1 February 1917, 182. Ben Singer provides a detailed account of critiques of the cinema during the teens in "Varieties of Middle Class Disaffection" (Unpublished paper presented at the Society for Cinema Studies conference, 1994). Reformers did also show an interest in the use of cinema as an educational tool during this period. See Constance D. Leupp, "The Motion Picture as Social Worker," *Survey* 25 (27 August 1910): 739–41; and Boyd Fisher, "Motion Pictures to Make Good Citizens," *American City* 7 (September 1912): 234–38.

166. "The Morals of the Movies: From the Standpoint," 662; "Movie Morals," *New Republic*, 25 August 1917, 101; "Movies Once More," *Outlook* 108 (28 October 1914): 449; and " 'Movie' Manners and Morals," *Outlook* 113 (26 July 1916): 695.

167. "The Moving Picture and the National Character," *American Review of Reviews* 42 (September 1910): 326.

168. *New York Sun*, 29 December 1913, 9.

169. Miriam Hansen, *Babel and Babylon: Spectatorship and American Silent Film* (Cambridge: Harvard University Press, 1991), 81, 83.

170. Ibid., 84

171. *New York Times*, 9 December 1913, 8.

172. *Variety*, 27 February 1914, 23.

173. *Moving Picture World*, 14 October 1916, 227.

174. *Motion Picture News*, 10 June 1916, 3541.

175. "*Traffic in Souls* Disappoints Many by Its Lack of Real Offense," *Minneapolis Journal*, 27 January 1914, n.p., BRC.

176. The character is identified in intertitles only as "Little Sister," so I have chosen to refer to her by this name. She is described as "Lorna" in most reviews, and subsequent writers have sometimes adopted this name for her. However, the film plays heavily on her status as a generic "little sister" for whom we are all held to be responsible. Like the other victims in the film, the "Country Girl" and the Swedish sisters, she is not individuated with a name, as are most of the other central characters. Nameless, the victims typify aspects of modern femininity, rather than particular individuals. Witness the number of other films that denote their heroines in a similar manner: *Little Lost Sister* and *The Little Girl Next Door*, for example. At the time of the film's release publicity for actor Ethel Grandin, who played Little Sister, also stressed her youth and ingenue qualities. See *Moving Picture World*, 6 December 1913, 1127; and *Moving Picture World*, 3 January 1914, 67. Robert C. Allen reports that Grandin later became a popular star in several serials. See Allen, "*Traffic in Souls*," 52.

177. *Motography*, 29 November 1913, 397.

178. *Moving Picture World*, 22 November 1913, 849.

179. At least one contemporary commentator did indeed cite candy stores among the sites where women were likely to encounter traffickers. See Janney, *The White Slave Traffic*, 99.

180. Addams, *A New Conscience*, 64.

181. Ibid., 55–56.

182. Robert O. Harland, *Vice Bondage of a Great City: or, The Wickedest City in the World* (Chicago: The Young People's Civic League, 1912), 68.

183. *Motography*, 29 November 1913, 397. *Variety* surmised that "Anthony Comstock will probably yell murder the first time he sees 'em." *Variety*, 28 November 1913, 12.

184. Janney, *The White Slave Traffic*, 97. See also Charles Edward Locke, *White Slavery in Los Angeles* (Los Angeles: Times Mirror Co., 1913), 9–10; Roe, *Panders*, 79–80; and M. Madeline Southard, *The White Slave Traffic versus the American Home* (Louisville, KY: Pentecostal Publishing, 1914), 16. A dance hall "with a subterranean passage connecting with a disorderly house" also featured prominently in *The Fight*. See *Variety*, 22 January 1915, 25.

185. Emma Norine Law, *The Shame of a Great Nation: The Story of the "White Slave Trade."* (Harrisburg, PA: United Evangelical Publishing House, 1909), 192–93. On efforts to reform dance halls, see Louise de Koven Bowen, "Dance Halls," *Survey* 26 (3 July 1911): 383–87; and Elisabeth Perry, " 'The General Motherhood of the Commonwealth': Dance Hall Reform in the Progressive Era," *American Quarterly* 37, no. 5 (1985): 719–33.

186. Mabel Condon, *"Traffic in Souls," Photoplay,* February 1914, 41.

187. Lee Grieveson reports that the two procurers aboard the immigrant ship are played by the film's director George Loane Tucker and its screenwriter Walter McNamara. See Grieveson, "Policing the Cinema: *Traffic in Souls* at Ellis Island," *Screen* 38, no. 2 (1997): 149–71.

188. *Motion Picture News*, 22 November 1913, 34.

189. Terry Ramsaye reports that George Loane Tucker, director and cowriter of *Traffic in Souls*, saw *The Lure* on Broadway, along with just about all of the white slavery dramas that autumn. Nonetheless, Jack Lodge has speculated that *Traffic in Souls* was filmed in May of 1913, several months prior to the stage premieres. See Ramsaye, *A Million and One Nights*, 613; and Lodge, " 'First of the Immortals,' " 41. For a summary of *The Lure*, see reviews in *Theatre*, September 1913, xi; and *New York Dramatic Mirror*, 20 August 1913, 6.

190. Jane Gail, the actress who played Mary Barton, received star billing in *Traffic in Souls* and appeared alone in advance publicity material for the film, further emphasizing the privileging of Mary Barton over her "Little Sister" (played by Ethel Grandin). Gail had been a major player at IMP after she was hired in January 1913. She acted in several other films directed by George Loane Tucker, besides *Traffic in Souls*. See Lodge, " 'First of the Immortals,' " 40. Lodge's useful filmography of Tucker's career shows that several of the actors who appear in *Traffic in Souls* were frequent collaborators with Tucker on other IMP productions. Kathleen Karr reports that Gail was also known during this period for playing a "dope fiend" in the stage play *Dope*. See Karr, "The Long Square-Up," 113.

191. Eustace Hale Ball, *Traffic in Souls: A Novel of Crime and Its Cure* (New York: G. W. Dillingham, 1914).

192. Staiger, *Bad Women*, 140.

193. *Variety*, 28 November 1913, 12.

194. Staiger, *Bad Women*, 136–37.

195. Southard, *The White Slave Traffic*, 10; and Harland, *Vice Bondage*, 19.

196. "There's a laugh on the Rockefeller investigators in the play in the personality of one of the white slavers, a physical counterpart of John D. himself so striking as to make the observer sit up and wonder whether the granger of Pocantico Hills [Rockefeller's estate] really came down to pose for the Universal." *Variety*, 28 November 1913, 12.

197. This ending is contained in the print housed at the National Film Archive in London. The significance of this finale is discussed in Ben Brewster, *"Traffic in Souls*: An Experiment in Feature-Length Narrative Construction," *Cinema Journal* 31, no. 1 (1990): 37–56; and Tom Gunning, "From the Kaleidoscope to the X-Ray: Urban Spectatorship, Poe, Benjamin, and *Traffic in Souls* (1913)," *Wide Angle* 19, no. 4 (1997): 25–61. I found no indication in Board of Censorship records that this shot was

among those excised at the board's request, so I am unable to ascertain why it is missing from prints in circulation in the United States.

198. Eileen Bowser ties Mary's use of her father's invention to the serials, where popular female detectives often employed similar quasi-scientific apparatuses. See Bowser, *The Transformation of Cinema*, 185–86. Jack Lodge reports that dictagraphic evidence had featured prominently in several recent court cases, and that an earlier Selig film, *Exposed by the Dictagraph* (1912), had also capitalized on this trend. He notes that a similar plot device had been used in an earlier IMP film, *The Rise of Officer 174* (1913), also directed by Tucker and scripted by Walter MacNamara, who wrote *Traffic in Souls*. See Lodge, " 'First of the Immortals,' " 40.

199. *The Toledo Blade*, 13 December 1913, n.p., BRTC.

200. *Motion Picture News*, 10 June 1916, 3541.

201. *New York Tribune*, 7 December 1913, sec. 3, 8; *New York Tribune*, 14 December 1913, sec. 3, 8; and *New York Tribune*, 22 February 1914, sec. 3, 8.

202. *New York Tribune*, 21 December 1913, sec. 3, 8.

203. Ibid.; and *New York Tribune*, 22 February 1914, sec. 3, 8.

204. *Variety*, 20 February 1914, 23.

205. *Moving Picture World*, 23 May 1914, 1134.

206. *Variety*, 12 December 1913, 12.

207. *New York Dramatic Mirror*, 24 September 1913, 31.

208. Lehman, *The White Slave Hell*, n.p.

209. Parts of this photo essay are reproduced in both Lehman, *The White Slave Hell*, and Roe, *Panders*.

210. Connelly, *The Response to Prostitution*, 119.

211. Lehman, *The White Slave Hell*, title page.

212. *New York Dramatic Mirror*, 24 September 1913, 31.

213. The incomplete print of *The Inside of the White Slave Traffic* that I viewed is held at the Library of Congress.

214. *Variety*, 12 December 1913, 12. Timothy J. Gilfoyle's exhaustive documentation of brothels on Manhattan in the teens shows that the Tenderloin stretched from Twenty-third Street to Fifty-seventh Street between Fifth and Eighth Avenues, with the greatest concentration of brothels on Eighth Avenue between Thirty-fourth Street and Forty-second Street. See Gilfoyle, *City of Eros: New York City, Prostitution and the Commercialization of Sex, 1790–1920* (New York: W. W. Norton, 1992), 202–3.

215. *Motion Picture News*, 20 December 1913, 31.

216. Ibid.

217. *New York World*, 21 December 1913, 1–2; and *New York Dramatic Mirror*, 24 December 1913, 27.

218. Joanne Meyerowitz, "Sexual Geography and Gender Economy: The Furnished Room Districts of Chicago, 1890–1930," *Gender and History* 2, no. 3 (1990): 274–96.

219. Grieveson, "Policing the Cinema."

220. More of these fictional, location scenes appear to survive in the existing print than candid footage.

221. Vice Commission of Minneapolis, *Report*.

222. *Motion Picture News*, 20 December 1913, 31.

223. Janney, *The White Slave Traffic*, 40.

224. Bell, *Fighting the Traffic in Young Girls*, 114.

225. *Variety*, 12 December 1913, 12.

226. Staiger, *Bad Women*, 145.

227. Connelly discusses what he calls the "country-girl-to-white slave theme" in more detail in *The Response to Prostitution*, 120–26.

228. John Regan, *Crimes of the White Slavers and the Results* (Chicago: J. Regan and Co., 1912), 171. See also Janney, *The White Slave Traffic*, 24; and Locke, *White Slavery in Los Angeles*, 9.

229. Janney, *The White Slave Traffic*, 90; Roe, *Panders*, 80–81; Addams, *A New Conscience*, 147; and Lehman, *The White Slave Hell*, 185.

230. *Moving Picture World*, 10 March 1917, 1596.

231. *Moving Picture World*, 24 March 1917, 1946.

232. *Paste-Pot and Shears*, 12 March 1917, 1. Folder 565, William Selig Collection, MHL.

233. Vice Commission of Philadelphia, *A Report on Existing Conditions*. Quoted in Lubove, "The Progressive and the Prostitute," 311.

234. Bingham, *The Girl That Disappears*, 7–9. Similar reports are presented in Locke, *White Slavery in Los Angeles*, 41; and Roe, *Panders*, 84. "The prodigal daughter" profiled elsewhere by Roe also spoke of the country's "lost" young women, but in slightly different terms. In Roe's account the wayward daughter was herself somewhat to blame and returned to the family home, chastened and wiser. See Roe, *The Great War on White Slavery*.

235. Judith R. Walkowitz, *City of Dreadful Delight: Narratives of Sexual Danger in Late-Victorian London* (London: Virago, 1992), 1–39. Walkowitz does not deal with white slavery here, but with specific scandals such as the "Jack the Ripper" case. Also see Elizabeth Wilson, *The Sphinx in the City: Urban Life, the Control of Disorder, and Women* (Berkeley and Los Angeles: University of California Press, 1991), 65–83.

236. Annette Kuhn stresses the importance of distinguishing between a film's *social audience* and the *spectatorial positions* offered therein, in "Women's Genres: Melodrama, Soap Opera, and Theory," *Screen* 25, no. 1 (1984): 18–28.

237. *Motion Picture News*, 20 December 1913, 31.

238. *Motion Picture News*, 10 June 1916, 3541.

239. *Moving Picture World*, 10 March 1917, 1478; and *Moving Picture World*, 24 March 1917, 1900.

240. *Paste-Pot and Shears*, 5 March 1917, 1. Folder 565, William Selig Collection, MHL.

241. "*Traffic in Souls* Disappoints Many. . . ."

242. *Moving Picture World*, 3 January 1914, 53; and *Moving Picture World*, 10 January 1914, 155. The speakers quoted are, respectively, Gertrude Howe Britton, president of the Juvenile Protective Association, and William L. Bodine, superintendent of compulsory education in Chicago.

243. *Moving Picture World*, 23 September 1916, 1961.

244. *Moving Picture World*, 28 March 1914, 1651.

245. *Moving Picture World*, 7 January 1914, 276.

246. "The White Slave Films: A Review." The comments were published in a letter to the editor written by Mrs. Barclay Hazard, head of the New York branch of the Florence Crittenton Mission for "unfortunate" women. Hazard's views were given even

wider currency when they were featured in "The Moral Havoc Wrought by Moving Picture Shows," *Current Opinion*, April 1914, 290.

247. True, *The Neglected Girl*, 68, 67.

248. Miner, *Slavery of Prostitution*, 85.

249. *Variety*, 2 January 1914, 14.

250. *Variety*, 27 February 1914, 23.

251. Ibid. Emphasis added.

252. *Moving Picture World*, 23 September 1916, 1961.

253. Laura Mulvey, "Pandora: Topographies of the Mask and Curiosity," in *Sexuality and Space*, ed. Beatriz Colomina (Princeton: Princeton Architectural Press, 1992), 65.

254. Ibid., 70.

255. Advertisement published in the *Toledo Blade*, 13 December 1913, n.p., BRC; and *Motion Picture News*, 10 June 1916, 3541.

256. Tom Gunning, "The Book That Refuses to Be Read: Images of the City in Early Cinema" (Unpublished paper presented at the Society for Cinema Studies conference, 1989), 15. Gunning develops this discussion further in "From the Kaleidoscope to the X-Ray."

257. Susan Buck-Morss, "The *Flâneur*, the Sandwichman and the Whore: The Politics of Loitering," *New German Critique* 39 (1986): 99–140. On the impossibility of the *"flâneuse,"* see also Janet Wolff, "The Invisible *Flâneuse*: Women and the Literature of Modernity," *Theory, Culture and Society* 2, no. 3 (1988): 37–46. Anne Friedberg notes that the *flâneuse*, or female urban wanderer, was not possible until shopping became an acceptable leisure-time activity for middle-class women around the turn of the century. See Friedberg, *Window Shopping: Cinema and the Postmodern* (Berkeley and Los Angeles: University of California Press, 1993), 36–37. Also see Rabinovitz, *For the Love of Pleasure*, 7–10.

258. Griselda Pollock, "Modernity and the Spaces of Femininity," in *Vision and Difference: Femininity, Feminism and the Histories of Art* (London and New York: Routledge, 1988), 84.

259. Hansen, *Babel and Babylon*, 117. The potential freedom that white slave films offered female viewers should not obscure the sexual, even pornographic, appeal they may have held for male spectators, who formed a significant portion of the audience for these films.

260. Giuliana Bruno, *Streetwalking on a Ruined Map: Cultural Theory and the City Films of Elvira Notari* (Princeton: Princeton University Press, 1993), 51.

Chapter Three
Ready-Made Customers: Female Movie Fans and the Serial Craze

1. *Moving Picture World*, 10 February 1917, 818.

2. For a discussion of similar prologues in earlier *Fantômas* serials, see Tom Gunning, "A Tale of Two Prologues: Actors and Roles, Detectives and Disguises in *Fantômas*, Film and Novel," *Velvet Light Trap* 37 (1996): 32–33. Noting that these self-referential prologues are followed by narratives themselves concerned with disguise, as will also be in the case in *The Mystery of the Double Cross*, Gunning suggests that "this relatively new protocol of film viewing as actor-watching becomes doubled (or

tripled) as one admires not only the actor's but also the character's skill at role playing" (33).

3. Michael Denning, *Mechanic Accents: Dime Novels and Working-Class Culture in America* (New York and London: Verso, 1987), 30–36; Raymond William Stedman, *The Serials: Suspense and Drama by Installment*, 2d ed. (Norman: University of Oklahoma Press, 1977), 3–11, 14–15, 35–38; Kalton Lahue, *Continued Next Week: A History of the Moving Picture Serial* (Norman: University of Oklahoma Press, 1964), 7–8, 15–16, 19, 28–33, 42–46, 59–61; and Ben Singer, "Fiction Tie-Ins and Narrative Intelligibility, 1911–1918," *Film History* 5, no. 4 (1993): 489–504.

4. Clara Laughlin, *The Work-a-Day Girl: A Study of Some Present-Day Conditions* (New York: Fleming H. Revell, 1913), 143. Quoted in Lois Banner, *American Beauty* (New York: Alfred Knopf, 1983), 200.

5. Eileen Bowser notes that several companies produced film *series* with common leading characters but self-contained stories prior to the appearance of *serials*, which had continuing plot lines and usually included print tie-ins. These included Kalem's *Girl Spy* series in 1909, Biograph's *Mr. and Mrs. Jones* series, also in 1909, and Yankee's 1910 *Girl Detective* series. See Bowser, *The Transformation of Cinema, 1907–1915* (New York: Charles Scribner's Sons, 1990), 206.

6. *New York Dramatic Mirror*, 28 January 1914, 30.

7. Philip Mindil, "Publicity for the Pictures," *Moving Picture World*, 11 July 1914, 217.

8. *Variety*, 10 April 1914, n.p., reprinted in *Variety Film Reviews* (New York: Garland, 1983).

9. *Variety*, 7 August 1914, n.p., reprinted in *Variety Film Reviews*.

10. Julian T. Baber, "Efficient Publicity Work," *Moving Picture World*, 30 May 1914, 1270.

11. *Moving Picture World*, 8 January 1916, 299.

12. Gardner W. Woods, "Magazines and Motion Pictures," *Moving Picture World*, 11 July 1914, 194.

13. *Kalem Kalendar*, December 1915, 6.

14. *Moving Picture World*, 28 March 1914, 1696, 1697; and *Motion Picture News*, 25 April 1914, 39.

15. *Moving Picture World*, 30 May 1914, 1201.

16. *Chicago Tribune*, 3 January 1914, 15.

17. *Photoplay*, May 1914, 131.

18. *Motion Picture Classic*, January 1916, 72.

19. *San Francisco Examiner*, 15 March 1914, City Life Section, 5; *San Francisco Examiner*, 29 March 1914, City Life Section, 6; and *San Francisco Examiner*, 22 March 1914, Editorial and Dramatic Section, 4.

20. *Chicago Tribune*, 2 January 1914, 8; and *Chicago Tribune*, 3 January 1914, 15.

21. *Motion Picture News*, 2 May 1914, 38.

22. Leslie Midkiff DeBauche, "Advertising and the Movies, 1908–1915," *Film Reader* 6 (1985): 115–24; and Janet Staiger, "Announcing Wares, Winning Patrons, Voicing Ideals: Thinking about the History and Theory of Film Advertising," *Cinema Journal* 29, no. 3 (1990): 3–31.

23. *New York Dramatic Mirror*, 28 January 1914, 30; *Moving Picture World*, 4 July 1914, 47; *Edison Kinetogram*, 15 April 1913, 17; *Motion Picture News*, 2 May 1914,

37; Charles J. Hite, "Advertising for the Exhibitor," *Moving Picture World*, 11 July 1914, 187; and *Moving Picture World*, 4 July 1914, 47.

24. Unidentified advertising flier, ca. 1914. Folder 560, William Selig Collection, MHL.

25. *Universal Weekly*, 27 June 1914, 29; and *Universal Weekly*, 29 August 1914, 33. See also *Universal Weekly*, 23 May 1914, 29.

26. *Moving Picture World*, 12 April 1913, 163; *Moving Picture World*, 27 June 1914, 1830; and *Variety*, 10 July 1914, n.p., reprinted in *Variety Film Reviews*.

27. *Chicago Tribune*, 1 January 1914, 21; *Chicago Tribune*, 17 January 1914, 8; and *Washington Star*, 14 January 1914, n.p., envelope 2603, RLC.

28. *San Francisco Examiner*, 1 April 1914, 10; *San Francisco Examiner*, 9 April 1914, 6; and *Variety*, 10 April 1914, n.p., reprinted in *Variety Film Reviews*.

29. *Variety*, 26 June 1914, n.p., reprinted in *Variety Film Reviews*.

30. *Motion Picture News*, 18 April 1914, 16; *Motion Picture News*, 25 April 1914, 38; *Moving Picture World*, 19 December 1914, 1642; and *Moving Picture World*, 19 December 1914, 1642–43.

31. *New York Dramatic Mirror*, 13 May 1914, 26; *Edison Kinetogram*, 1 June 1913, 16; and *Universal Weekly*, 27 June 1914, 29.

32. *New York Dramatic Mirror*, 28 January 1914, 30.

33. *Motion Picture News*, 11 April 1914, 28; and *Moving Picture World*, 18 July 1914, 389.

34. *New York Dramatic Mirror*, 28 January 1914, 30.

35. *Moving Picture World*, 17 January 1914, 266.

36. *Moving Picture World*, 4 April 1914, 38.

37. Ben Singer, "Serial Melodrama and Narrative *Gesellschaft*," *Velvet Light Trap* 37 (1996): 76.

38. The advertisement is reproduced in Kalton C. Lahue, *Bound and Gagged: The Story of the Silent Serials* (South Brunswick and New York: A. S. Barnes and Co., 1968), 114.

39. *Moving Picture World*, 5 December 1914, 1351.

40. Lahue, *Bound and Gagged*, 85.

41. *Moving Picture World*, 10 February 1917, 818; *Moving Picture World*, 6 January 1917, 65; and *Moving Picture World*, 8 January 1916, 214.

42. *Moving Picture World*, 5 December 1914, 1351; *Moving Picture World*, 5 December 1914, 1351; *Moving Picture World*, 7 November 1914, 791; *New York Dramatic Mirror*, 31 December 1913, 29; *New York Dramatic Mirror*, 6 May 1914, 23; and *Motion Picture News*, 25 April 1914, 39.

43. Epes Winthrop Sargent, *Picture Theatre Advertising* (New York: Chalmers Publishing, 1915), 264.

44. *Moving Picture World*, 10 August 1912, 546; *Moving Picture World*, 7 June 1913, 1031; and *Moving Picture World*, 7 February 1914, 677.

45. *Moving Picture World*, 10 August 1912, 545; *Moving Picture World*, 28 February 1914, 1088; and *Moving Picture World*, 7 September 1912, 976.

46. "The Standards and Policy of the National Board of Review of Motion Pictures," 1 October 1916, 10. Box 171, NBRMPC.

47. *Moving Picture World*, 5 September 1914, 1347.

48. *Moving Picture World*, 6 January 1917, 64; *Edison Kinetogram*, 1 August 1912, 16–17; and *New York Dramatic Mirror*, 2 September 1914, 26.

49. *Chicago Tribune*, 9 January 1914, 9.

50. *Moving Picture World*, 7 September 1912, 976.

51. *New York Dramatic Mirror*, 1 April 1914, 42; and *Moving Picture World*, 5 September 1914, 1347.

52. *Moving Picture World*, 2 January 1915, 80.

53. *Moving Picture World*, 4 April 1914, 38.

54. *Chicago Tribune*, 3 January 1914, 15; *San Francisco Examiner*, 5 April 1914, Editorial and Dramatic Section, 9; and *Chicago Tribune*, 16 January 1914, 9.

55. *Moving Picture World*, 17 January 1914, 266.

56. *Moving Picture World*, 16 January 1915, 388; *Moving Picture World*, 23 January 1915, 498; and *Moving Picture World*, 20 February 1915, 1148.

57. *Photoplay*, May 1914, 131.

58. *Motion Picture Classic*, January 1916, 72.

59. *Moving Picture World*, 13 February 1915, 987; and *Moving Picture World*, 23 January 1915, 498. MacDonald refers to "a series of flashbacks" when describing what is likely crosscutting.

60. Ben Singer, "Modernity, Hyperstimulus, and the Rise of Popular Sensationalism," in *Cinema and the Invention of Modern Life*, ed. Leo Charney and Vanessa R. Schwartz (Berkeley and Los Angeles: University of California Press, 1995), 72–99. For a fuller discussion of the connections between serials and sensationalism, see Singer's book *Melodrama and Modernity: Early Pulp Cinema and the Social Contexts of Sensationalism* (forthcoming from Columbia University Press). *Moving Picture World*, 4 April 1914, 38.

61. *Moving Picture World*, 19 September 1914, 1621.

62. *Moving Picture World*, 15 January 1916, 365.

63. Unidentified newspaper clipping, n.d., n.p., vol. 306, RLSBC; and *San Francisco Examiner*, 19 January 1915, 7.

64. *Universal Weekly*, 1 August 1914, 29.

65. *Chicago Tribune*, 3 January 1914, 15.

66. *Washington Star*, 29 December 1913, n.p., envelope 2603, RLC.

67. *Chicago Tribune*, 14 January 1914, 7; and *Chicago Tribune*, 1 January 1914, 21.

68. *Chicago Tribune*, 17 January 1914, 8.

69. *Chicago Tribune*, 29 January 1914, 13.

70. *Chicago Tribune*, 9 February 1914, 4; and *Chicago Tribune*, 16 February 1914, 7.

71. *San Francisco Examiner*, 3 January 1915, Editorial and City Life Section, 3.

72. *San Francisco Examiner*, 4 January 1915, 10.

73. *San Francisco Examiner*, 3 January 1915, Editorial and City Life Section, 3; *San Francisco Examiner*, 10 January 1915, Editorial and Dramatic Section, 3; and *San Francisco Examiner*, 17 January 1915, Editorial and Dramatic Section, 3.

74. *San Francisco Examiner*, 19 January 1915, 7.

75. *Edison Kinetogram*, 15 April 1913, 17.

76. *Edison Kinetogram*, 1 September 1913, 18.

77. *Moving Picture World*, 11 March 1916, 1693.

78. *New York Dramatic Mirror*, 26 August 1914, 26. *Moving Picture World* summaries of the twelfth and thirteenth episodes can be found in 5 September 1914, 1347, and 19 September 1914, 1621, respectively.

79. See Singer, "Fiction Tie-In and Narrative Intelligibility."

80. Denning, *Mechanic Accents*, 71.

81. Ellen Gruber Garvey, *The Adman in the Parlor: Magazines and the Gendering of Consumer Culture, 1880s to 1910s* (New York: Oxford University Press, 1996), 51–79.

82. *Ladies' World*, August 1912, 1, 3–4. See also Stedman, *The Serials*, 14–15; and Lahue, *Continued Next Week*, 3–6.

83. *San Francisco Examiner*, 15 March 1914, City Life Section, 5.

84. *San Francisco Examiner*, 22 March 1914, City Life Section, 5.

85. *New York Dramatic Mirror*, 1 April 1914, 42; and *Motion Picture News*, 18 April 1914, 41.

86. *Chicago Tribune*, 28 June 1914, pt. 5, 1; Stedman, *The Serials*, 15–16; and *Motion Picture Classic*, January 1916, 72. Other contests invited fans to participate in an illusory Hollywood glamour culture. Fans of Reliance's *Runaway Jane* vied to win a trip to the Pan-Pacific Exposition in San Francisco and the San Diego Exposition. Along the way winners would be pampered by maids, manicurists, hair stylists, and dressmakers. See Lahue, *Bound and Gagged*, 126.

87. John Fiske, "The Cultural Economy of Fandom," in *The Adoring Audience: Fan Culture and Popular Media*, ed. Lisa Lewis (New York and London: Routledge, 1992), 30, 47.

88. Peter Brooks, "The Mark of the Beast: Prostitution, Serialization and Narrative," in *Reading for the Plot: Design and Intention in Narrative* (New York: Vintage, 1985), 163.

89. *Universal Weekly*, 2 May 1914, 9.

90. *Universal Weekly*, 11 July 1914, 25.

91. Mary Ann Doane, "The Economy of Desire: The Commodity Form in/of the Cinema," *Quarterly Review of Film and Video* 11, no. 1 (1989): 27.

92. *Edison Kinetogram*, 15 April 1913, 17; and unidentified advertisement, ca. 1913, vol. 190, RLSBC.

93. *Motion Picture Magazine*, March 1917, 115.

94. Lahue, *Bound and Gagged*, 138–40; Clipping files, MHL; *Edison Kinetogram*, 15 April 1913, 17; unidentified advertisement, ca. 1913, vol. 190, RLSBC; and *Chicago Examiner*, 6 June 1915, pt. 5, p. 4.

95. Photographs of the "crolette" are reproduced in Lahue, *Bound and Gagged*, 102 and 104.

96. Jane Gaines, "The Queen Christina Tie-Ups: Convergence of Show Window and Screen," *Quarterly Review of Film and Video* 11, no. 1 (1989): 38, 56.

97. "The Real Perils of Pearl White," *Literary Digest*, 5 December 1914, 1147.

98. There are considerable discrepancies between the original episodes of *The Perils of Pauline* and those that survive in Blackhawk editions released by Grapevine Video. Surviving prints are based not on the original 35mm 1914 release version of *The Perils of Pauline* but on a 28mm version that Pathé recut and rereleased after the initial run. The original twenty installments were pared down to nine episodes, some of which integrate material from two or three of the original chapters; other material is left

out entirely. (See *Blackhawk Bulletin*, July 1974, 63.) While I have relied on these surviving versions for visual descriptions of the action, I have attempted to reconstruct the original episode demarcations, based on plot summaries available from reviews and written commentaries published in 1914. When describing plot details, I have endeavored to cite the original episode number. Similarly, although I will quote from intertitles, I cannot vouch for their historical accuracy. Intertitles in surviving prints appear to be English retranslations of French translations of the original, and therefore potentially quite different from those which American audiences saw in 1914. Most notably, Stanford Marvin's secretary is referred to as "Koerner" in surviving prints, whereas all contemporary sources list his name as "Owen," the name by which I will also refer to him.

99. *Moving Picture World*, 28 March 1914, 1698.

100. *San Francisco Examiner*, 14 April 1914, 7.

101. *Edison Kinetogram*, 15 July 1912, 9, 17; *Moving Picture World*, 20 July 1912, 268; and *Moving Picture World*, 10 August 1912, 546.

102. The novelization of *What Happened to Mary?* devotes even greater attention to this aspect of the narrative, for the entire opening chapter, entitled "Mary's First Adventure," chronicles her kidnapping. After Mary's abduction, her wealthy grandfather dies only moments after signing a will leaving his entire inheritance to Mary should she be found before her twenty-first birthday. Even before her departure from Peart's ice cream shop and the sure drudgery that awaits her there, all of the ingredients of Mary's story are in place: forcible separation from family, death of a patriarch, unknown inheritance. See Robert Carlton Brown, *What Happened to Mary? A Novelization from the Play and the Stories Appearing in* The Ladies' World (New York: Edward J. Clode, 1913), 17.

103. *Moving Picture World*, 20 July 1912, 268.

104. *Ladies' World*, August 1912, 3.

105. *Moving Picture World*, 20 July 1912, 268.

106. Nan Enstad argues that serial heroines appealed to working-class women viewers because the heroines were themselves from this same background, a view that must surely be revised since virtually all of the heroines in this early period either are daughters of wealthy families or later find that they are heiresses to great fortunes, and few, apart from Mary and Helen, are shown to work for a living. See Enstad, "Dressed for Adventure: Working Women and Silent Movie Serials in the 1910s," *Feminist Studies* 21, no. 1 (1995): 67–90.

107. As Robert C. Allen has pointed out, mistaken parentage is also a familiar plot device in more contemporary soap operas. See Allen, *Speaking of Soap Operas* (Chapel Hill: University of North Carolina Press, 1985), 74.

108. *Moving Picture World*, 4 July 1914, 47; and *Moving Picture World*, 14 November 1914, 912.

109. Enstad, "Dressed for Adventure," 76.

110. Ben Singer makes a similar point in "Female Power in the Serial-Queen Melodrama: The Etiology of an Anomaly," *Camera Obscura* 22 (1990): 122–23.

111. *Moving Picture World*, 4 April 1914, 38.

112. *Adventures of Kathlyn*, Herald no. 1, "The Unwelcome Throne." Selig Collection, Folder 560, MHL.

113. *Adventures of Kathlyn*, Herald no. 2, "The Court of Death." Selig Collection, Folder 560, MHL.

114. *Adventures of Kathlyn*, Herald no. 13, "The Two Ordeals." Selig Collection, Folder 560, MHL.

115. *San Francisco Examiner*, 4 January 1915, 10; and *Photoplay*, May 1914, 131.

116. *New York Dramatic Mirror*, 2 September 1914, 26.

117. *Ladies' World*, July 1913, 36.

118. *Moving Picture World*, 26 December 1914, 1846.

119. *Moving Picture World*, 25 April 1914, 572.

120. *San Francisco Examiner*, 22 March 1914, Editorial and Dramatic Section, 4.

121. *Moving Picture World*, 12 December 1914, 1529. Arthur B. Reeve, who penned Kennedy's adventures for *Cosmopolitan*, cowrote the Pathé serial with Charles L. Goddard.

122. *San Francisco Examiner*, 19 January 1915, 7.

123. *Moving Picture World*, 9 January 1915, 278; and *Moving Picture World*, 16 January 1915, 388.

124. *San Francisco Examiner*, 10 January 1915, Editorial and Dramatic Section, 3.

125. *Moving Picture World*, 16 January 1915, 388; and *Moving Picture World*, 9 January 1915, 278.

126. *Moving Picture World*, 30 January 1915, 740; *Moving Picture World*, 20 February 1915, 1198, 1200; and *Moving Picture World*, 20 March 1915, 1774, 1766.

127. *Moving Picture World*, 30 January 1915, 740.

128. Only portions of this episode survive. Full details of the episode are contained in the reviews: *Moving Picture World*, 30 January 1915, 740; and *Moving Picture World*, 13 February 1915, 987.

129. *Moving Picture World*, 20 January 1915, 740.

130. *Moving Picture World*, 13 February 1915, 1052.

131. These episodes do not survive. Summaries of their contents can be found in *Edison Kinetogram*, 15 November 1912, 8, 15; *Edison Kinetogram*, 15 December 1912, 12; and *Moving Picture World*, 11 January 1913, 158.

132. Mabel Condon, " 'True Blue' Mary Fuller," *Photoplay Magazine*, May 1914, 63, 64. The absence of working women among early serial heroines is all the more remarkable given the predominance of female wage-earners in nineteenth-century serialized story papers. See Denning, *Mechanic Accents*, 185–200.

133. A print of this episode survives at the Museum of Modern Art's Film Study Center.

134. *Ladies' World*, March 1913, 15, 52. A comparison of this episode with the chapter printed in the *Ladies' World* suggests substantial differences between the two stories, something Nan Enstad fails to account for in her analysis of the *Mary* plots, which is based solely upon the magazine chapters. See Enstad, "Dressed for Adventure," 75–81.

135. Lynne Kirby, *Parallel Tracks: The Railroad and Silent Cinema* (Durham: Duke University Press, 1997), 114.

136. Nan Enstad suggests that Helen also exuded a sexual autonomy that opened up the possibility of lesbian spectatorship. See Enstad, "Dressed for Adventure," 83–86.

137. Pearl White was, according to Anthony Slide, among the very earliest motion picture players to receive mention in the trade press, warranting an article in *Moving*

Picture World in December 1910, long before her association with serials. Slide, "The Evolution of the Film Star," *Films in Review* 25 (1974): 591–94. Quoted in Janet Staiger, "Seeing Stars," *Velvet Light Trap* 20 (1983): 11.

138. Staiger, "Seeing Stars," 10–14; Richard deCordova, "The Emergence of the Star System in America," *Wide Angle* 6, no. 4 (1985): 4–13; Q. David Bowers, "Souvenir Postcards and the Development of the Star System, 1912–1914," *Film History* 3, no. 1 (1989): 39–45; deCordova, *Picture Personalities: The Emergence of the Star System in America* (Urbana and Chicago: University of Illinois Press, 1990), 50–116; Bowser, *The Transformation of Cinema*, 103–19; Catherine E. Kerr, "Incorporating the Star: The Intersection of Business and Aesthetic Strategies in Early American Film," *Business History Review* 64, no. 3 (1990): 383–410; Richard Kozsarski, *An Evening's Entertainment: The Age of the Silent Feature Picture, 1915–1928* (New York: Charles Scribner's Sons, 1990), 259–62; and Kathryn Fuller, *At the Picture Show: Small-Town Audiences and the Creation of Movie Fan Culture* (Washington: Smithsonian Institution Press, 1996).

139. DeCordova, "The Emergence of the Star System," 11, 13; and deCordova, *Picture Personalities*, 98–107.

140. Bowser, *The Transformation of Cinema*, 107.

141. Richard deCordova points out that many early players also shared names with their characters. See *Picture Personalities*, 89.

142. Gaylyn Studlar, "The Perils of Pleasure? Fan Magazine Discourse as Women's Commodified Culture in the 1920s," *Wide Angle* 13, no. 1 (1991): 28.

143. Fuller, *At the Picture Show*, 110.

144. Gaylyn Studlar, *This Mad Masquerade: Stardom and Masculinity in the Jazz Age* (New York: Columbia University Press, 1996), 90–95, 98–114.

145. Even given their obvious appeal to female fans, the fascination that serial actresses might also have held for male fans should not be underestimated, something that both Ben Singer and Kathryn Fuller have stressed. Men, just as much as women, might have found interest in following the exploits of athletic, adventuresome heroines who seemed to embody the spirit of modernity. See Singer, "Female Power in the Serial-Queen Melodrama," 115; and Fuller, *At the Picture Show*, 180–81.

146. *Moving Picture World*, 11 March 1916, 1668. Traditional histories of the serials also recount the dangers actresses faced while filming, reproducing this discourse. See Lahue, *Continued Next Week*, 11–15, 17–18.

147. Mary B. Mullet, "The Heroine of a Thousand Dangerous Stunts," *American Magazine*, September 1921, 32. See also Frank V. Bruner, "What Sort of Fellow Is Pearl White?" *Photo-Play Journal*, February 1919, n.p., vol. 306, RLSBC; and Pearl White, "Putting It Over," *Motion Picture Magazine*, February 1917, 61–62.

148. *New York Clipper*, 20 December 1913, 15.

149. *Moving Picture World*, 6 January 1917, 65.

150. *Moving Picture World*, 1 January 1916, 46; *Moving Picture World*, 15 January 1916, 405; and *Moving Picture World*, 11 March 1916, 1668.

151. Unidentified press clipping, March 1916, Helen Holmes file, MHL; *New York Dramatic Mirror*, 6 May 1914, n.p., vol. 331, RLSBC; and Bertha H. Smith, "A Nervy Movie Lady," *Sunset* 32 (June 1914): 1325.

152. *Moving Picture World*, 16 January 1915, 382.

153. *Moving Pictures Stories*, 21 February 1913, 31; *Montgomery Journal*, 10 May 1913, n.p., vol. 331, RLSBC; *Moving Picture World*, 19 February 1916, 1115; Richard Willis, "Kathlyn the Intrepid," *Photoplay Magazine*, April 1914, 45; *Moving Picture World*, 23 August 1913, 832; and Moving *Picture World*, 11 July 1914, 263.

154. Kathlyn Williams, "Kathlyn's Own Story," *Photoplay Magazine*, April 1914, 39.

155. *Photo-Play Journal*, May 1917, n.p., vol. 331, RLSBC.

156. *Photoplay*, December 1917, n.p., envelope 737, RLC.

157. *Moving Picture World*, 23 August 1913, 832.

158. "Film Star Gives Advice to Girls," *San Antonio Light*, 1 July 1912, n.p., vol. 331, RLSBC. The serial stars anticipated efforts by many female stars in the late 1910s to gain a greater creative role in the industry. See Anthony Slide, *The Silent Feminists: America's First Women Directors* (Lanham, MD: Scarecrow Press, 1996).

159. *Moving Picture World*, 16 January 1915, 382.

160. *Motion Picture Magazine*, May 1915, 119; and *Moving Picture World*, 19 February 1916, 1115.

161. Brian Duryea, "The Necessity of Thrills," *Green Book*, April 1916, 741–43, envelope 737, vol. 1, RLC.

162. "Some Confessions by Kathlyn Williams," *Movie Pictorial*, 4 July 1914, n.p., vol. 308, RLSBC; and Willis, "Kathlyn the Intrepid," 45.

163. *Moving Picture World*, 13 June 1914, 1559.

164. Hector Ames, "The Champion Heroine of Movie Perils, Exploits, Plots and Conspiracies," *Motion Picture Classic*, June 1916, n.p., vol. 306, RLSBC; and *Moving Picture Stories*, 4 July 1913, 31.

165. Willis, "Kathlyn the Intrepid," 45; and *Moving Picture World*, 13 June 1914, 1517.

166. Unidentified newspaper clipping, 19 December 1915, n.p., vol. 308, RLSBC; and "Photo-Player Puts Pep in Perilous Pictures," *State Journal* (Madison, WI), 24 May 1915, n.p., envelope 737, vol. 1, RLC.

167. "A Charming Dare-Devil," *Pictures and the Picturegoer*, 13 March 1915, 504–5, MHL; and Frederick James Smith, "A Pearl in the Rough," *Motion Picture Classic*, February 1919, n.p., vol. 306, RLSBC.

168. Alan Burden, "The Girl Who Keeps the Railroad," *Photoplay*, July 1915, 91.

169. Bruner, "What Sort of Fellow Is Pearl White?"

170. "Kathlyn Williams, the Jungle Actress," *Picture-Play Weekly*, 17 April 1915, 1–4, vol. 308, RLSBC.

171. *Motion Picture Magazine*, August 1916, 158.

172. Smith, "A Nervy Movie Lady," 1323.

173. "Action Is the Spice of Life, Says Miss Holmes," *New York Telegraph*, 21 November 1915, n.p., envelope 737, vol. 1, RLC.

174. DeCordova, *Picture Personalities*.

175. Willis, "Kathlyn the Intrepid," 45; and Ames, "The Champion Heroine of Movie Perils, Exploits, Plots and Conspiracies."

176. *New York Tribune*, 7 December 1919, n.p., vol. 331, RLSBC.

177. *Moving Picture Stories*, 11 April 1913, 14.

178. Pearl Gaddis, "How Helen Holmes Became Mrs. Mack and a Picture Star," *Motion Picture Magazine*, March 1917, 102–6.

179. "Can She Bake a Cherry Pie, Billy Boy?" *Photoplay,* February 1915, n.p., envelope 2603, RLC.

180. Hector Ames, "Kathlyn Williams, Builder," *Motion Picture Magazine,* July 1916, 89. Also see Roberta Courtlandt, "At Home with Helen," *Motion Picture Classic,* August 1917, n.p., vol. 308, RLSBC.

181. "Film Play Work Hard on Tires," *Los Angeles Examiner,* n.d., n.p., envelope 737, vol. 1, RLC.

182. "The Mother Love That Spoiled a Movie Thriller," unidentified newspaper clipping, 1917, envelope 737, vol. 1, RLC.

183. Studlar, "The Perils of Pleasure?" 28.

Chapter Four
Civic Housekeeping: Women's Suffrage, Female Viewers, and the Body Politic

1. "Bring Out Picture Play," *Woman's Journal,* 10 October 1914.

2. Ibid.

3. Kay Sloan, *The Loud Silents: Origins of the Social Problem Film* (Urbana and Chicago: University of Illinois Press, 1988), 100. Sloan discusses other uses of film by progressive causes throughout the book. Also see Sloan, "A Cinema in Search of Itself: Ideology of the Social Problem Film during the Silent Era," *Cineaste* 14, no. 2 (1985): 34–37, 56; Kevin Brownlow, *Behind the Mask of Innocence. Sex, Violence, Prejudice, Crime: Films of Social Conscience in the Silent Era* (New York: Alfred Knopf, 1990), esp. 225–37; and Steven J. Ross, "Struggles for the Screen: Workers, Radicals, and the Political Uses of Silent Film," *American Historical Review* 96, no. 2 (1991): 333–67.

4. Sloan, *The Loud Silents,* 108, 116; Eleanor Flexner, *A Century of Struggle: The Woman's Rights Movement in the United States* (Cambridge: Harvard University Press, 1959), 254–59; William L. O'Neill, "The Fight for Suffrage," *Wilson Quarterly* 10, no. 4 (1986): 103–6; and Sara M. Evans, *Born for Liberty: A History of Women in America* (New York: The Free Press, 1989), 152–56, 164–72. Wyoming, Colorado, Utah, and Idaho granted women the vote in 1869, 1893, 1895, and 1896, respectively; in 1910, after a fourteen-year hiatus, Washington State enacted women's suffrage, followed by California in 1911, then Kansas, Oregon, and Arizona in 1912.

5. Arguments against women's suffrage during this period are examined in detail in Flexner, *A Century of Struggle,* 248–93; Aileen Kraditor, *The Ideas of the Woman Suffrage Movement 1890–1920* (New York: Columbia University Press, 1965), 1–68, 96–121; Mariam Darce Frenier, "American Anti-Feminist Women: Comparing the Rhetoric of Opponents of the Equal Rights Amendment with That of Opponents of Women's Suffrage," *Women's Studies International Forum* 7, no. 6 (1984): 456–58; Susan E. Marshall, " 'Ladies against Women': Mobilization Dilemmas of Antifeminist Movements," *Social Problems* 32, no. 4 (1985): 348–62; and Manuela Thurner, " 'Better Citizens without the Ballot': American Antisuffrage Women and Their Rationale during the Progressive Era," *Journal of Women's History* 5, no. 1 (1993): 33–60.

6. Jean Bethke Elshtain, "Moral Woman and Immoral Man: A Consideration of the Public-Private Split and Its Political Ramifications," *Politics and Society* 4, no. 4 (1974): 461. Elshtain discusses the particular philosophical implications of the suffrage

campaign in *Public Man, Private Woman: Women in Social and Political Thought* (Princeton: Princeton University Press, 1981), 229–39.

7. "Do You, as a Woman, Want to Vote?" *Ladies' Home Journal*, 11 January 1911, 17.

8. Quoted in Kraditor, *The Ideas of the Woman Suffrage Movement*, 25.

9. Thurner, " 'Better Citizens,' " 39–41.

10. Monique Canto, "The Politics of Women's Bodies: Reflections on Plato," in *The Female Body in Western Culture: Contemporary Perspectives*, ed. Susan Rubin Suleiman (Cambridge: Harvard University Press, 1985), 339–53.

11. I am indebted to Kay Sloan, Gretchen Bataille, and Martin F. Norden, who have done a considerable amount of work in identifying early women's suffrage comedies, most of which no longer survive. See Sloan, *The Loud Silents*, 99–123; Gretchen Bataille, "Preliminary Investigations: Early Suffrage Films," *Women and Film* 1, nos. 3–4 (1973): 42–44; Sloan, "Sexual Warfare in the Silent Cinema: Comedies and Melodramas of Woman Suffrage," *American Quarterly* 33 (1981): 412–36; and Martin F. Norden, " 'A Good Travesty upon the Suffragette Movement': Women's Suffrage Films as Genre," *Journal of Popular Film and Television* 13, no. 4 (1986): 171–77. The only extant prints I have been able to view are *A Busy Day, A Cure for Suffragettes, The Men Haters' Club, Suffragette Minstrels, A Suffragette in Spite of Himself*, and portions of two reels of *How They Got the Vote*. My accounts of other suffrage comedies are based exclusively on contemporary reviews and publicity materials.

12. *Moving Picture World*, 22 June 1907, 252; *Moving Picture World*, 27 November 1909, 769, 771; and *Moving Picture World*, 9 March 1912, 866.

13. *Moving Picture World*, 27 November 1909, 769, 771.

14. Ibid.

15. *Moving Picture World*, 30 May 1914, 1246.

16. Ibid., 1296; and *New York Dramatic Mirror*, 27 May 1914, 37.

17. *Moving Picture World*, 25 February 1911, 434. Several French suffrage comedies, including *The Reformation of the Suffragettes* and *For the Cause of Suffrage*, were exhibited in the United States. Although the context in which they were produced differs from that of American comedies, their American release suggests that exhibitors saw the relevance of their commentary to the stateside situation. Many reviews confirm this view as well.

18. *Moving Picture World*, 28 January 1911, 194.

19. *Moving Picture World*, 6 March 1909, 282.

20. Unidentified advertising herald. Folder 556, Selig Collection, MHL.

21. *Moving Picture World*, 8 April 1911, 787.

22. Advertising herald. Folder 556, Selig Collection, MHL.

23. *Moving Picture World*, 22 June 1907, 252.

24. *Universal Weekly*, 20 December 1913, 20. See also *Moving Picture World*, 20 December 1913, 1413.

25. *Moving Picture World*, 27 November 1909, 769, 771.

26. *Universal Weekly*, 14 February 1914, 11.

27. *Moving Picture World*, 1 July 1911, 1522; *Moving Picture World*, 8 June 1912, 890; and *Moving Picture World*, 22 June 1912, 1128.

28. *Moving Picture World*, 8 April 1911, 787.

29. *Moving Picture World*, 17 January 1914, 296; and *"The Militant," Photoplay*, March 1914, 65–75.

30. *Moving Picture World*, 25 April 1914, 494.

31. *Moving Picture World*, 4 April 1914, 176–77.

32. *"A Militant Suffragette," Photoplay*, January 1913, 46.

33. *Moving Picture World*, 2 May 1908, 401.

34. Mary Russo, "Female Grotesques: Carnival and Theory," in *Feminist Studies/Critical Studies*, ed. Teresa de Lauretis (Bloomington: Indiana University Press, 1986), 217.

35. See, for instance, "Emmeline, Christabel and Sylvia: The Shrieking Sisterhood of Suffragettes," *Current Literature* 45 (August 1908): 159–62. The title refers to British activist Emmeline Pankhurst and her daughters, Christabel and Sylvia.

36. *Edison Kinetogram*, 1 January 1913, 4. See also *Moving Picture World*, 18 January 1913, 263.

37. *Edison Kinetogram*, 1 January 1913, 4.

38. *Moving Picture World*, 16 August 1913, 722. See also *Moving Picture World*, 20 September 1913, 1285.

39. *Moving Picture World*, 16 November 1912, 658.

40. Quoted in "Ten Thousand Women Marching for Votes," *Literary Digest* 44 (18 May 1912): 1026.

41. The poster is reproduced in Paula Hays Harper, "Votes for Women? A Graphic Episode in the Battle of the Sexes," in *Art and Architecture in the Service of Politics*, ed. Henry A. Millon and Linda Nochlin (Cambridge: MIT Press, 1978), 152.

42. Many comedies in the teens, besides those directly concerned with suffrage, play upon transvestism and gender role reversal. This suggests the degree to which masculine and feminine identities were destabilized during these years. The suffrage debate proved to be only one arena in which new gender identities might be negotiated. In a somewhat loftier vein, Sandra M. Gilbert notes the persistence of transvestism in early-twentieth-century literature. See Gilbert, "Costumes of the Mind: Transvestism as Metaphor in Modern Literature," in *Writing and Sexual Difference*, ed. Elizabeth Abel (Chicago: University of Chicago Press, 1982), 193–219.

43. *Moving Picture World*, 6 March 1909, 282; and *Moving Picture World*, 23 October 1909, 581.

44. *"A Militant Suffragette."*

45. *Moving Picture World*, 6 March 1909, 282.

46. *Moving Picture World*, 23 October 1909, 581.

47. *Moving Picture World* 6 November 1909, 644.

48. *Moving Picture World*, 8 June 1912, 890. See also *Moving Picture World*, 22 June 1912, 1128.

49. Michael Monahan, editor of *Papyrus Magazine*, quoted in " 'The American Peril,' " *Woman's Journal*, 4 July 1914.

50. In the prints of *A Busy Day* I have viewed at the Museum of Modern Art and the National Film Archive in London, Chaplin is not directly identified as a suffragist in the intertitles. However, Kay Sloan reports that the film's original title was intended to be *The Militant Suffragist*, until it was discovered that the Pathé film *A Militant Suffragette* was also to be released in 1914 (Sloan, *The Loud Silents*, 104). Indeed, the National Film Archive print survives with this latter title. Even without such an

explanatory title, however, contemporary audiences would most likely have understood contextual references to "mannish" suffragists disrupting public parades.

51. Chaplin's appearance as a woman in *A Busy Day* should be distinguished from his other drag roles around the same time. In *The Masquerader* (Keystone, 1914) and *A Woman* (Essanay, 1915), both released after *A Busy Day*, Chaplin plays a male character who disguises himself as a woman within the narrative. Both films feature scenes where the masquerade is revealed either to viewers or to characters on-screen, which is *not* the case in *A Busy Day*, where Chaplin plays a woman. See Rebecca Bell-Metereau, *Hollywood Androgyny* (New York: Columbia University Press, 1985), 25–26. Bell-Metereau unfortunately does not discuss *A Busy Day*.

52. Annette Kuhn, *The Power of the Image: Essays on Representation and Sexuality* (London and New York: Routledge and Kegan Paul, 1985), 57. Other theorists, notably Marjorie Garber, focus on the culturally transgressive nature of cross-dressing, rather than its more conservative implications. See Garber, *Vested Interests: Cross-Dressing and Cultural Anxiety* (New York: Harper Collins, 1992).

53. "*Votes for Women*," *Photoplay*, July 1912, 41.

54. "Bring Out Picture Play."

55. Ibid.

56. Flexner, *A Century of Struggle*, 248–53; Michael McGerr, "Political Style and Women's Power, 1830–1930," *Journal of American History* 77, no. 3 (1990): 873–80; and Bertha Damaris Knobe, "Spectacular Woman Suffrage in America," *Independent*, 12 October 1911, 804–10.

57. "Ten Thousand Women Marching for Votes"; "Marching for Equal Suffrage," *Hearst's Magazine* 21 (June 1912); and "Parading in New York for Woman Suffrage," *Current Literature*, June 1912, 627–28. The first article reports that this march was "the largest demonstration of its kind this country has witnessed" (1024).

58. Karen J. Blair, "Pageantry for Women's Rights: The Career of Hazel MacKaye, 1913–1923," *Theatre Survey* 31 (1990): 36–38; and Christine A. Lunardini, *From Equal Suffrage to Equal Rights: Alice Paul and the National Woman's Party, 1910–1928* (New York: New York University Press, 1986), 27–31. The pageant and its accompanying march were organized by Alice Paul, then head of NAWSA's Congressional Committee. Paul had lived in England and was deeply influenced by the militancy of the British campaign. In April 1913 she formed the Congressional Union for Woman Suffrage, later to become the National Woman's Party, a group that advocated (and sometimes practiced) British-style militancy in the American suffrage movement. Unlike NAWSA and the WPU, however, the NWP did not include motion pictures in its crusade. For information on Paul and the NWP, see Lunardini, *From Equal Suffrage to Equal Rights*; Sally Hunter Graham, "Woodrow Wilson, Alice Paul and the Woman Suffrage Movement," *Political Science Quarterly* 98, no. 4 (1983–84): 665–79; and Linda G. Ford, *Iron-Jawed Angels: The Suffrage Militancy of the National Woman's Party, 1912–1920* (New York: University Press of America, 1991).

59. Sloan, *The Loud Silents*, 109. Suffrage stage plays are collected in Bettina Friedl, ed., *On to Victory: Propaganda Plays of the Woman Suffrage Movement* (Boston: Northeastern University Press, 1989).

60. Quoted in Lisa Tickner, *The Spectacle of Women: Imagery of the Suffrage Campaign, 1907–1914* (Chicago: University of Chicago Press, 1988), 58.

61. Knobe, "Spectacular Woman Suffrage," 804, 810.

62. Martha Vicinus, "Male Space and Women's Bodies: The Suffragette Movement," in *Independent Women: Work and Community for Single Women, 1850–1920* (Chicago: University of Chicago Press, 1985), 256. Like Tickner, Vicinus discusses the more militant British campaign.

63. Tickner, *The Spectacle of Women*, 52–60.

64. Ibid., 151.

65. "How It Seemed to March in the Suffrage Parade. By One of the Marchers," *Outlook* 111 (3 November 1915): 554.

66. Lunardini, *From Equal Suffrage to Equal Rights*, 27–31; O'Neill, "The Fight for Suffrage," 105; and Flexner, *A Century of Struggle*, 264.

67. Vicinus, "Male Space and Women's Bodies," 264.

68. Sloan, *The Loud Silents*, 101–3.

69. *Moving Picture News*, 22 March 1913, 13; and *Moving Picture World*, 29 March 1913, 338.

70. *Motography*, August 1911, 81.

71. *New York Tribune*, 10 April 1913, 6; and *Moving Picture Stories*, 18 April 1913, 32. For information on the Kinetophone, see Charles Musser, *Thomas A. Edison and His Kinetographic Motion Pictures* (New Brunswick, NJ: Rutgers University Press, 1995), 52.

72. *New York Dramatic Mirror*, 28 January 1914, 29.

73. "*Votes for Women.*"

74. *Moving Picture World*, 15 November 1913, 763; *Moving Picture World*, 8 November 1913, 626; and *Moving Picture World*, 29 November 1913, 1079.

75. *Moving Picture World*, 1 June 1912, 811.

76. "Dr. Shaw Tells about Acting," *Woman's Journal*, 26 December 1914; and *New York Tribune*, 6 November 1913, 7.

77. *New York Times*, 6 November 1913, 9; *New York Tribune*, 6 November 1913, 7; *Moving Picture World*, 15 November 1913, 741; and *Motography*, 29 November 1913, 406–7.

78. *Moving Picture World*, 3 January 1914, 34. See also *Variety*, 20 March 1914, 23.

79. Lyman Abbott, "The Assault on Womanhood," *Outlook* 91 (3 April 1909): 784, 788. For an exemplary analysis of the ideological implications of feminist oratory in the nineteenth century, see Mary Loeffelholz, "Posing the Woman Citizen: The Contradictions of Stanton's Feminism," *Genders* 7 (1990): 87–98.

80. Tom Gunning, *D. W. Griffith and the Origins of American Narrative Film: The Early Years at Biograph* (Urbana and Chicago: University of Illinois Press, 1991), 91–94; and Miriam Hansen, *Babel and Babylon: Spectatorship and American Silent Film* (Cambridge: Harvard University Press, 1991), 96. Gunning makes the point that lecturers were eventually dropped because it was felt that they ultimately detracted from the creation of an illusory diegesis.

81. "Dr. Shaw Tells about Acting."

82. *Motography*, 29 November 1913, 406–7; and *New York Times*, 6 November 1913, 9.

83. *New York Times*, 6 November 1913, 9; and Sloan, *The Loud Silents*, 116. Pankhurst spoke mainly about white slavery.

84. *Moving Picture World*, 7 November 1914, 764.

85. "Bring Out Picture Play."

86. *Motography*, 28 September 1912, 252; and *Variety*, 20 March 1914, 23.

87. *Moving Picture World*, 4 March 1911, 472.

88. Daniel Levine, *Jane Addams and the Liberal Tradition* (Madison: State Historical Society of Wisconsin, 1971), 186. Sadly, no detailed account of Addams's presentation appears to survive.

89. Quoted in *Moving Picture World*, 5 March 1910, 370–71.

90. *Moving Picture World*, 18 May 1912, 617. According to Sloan, Addams and Shaw were reluctant to produce films when first approached by Reliance, not only because of their apprehensions about the medium, but also because Reliance had produced an antisuffrage comedy, *Bedelia and the Suffragette*, just a few months earlier. See Sloan, *The Loud Silents*, 111.

91. "Chicago Women Voters Clean Up Film Plays," *Woman's Journal*, 1 April 1916, 106.

92. Boyd Fisher, "Motion Pictures to Make Good Citizens," *American City* 7 (September 1912): 234.

93. *Moving Picture World*, 7 November 1914, 764.

94. Mrs. Medill McCormick, *"Your Girl and Mine," Woman's Journal*, 7 November 1914; and Sloan, *The Loud Silents*, 113, 117, 120–21.

95. *Moving Picture World*, 15 November 1913, 741.

96. *Motion Picture News*, 19 December 1914, 37. Quoted in Eileen Bowser, *The Transformation of Cinema, 1907–1915* (New York: Charles Scribner's Sons, 1990), 124.

97. *New York Dramatic Mirror*, 30 December 1914, 27. Emphasis added. The review is uncredited, but I am assuming from its tone that the author is male.

98. *Variety*, 19 December 1914, 28. For a different account of the premiere, see the *Woman's Journal*, 26 December 1914.

99. *New York Tribune*, 10 April 1913, 6. The item was also reproduced in *Moving Picture News*, 19 April 1913, 11.

100. *Moving Picture World*, 18 May 1912, 617.

101. *Moving Picture World*, 8 June 1912, 962. No prints of *Suffrage and the Man*, *Votes for Women*, or *Your Girl and Mine* are known to survive. My accounts are drawn exclusively from contemporary reviews and publicity materials.

102. *Moving Picture World*, 25 May 1912, 796.

103. *Moving Picture World*, 1 June 1912, 811; *Moving Picture News*, 18 May 1912, 30; and *Photoplay*, July 1912, 35–41. No print of *Votes for Women* is known to survive.

104. Allen F. Davis, *American Heroine: The Life and Legend of Jane Addams* (New York: Oxford University Press, 1973), 187; and Kraditor, *The Ideas of the Woman Suffrage Movement*, 86.

105. Susan Walker Fitzgerald, "Women in the Home," n.d., reprinted in *One Half of the People: The Fight for Woman Suffrage*, ed. Ann Frior Scott and Andrew MacKay Scott (Urbana and Chicago: University of Illinois Press, 1975), 114–15.

106. Quoted in Kraditor, *The Ideas of the Woman Suffrage Movement*, 24.

107. Kraditor, *The Ideas of the Woman Suffrage Movement*, 44–52. For information on often more radical nineteenth-century suffrage arguments, see Ellen Dubois, "The Radicalism of the Woman Suffrage Movement: Notes toward the Reconstruction of Nineteenth-Century Feminism," *Feminist Studies* 3, nos. 1–2 (1975): 63–71; and Du-

bois, *Feminism and Suffrage: The Emergence of an Independent Women's Movement in America, 1848–1869* (Ithaca: Cornell University Press, 1978).

108. Mary Holland Kincaid, "The Feminine Charms of the Woman Militant," *Good Housekeeping* 54 (February 1912): 146–55. Also see "Why I Want the Ballot. By a Home Woman," *Woman's Home Companion* 38 (April 1911): 4; and Sarah Comstock, "The Woman Who Votes," pts. I–III, *Collier's* 43 (17 April 1909): 14–15; (1 May 1909): 14–15; and(8 May 1909): 23, 31–32. The series purports to show "the Western woman voter's equal interest in jelly-making and politics." (pt. I, 14).

109. The poster is reproduced in Harper, "Votes for Women," 152, and in Alice Sheppard, *Cartooning for Suffrage* (Albuquerque: University of New Mexico Press, 1994).

110. *Moving Picture World*, 7 November 1914, 764–65; *Variety*, 18 December 1914, 25; and *New York Dramatic Mirror*, 30 December 1914, 27.

111. *Moving Picture World*, 7 November 1914, 764.

112. *Variety*, 18 December 1914, 25.

113. Unidentified newspaper review quoted in Vachel Lindsay, *The Art of the Moving Picture* (1915; rpt. New York: Liveright, 1970), 257.

114. "Bring Out Picture Play."

115. Lindsay, *The Art of the Moving Picture*, 256.

116. *Moving Picture World*, 7 November 1914, 765. Ruth McCormick evidently had to defend *Your Girl and Mine* against criticism of its presentation of American law. See "Photo Play Gives Laws Faithfully," *Woman's Journal*, 15 May 1915.

117. Julia Ward Howe, "Woman and the Suffrage: The Case for Woman Suffrage," *Outlook* 91 (3 April 1909): 781.

118. Sheila Rothman illustrates the connection between new conceptions of "educated motherhood" and the suffrage campaign during the Progressive Era in *Woman's Proper Place: A History of Changing Ideals and Practices* (New York: Basic Books, 1978), 127–32. Ellen Dubois argues that the working woman became an image of womanhood as potent as that of the mother once working-class women were recognized by the suffrage movement in the twentieth century. See Dubois, "Harriot Stanton Blatch and the Transformation of Class Relations among Woman Suffragists," in *Gender, Class, Race and Reform in the Progressive Era*, ed. Noralee Frankel and Nancy S. Dye (Lexington: University of Kentucky Press, 1991), 162–79.

119. Davis, *American Heroine*, 184.

120. Quoted in Howe, "Woman and the Suffrage," 781.

121. Ibid., 783.

122. Howe praises the legislative victories achieved in states where women were already granted limited voting rights, and points to newly enacted laws restricting alcohol licensing, gambling, obscene literature, and cruelty to animals as evidence of a positive "feminine" influence in political matters. See ibid., 782.

123. Paula Baker, "The Domestication of Politics: Women and American Political Society, 1780–1920," *American Historical Review* 89, no. 3 (1984): 642.

124. It is not clear who is responsible for the screenplay of *Eighty Million Women Want——?* Despite the title's reference to Rheta Childe Dorr's book, *What Eight Million Women Want* (Boston: Small, Maynard and Co., 1910), the film's opening intertitles claim that the plot is "from a story by Kate Corbaley." *Motion Picture News* and *Motography* both report that the screenplay was written by Florence Maule Cooley; the latter

suggests that Blatch collaborated as well. (*Motion Picture News*, 22 November 1913, 35; and *Motography*, 29 November 1913, 406.) This information is also verified in *The American Film Institute Catalog of Motion Pictures Produced in the United States: Feature Films, 1911–1920* (New York: R. R. Bowker, 1988), 238. However, Kevin Brownlow reports that B. P. Schulberg (later "discoverer" of Clara Bow) wrote the screenplay at Emmeline Pankhurst's request (Brownlow, *Behind the Mask of Innocence*, 229).

125. *Motion Picture News*, 22 November 1913, 35.

126. *Moving Picture World*, 8 November 1913, 660.

127. *Motion Picture News*, 22 November 1913, 35.

128. *Motography*, 29 November 1913, 407.

129. In addition to advocating "Votes for Women" in the final chapter of the work, Dorr calls for wide-ranging social reform, all in the name of women. She advocates stricter labor laws and improved factory conditions for working women, the eradication of prostitution and white slavery, improved treatment of women in domestic service, and the revision of unfair laws governing property and inheritance.

130. *Moving Picture World*, 8 November 1913, 619.

131. Ibid., 660.

132. *Motography*, 29 November 1913, 406.

133. Edward S. Martin, "What Suffragists Want," *Ladies' Home Journal*, April 1913, 25.

134. Wallace Irwin, "Satan and the Suffragette," *Collier's* 43 (10 April 1909): 17.

135. Stephen Heath, "Film and System: Terms of Analysis," pt. 1, *Screen* 16, no. 1 (1975): 7–77.

136. *Motion Picture News*, 22 November 1913, 35. The comment refers to evidence of corruption at Tammany Hall, Democratic headquarters in New York City.

137. Prompted by the similarities between these two plots, Jack Lodge surmises that *Eighty Million Women Want——?* was "a bare-faced crib from *Traffic [in Souls].*" This despite the evidence that *Eighty Million Women Want——?* was released two weeks prior to the film it was supposedly imitating. For Lodge this merely means that *Traffic in Souls* circulated in New York prior to its official release. I have found no evidence to support his conclusions. The detective plots, though they bear some interesting congruences, differ substantially in the main. See Lodge, " 'First of the Immortals': The Career of George Loane Tucker," *Griffithiana* 37 (December 1989): 41.

Conclusion

1. Mary Heaton Vorse, "Some Picture Show Audiences," *Outlook* 98 (24 June 1911): 441.

2. Ibid., 443.

3. Ibid., 446.

4. Miriam Hansen, *Babel and Babylon: Spectatorship in American Silent Film* (Cambridge: Harvard University Press, 1991), 118.

5. Gaylyn Studlar, "The Perils of Pleasure? Fan Magazine Discourse as Women's Commodified Culture in the 1920's," *Wide Angle* 13, no. 1 (1991): 6–33.

Selected Bibliography

Archival Collections

Billy Rose Theater Collection, New York Public Library for the Performing Arts
Film and Television Archive, University of California at Los Angeles
Film Department, International Museum of Photography, George Eastman House
George Amberg Memorial Study Center, New York University
Margaret Herrick Library, Center for Motion Picture Study, Academy of Motion Picture
    Arts and Sciences, Los Angeles
Motion Picture, Broadcasting and Recorded Sound Division, Library of Congress
Museum of Modern Art Film Study Center, New York
National Board of Review of Motion Pictures Collection, Rare Books and Manuscripts
    Division, New York Public Library
National Film Archive, London

Film Industry Trade Papers

Eclair Bulletin
Edison Kinetogram
Kalem Kalendar
Motion Picture News
Motion Picture Story Magazine, later *Motion Picture Magazine*
Moving Picture World
New York Clipper
New York Dramatic Mirror
Nickelodeon, later *Motography*
Paramount's Picture Progress
Photoplay
Selig's Paste Pot and Shears
Universal Weekly
Variety
Wid's Daily

Newspapers

Chicago Tribune
New York Evening Post
New York Herald
New York Sun
New York Times
New York Tribune
New York World
San Francisco Examiner

Primary Sources

Abbott, Lyman. "The Assault on Womanhood." *Outlook* 91 (3 April 1909): 784–88.
———. "The Profession of Motherhood." *Outlook* 91 (10 April 1909): 836–40.
"A Booming Industry," *Outlook* 110 (21 July 1915): 645.
Addams, Jane. *Jane Addams: A Centennial Reader.* New York: Macmillan, 1960.
———. *A New Conscience and an Ancient Evil.* New York: Macmillan, 1912.
———. "Some Reflections on the Failure of the Modern City to Provide Recreation for Young Girls." *Charities and the Commons* 21 (5 December 1909): 365.
———. *The Spirit of Youth and City Streets.* New York: 1909.
" 'The American Peril.' " *Woman's Journal,* 4 July 1914.
Ames, Hector. "Kathlyn Williams, Builder." *Motion Picture Magazine,* July 1916, 89.
Austin, Annette. "The Drifting Daughter: Why Many Girls Leave Home to Work in the City and Why They and Many Others Do Not Marry." *Ladies' World,* October 1912, 5–6.
Ball, Eustace Hale. *The Art of the Photoplay.* New York: Veritas, 1913.
———. *Traffic in Souls: A Novel of Crime and Its Cure.* New York: G. W. Dillingham, 1914.
Barry, John F., and Epes W. Sargent. *Building Theatre Patronage: Management and Merchandising.* New York: Chalmers Publishing, 1927.
Beaton, Ralph. *The Anti-Vice Crusader and Social Reformer: A Treatise on the Social Evil.* Dallas: Southwestern Publishing, 1918.
Bell, Ernest A. *Fighting the Traffic in Young Girls; or, War on the White Slave Trade.* Chicago: L. S. Ball, 1910.
"The Best Known Girl in America: Mary Pickford Tells What It Means to Be a 'Movie' Actress." *Ladies' Home Journal* 32 (January 1915): 9.
Bingham, Theodore A. *The Girl That Disappears: The Real Facts about the White Slave Traffic.* Boston: R. G. Badger, 1911.
Bowen, Louise de Koven. "Dance Halls." *Survey* 26 (3 July 1911): 383–87.
———. *Five and Ten Cent Theaters: Two Investigations.* Chicago: The Juvenile Protective Association, 1911.
———. *Safeguards for City Youth at Work and at Play.* New York: Macmillan, 1914.
" 'Breaking into the Game': Told by A Girl Who Didn't Break In." *Photoplay,* August 1914, 131–35.
"Bring Out Picture Play." *Woman's Journal,* 10 October 1914.
Brown, Robert Carlton. *What Happened to Mary? A Novelization from the Play and the Stories Appearing in* The Ladies' World. New York: Edward J. Clode, 1913.
Burden, Alan. "The Girl Who Keeps the Railroad." *Photoplay,* July 1915, 91.
California State Recreational Inquiry Committee. *Report.* California State Printing Office, 1914.
"Chicago Women Voters Clean Up Film Plays." *Woman's Journal,* 1 April 1916, 106.
Clark, Margeurite. "Eat and Keep Well: The Suggestions of a Famous Photoplay Star." *Picture Progress,* November 1916, 4.
The Cleveland Foundation Committee. *Commercial Recreation.* Cleveland: Cleveland Foundation Committee, 1920.
Cocks, Orrin G. "Applying Standards to Motion Picture Films." *Survey* 32 (27 June 1914): 337–38.

Collier, John. "Censorship and the National Board." *Survey* 35 (2 October 1915): 9–14.

Committee of Fifteen. *The Social Evil, with Special Reference to Conditions Existing in the City of New York.* 2d ed. New York and London: G. P. Putnam's Sons, 1912.

Comstock, Sarah. "The Woman Who Votes." Pts. I–III. *Collier's* 43 (17 April 1909): 14–15; (1 May 1909): 14–15; and (8 May 1909): 23, 31–32.

Condon, Mabel. "*Traffic in Souls.*" *Photoplay*, February 1914, 41.

———. " 'True Blue' Mary Fuller." *Photoplay*, May 1914, 63–64.

"Conference on the White Slave Trade." *Survey* 25 (20 August 1910): 714–15.

"Control and Women." *Life*, 1 February 1917, 184.

The Dangers of A Large City; or, The System of the Underworld: Exposing the White Slave Traffic. Chicago, n.d. Collection of the author.

Davis, Michael M. *The Exploitation of Pleasure: A Study of Commercial Recreation in New York City.* New York: Russell Sage Foundation, 1911.

Deland, Margaret. "The Third Way in Woman Suffrage." *Ladies' Home Journal* (January 1913): 11.

Dench, Ernest A. *Advertising by Motion Pictures.* Cincinnati: Standard Publishing, 1916.

———. "Extras! Extras! Extras!" *Motion Picture Classic*, July 1916, 57–58.

"Dr. Shaw Tells about Acting." *Woman's Journal*, 26 December 1914.

Dorr, Rheta Childe. *What Eight Million Women Want.* New York: Small, Maynard and Co., 1910.

"Do You, as a Woman, Want to Vote?" *Ladies' Home Journal*, 11 January 1911, 17.

"Dramatizing Vice." *Literary Digest* 47 (1913): 577–78.

Duey, Helen. "The Movement for Better Films." *Woman's Home Companion* 42 (March 1915): 3, 64.

Dunbar, Olivia Howard. "The Lure of the Films." *Harper's Weekly* 57 (18 January 1913): 20, 22.

Edwards, Richard Henry. *Popular Amusements.* New York: Association Press, 1915.

"Emmeline, Christabel and Sylvia: The Shrieking Sisterhood of Suffragettes." *Current Literature* 45 (August 1908): 159–62.

Fisher, Boyd. "Motion Pictures to Make Good Citizens." *American City* 7 (September 1912): 234–38.

———. "The Regulation of Motion Picture Theaters." *American City* 7 (September 1912): 520–22.

"Five 'White Slave' Trade Investigations." *McClure's* 35 (July 1910): 346.

Foster, William Trufant. *Vaudeville and Motion Picture Shows: A Study of Theatres in Portland, Oregon.* Portland: Reed College, 1914.

Frohman, Daniel. "The 'Movies' and the Theatre." *Woman's Home Companion* 40 (November 1913): 5.

Fuller, Mary. "My Adventures as a Motion-Picture Heroine." *Collier's* 48 (30 December 1911): 16–17.

Gaddis, Pearl. "How Helen Holmes Became Mrs. Mack and a Picture Star." *Motion Picture Magazine*, March 1917, 102–6.

Gleason, Arthur. "The Story of Rosalinda." *Collier's* 51 (10 May 1913): 16+.

Goddard, Charles. *The Perils of Pauline: A Motion Picture Novel.* New York: Heart's International Library Co., 1914.

Goldman, Emma. "The Traffic in Women." 1917. Reprinted in *The Traffic in Women and Other Essays on Feminism*, 19–32. New York: Times Change Press, 1970.

Hard, William, with Rheta Childe Dorr. "The Woman's Invasion." Pts. I–VI. *Everybody's Magazine* 19 (November 1908): 579–91; (December 1908): 798–810; 20 (January 1909): 73–85; (February 1909): 236–48; (March 1909): 372–86; and (April 1909): 521–32.

Harland, Robert O. *Vice Bondage of a Great City; or, The Wickedest City in the World*. Chicago: The Young People's Civic League, 1912.

Harrison, Thekla D. "On Etiquette, As It Were. Or Advice to a Young Man and a Young Lady upon Entering a Picture Show." *Motion Picture Supplement* 1, no. 1 (September 1915): 40–41.

Hodges, James. *Opening and Operating a Motion Picture Theatre, How It Is Done Successfully*. New York: Scenario Publishing, 1912.

Hornblow, Arthur, Jr. "Have You a Movie Camera Face?" *Motion Picture Classic*, May 1916, 14–15.

———. "How They Got In." *Motion Picture Classic*, November 1916, 23–25.

Horstmann, Henry Charles. *Motion Picture Operation, Stage Electrics and Illusions: A Practical Hand-Book and Guide for Theater Electricians, Motion Picture Operators and Managers of Theaters and Productions*. Chicago: Frederick J. Drake & Co., 1917.

Howe, Frederic C. "What to Do with the Motion-Picture Show: Shall It Be Censored?" *Outlook* 107 (20 June 1914): 412–16.

Howe, Julia Ward. "Woman and the Suffrage: The Case for Woman Suffrage." *Outlook* 91 (3 April 1909): 780–84.

"How It Seemed to March in the Suffrage Parade. By One of the Marchers." *Outlook* 111 (3 November 1915): 554.

Hulfish, David S. *Motion-Picture Work: A General Treatise on Picture Taking, Picture Making, Photo-Plays, and Theater Management and Operation*. Chicago: American School of Correspondence, 1913.

"The Immoral Morality of the 'Movies.'" *Current Opinion*, October 1915, 244.

Irwin, Wallace. "Satan and the Suffragette." *Collier's* 43 (10 April 1909): 17.

———. "A Woman's Place Is in the Home." *Ladies' World*, May 1914, 3.

Israels, Belle Lindner. "The Way of the Girl." *Survey* 22 (3 July 1909): 486–88.

"Is White Slavery Nothing More Than a Myth?" *Current Opinion*, November 1913, 348.

"It's a Long Way to Filmland." *Motion Picture Supplement*, October 1915, 69.

Janney, O. Edward. *The White Slave Traffic in America*. New York: National Vigilance Committee, 1912.

Johnson, Jane Stannard. "Woman's Duty to Motion Pictures." *Ladies' World*, January 1915, 18.

Johnson, William Allen. "In Motion Picture Land." *Everybody's Magazine* 33 (October 1915): 437–48.

Juvenile Protection Association of Cincinnati. *Recreation Survey of Cincinnati*. Cincinnati, OH, 1913.

Kauffman, Reginald Wright. *The Girl That Goes Wrong*. New York: Moffat, Yard, 1911.

———. *The House of Bondage*. New York: Grosset and Dunlap, 1910.

Kincaid, Mary Holland. "The Feminine Charms of the Woman Militant." *Good Housekeeping* 54 (February 1912): 146–55.

Kneeland, George J. *Commercialized Prostitution in New York City.* Rev. ed. New York: The Century Co., 1917.

Knobe, Bertha Damaris. "Spectacular Woman Suffrage in America." *Independent*, 12 October 1911, 804–10.

Laidlaw, Harriet Burton. "My Little Sister." *Survey*, 3 May 1913, 199–202.

Law, Emma Norine. *The Shame of a Great Nation: The Story of the "White Slave Trade".* Harrisburg, PA: United Evangelical Publishing House, 1909.

Lehman, Rev. Frederick M. *The White Slave Hell; or, With Christ at Midnight in the Slums of Chicago.* Chicago: The Christian Witness Co., 1910.

Leupp, Constance D. "The Motion Picture as Social Worker." *Survey* 25 (27 August 1910): 739–41.

Lindsay, Vachel. *The Art of the Moving Picture.* 1915. Reprint, New York: Liveright, 1970.

Locke, Charles Edward. *White Slavery in Los Angeles.* Los Angeles: Times Mirror Co., 1913.

MacGrath, Harold. *The Adventures of Kathlyn.* Indianapolis: Bobbs-Merrill, 1914.

Madison Board of Commerce. *Madison, "The Four Lake City," Recreational Survey.* Madison, WI, 1915.

"Making the Most of Moving Pictures." *Woman's Home Companion* 39 (April 1912): 12, 100.

"Man's Commerce in Women: Mr. Rockefeller's Bureau of Social Hygiene Issues Its First Report." *McClure's* 41 (August 1913): 185–89.

"Marching for Equal Suffrage." *Hearst's Magazine* 21 (June 1912).

Marple, Albert. "Making Pictures in California." *Motion Picture Classic*, April 1916, 37–39, 73.

Martin, Edward S. "What Suffragists Want." *Ladies' Home Journal*, April 1913, 25.

McCormick, Mrs. Medill. "*Your Girl and Mine*." *Woman's Journal*, 7 November 1914.

Merwin, B. "Family Vote: How the Suffrage Question Came Home to the Wainwrights." *Woman's Home Companion* 37 (April 1910): 8, 64.

"*The Militant*." *Photoplay*, March 1914, 65–75.

"*A Militant Suffragette*." *Photoplay*, January 1913, 46.

Miner, Maude. *Slavery of Prostitution: A Plea for Emancipation.* New York: Macmillan, 1916.

"Modern Americans." *Collier's* 51 (26 July 1913): 15.

"The Moral Havoc Wrought by Moving Picture Shows." *Current Opinion*, April 1914, 290.

"The Morals of the Movies." *Outlook* 107 (20 June 1914): 387–88.

"The Morals of the Movies: From the Standpoint of the Manager in the Small Town." *Survey* 33 (4 March 1916): 662.

"Movie Crimes against Good Taste." *Literary Digest* 51 (18 September 1915): 591–92.

" 'Movie' Manners and Morals." *Outlook* 113 (26 July 1916): 694–95.

"Movie Morals." *New Republic*, 25 August 1917, 100–101.

"Movies Once More." *Outlook* 108 (28 October 1914): 449.

"The Moving Picture and the National Character." *American Review of Reviews* 42 (September 1910): 326.

"The Moving Picture Shows." *Harper's Weekly* 55 (16 September 1911): 6.

"The Moving-Picture Show: What It Ought to Mean in Your Town, and What It Really Does Mean." *Woman's Home Companion* 38 (October 1911): 21–22.

Mullet, Mary B. "The Heroine of a Thousand Dangerous Stunts." *American Magazine*, September 1921, 32.

Münsterberg, Hugo. *The Film: A Psychological Study.* 1916. Reprint, New York: Dover, 1970.

"Not Worrying about Her Rights." *Collier's* 43 (1 May 1909): 8.

O'Higgins, Harvey J. "The Case of Fanny." *Collier's* 50 (2 March 1912): 11+.

Page, William A. "The Movie-Struck Girl." *Woman's Home Companion* 45 (June 1918): 18, 75.

"Parading in New York for Woman Suffrage." *Current Literature*, June 1912, 627–28.

Park, Robert. "The City: Suggestions for the Investigation of Human Behavior in the Urban Environment." 1916. Reprinted in *Classic Essays on the Culture of Cities*, edited by Richard Sennett, 91–123. New York: Appleton-Century-Crofts, 1969.

Phelan, John Joseph. *Motion Pictures as a Phase of Commercial Amusement in Toledo, Ohio.* Toledo: Little Book Press, 1919.

Phelps, Guy F. *Ethel Vale: The White Slave.* Chicago: The Christian Witness Co., 1910.

"A Philadelphia Warning to Girls." *Literary Digest* 46 (1 February 1913): 234.

"Photo Play Gives Laws Faithfully." *Woman's Journal*, 15 May 1915.

"Popular Gullibility as Exhibited in the New White Slavery Hysteria." *Current Opinion*, February 1914, 129.

Rathbun, John B. *Motion Picture Making and Exhibiting.* Chicago: Charles C. Thompson Company, 1914.

"The Real Perils of Pearl White." *Literary Digest*, 5 December 1914, 1147.

Reeve, Arthur B. *The Exploits of Elaine.* New York and London: Harper and Brothers, 1914.

Regan, John. *Crimes of the White Slavers and the Results.* Chicago: J. Regan and Co., 1912.

Richardson, Anna Steese. "The City as the Country Girl Finds It." *Ladies' World*, July 1912, 10, 26.

———. " 'Filmitis,' the Modern Malady—Its Symptoms and Its Cure." *McClure's* 47 (January 1916): 12–14, 70.

———. "Who Gets Your Dime?" *McClure's* 46 (November 1915): 21–22, 73–74.

Richardson, Bertha June. *The Woman Who Spends: A Study of Her Economic Function.* Rev. ed. Boston: Whitcomb and Barrows, 1910.

Richardson, Frank Herbert. *The Motion Picture Handbook: A Guide for Managers and Operators of Motion Picture Theatres.* 3d ed. New York: Moving Picture World, 1916.

———. "Women and Children." *Moving Picture World*, 21 February 1914, 962.

Rippey, S. C. "The Case of Angeline." *Outlook* 106 (31 January 1914): 255–56.

"The Rockefeller Grand Jury Report: Showing the Conditions of the 'White Slave' Trade in New York City." *McClure's* 35 (August 1910): 471–73.

Roe, Clifford G. *The Great War on White Slavery.* ca. 1911. Reprint, New York: Garland, 1979.

———. *Panders and Their White Slaves*. New York: Fleming H. Revel Co., 1910.

Sanger, William. *The History of Prostitution: Its Extent, Causes, and Effects throughout the World*. New York: Harper and Brothers, 1858.

Sargent, Epes Winthrop. *Picture Theatre Advertising*. New York: Chalmers Publishing, 1915.

Scranton, W. A. "Etiquette: On the Proper Way for Two Women to Spend an Evening in a Moving Picture Theatre." *Motion Picture Magazine*, May 1916, 65–70.

"Sex-O'Clock in America." *Current Opinion*, August 1913, 113–14.

"The Slave Traffic in America." *Outlook* 93 (6 November 1909): 528–29.

Smith, Bertha H. "A Nervy Movie Lady." *Sunset* 32 (June 1914): 1323–25.

Smith, Helen G. "The Extra Girl Is Handed a Few Snickers." *Photoplay*, March 1920, 107–8.

"Social Evil in a Smaller City." *Survey* 26 (16 May 1911): 212.

Southard, M. Madeline. *The White Slave Traffic versus the American Home*. Louisville, KY: Pentecostal Publishing, 1914.

"The Spectator." *Outlook* 103 (25 January 1913): 230.

Spingarn, Arthur B. *Laws Relating to Sex Morality in New York City*. 1915. Rev. ed. New York: The Century Co., 1926.

State of Wisconsin. *Report of the Wisconsin Vice Committee*. Madison, 1914.

"Ten Thousand Women Marching for Votes." *Literary Digest* 44 (18 May 1912): 1024–26.

"This Little Girl Earns $100,000 a Year." *McClure's*, May 1915.

Todd, Harry Coulter. *The White Slave: A Novel*. New York: Neale Publishing, 1913.

True, Ruth S. *The Neglected Girl*. New York: Russell Sage Foundation, 1914.

Turner, George Kibbe. "The City of Chicago: A Study of the Great Immoralities." *McClure's* 28 (April 1907): 575–92.

———. "The Daughters of the Poor." *McClure's* 34 (November 1909): 45–61.

"The Utter Hopelessness of the Movies." *Life*, 1 February 1917, 182.

Vice Commission of Chicago. *The Social Evil in Chicago: A Study of Existing Conditions*. Chicago: Gunthorp-Warren, 1911.

Vice Commission of Minneapolis. *Report of the Vice Commision of Minneapolis*. Minneapolis, 1911. Reprinted in *The Prostitute and the Social Reformer: Commerical Vice in the Progressive Era*. New York: Arno Press, 1974.

Vice Commission of Philadelphia. *A Report on Existing Conditions*. Philadelphia, 1913. Reprinted in *The Prostitute and the Social Reformer: Commerical Vice in the Progressive Era*. New York: Arno Press, 1974.

Vorse, Mary Heaton. "Some Picture Show Audiences." *Outlook* 98 (24 June 1911): 441–47.

"*Votes for Women*." *Photoplay*, July 1912, 41.

"Wages and Sin," *Literary Digest* 46 (22 March 1913): 621–24.

"When You Dance: Some Gowns and Hats. Suggestions by Florence Walton." *Picture Progress*, November 1916, 12–13.

White, Pearl. "Putting It Over," *Motion Picture Magazine*, February 1917, 61–62.

"The White Slave Films." *Outlook* 106 (17 January 1914): 121.

"The White Slave Films: A Review." *Outlook* 106 (14 February 1914): 347–48, 350.

"Why I Want the Ballot. By a Home Woman." *Woman's Home Companion* 38 (April 1911): 4.

"Will You Stand with Me?" *Woman's Home Companion* 43 (May 1916).

Williams, Kathlyn. "Kathlyn's Own Story." *Photoplay*, April 1914, 39.

Willis, Richard. "Kathlyn the Intrepid." *Photoplay*, April 1914, 45.

"The Working Girl," *Collier's* 51 (28 June 1913): 13.

Secondary Sources

Abel, Richard. *The Ciné Goes to Town: French Cinema, 1896–1914*. Berkeley and Los Angeles: University of California Press, 1994.

———. "Scenes from Domestic Life in Early French Cinema." *Screen* 30, no. 3 (1989): 4–28.

———. "The Thrills of *Grand Peur*: Crime Series and Serials in the Belle Epoque." *Velvet Light Trap* 37 (1996): 3–9.

Abelson, Elaine S. *When Ladies Go A-Thieving: Middle-Class Shoplifters in the Victorian Department Store*. New York and London: Oxford University Press, 1989.

Abrams, Richard M. *The Burdens of Progress, 1900–1929*. Glenview, IL: Scott Foresman, 1978.

———, ed. *The Issues of the Populist and Progressive Eras, 1892–1912*. Columbia: University of South Carolina Press, 1970.

Allen, Jeanne Thomas. "The Film Viewer as Consumer." *Quarterly Review of Film Studies* 5, no. 4 (1980): 481–501.

Allen, Robert C. *Horrible Prettiness: Burlesque and American Culture*. Chapel Hill: University of North Carolina Press, 1991.

———. " 'The Leg Business': Transgression and Containment in American Burlesque." *Camera Obscura* 23 (1990): 42–69.

———. "Manhattan Myopia; or, Oh! Iowa!" *Cinema Journal* 35, no. 3 (1996): 75–103.

———. "Motion Picture Exhibition in Manhattan, 1906–1912: Beyond the Nickelodeon." In *The American Movie Industry: The Business of Motion Pictures*, edited by Gorham Kindem, 12–24. Carbondale: Southern Illinois University Press, 1982.

———. "The Movies in Vaudeville: Historical Context of the Movies as Popular Entertainment." In *The American Film Industry*, edited by Tino Balio, 57–82. 2d ed. Madison: University of Wisconsin Press, 1985.

———. *Speaking of Soap Operas*. Chapel Hill: University of North Carolina Press, 1985.

———. "*Traffic in Souls*." *Sight and Sound* 44, no. 1 (1974–75): 50–52.

———. *Vaudeville and Film, 1895–1915: A Study in Media Interaction*. New York: Arno Press, 1980.

Anderson, Robert L. *The Diggs-Caminetti Case, 1913–1917: For Any Other Immoral Purpose*. Lewiston, NY: Edwin Mellen, 1990.

Ardener, Shirley. "Ground Rules and Social Maps for Women: An Introduction." In *Women and Space: Ground Rules and Social Maps*, edited by Shirley Ardener, 11–24. New York: St. Martin's Press, 1981.

Armour, Robert A. "The Effects of Censorship Pressure on the New York Nickelodeon Market, 1907–1909." *Film History* 4, no. 2 (1990): 113–21.

Austin, Bruce A. *Immediate Seating: A Look at Movie Audiences*. Belmont, CA: Wadsworth, 1989.

Bacci, Carol. "Feminism and the 'Eroticization' of the Middle-Class Woman: The Intersection of Class and Gender Attitudes." *Women's Studies International Forum* 11, no. 1 (1988): 43–53.

Baker, Paula. "The Domestication of Politics: Women and American Political Society, 1780–1920." *American Historical Review* 89, no. 3 (1984): 620–47.

Balides, Constance. "Making Dust in the Archives: Feminism, History, and Early American Cinema." Ph.D. diss., University of Wisconsin at Milwaukee, 1993.

———. "Scenarios of Exposure in the Practice of Everyday Life: Women in the Cinema of Attractions." *Screen* 34, no. 1 (1993): 19–37.

Banner, Lois. *American Beauty.* New York: Alfred Knopf, 1983.

Banta, Martha. *Imaging American Women: Ideas and Ideals in Cultural History.* New York: Columbia University Press, 1987.

Barrett, James R. "Americanization from the Bottom Up: Immigration and the Remaking of the Working Class in the United States, 1880–1930." *Journal of American History* 79, no. 3 (1992): 996–1020.

Barry, Kathleen. *Female Sexual Slavery.* New York: New York University Press, 1984.

Barth, Gunther. *City People: The Rise of Modern City Culture in Nineteenth-Century America.* New York: Oxford University Press, 1980.

Bataille, Gretchen. "Preliminary Investigations: Early Suffrage Films." *Women and Film* 1, nos. 3–4 (1973): 42–44.

Beckman, Marlene. "The White Slave Traffic Act: The Historical Impact of a Federal Crime Policy on Women." *Women and Politics* 4, no. 3 (1984): 85–101.

Bell-Metereau, Rebecca. *Hollywood Androgyny.* New York: Columbia University Press, 1985.

Benson, Susan Porter. *Counter Cultures: Saleswomen, Managers, and Customers in American Department Stores, 1890–1940.* Urbana: University of Illinois Press, 1986.

Berman, David K. "Male Support for Woman Suffrage: An Analysis of Voting Patterns in the Mountain West." *Social Science History* 11, no. 3 (1987): 281–94.

Blair, Karen J. *Clubwoman as Feminist: True Womanhood Redefined, 1868–1914.* New York: Holmes and Meier, 1980.

———. "Pageantry for Women's Rights: The Career of Hazel MacKaye, 1913–1923." *Theatre Survey* 31, no. 1 (1990): 23–46.

Boller, Paul F., Jr. "The Sound of Silents." *American Heritage* 36, no. 5 (1985): 98–107.

Bordwell, David, Janet Staiger, and Kristin Thompson. *The Classical Hollywood Cinema, 1917–1960.* New York: Columbia University Press, 1985.

Bowers, Q. David. *Nickelodeon Theatres and Their Music.* Vestal, NY: Vestal Press, 1986.

———. "Souvenir Postcards and the Development of the Star System, 1912–1914." *Film History* 3, no. 1 (1989): 39–45.

Bowlby, Rachel. *Just Looking: Consumer Culture in Dreiser, Gissing and Zola.* New York: Methuen, 1983.

Bowser, Eileen. *The Transformation of Cinema, 1907–1915.* Vol. 2, *History of the American Cinema.* New York: Charles Scribner's Sons, 1990.

———, ed. *Biograph Bulletins, 1908–1912.* New York: Octagon Books, 1973.

Brandon, Ruth. *The New Women and the Old Men: Love, Sex and the Woman Question.* New York: W. W. Norton, 1990.

Brewster, Ben. "*Traffic in Souls*: An Experiment in Feature-Length Narrative Construction." *Cinema Journal* 31, no. 1 (1990): 37–56.

Bristow, Edward J. *Prostitution and Prejudice: The Jewish Fight against White Slavery, 1870–1939*. Oxford: Clarendon Press, 1982.

Brooks, Peter. "The Mark of the Beast: Prostitution, Serialization and Narrative." In *Reading for the Plot: Design and Intention in Narrative*, 143–70. New York: Vintage, 1985.

Brownlow, Kevin. *Behind the Mask of Innocence: Sex, Violence, Prejudice, Crime: Films of Social Conscience in the Silent Era*. New York: Alfred Knopf, 1990.

Bruno, Giuliana. *Streetwalking on a Ruined Map: Cultural Theory and the City Films of Elvira Notari*. Princeton: Princeton University Press, 1993.

Buck-Morss, Susan. "The *Flâneur*, the Sandwichman and the Whore: The Politics of Loitering." *New German Critique* 39 (1986): 99–140.

Burch, Noel. *Life to Those Shadows*. Translated by Ben Brewster. Berkeley and Los Angeles: University of California Press, 1990.

Burnham, John C. "The Progressive Era Revolution in American Attitudes towards Sex." *Journal of American History* 9, no. 4 (March 1973): 885–908.

Callahan, Vicki. "Zones of Anxiety: Movement, Musidora, and the Crime Serials of Louis Feuillade." *Velvet Light Trap* 37 (1996): 37–50.

Canto, Monique. "The Politics of Women's Bodies: Reflections on Plato." In *The Female Body in Western Culture: Contemporary Perspectives*, edited by Susan Rubin Suleiman, 339–53. Cambridge: Harvard University Press, 1985.

Carbine, Mary. " 'The Finest Outside the Loop': Motion Picture Exhibition in Chicago's Black Metropolis, 1905–1928." *Camera Obscura* 23 (1990): 8–41.

Cassady, Ralph, Jr. "Monopoly in Motion Picture Production and Distribution: 1908–1915." 1959. Reprinted in *The American Movie Industry: The Business of Motion Pictures*, edited by Gorham Kindem, 25–75. Carbondale and Edwardsville: Southern Illinois University Press, 1982.

Connelly, Mark Thomas. *The Response to Prostitution in the Progressive Era*. Chapel Hill: University of North Carolina Press, 1980.

Coontz, Stephanie. *The Social Origins of Private Life: A History of American Families, 1600–1900*. New York and London: Verso, 1988.

Cordasco, Francesco. *The White Slave Trade and the Immigrants: A Chapter in American Social History*. Detroit: Blaire-Ethridge Books, 1981.

Cott, Nancy F. *The Grounding of Modern Feminism*. New Haven: Yale University Press, 1987.

Couvares, Francis G. "The Good Censor: Race, Sex, and Censorship in the Early Cinema." *Yale Journal of Criticism* 7, no. 2 (1994): 233–51.

———. *The Remaking of Pittsburgh*. Albany: State University of New York Press, 1984.

Crunden, Robert M. *Ministers of Reform: The Progressives' Achievement in American Civilization, 1889–1920*. New York: Basic Books, 1982.

Czitrom, Daniel. "The Politics of Performance: From Theater Licensing to Movie Censorship in Turn-of-the-Century New York." *American Quarterly* 44, no. 4 (1992): 525–53.

————. "The Redemption of Leisure: The National Board of Censorship and the Rise of Motion Pictures in New York City, 1900–1920." *Studies in Visual Communication* 10, no. 4 (1984): 2–6.

Damon-Moore, Helen. *Magazines for the Millions: Gender and Commerce in the Ladies' Home Journal and the Saturday Evening Post, 1880–1910*. Albany: State University of New York Press, 1994.

Davis, Allen F. *American Heroine: The Life and Legend of Jane Addams*. New York: Oxford University Press, 1973.

DeBauche, Leslie Midkiff. "Advertising and the Movies, 1908–1915." *Film Reader* 6 (1985): 115–24.

deCordova, Richard. "The Emergence of the Star System in America." *Wide Angle* 6, no. 4 (1985): 4–13.

————. *Picture Personalities: The Emergence of the Star System in America*. Urbana and Chicago: University of Illinois Press, 1990.

Degler, Carl. *At Odds: Women and the Family in America from the Revolution to the Present*. New York: Oxford University Press, 1980.

Denning, Michael. *Mechanic Accents: Dime Novels and Working-Class Culture in America*. New York and London: Verso, 1987.

de Young, Mary. " 'Help, I'm Being Held Captive!' The White Slave Fairy Tale of the Progressive Era." *Journal of American Culture* 6, no. 1 (1983): 96–99.

Doane, Mary Ann. *The Desire to Desire: The Woman's Film of the 1940s*. Bloomington: Indiana University Press, 1987.

————. "An Economy of Desire: The Commodity Form in/of the Cinema." *Quarterly Review of Film and Video* 11, no. 1 (1989): 23–33.

Dorsett, Lyle, ed. *The Challenge of the City, 1860–1910*. Lexington, MA: Heath, 1968.

Dubois, Ellen Carol. *Feminism and Suffrage: The Emergence of an Independent Women's Movement in America, 1848–1869*. Ithaca: Cornell University Press, 1978.

————. "Harriot Stanton Blatch and the Transformation of Class Relations among Woman Suffragists." In *Gender, Class, Race and Reform in the Progressive Era*, edited by Noralee Frankel and Nancy S. Dye, 162–79. Lexington: University of Kentucky Press, 1991.

————. "The Radicalism of the Woman Suffrage Movement: Notes toward the Reconstruction of Nineteenth-Century Feminism." *Feminist Studies* 3, nos. 1–2 (1975): 63–71.

Dyer, Richard. "The Colour of Virtue: Lillian Gish, Whiteness and Femininity." In *Women and Film: A Sight and Sound Reader*, edited by Pam Cook and Philip Dodd, 1–9. Philadelphia: Temple University Press, 1993.

————. *Heavenly Bodies: Film Stars and Society*. New York: St. Martin's Press, 1986.

————. *Stars*. London: British Film Institute, 1979.

Eckert, Charles. "The Carole Lombard in Macy's Window." *Quarterly Review of Film Studies* 3, no. 1 (1978): 1–21.

Elshtain, Jean Bethke. "Moral Woman and Immoral Man: A Consideration of the Public-Private Split and Its Political Ramifications." *Politics and Society* 4, no. 4 (1974): 453–73.

————. *Public Man, Private Woman: Women in Social and Political Thought*. Princeton: Princeton University Press, 1981.

Enstad, Nan. "Dressed for Adventure: Working Women and Silent Movie Serials in the 1910s." *Feminist Studies* 21, no. 1 (1995): 67–90.

Epstein, Barbara Leslie. *The Politics of Domesticity: Women, Evangelism, and Temperance in Nineteenth-Century America*. Middletown, CT: Wesleyan University Press, 1981.

Erenberg, Lewis. " 'Ain't We Got Fun?' " *Chicago History* 14, no. 4 (1985–86): 4–21.

———. " 'Everybody's Doin' It': The Pre–World War I Dance Craze, the Castles and the Modern American Girl." *Feminist Studies* 3, nos. 1–2 (1975): 155–70.

———. *Steppin' Out: New York Night Life and the Transformation of American Culture 1890–1930*. Chicago: University of Chicago Press, 1981.

Evans, Sara M. *Born for Liberty: A History of Women in America*. New York: The Free Press, 1989.

Everson, William. *American Silent Film*. New York: Oxford University Press, 1978.

Ewen, Elizabeth. "City Lights: Immigrant Women and the Rise of the Movies." *Signs* 5, no. 3 (1980): 42–56.

———. *Immigrant Women in the Land of Dollars: Life and Culture on the Lower East Side, 1890–1920*. New York: Monthly Review Press, 1985.

Feldman, Charles Matthew. *The National Board of Censorship (Review) of Motion Pictures, 1909–1922*. New York: Arno Press, 1977.

Feldman, Egal. "Prostitution, the Alien Woman and the Progressive Imagination, 1910–1915." *American Quarterly* 19, no. 2 (1967): 192–206.

Fishbein, Leslie. "The Demise of the Cult of True Womanhood in Early American Film, 1900–1930." *Journal of Popular Film and Television* 12, no. 2 (1984): 66–72.

———. "From Sodom to Salvation: The Image of New York City in Films about Fallen Women, 1899–1934." *New York History* 70 (1989): 171–90.

———. "The Harlot's Progress: Myth and Reality in European and American Film, 1900–1934." *American Studies* 27, no. 2 (1986): 5–17.

Fisher, Robert. "Film Censorship and Progressive Reform: The National Board of Censorship of Motion Pictures, 1909–1922." *Journal of Popular Film and Television* 4, no. 2 (1975): 143–56.

Fiske, John. "The Cultural Economy of Fandom." In *The Adoring Audience: Fan Culture and Popular Media*, edited by Lisa A. Lewis, 30–49. New York and London: Routledge, 1992.

Flexner, Eleanor. *A Century of Struggle: The Woman's Rights Movement in the United States*. Cambridge: Harvard University Press, 1959.

Ford, Linda G. *Iron-Jawed Angels: The Suffrage Militancy of the National Woman's Party, 1912–1920*. New York: University Press of America, 1991.

Frankel, Noralee, and Nancy S. Dye, eds. *Gender, Class, Race, and Reform in the Progressive Era*. Lexington: University of Kentucky Press, 1991.

Frankfort, Roberta. *Collegiate Women: Domesticity and Career in Turn-of-the-Century America*. New York: New York University Press, 1977.

Frenier, Mariam Darce. "American Anti-Feminist Women: Comparing the Rhetoric of Opponents of the Equal Rights Amendment with that of Opponents of Women's Suffrage." *Women's Studies International Forum* 7, no. 6 (1984): 455–65.

Friedberg, Anne. *Window Shopping: Cinema and the Postmodern*. Berkeley and Los Angeles: University of California Press, 1993.

Friedl, Bettina, ed. *On to Victory: Propaganda Plays of the Woman Suffrage Movement.* Boston: Northeastern University Press, 1989.

Fuller, Kathryn H. *At the Picture Show: Small-Town Audiences and the Creation of Movie Fan Culture.* Washington: Smithsonian Institution Press, 1996.

———. "Boundaries of Participation: The Problem of Spectatorship and American Film Audiences, 1905–1930." *Film and History* 20, no. 4 (1990): 75–86.

———. "You Can Have the Strand. . . ." *Film History* 6, no. 2 (1994): 166–77.

Gaines, Jane. "From Elephants to Lux Soap: The Programming and 'Flow' of Early Motion Picture Exploitation." *Velvet Light Trap* 25 (1990): 29–43.

———. "The Queen Christina Tie-Ups: Convergence of Show Window and Screen." *Quarterly Review of Film and Video* 11, no. 1 (1989): 35–60.

Gaines, Jane, and Charlotte Herzog. "Puffed Sleeves before Teatime: Joan Crawford, Adrian and Women Audiences." *Wide Angle* 6, no. 4 (1985): 24–33.

Garber, Marjorie. *Vested Interests: Cross-Dressing and Cultural Anxiety.* New York: Harper Collins, 1992.

Garvey, Ellen Gruber. *The Adman in the Parlor: Magazines and the Gendering of Consumer Culture, 1880s to 1910s.* New York: Oxford University Press, 1996.

Geary, Helen Brophy. "After the Last Picture Show." *Chronicles of Oklahoma* 61, no. 1 (1983): 4–27.

Gilbert, Sandra M. "Costumes of the Mind: Transvestism as Metaphor in Modern Literature." In *Writing and Sexual Difference*, edited by Elizabeth Abel, 193–219. Chicago: University of Chicago Press, 1982.

Gilfoyle, Timothy J. *City of Eros: New York City, Prostitution and the Commercialization of Sex, 1790–1920.* New York: W. W. Norton, 1992.

———. "The Moral Origins of Political Surveillance: The Preventive Society in New York City, 1867–1918." *American Quarterly* 38, no. 4 (1986): 637–52.

Glassberg, David. *American Historical Pageantry: The Uses of Tradition in the Early Twentieth Century.* Chapel Hill: University of North Carolina Press, 1990.

———. "History and the Public: Legacies of the Progressive Era." *Journal of American History* 73 (1987): 957–80.

Goldstein, Cynthia. "Early Film Censorship: Margaret Sanger, *Birth Control* and the Law." In *Current Research in Film Audiences, Economics, and the Law*, edited by Bruce A. Austin, 188–200. Vol. 2. Norwood, NJ: Ablex Publishing, 1988.

Gomery, Douglas. "Movie Audiences, Urban Geography and the History of the American Film." *Velvet Light Trap* 19 (1982): 23–29.

———. *Shared Pleasures: A History of Movie Presentation in the United States.* Madison: University of Wisconsin Press, 1992.

Gordon, Lynn. "The Gibson Girl Goes to College: Popular Culture and Women's Higher Education in the Progressive Era, 1890–1920." *American Quarterly* 39 (1987): 211–30.

Graham, Sally Hunter. "Woodrow Wilson, Alice Paul and the Woman Suffrage Movement." *Political Science Quarterly* 98, no. 4 (1983–84): 665–79.

Grieveson, Lee. "Policing the Cinema: *Traffic in Souls* at Ellis Island." *Screen* 38, no. 2 (1997): 149–71.

Griffin, Clyde. "The Progressive Ethos." In *The Development of an American Culture*, edited by Stanley Coben and Lorman Ratner, 144–80. 2d ed. New York: St. Martin's Press, 1983.

Grittner, Fredrick K. *White Slavery: Myth, Ideology and American Law.* New York: Garland, 1990.

Gunning, Tom. "An Aesthetic of Astonishment: Early Film and Its (In)credulous Spectator." *Art and Text* 34 (1989): 31–45.

———. "The Cinema of Attraction: Early Film, Its Spectator and the Avant-Garde." *Wide Angle* 8, nos. 3–4 (1986): 63–70.

———. "D. W. Griffith and the Narrator System: Narrative Structure and Industry Organization in Biograph Films, 1908–1909." Ph.D. diss., New York University, 1985.

———. *D. W. Griffith and the Origins of American Narrative Film: The Early Years at Biograph.* Urbana and Chicago: University of Illinois Press, 1991.

———. "Film History and Film Analysis: The Individual Film in the Course of Time." *Wide Angle* 12, no. 3 (1990): 4–19.

———. "From the Kaleidoscope to the X-Ray: Urban Spectatorship, Poe, Benjamin, and *Traffic in Souls* (1913)." *Wide Angle* 19, no. 4 (1997): 25–61.

———. "From the Opium Den to the Theatre of Morality: Moral Discourse and Film Process in Early American Cinema." *Art and Text* 30 (1988): 30–40.

———. "A Tale of Two Prologues: Actors and Roles, Detectives and Disguises in *Fantômas*, Film and Novel." *Velvet Light Trap* 37 (1996): 30–36.

———. "Tracing the Individual Body: Photography, Detectives, and Early Cinema." In *Cinema and the Invention of Modern Life*, edited by Leo Charney and Vanessa R. Schwartz, 15–45. Berkeley and Los Angeles: University of California Press, 1995.

———. "Weaving a Narrative: Style and Economic Background in Griffith's Biograph Films." *Quarterly Review of Film Studies* 6, no. 1 (1981): 11–25.

———. "The Whole Town's Gawking: Early Cinema and the Visual Experience of Modernity." *Yale Journal of Criticism* 7, no. 2 (1994): 189–201.

Gutman, Herbert. *Work, Culture and Society in Industrializing America.* New York: Alfred Knopf, 1976.

Haag, Pamela Susan. " 'Commerce in Souls': Vice, Virtue, and Women's Wage Work in Baltimore, 1990–1915." *Maryland Historical Magazine* 86, no. 3 (1991): 292–308.

Hagan, John. "Erotic Tendencies in Film, 1900–1906." In *Cinema 1900–1906: An Analytical Study*, edited by Roger Holman, 231–38. Vol. 1. Brussels: FIAF, 1982.

Hagedorn, Roger. "Technology and Economic Exploitation: The Serial as a Form of Narrative Presentation." *Wide Angle* 10, no. 4 (1988): 4–12.

Hall, Ben M. *The Best Remaining Seats: The Story of the Golden Age of the Movie Palace.* New York: Clarkson N. Potter, 1961.

Handel, Leo A. *Hollywood Looks at Its Audience: A Report on Film Audience Research.* Urbana: University of Illinois Press, 1950.

Hansen, Miriam. "The Adventures of Goldilocks: Spectatorship, Consumerism, and Public Life." *Camera Obscura* 22 (1990): 51–71.

———. *Babel and Babylon: Spectatorship and American Silent Film.* Cambridge: Harvard University Press, 1991.

———. "Early Cinema, Late Cinema: Permutations of the Public Sphere." *Screen* 34, no. 3 (1993): 197–210.

———. "Early Silent Cinema: Whose Public Sphere?" *New German Critique* 29 (1983): 147–84.

———. "The Hieroglyph and the Whore: D. W. Griffith's *Intolerance*." *South Atlantic Quarterly* 88, no. 2 (1989): 361–92.

———. "Reinventing the Nickelodeon: Notes on Kluge and Early Cinema." *October* 46 (1988): 179–98.

Hanson, Stephen L. "Serials and *The Perils of Pauline*." In *Magill's Survey of Cinema*, vol. 1, edited by Frank N. Magill, 95–100. Englewood Cliffs, NJ: Salem Press, 1982.

Hapke, Laura. *Conventions of Denial: Prostitution in Late Nineteenth-Century American Anti-Vice Narratives*. Michigan Occasional Papers in Women's Studies, no. 24. Ann Arbor, Women's Studies Program, University of Michigan, 1982.

Harper, Paula Hays. "Votes for Women? A Graphic Episode in the Battle of the Sexes." In *Art and Architecture in the Service of Politics*, edited by Henry A. Millon and Linda Nochlin, 150–61. Cambridge: MIT Press, 1978.

Harris, Barbara J. *Beyond Her Sphere: Women and the Professions in American History*. Westport, CT: Greenwood Press, 1979.

Hartmann, Susan. *The Paradox of Women's Progress, 1820–1920*. St. Charles, MO: Forum Press, 1974.

Havig, Alan. "The Commercial Amusement Audience in Early Twentieth-Century American Cities." *Journal of American Culture* 5, no. 1 (1982): 1–19.

———. "Mass Commercial Amusements in Kansas City before World War I." *Missouri Historical Review* 75, no. 3 (1981): 316–45.

Heath, Stephen. "Film and System: Terms of Analysis." Pt. 1. *Screen* 16, no. 1 (1975): 7–77.

———. "Narrative Space." In *Questions of Cinema*, 19–75. Bloomington: Indiana University Press, 1981.

Heller, Adele, and Lois Rudnick, eds. *1915, The Cultural Moment: The New Politics, the New Woman, the New Psychology*. New Brunswick, NJ: Rutgers University Press, 1991.

Helly, Dorothy O., and Susan M. Reverby, eds. *Gendered Domains: Rethinking Public and Private in Women's History*. Ithaca: Cornell University Press, 1992.

Herzog, Charlotte, "The Archaeology of Cinema Architecture: The Origins of the Movie Theater." *Quarterly Review of Film Studies* (Winter 1984): 11–32.

———. "The Movie Palace and the Theatrical Sources of Its Architectural Style." *Cinema Journal* 20, no. 2 (1981): 15–37.

Higashi, Sumiko. *Cecil B. DeMille and American Culture: The Silent Era*. Berkeley and Los Angeles: University of California Press, 1994.

———. "Cecil B. DeMille and the Lasky Company: Legitimating Feature Film as Art." *Film History* 4, no. 3 (1990): 181–97.

———. "Cinderella vs. Statistics: The Silent Movie Heroine as Jazz-Age Working Girl." In *Woman's Being, Woman's Place: Female Identity and Vocation in American History*, edited by Mary Kelley, 109–26. Boston: G. K. Hall, 1979.

———. "Dialogue: Manhattan's Nickelodeons." *Cinema Journal* 35, no. 3 (1996): 72–73.

———. "Ethnicity, Class and Gender in Film: DeMille's *The Cheat*." In *Unspeakable Images: Ethnicity and the American Cinema*, edited by Lester D. Friedman, 112–39. Urbana and Chicago: University of Illinois Press, 1991.

———. *Virgins, Vamps and Flappers: The American Silent Movie Heroine*. St. Albans, VT: Eden Press Women's Publications, 1977.

Hill, Charles, and Steven Cohen. "John A. Fitch and the Pittsburgh Survey." *Western Pennsylvania Historical Magazine* 67, no. 1 (1984): 17–32.

Hobson, Barbara Meil. *Uneasy Virtue: The Politics of Prostitution and the American Reform Tradition*. New York: Basic Books, 1987.

Hofstadter, Richard. *The Age of Reform: From Bryan to F.D.R.* New York: Alfred Knopf, 1956.

———, ed. *The Progressive Movement, 1900–1915*. Englewood Cliffs, NJ: Prentice-Hall, 1963.

Honey, Maureen, ed. *Breaking the Ties That Bind: Popular Stories of the New Woman, 1915–1930*. Norman: University of Oklahoma Press, 1992.

Izod, John. *Hollywood and the Box Office, 1895–1986*. New York: Columbia University Press, 1988.

Jenkins, William D. "Housewifery and Motherhood: The Question of Role Change in the Progressive Era." In *Woman's Being, Woman's Place: Female Identity and Vocation in American History*, edited by Mary Kelley, 142–53. Boston: G. K. Hall, 1979.

Jesionowski, Joyce. *Thinking in Pictures: Dramatic Structure in D. W. Griffith's Biograph Films*. Berkeley and Los Angeles: University of California Press, 1987.

Johnson, Claudia D. "That Guilty Third Tier: Prostitution in Nineteenth-Century American Theaters." In *Victorian America*, edited by Daniel Walker Howe, 111–20. Philadelphia: University of Pennsylvania Press, 1976.

Jones, Jarnes B., Jr. "Municipal Vice: The Management of Prostitution in Tennessee's Urban Experience. Part I: The Experience of Nashville and Memphis, 1854–1917." *Tennessee Historical Quarterly* 50, no. 1 (1991): 33–41.

Jowett, Garth S. " 'A Capacity for Evil': The 1915 Supreme Court Mutual Decision." *Historical Journal of Film, Radio and Television* 9, no. 1 (1989): 59–78.

———. *Film: The Democratic Art*. Boston: Little, Brown, 1976.

———. "The First Motion Picture Audiences." *Journal of Popular Film* (1974): 39–54.

Karr, Kathleen. "The Long Square-Up: Exploitation Trends in the Silent Films." *Journal of Popular Film* 3, no. 2 (1974): 107–28.

Keil, Charlie. "Advertising Independence: Industrial Performance and Advertising Strategies of the Independent Movement." *Film History* 5, no. 4 (1993): 472–88.

———. "American Cinema from 1907–1913: The Nature of Transition." Ph.D. diss., University of Wisconsin at Madison, 1995.

———. "Reframing *The Italian*: Questions of Audience Address in Early Cinema." *Journal of Film and Video* 42, no. 1 (1990): 36–48.

Keller, Alexandra. "Disseminations of Modernity: Representation and Consumer Desire in Early Mail-Order Catalogues." In *Cinema and the Invention of Modern Life*, edited by Leo Charney and Vanessa R. Schwartz, 156–82. Berkeley and Los Angeles: University of California Press, 1995.

Kennedy, David M. "The Progressive Era." *Historian* 37 (1985): 453–68.

Kerber, Linda. "Separate Spheres, Female Worlds, Woman's Place: The Rhetoric of Women's History." *Journal of American History* 75, nos. 1–2 (1988): 9–39.

Kern, Stephen. *The Culture of Time and Space, 1880–1918*. Cambridge: Harvard University Press, 1983.

Kerr, Catherine E. "Incorporating the Star: The Intersection of Business and Aesthetic Strategies in Early American Film." *Business History Review* 64, no. 3 (1990): 383–410.

Kessler-Harris, Alice. "Independence and Virtue in the Lives of Wage-Earning Women: The United States 1870–1930." In *Women in Culture and Politics: A Century of Change*, edited by Judith Friedlander, Blanche Wiesen Cook, Alice Kessler-Harris, and Carroll Smith-Rosenberg, 3–17. Bloomington: Indiana University Press, 1986.

———. *Out to Work: A History of Wage-Earning Women in the United States*. New York: Oxford University Press, 1982.

Kimmel, Michael. "Men's Responses to Feminism at the Turn of the Century." *Gender and Society* 1 (1987): 261–83.

Kinnard, Roy. *Fifty Years of Serial Thrills*. Metuchen, NJ: Scarecrow Press, 1983.

Kirby, Lynne. "Gender and Advertising in American Silent Film: From Early Cinema to *The Crowd*." *Discourse* 13, no. 2 (1991): 3–20.

———. "Male Hysteria and Early Cinema." *Camera Obscura* 17, (1988): 113–31.

———. *Parallel Tracks: The Railroad and Silent Cinema*. Durham: Duke University Press, 1997.

———. "Temporality, Sexuality and Narrative in *The General*." *Wide Angle* 9, no. 1 (1987): 32–40.

Kirschner, Don. "The Ambiguous Legacy: Social Justice and Social Control in the Progressive Era." *Historical Reflections* 2, no. 1 (1975): 69–88.

———. "The Perils of Pleasure: Commercial Recreation, Social Disorder and Moral Reform in the Progressive Era." *American Studies* 21, no. 2 (1980): 27–42.

Koszarski, Richard. *An Evening's Entertainment: The Age of the Silent Feature Picture, 1915–1928*. Vol. 3, *History of the American Cinema*. New York: Charles Scribner's Sons, 1990.

Kraditor, Aileen. *The Ideas of the Woman Suffrage Movement, 1890–1920*. New York: Columbia University Press, 1965.

———, ed. *Up From the Pedestal: Selected Writings in the History of American Feminism*. Chicago: University of Chicago Press, 1968.

Kryder, LeeAnne Giannone. "Self-Assertion and Social Commitment: The Significance of Work to the Progressive Era's New Woman." *Journal of American Culture* 6, no. 2 (1983): 25–30.

Kuhn, Annette. *Cinema, Censorship, Sexuality, 1909–1925*. London: Routledge, 1988.

———. *The Power of the Image: Essays on Representation and Sexuality*. London and New York: Routledge and Kegan Paul, 1985.

———. "Women's Genres: Melodrama, Soap Opera, and Theory." *Screen* 25, no. 1 (1984): 18–28.

Lahue, Kalton C. *Bound and Gagged: The Story of the Silent Serials*. South Brunswick and New York: A. S. Barnes and Co., 1968.

———. *Continued Next Week: A History of the Moving Picture Serial*. Norman: University of Oklahoma Press, 1964.

Langum, David J. *Crossing Over the Line: Legislating Morality and the Mann Act*. Chicago: University of Chicago Press, 1994.

La Place, Maria. "Producing and Consuming the Woman's Film: Discursive Struggle in *Now, Voyager*." In *Home Is Where the Heart Is: Studies in Melodrama and the*

Woman's Film, edited by Christine Gledhill, 138–66. London: British Film Institute, 1987.

Leach, William. *Land of Desire: Merchants, Power, and the Rise of a New American Culture*. New York: Pantheon Books, 1993.

————. "Transformations in a Culture of Consumption: Women and Department Stores, 1890–1925." *Journal of American History* 71 (1984): 317–42.

————. *True Love and Perfect Union: The Feminist Reformation of Sex and Society*. New York: Basic Books, 1980.

Lears, T. J. Jackson. "From Salvation to Self-Realization: Advertising and the Therapeutic Roots of Consumer Culture." In *The Culture of Consumption: Critical Essays in American History, 1880–1980*, edited by Richard Wightman Fox and T. J. Jackson Lears. New York: Pantheon, 1983.

Leonard, Henry B. "The Immigrants' Protective League of Chicago, 1908–1921." *Journal of the Illinois State Historical Society* 66 (1973): 271–84.

Levine, Daniel. *Jane Addams and the Liberal Tradition*. Madison: State Historical Society of Wisconsin, 1971.

Levine, Lawrence W. *Highbrow/Lowbrow: The Emergence of Cultural Hierarchy in America*. Cambridge: Harvard University Press, 1988.

Lodge, Jack. " 'First of the Immortals': The Career of George Loane Tucker." *Griffithiana* 37 (December 1989): 36–68.

Loeffelholz, Mary. "Posing the Woman Citizen: The Contradictions of Stanton's Feminism." *Genders* 7 (1990): 87–98.

Lubove, Roy. "The Progressive and the Prostitute." *Historian* 24, no. 3 (1962): 308–30.

Lunardini, Christine A. *From Equal Suffrage to Equal Rights: Alice Paul and the National Woman's Party, 1910–1928*. New York: New York University Press, 1986.

Lunbeck, Elizabeth. " 'A New Generation of Women': Progressive Psychiatrists and the Hyper-Sexual Female." *Feminist Studies* 13, no. 3 (1987): 513–43.

MacDonald, Norbert. "The Diggs-Caminetti Case of 1913 and Subsequent Interpretation of the White Slave Trade Act." *Pacific Historian* 29, no. 1 (1985): 30–39.

Mackey, Thomas C. *Red Lights Out: A Legal History of Prostitution, Disorderly Houses, and Vice Districts, 1870–1917*. New York: Garland, 1987.

Maltby, Richard. "The Social Evil, the Moral Order, and the Melodramatic Imagination, 1890–1915." In *Melodrama: Stage, Picture, Screen*, edited by Jacky Bratton, Jim Cook, and Christine Gledhill, 214–30. London: British Film Institute, 1994.

Marsh, John L. "Vaudefilm: Its Contribution to a Moviegoing America." *Journal of Popular Culture* 18, no. 4 (1985): 17–29.

Marshall, Susan E. " 'Ladies against Women': Mobilization Dilemmas of Antifeminist Movements." *Social Problems* 32, no. 4 (1985): 348–62.

May, Elaine Tyler. *Great Expectations: Marriage and Divorce in Post-Victorian America*. Chicago: University of Chicago Press, 1980.

May, Lary. *Screening Out the Past: The Birth of Mass Culture and the Motion Picture Industry*. 2d ed. Chicago: University of Chicago Press, 1982.

Mayne, Judith. "Immigrants and Spectators." *Wide Angle* 5, no. 2 (1982): 32–41.

————. *Public Novels, Private Films*. Athens: University of Georgia Press, 1988.

———. "Uncovering the Female Body." In *Before Hollywood: Turn-of-the-Century Film from American Archives*, edited by Jay Leyda and Charles Musser, 63–67. New York: American Federation of the Arts, 1986.

———. *Woman at the Keyhole: Feminism and Cinema*. Bloomington: Indiana University Press, 1990.

McCarthy, Kathleen D. "Nickel Vice and Virtue: Movie Censorship in Chicago, 1907–1915." *Journal of Popular Film* 5, no. 1 (1976): 37–56.

McCarthy, Michael. "Urban Optimism and Reform Thought in the Progressive Era." *Historian* 51, no. 2 (1989): 239–62.

McDonagh, Eileen L., and Douglas H. Price. "Woman Suffrage in the Progressive Era: Patterns of Opposition and Support in Referenda Voting, 1910–1918." *American Political Science Review* 79, no. 2 (1985): 415–35.

McGerr, Michael. "Political Style and Women's Power, 1830–1930." *Journal of American History* 77, no. 3 (1990): 864–85.

McGovern, James. "The American Woman's Pre–World War I Freedom in Manners and Morals." *Journal of American History* 55, no. 2 (September 1968): 315–33.

McKanna, Clare V., Jr. "Hold Back the Tide: Vice Control in San Diego, 1870–1930." *Pacific Historian* 28, no. 3 (1984): 54–64.

———. "Prostitutes, Progressives, and Police: The Viability of Vice in San Diego, 1900–1930." *Journal of San Diego History* 35, no. 1 (1989): 44–65.

Mellencamp, Patricia. "Female Bodies and Women's Past-Times, 1890–1920." *East-West Film Journal* 6, no. 1 (1992): 17–65.

Meloy, Arthur S. *Theaters and Motion Picture Houses*. New York: Architects' Supply and Publishing Company, 1916.

Merritt, Russell. "Nickelodeon Theatres, 1905–1914: Building an Audience for the Movies." In *The American Film Industry*, edited by Tino Balio, 83–102. 2d ed. Madison: University of Wisconsin Press, 1985.

Meyerowitz, Joanne. "Sexual Geography and Gender Economy: The Furnished Room Districts of Chicago, 1890–1930." *Gender and History* 2, no. 3 (1990): 274–96.

———. *Women Adrift: Independent Wage-Earners in Chicago, 1880–1930*. Chicago: University of Chicago Press, 1988.

———. "Women and Migration: Autonomous Female Migrants to Chicago, 1880–1930." *Journal of Urban History* 13, no. 2 (1987): 147–68.

Micklish, Janet, and Patricia Searles. " 'A Thoroughbred Girl': Images of Female Gender Roles in Turn-of-the-Century Mass Media." *Women's Studies* 10, no. 3 (1984): 261–81.

Miller, D. A. *The Novel and the Police*. Berkeley and Los Angeles: University of California Press, 1988.

Mintz, Steven, and Susan Kellogg. *Domestic Revolutions: A Social History of American Family Life*. New York: The Free Press, 1988.

Mohl, Raymond A. *The New City: Urban America in the Industrial Age, 1860–1920*. Arlington Heights, IL: Harlan Davidson, 1985.

Monroy, Douglas. " 'Our Children Get So Different Here': Film, Fashion, Popular Culture, and the Process of Cultural Syncretization in Mexican Los Angeles, 1900–1935." *Aztlan: A Journal of Chicano Studies* 19, no. 1 (1988–90): 79–108.

Morton, Marian J. "Seduced and Abandoned in an American City: Cleveland and Its Fallen Women, 1869–1939." *Journal of Urban History* 11, no. 4 (1985): 443–69.

Mottram, Ron. *Danish Film before Dreyer.* Metuchen, NJ: Scarecrow Press, 1988.

Mulvey, Laura. "Pandora: Topographies of the Mask and Curiosity." In *Sexuality and Space*, edited by Beatriz Colomina, 53–71. Princeton: Princeton Architectural Press, 1992.

———. "Visual Pleasure and Narrative Cinema." *Screen* 16, no. 4 (1975): 6–18.

Musser, Charles. *The Emergence of Cinema: The American Screen to 1907.* New York: Charles Scribner's Sons, 1990.

———. "The Nickelodeon Era Begins: Establishing the Framework for Hollywood's Mode of Representation." *Framework* 22–23 (1983): 4–11.

———. "Pre-Classical American Cinema: Its Changing Modes of Film Production." *Persistence of Vision* 9 (1991): 46–65.

———. *Thomas A. Edison and His Kinetographic Motion Pictures.* New Brunswick, NJ: Rutgers University Press, 1995.

Nasaw, David. "Learning to Go to the Movies." *American Heritage* 44, no. 7 (1993): 78–92.

Nicholson, Linda. *Gender and History: The Limits of Social Theory in the Age of the Family.* New York: Columbia University Press, 1986.

Noble, David W. *The Progressive Mind.* Chicago: Rand McNally, 1970.

Norden, Martin F. " 'A Good Travesty upon the Suffragette Movement': Women's Suffrage Films as Genre." *Journal of Popular Film and Television* 13, no. 4 (1986): 171–77.

———. "New York Mayor William J. Gaynor and His City's Film Industry." *Film Reader*, 6 (1985): 79–91.

———. "Women in the Early Film Industry." *Wide Angle* 6, no. 3 (1984): 58–67.

Norton, Mary Beth, ed. *Major Problems in American Women's History: Documents and Essays.* Lexington, MA: D. C. Heath, 1989.

Odean, Kathleen. "White Slavers in Minnesota: A Psychological Reading of the Legend." *Midwestern Journal of Language and Folklore* 11, no. 1 (1985): 20–30.

Ogihara, Junko. "The Exhibition of Films for Japanese Americans in Los Angeles during the Silent Film Era." *Film History* 4, no. 2 (1990): 81–87.

O'Malley, Paul. "Neighborhood Nickelodeons: Residential Theaters in South Denver from 1907 to 1917." *Colorado Heritage* 3 (1984): 44–58.

O'Neill, William L. "The Fight for Suffrage." *Wilson Quarterly* 10, no. 4 (1986): 99–109.

———. *The Progressive Years: America Comes of Age.* New York: Dodd Mead, 1975.

Parker, Alison M. "Mothering the Movies: Women Reformers and Popular Culture." In *Movie Censorship and American Culture*, edited by Francis G. Couvares, 73–96. Washington and London: Smithsonian Institution Press, 1996.

Pearson, Roberta E. "Cultivated Folks and the Better Classes: Class Conflict and Representation in Early American Film." *Journal of Popular Film and Television* 15, no. 3 (1987): 120–28.

———. *Eloquent Gestures: The Transformation of Performance Style in the Griffith Biograph Films.* Berkeley and Los Angeles: University of California Press, 1992.

———. "Transitional Cinema." In *The Oxford History of World Cinema*, edited by Geoffrey Nowell-Smith, 23–42. Oxford and New York: Oxford University Press, 1996.

Peiss, Kathy. " 'Charity Girls' and City Pleasures: Historical Notes on Working-Class Sexuality, 1880–1920." In *Passion and Power: Sexuality in History*, edited by Kathy Peiss and Christina Simmons, 57–69. Philadelphia: Temple University Press, 1989.

———. *Cheap Amusements: Working Women and Leisure in Turn-of-the-Century New York*. Philadelphia: Temple University Press, 1986.

———. "Commercial Leisure and the 'Woman Question.' " In *For Fun and Profit: The Transformation of Leisure into Consumption*, edited by Richard Butsch, 105–17. Philadelphia: Temple University Press, 1990.

Perry, Elisabeth. "Cleaning Up the Dance Halls." *History Today* 39 (October 1989): 20–26.

———. " 'The General Motherhood of the Commonwealth': Dance Hall Reform in the Progressive Era." *American Quarterly* 37, no. 5 (1985): 719–33.

Peters, John Durham. "Satan and Savior: Mass Communication in Progressive Thought." *Critical Studies in Mass Communication* 6 (1989): 247–63.

Pivar, David J. *Purity Crusade: Sexual Morality and Social Control, 1868–1900*. Westport, CT: Greenwood Press, 1973.

Pollock, Griselda. "Modernity and the Spaces of Femininity." In *Vision and Difference: Femininity, Feminism and the Histories of Art*. London and New York: Routledge, 1988.

Pratt, George C. *Spellbound in Darkness: A History of the Silent Film*. Rev. ed. Greenwich, CT: New York Graphic Society, 1973.

Rabinovitz, Lauren. *For the Love of Pleasure: Women, Movies and Culture in Turn-of-the Century Chicago*. New Brunswick, NJ: Rutgers University Press, 1998.

———. "Temptations of Pleasure: Nickelodeons, Amusement Parks and the Sights of Female Sexuality." *Camera Obscura* 23 (1991): 71–89.

Rainey, Buck. *Those Fabulous Serial Heroines: Their Lives and Films*. Metuchen, NJ: Scarecrow Press, 1990.

Ramsaye, Terry. *A Million and One Nights: A History of the Motion Picture through 1925*. New York: Simon and Schuster, 1926.

Riegel, Robert E. "Changing American Attitudes towards Prostitution." *Journal of the History of Ideas* 29 (July–September 1968): 437–52.

Riley, Denise. *"Am I That Name?": Feminism and the Category of "Women"*. Minneapolis: University of Minnesota Press, 1988.

Riley, Glenda. *A Perspective on Women's History: 1865 to the Present*. Vol. 2, *Inventing the American Woman*. Arlington Heights, IL: Harlan Davidson, 1986.

Robinson, David. *From Peep Show to Palace: The Birth of American Film*. New York: Columbia University Press, 1996.

Rogers, Daniel T. "In Search of Progressivism." *Reviews in American History* 10 (1982): 113–32.

Rosen, Ruth. *The Lost Sisterhood: Prostitution in America, 1900–1918*. Baltimore: Johns Hopkins University Press, 1982.

Rosenberg, Rosalind. *Divided Lives: American Women in the Twentieth Century*. New York: Hill and Wang, 1992.

Rosenbloom, Nancy J. "Between Reform and Regulation: The Struggle over Film Censorship in Progressive America, 1909–1922." *Film History* 1, no. 4 (1987): 307–25.

———. "In Defense of Moving Pictures: The People's Institute, The National Board of Censorship and the Problems of Leisure in Urban America." *American Studies* 33, no. 2 (1992): 41–61.

———. "Progressive Reform, Censorship and the Motion Picture Industry, 1909–1917." In *Popular Culture and Political Change in Modern America*, edited by Ronald Edsforth and Larry Bennett, 41–60. Albany: State University of New York Press, 1991.

Rosenzweig, Roy. *Eight Hours for What We Will: Work and Leisure in an Industrial City, 1870–1920*. New York: Cambridge University Press, 1983.

Ross, Steven J. "Struggles for the Screen: Workers, Radicals, and the Political Uses of Silent Film." *American Historical Review* 96, no. 2 (1991): 333–67.

———. *Working-Class Hollywood: Silent Film and the Shaping of Class in America*. Princeton: Princeton University Press, 1998.

Rothman, Sheila. *Woman's Proper Place: A History of Changing Ideals and Practices*. New York: Basic Books, 1978.

Russo, Mary. "Female Grotesques: Carnival and Theory." In *Feminist Studies/Critical Studies*, edited by Teresa de Lauretis, 213–29. Bloomington: Indiana University Press, 1986.

Ryan, Mary P. "Gender and Public Access: Women's Politics in Nineteenth-Century America." In *Habermas and the Public Sphere*, edited by Craig Calhoun, 259–88. Cambridge: MIT Press, 1992.

———. *Womanhood in America*. 2d ed. New York: New Viewpoints, 1979.

———. *Women in Public: Between Banners and Ballots, 1825–1880*. Baltimore: Johns Hopkins University Press, 1990.

Ryan, Thomas G. "Male Opponents and Supporters of Woman Suffrage: Iowa in 1916." *Annals of Iowa* 45, no. 7 (1981): 537–50.

Scanlon, Jennifer. *Inarticulate Longings: The Ladies' Home Journal, Gender, and the Promises of Consumer Culture*. New York: Routledge, 1995.

Schaefer, Eric. "Of Hygiene and Hollywood: Origins of the Exploitation Film." *Velvet Light Trap* 30 (1990): 34–47.

Schneider, Donald. "The Controversy of Sunday Movies in Hastings, 1913–1929." *Nebraska History* 69, no. 2 (1988): 60–72.

Schutz, Wayne. *The Motion Picture Serial: An Annotated Bibliography*. Metuchen, NJ: Scarecrow Press, 1992.

Scott, Ann Frior, and Andrew MacKay Scott, eds. *One Half of the People: The Fight for Woman Suffrage*. Urbana and Chicago: University of Illinois Press, 1975.

Scott, Joan Wallach. *Gender and the Politics of History*. New York: Columbia University Press, 1988.

Sharpless, John, and John Rury. "The Political Economy of Women's Work 1900–1920." *Social Science History* 4, no. 3 (1980): 317–46.

Sheppard, Alice. *Cartooning for Suffrage*. Albuquerque: University of New Mexico Press, 1994.

Singer, Ben. "Female Power in the Serial-Queen Melodrama: The Etiology of an Anomaly." *Camera Obscura* 22 (1990): 91–129.

————. "Fiction Tie-Ins and Narrative Intelligibility, 1911–1918." *Film History* 5, no. 4 (1993): 489–504.

————. "Manhattan Melodrama." *Cinema Journal* 36, no. 4 (1997): 107–12.

————. "Manhattan Nickelodeons: New Data on Audiences and Exhibitors." *Cinema Journal* 34, no. 3 (1995): 5–35.

————. "Modernity, Hyperstimulus, and the Rise of Popular Sensationalism." In *Cinema and the Invention of Modern Life*, edited by Leo Charney and Vanessa R. Schwartz, 72–99. Berkeley and Los Angeles: University of California Press, 1995.

————. "New York, Just Like I Pictured It. . . ." *Cinema Journal* 35, no. 3 (1996): 104–28.

————. "Serial Melodrama and Narrative *Gesellschaft*." *Velvet Light Trap* 37 (1996): 72–80.

————. "Serials." In *The Oxford History of World Cinema*, edited by Geoffrey Nowell-Smith, 105–11. London and New York: Oxford University Press, 1996.

Singer, Stan. "Vaudeville in Los Angeles, 1910–1926: Theaters, Management, and the Orpheum." *Pacific Historical Review* 61, no. 1 (1992): 103–13.

Sklar, Robert. *Movie-Made America: A Cultural History of American Movies*. New York: Vintage, 1976.

Slide, Anthony. *Aspects of American Film History prior to 1920*. Metuchen, NJ: Scarecrow Press, 1978.

————. *Early American Cinema*. New York: A. S. Barnes, 1970.

————. *The Silent Feminists: America's First Women Directors*. Lanham, MD: The Scarecrow Press, 1996.

————, ed. *Selected Film Criticism, 1912–1920*. Metuchen, NJ: The Scarecrow Press, 1982.

Sloan, Kay. "A Cinema in Search of Itself: Ideology of the Social Problem Film during the Silent Era." *Cineaste* 14, no. 2 (1985): 34–37, 56.

————. *The Loud Silents: Origins of the Social Problem Film*. Urbana and Chicago: University of Illinois Press, 1988.

————. "Sexual Warfare in the Silent Cinema: Comedies and Melodramas of Woman Suffrage." *American Quarterly* 33 (1981): 412–36.

Somers, Dale A. "The Leisure Revolution: Recreation in the American City, 1820–1920." *Journal of Popular Culture* 5 (1971): 125–47.

Spain, Daphne. *Gendered Spaces*. Chapel Hill: University of North Carolina Press, 1992.

Stacey, Jackie. *Star Gazing: Hollywood Cinema and Female Spectatorship*. New York and London: Routledge, 1994.

Staiger, Janet. "Announcing Wares, Winning Patrons, Voicing Ideals: Thinking about the History and Theory of Film Advertising." *Cinema Journal* 29, no. 3 (1990): 3–31.

————. *Bad Women: Regulating Sexuality in Early American Cinema*. Minneapolis: University of Minnesota Press, 1995.

————. "Blueprints for Feature Films." In *The American Film Industry*, edited by Tino Balio, 173–94. 2d ed. Madison: University of Wisconsin Press, 1985.

————. "Combination and Litigation: Structures of U.S. Film Distribution, 1896–1917." *Cinema Journal* 23, no. 2 (1984): 41–72.

Staiger, Janet. "Dividing Labor for Production Control: Thomas Ince and the Rise of the Studio System." In *The American Movie Industry: The Business of Motion Pictures*, edited by Gorham Kindem, 94–103. Carbondale: Southern Illinois University Press, 1982.

———. " 'The Eyes Are Really the Focus': Photoplay Acting and Film Form and Style." *Wide Angle* 6, no. 4 (1985): 14–23.

———. "Mass-Produced Photoplays: Economic and Signifying Practices in the First Years of Hollywood." In *The Hollywood Film Industry*, edited by Paul Kerr, 99–119. London: British Film Institute, 1986.

———. "Seeing Stars." *Velvet Light Trap* 20 (1983): 10–15.

Stamp, Shelley. "Moral Coercion, or the Board of Censorship Ponders the Vice Question." In *Regulating Hollywood: Censorship and Control in the Studio Era*, edited by Matthew Bernstein, 41–58. New Brunswick, NJ: Rutgers University Press, 1999.

Stamp Lindsey, Shelley. "*Eighty Million Women Want——?*: Women's Suffrage, Female Viewers and the Body Politic." *Quarterly Review of Film and Video* 16, no. 1 (1995): 1–22.

———. "Is Any Girl Safe? Female Spectators at the White Slave Films." *Screen* 37, no. 1 (1996): 1–15.

———. " 'Oil Upon the Flames of Vice': The Battle over White Slave Films in New York City." *Film History* 9, no. 4 (1997): 351–64.

———. "Wages and Sin: *Traffic in Souls* and the White Slavery Scare." *Persistence of Vision* 9 (1991): 90–102.

Stansell, Christine. "Men, Women and the Uses of the Streets." *Feminist Studies* 8, no. 2 (1982): 308–35.

Stedman, Raymond William. *The Serials: Suspense and Drama by Installment*. 2d ed. Norman: University of Oklahoma Press, 1977.

Stromgren, Richard L. "The *Moving Picture World* of W. Stephen Bush." *Film History* 2, no. 1 (1988): 13–22.

Studlar, Gaylyn. "The Perils of Pleasure? Fan Magazine Discourse as Women's Commodified Culture in the 1920s." *Wide Angle* 13, no. 1 (1991): 6–33.

———. *This Mad Masquerade: Stardom and Masculinity in the Jazz Age*. New York: Columbia University Press, 1996.

Susman, Warren. *Culture as History: The Transformation of American Society in the Twentieth Century*. New York: Pantheon, 1984.

Swartz, Mark E. "Motion Pictures on the Move." *Journal of American Culture* 9, no. 4 (1986): 1–7.

———. "An Overview of Cinema on the Fairgrounds." *Journal of Popular Film and Television* 15, no. 3 (1987): 102–8.

Szuberla, Guy. "Ladies, Gentlemen, Flirts, Mashers, Snoozers, and the Breaking of Etiquette's Code." *Prospects* 15 (1990): 169–96.

Taylor, William R. "The Evolution of Public Space in New York City: The Commercial Showcase of America." In *Consuming Visions: Accumulation and Display of Goods in America, 1880–1920*, edited by Simon J. Bronner, 287–309. New York: W. W. Norton, 1989.

Teaford, Jon C. *The Twentieth-Century American City: Problem, Promise and Reality*. Baltimore: Johns Hopkins University Press, 1986.

Tentler, Leslie Woodcock. *Wage-Earning Women: Industrial Work and Family Life in the United States, 1900–1930*. New York: Oxford University Press, 1979.

Thissen, Judith. "Oy, Myopia!" *Cinema Journal* 36, no. 4 (1997): 102–7.

Thurner, Manuela. " 'Better Citizens without the Ballot': American Antisuffrage Women and Their Rationale during the Progressive Era." *Journal of Women's History* 5, no. 1 (1993): 33–60.

Tickner, Lisa. *The Spectacle of Women: Imagery of the Suffrage Campaign, 1907–1914*. Chicago: University of Chicago Press, 1988.

Todd, Ellen Wiley. *The "New Woman" Revised: Painting and Gender Politics on Fourteenth Street*. Berkeley and Los Angeles: University of California Press, 1993.

Uricchio, William, and Roberta E. Pearson. "Dante's Inferno and Caesar's Ghost: Intertextuality and Conditions of Reception in Early American Cinema." *Journal of Communication Inquiry* 14, no. 2 (1990): 71–85.

———. " 'Films of Quality,' 'High Art Films,' and 'Films de Luxe': Intertextuality and Reading Positions in the Vitagraph Films." *Journal of Film and Video* 41, no. 4 (1989): 15–31.

———. "New York? New York!" *Cinema Journal* 36, no. 4 (1997): 98–102.

———. *Reframing Culture: The Case of the Vitagraph Quality Films*. Princeton: Princeton University Press, 1993.

Usai, Paolo Cherchi, and Lorenzo Codelli, eds. *The Path to Hollywood, 1911–1920*. Rome: Edizioni Biblioteca dell-Immagine, 1988.

Valentine, Maggie. *The Show Starts on the Sidewalk: An Architectural History of the Movie Theatre, Starring S. Charles Lee*. New Haven: Yale University Press, 1994.

Vicinus, Martha. *Independent Women: Work and Community for Single Women, 1850–1920*. Chicago: University of Chicago Press, 1985.

Waldman, Diane. "From Midnight Shows to Marriage Vows: Women, Exploitation and Exhibition." *Wide Angle* 6, no. 2 (1984): 40–48.

Walkowitz, Judith R. *City of Dreadful Delight: Narratives of Sexual Danger in Late-Victorian London*. London: Virago, 1992.

———. *Prostitution and Victorian Society: Women, Class and the State*. New York: Cambridge University Press, 1980.

Waller, Gregory A. "Another Audience: Black Moviegoing, 1907–1916." *Cinema Journal* 31, no. 2 (1992): 3–25.

———. *Main Street Amusements: Movies and Commercial Entertainment in a Southern City, 1896–1930*. Washington: Smithsonian Institution Press, 1995.

———. "Situating Motion Pictures in the Pre-Nickelodeon Period: Lexington Kentucky, 1897–1906." *Velvet Light Trap* 25 (1990): 12–28.

Ward, David. "Social Reform, Social Surveys, and the Discovery of the Modern City." *Annals of the Association of American Geographers* 80, no. 4 (1990): 491–503.

Wekerle, Gerda R., Rebecca Peterson, and David Morley, eds. *New Space for Women*. Boulder, CO: Westview Press, 1980.

Welter, Barbara. "The Cult of True Womanhood: 1820–1860." *American Quarterly* 18 (1966): 151–74.

Wertheimer, John. "Mutual Film Reviewed: The Movies, Censorship, and Free Speech in Progressive America." *American Journal of Legal History* 37, no. 2 (1993): 158–89.

Wiebe, Robert H. *The Search for Order, 1877–1920*. New York: Hill and Wang, 1967.

Wilson, Elizabeth. *The Sphinx in the City: Urban Life, the Control of Disorder, and Women.* Berkeley and Los Angeles: University of California Press, 1991.

Wilson, Harold S. *McClure's Magazine and the Muckrakers.* Princeton: Princeton University Press, 1970.

Wilson, Margaret Gibbons. *The American Woman in Transition: The Urban Influence, 1870–1920.* Westport, CT: Greenwood Press, 1979.

Woal, Linda. "When a Dime Could Buy a Dream: Siegmund Lubin and the Birth of Motion Picture Exhibition." *Film History* 6, no. 2 (1994): 152–65.

Wolff, Janet. *Feminine Sentences: Essays on Women and Culture.* Cambridge, UK: Polity Press, 1990.

———. "The Invisible *Flâneuse*: Women and the Literature of Modernity." *Theory, Culture and Society* 2, no. 3 (1988): 37–46.

Index